DataCAD
for the
Architect

2nd Edition

COMPUTER
GRAPHICS
TECHNOLOGY
AND
MANAGEMENT
SERIES

Computer Graphics Technology and Management Series

AutoCAD: Methods and Macros—2nd Edition
by Jeff Guenther and John Ocoboc

AutoCAD Programming—2nd Edition
by Dennis Jump

Understanding Electronic Photography
by John J. Larish

VersaCAD on the Mac
by Carol Buehrens

VersaCAD Tutorial:
A Practical Approach to Computer-Aided Design
by Carol Buehrens

The C-4 Handbook: CAD, CAM, CAE, CIM
by Carl Machover

DataCAD
for the
Architect
2nd Edition

Carol Buehrens

DataCAD for the Architect is written for use with the DataCAD drafting and design software, release 4.0 and IBM compatible type personal computers. This book is designed to provide tutorial information about the DataCAD software program. Every effort has been made to make this book as correct and as complete as possible. Because software programs are subject to frequent change, there might be subtle differences in the operations described in this text.

SECOND EDITION
FIRST PRINTING

© 1991 by **Carol Buehrens**.
Published by McGraw-Hill, Inc.

Library of Congress Cataloging-in-Publication Data

Buehrens, Carol.
    DataCAD for the architect / by Carol Buehrens. — 2nd ed.
      p.   cm.
    Includes index.
    ISBN 0-8306-3746-X (pbk.)
    1. DataCAD (Computer program)   2. Architectural design—Data
processing.   3. Architectural drawing—Data processing.   I. Title.
NA2728.B84   1991
720′.28′402855369—dc20   90-26145
                                                              CIP

For information about other McGraw-Hill materials, call 1-800-2-MCGRAW in the U.S. In other countries call your nearest McGraw-Hill office.

Vice President & Editorial Director: Larry Hagar
Book Editors: David Gauthier, Eileen Baylus
Production: Katherine G. Brown
Book Design: Jaclyn J. Boone
Cover photograph courtesy of CADKEY Inc., Manchester, CT.   EL2

Contents

Lesson 4: Windowing

Lesson 5: Adding symbols

Lesson 16: Detailing the model with doors and windows   337

Appendices

About the author

Carol Buehrens is a CADD Course Designer/Training Specialist and owner of Desktop Productions, Yorba Linda, California. She designs courseware and professional texts for a wide variety of engineers from both the architectural and mechanical industries.

With 15 years of design and manufacturing experience, Carol has devoted 12 years to computer-aided design and drafting training and design technology.

With 15 years of design and manufacturing experience, Carol has devoted 12 years to computer-aided design and drafting training and design technology.

Carol began her interest in this highly specialized area as a general machinist, from which she entered into the design drafting field. In 1975, she became directly involved in CADD/CAM.

Since then, she has created CADD training programs for McDonnell Douglas Automation Company, Northrop Corporation—Advanced Systems, Bechtel Corporation, GE/Calma Corporation, Calcomp, and CR/CADD. She has also authored books through these corporations for 10 different mainframe, minicomputer, and microcomputer CADD software programs, including the *VersaCAD Tutorial—A Practical Approach to Computer-Aided Design*, published by TAB Books.

Acknowledgments

The author wishes to thank CADKEY for their support during the development of this book, and on continued support on the daily use of DataCAD. Special thanks to Mark Hyjek and Clay Rogers who were always available for questions and returned many phone calls.

To our many users and students of DataCAD, who are architects or work in the architectural field, thank you for comments and suggestions. The author would also like to thank the architects who took time out of their busy schedules to review this book.

Special thanks to Karl Buehrens, my husband, for the encouragement given throughout this project. And to Adam and Lora Buehrens, who gave mommy plenty of hugs and kisses to keep her going.

Overview

DataCAD for the Architect is a tutorial book designed for use with the DataCAD computer-aided drafting and design software package. This book contains easy-to-follow, fully illustrated instructions that take the reader from the beginning to the advanced level of using DataCAD to create architectural projects.

This overview is designed to help you understand how this book is formatted, and what you can expect to learn from it.

The DataCAD software program

DataCAD is a microcomputer-based software program that helps you draw with increased efficiency and precision. It allows you to use the computer as a design and drafting tool.

Like any new tool, you will be required to learn new concepts and skills in order to use it. Once you understand the basic concepts used in computer drafting, using DataCAD will become easier. Then, with practice, you will become a proficient and expert user of the DataCAD program!

DataCAD release version 4.0

This book is designed to be used with the DataCAD release version called 4.0.

If you have an earlier or later release of DataCAD

You can still use this book if you have a different release version than 4.0! You will notice, however, slight changes in the menu options or particular procedure followed in the operation of the menu options.

DataCAD 128

If you have the special release of DataCAD 128, you will be happy to find this book contains inserts just for you. The DataCAD 128 software is an entry level, low-cost software package that operates like the regular Data-CAD package, but it limits the file size to 128,000 bytes (128 k).

Some of the drawing projects in this book might exceed the 128,000 bytes allowed by this software. Because of this, there are special hints included during these steps that will allow you to use DataCAD 128 to its fullest potential.

The DataCAD 128 user hints will appear as the following example:

DataCAD 128 alert!

If you have DataCAD 128, you will want to turn off the Furn and Plumb layers before completing the HIDE procedure. This will help you keep your file size within the 128 k limit.

The "DataCAD for the Architect" book

DataCAD for the Architect is designed as a self-teaching guide to using the DataCAD software program. You can follow the steps and work through the projects independently or with the aid of a classroom instructor.

This book also is designed as a continued reference, and contains a special section called *The DataCAD Operations Guide*, which contains easy steps to follow for daily use of DataCAD.

Beginning assumptions

This book assumes that you have little or no experience drawing with DataCAD. You might or might not be an experienced computer user. This does not matter. Drawing with DataCAD does not require you to be a computer expert.

If you already have used DataCAD a little, then you will be happy to find that this book can answer the many questions you might have. If you have been using DataCAD for an extended period of time, you will find the second section of the book—*The DataCAD Operations Guide*—most helpful.

Another assumption is that you have the DataCAD program loaded on your computer, and have it configured to work with your hardware. This is accomplished by following the procedures outlined in your *DataCAD User's Manual*, or in a special installation insert that was supplied with your program.

How this book is organized

This book is divided into 16 lessons. These lessons take you from beginning concepts of DataCAD, to more advanced uses and operations. The lessons are systematic, meaning that they tend to build on each other, and are presented from easy to harder skills sequentially.

Lesson 1. Beginning DataCAD Introduces DataCAD and the basic concepts for CAD drawing. You will start the DataCAD program, create a drawing file, use the mouse input device to draw lines, look at menus, erase, and file the drawing.

Lesson 2. Initial drawing setup You will create two drawing setups. The first will be for $1/4'' = 1'$ scale drawings, which will be used for creating floor plans. The second will be for $1'' = 20'$ scale drawings, which will be used for site layouts.

Lesson 3. Basic drafting techniques Guides you through using basic drawing capabilities for creating walls, doors, and windows.

Lesson 4. Windowing You will use the different window techniques for controlling the view window of your drawing.

Lesson 5. Adding symbols You will retrieve, add, and rotate symbols as you place them into your drawing. DataCAD comes with a variety of developed symbols that you can use.

Lesson 6. Adding dimension and text Your projects need to be dimensioned, and this lesson shows you how.

Lesson 7. Viewing your drawing in 3-D Your house is created, and now you want to see what it really looks like in 3-D. You will look at your drawing in perspective and from a bird's-eye view. You will also remove hidden lines so that your walls look "solid."

Lesson 8. Plotting your drawing Now you will learn how to send your drawing to the plotter, and get a finished product!

Lesson 9. Creating site plans Most of the site information for your layout is provided by the civil engineer—but are his calculations correct? You will learn to use the formulas that are given to you to draw the initial site plan.

Lesson 10. Creating 3-dimensional lines You have been creating your drawing in the orthographic view. Now you can view your drawing in 3-D and create lines that are 3-dimensional.

Lesson 11. Copying techniques What is the easiest way to create a drawing that has repeated items in it? This lesson shows you how to do this and more. You also will learn how to modify the items you copied.

Lesson 12. Detail drawings You will create your own detail, learn how to crosshatch, reduce the size of items, find out how to measure lines, and other more advanced techniques that DataCAD provides.

Lesson 13. Creating templates and symbols Make your own symbols, organized in templates, for your DataCAD drawings. You also can extract reports from your symbols. This lesson provides you with the skills necessary to use and modify these reports.

Lesson 14. Creating your default drawings Design Default Drawings for your own office or classroom use. All of the steps you need are included here, with explanations provided for the customization of these defaults to your own standards.

Lesson 15. The DataCAD modeler Create a building that is entirely modeled with slabs, voids, mesh surfaces, and more.

Lesson 16. Detailing the model with doors and windows Now that you have created your model, you can add fully detailed doors and windows for a finishing touch!

Hands-on learning

It is hard to learn a skill by reading about it. Reading helps us achieve a knowledge about a subject, but skills are learned by doing. This is called "hands-on learning."

To make it easier for you to acquire your new DataCAD drawing skills, this book is designed to help you "do" by putting your "hands on" the DataCAD system. You will be guided through performing actual skills with easy-to-read instructions.

Classroom environment

Because the book is divided into concept "lessons," the book is easily fitted into the classroom curriculum. If you have bought this book as part of your CAD drafting course, you will find it easy to use and reference as course text.

Step-by-step tutorials

Step-by-step tutorials help you perform DataCAD operations, providing you with easy to read instructions. Each step is numbered and an abundance of illustrations are included.

"Self-paced" design

We all learn at different speeds. We tend to want to decide for ourselves the amount of time we want to spend on a subject or on learning a new skill.

All age groups, in fact, acquire new information at speeds comfortable to them as individuals.

This book was designed with this type of learning strategy in mind. It allows you to advance at your own speed. You can look back at certain lessons for reference to go over a skill on which you want to spend more time.

How to use this book

Each lesson contains 4 basic elements:

1. Learning objectives.
2. Concept explanation.
3. Project and tutorial.
4. Exercise with multiple choice questions.

What you should do

☐ Read the objectives at the beginning of each lesson, describing what you will be doing.

☐ Read the concept explanation.

☐ It is very helpful if you briefly review the tutorial you will be following, so that there are no surprises.

☐ Sit down at the computer and follow the step-by-step instructions provided you. (Make notes, if you want to, right in your book.)

☐ Refer to the *DataCAD Operations Guide*, which is in the back section of the book, when instructed to do so. Later, this guide will be your reference tool for on-the-job usage.

☐ Check your project, after you have completed the tutorial, to make sure it is correct. If it is not correct, go over the steps again. Be sure to carefully read the instructions and illustrations.

☐ Complete the exercise found at the end of each lesson. If you do not remember the answer, look back at the tutorial or explanation to find it. You might also want to look at the DataCAD menus.

☐ Look in the *DataCAD User's Manual* to find more information about the options you are using.

Throughout this book you will be given instructions that are new to you. It is important to understand the format in which the tutorials will be presented.

Numbering scheme

Your instructions will appear following a "step" number (e.g., Step 1, Step 2). This signifies that:

1. There is an action you should perform.
   (e.g., Step 1 - Pick the LineType option.)

2. An action has occurred.
   (e.g., Step 2 - The menu in Fig. 3-10 is displayed.)

If the number is followed by a parenthesis (e.g., 1), 2), 3)), then important information is being conveyed to you that you should read. (Such as above.)

Instruction terms

Certain terms will be used that indicate what you are being instructed to do. Basically, these terms are:

1. Press – you should press the key found on the keyboard.
2. Pick – you should pick an item on the drawing with the mouse button 1 or pick an option from a menu. Again, you would use mouse button 1.
3. Object Snap – you should put the cursor by an item, and press mouse button 2. This action will grab on to the item.
4. Type in – you should type in a value from the keyboard. When necessary, the value should be followed by pressing the [**Enter**] key.

Drawing projects

Most lessons include drawing projects that have been designed to help you practice the particular skills being taught.

If you choose to create your own drawing projects, remember to be careful in selecting projects that fit the criteria for the lesson. Many drawings can be found in architectural drafting books that work quite well for practice.

Exercises

Each lesson is followed by a multiple choice exercise. These exercises allow you to recall the operations you learned during the lesson. The answers for these exercises are found in Appendix C.

Lesson 1
Beginning DataCAD

What you will be doing

You will be learning about the components of your computer system, and a little on how DataCAD system is structured. You will start DataCAD and use simple techniques to draw lines. You will use the mouse input device to pick menu options, line start and endpoints, change from the main menus, and to Quit an operation.

Objectives

Your lesson objectives are to:

- Learn the basics of DataCAD.
- Start DataCAD.
- Use the mouse input device.
- Set the Object Snap options.
- Object snap onto lines.
- Erase lines by entity, area, and polygon fence.

Remember to refer to the section called *The DataCAD Operations Guide* when instructed. This section is your *quick* guide to DataCAD operations.

Introduction to your computer system

Although computers are not exactly the same, most computer systems are made up of 5 major pieces, as shown in FIG. 1-1. They are:

1. Display Screen
2. Processor
3. Disk Drives
4. Keyboard
5. Mouse

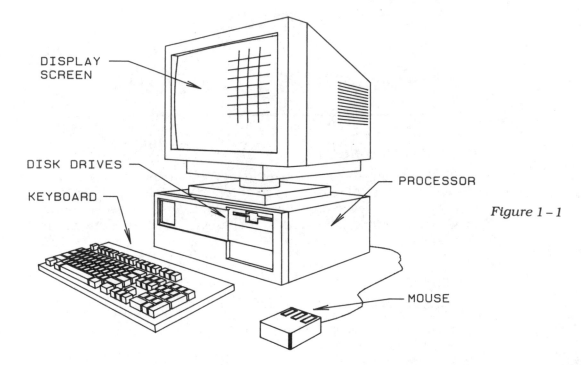

Figure 1 – 1

The first thing you might notice about your computer is the many special keys on the keyboard. Many of these keys, which are not found on the everyday typewriter, assist you in the operation of DataCAD. Some of these helpful keys are noted in FIG. 1-2. Your keyboard might look slightly different than this. Locate these keys on your own keyboard.

DataCAD directory structure

Your DataCAD system is organized like you might organize your file cabinets. In fact, every file on your computer can and should be organized in a well-planned system, in order for you and your computer to easily find your important files.

Figure 1 – 2

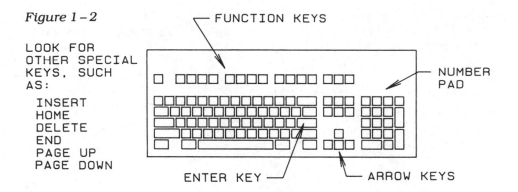

LOOK FOR
OTHER SPECIAL
KEYS, SUCH
AS:

INSERT
HOME
DELETE
END
PAGE UP
PAGE DOWN

FUNCTION KEYS

NUMBER PAD

ENTER KEY

ARROW KEYS

You can think of the organization of your computer, as a filing cabinet, as shown in FIG. 1-3.

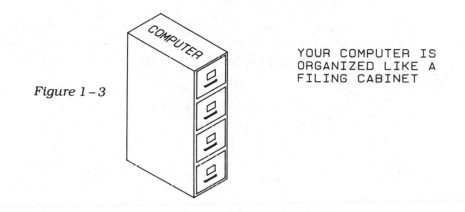

Figure 1 – 3

YOUR COMPUTER IS
ORGANIZED LIKE A
FILING CABINET

Directories, which help to organize the data in your computer, can be thought of as the individual drawers in the cabinet. This is illustrated in FIG. 1-4.

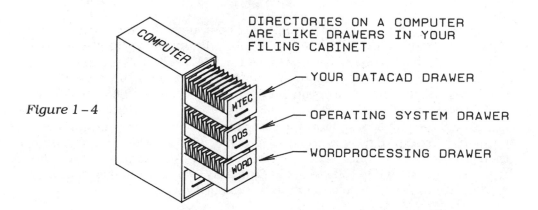

Figure 1 – 4

DIRECTORIES ON A COMPUTER
ARE LIKE DRAWERS IN YOUR
FILING CABINET

YOUR DATACAD DRAWER

OPERATING SYSTEM DRAWER

WORDPROCESSING DRAWER

Each drawer of your file cabinet can obtain file folders, as indicated in FIG. 1-5. These folders also can be compared to as subdirectories (or "directories within directories") on your computer.

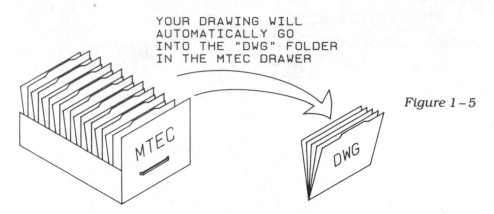

YOUR DRAWING WILL
AUTOMATICALLY GO
INTO THE "DWG" FOLDER
IN THE MTEC DRAWER

Figure 1 – 5

The folder can contain your files, just as the subdirectories contain the data files for your drawings (drawing files) and software programs, or even additional directories. See FIG. 1-6.

THE "DWG" FOLDER CONTAINS YOUR DRAWING FILES

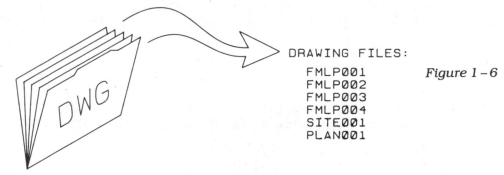

DRAWING FILES:

    FMLP001   *Figure 1 – 6*
    FMLP002
    FMLP003
    FMLP004
    SITE001
    PLAN001

In FIG. 1-7, a typical organization of a computer directory structure is illustrated. Your computer might be organized similar to this. Notice the types of files that are found in the various DataCAD "MTEC" subdirectories.

In conclusion, directories are a way to organize your files. You group your files into directories, like you would group your paper files into folders and drawers of a filing cabinet.

FILES are the actual data. Files are the drawings and programs you have on the computer. If you create a drawing called XYZ on the computer, then you have a file called XYZ. It is that simple. All of this is transparent to you, of course, while you are using DataCAD. DataCAD makes your files for you. You don't have to be a computer expert!

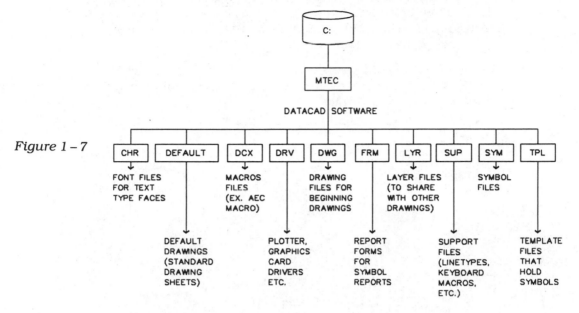

EXPLANATION OF DIRECTORY TREE STRUCTURE

Figure 1 – 7

Now that you know a little about how the components of your computer, and how your computer might be organized, you are ready to start using DataCAD.

Starting DataCAD

Step 1 – Starting DataCAD is easy. When you turn on your computer, you will receive a **C:** prompt. This indicates you are using the hard drive. To make sure you are in the proper directory to run Data-CAD, at the **C:** prompt simply type in the following, and press [**Enter**].

cd \ mtec

Step 2 – Remember, you must press the [**Enter**] key when you type something in. This signals the computer to read the command you gave it.

Step 3 – If you have DataCAD version 4.0 or later, you can type in and [**Enter**] the following:

rundcad

If you have DataCAD 128, or version 3.6 or earlier, you can type in and [**Enter**] the follwing:

dcad

Step 4 – The next thing that will appear on your screen is the copyrite menu. This is the copyrite agreement that you made with CADKEY Inc. when purchasing DataCAD. Read this message, then press [**Enter**] to continue.

Step 5 – The DataCAD opening screen will be displayed, as indicated in FIG. 1-8. If there are any existing drawings, they will be listed in the left column of the screen.

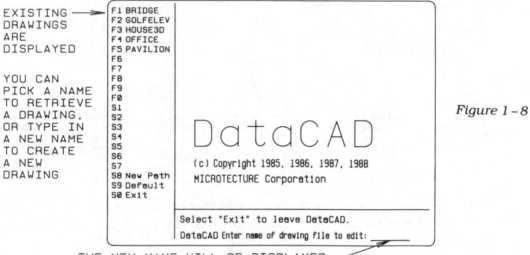

Figure 1 – 8

Beginning a drawing

To begin a new drawing, all you have to do is type in a new drawing name. Drawing names can only be 8 characters long. Because of this, you will want to develop special naming conventions for your drawings. For practice drawings, you can use a simple naming convention.

Step 1 – Type in the name of your new drawing:

fml-prac   (Your **F**irst **M**iddle and **L**ast initials, **PRAC**tice)

User note: Certain characters are *illegal* in names of files. These characters include:

.   ,   ?
:   ;   \
/   and spaces

The characters that *are legal* include:

A thru Z	0 thru 9	-	@
%	'	$	{ }
#	( )	!	&

The main menu screen

Once you begin a drawing, the DataCAD main menu screen will be displayed. There are 4 major areas that make up this screen, as indicated in FIG. 1-9. They are:

- Menu Window – your menus will always appear in this column.
- Drawing Area – Your drawing is displayed here.
- Status Area – This area informs you of your present settings: the active layer, the present viewing scale, the selection set, and the SWOTHLUD status.
- Message Area – Your coordinate readout, system messages, and user prompt appear here.

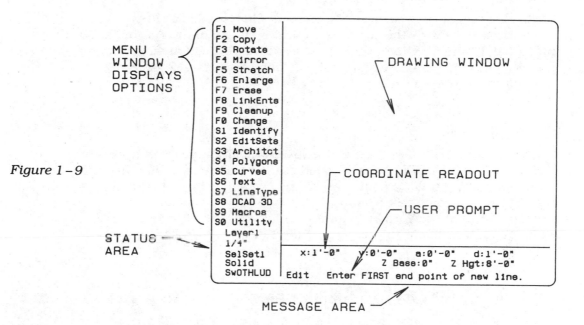

Figure 1–9

What is SWOTHLUD?

The word SWOTHLUD, which appears at the lower left corner of the status area, represents the current setting status. Each letter stands for a particular setting. It keeps you informed "at a glance" of what settings you have active.

The letters "SWOTHLUD" stand for:

Snap – Increment snapping is on.
Walls – You are creating walls (compared to lines).
Ortho – Ortho lock is on (45° angle lock).

Text – Text is displayed on screen (instead of boxes only).
Hatch – Hatch is displayed on screen.
Line weight – Thicknesses of lines are displayed.
User linetypes – Linetypes are displayed (compared to appearing as solid).
Dimensions – Dimensions are displayed on screen.

When a switch is active (e.g., walls are being drawn), the letter will appear capitalized. If the switch is off (e.g., walls are not being drawn, lines are), the letter will appear in lowercase (e.g., SwOTHLUD). You will see how this works later in this lesson.

The screen cursor

Notice that there is a small + on your screen. This is called a *cursor*. When you move your mouse, the cursor on your screen will move. As you found out earlier, if you move the cursor into the MENU OPTION area, the option closest to the cursor will be highlighted. The cursor is also used to pick items in the drawing area.

Drawing lines

Notice that the "W" in the status line (SWOTHLUD) appears in upper- or lowercase (SwOTHLUD). As mentioned earlier, this means that you will either be drawing walls (a double set of lines) or single lines. (Other letters might appear in lowercase also.)

You will want the W to be in lowercase for your first drawing lesson. If it is in uppercase, follow the next step, Step 1, to change this status. If your W is in lowercase, skip this step and go to Step 2.

If the W (in SWOTHLUD) is uppercase –

Step 1 – Press the double line key [=] (equal sign). This will turn off the walls mode for now.

Notice that the user prompt (bottom of screen) is asking you to pick a point to draw a line. To draw lines, all you have to do is point with the cursor and press mouse button **1**. This is called *picking*. You can continue drawing lines, always picking the next point with mouse number **1**. To quit drawing the line, you simply press mouse button **3**.
Let's try it!

Step 2 – Move the cursor to the desired area in the Drawing Window you wish to begin drawing a line.

Step 3 – Press mouse button **1**. Move your cursor. You will be drawing a line! Press mouse button **1** again to indicate the second point of your line.

Step 4 – Continue making multiple lines, moving the cursor, and using mouse button **1**, as shown in FIG. 1-10.

Step 5 – To end your line, press mouse button **3**.

Figure 1 – 10

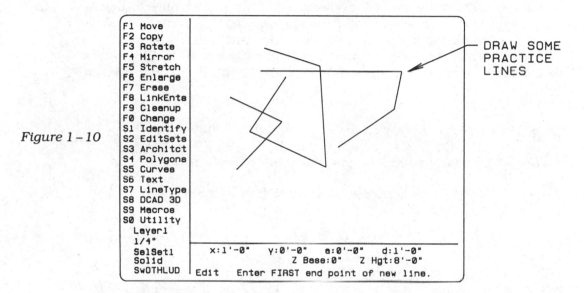

Your three-button mouse

You just used your mouse to pick points on the screen for your lines, and to detach the line. These are only two of the uses for your mouse. The three buttons, and their uses, are described in FIG. 1-11.

Figure 1 – 11

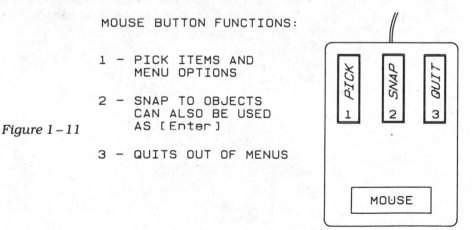

MOUSE BUTTON FUNCTIONS:

1 – PICK ITEMS AND MENU OPTIONS

2 – SNAP TO OBJECTS CAN ALSO BE USED AS [Enter]

3 – QUITS OUT OF MENUS

If you have a two-button mouse:

Mouse button 1 - Picks

Button 2 - Quits

To object snap, hold the cursor by the item you wish to grab, and press the **N** key on your keyboard.

The first button, as you found out, is used to "*pick*". You can pick a location on the screen for a line or wall, or you can pick an option from the menu.

The second button is used to object snap to an existing object, such as a line. Object snap means to "*grab onto an object.*"

The third button is used to *quit* a line, or "quit" from a menu.

(The third button actually selects the option found in the S0 position of the menu window. In many submenus, this option is "**Exit**," which appears as though you "Quit" a menu.)

Let's try it!

Step 1 – Make sure there are a few lines in your drawing area.

Step 2 – Pick a start point for a line, using mouse button **1**.

Step 3 – Move the cursor close to an existing line, as shown in FIG. 1-12.

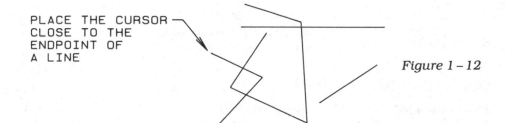

PLACE THE CURSOR
CLOSE TO THE
ENDPOINT OF
A LINE

Figure 1 – 12

Step 4 – Press mouse button **2**. If you have a 2 button mouse, press **N** on your keyboard. The first endpoint of the line will snap onto the endpoint of the existing line, as in FIG. 1-13.

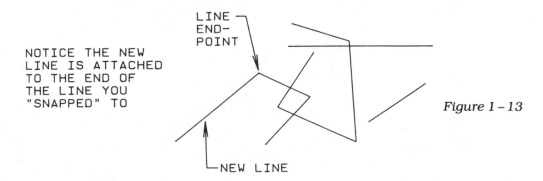

LINE
END-
POINT

NOTICE THE NEW
LINE IS ATTACHED
TO THE END OF
THE LINE YOU
"SNAPPED" TO

Figure 1 – 13

NEW LINE

Quick erasing

You can quickly erase entities you drew by using the < key. To erase all the lines you drew as a multiple line during a single series (without pressing mouse button **3** to detach your line), you would use the [**Shift**] and < keys together. Lines drawn as a single series are called a *group* of lines.

Step 1 – Press the < key. Did one of your lines disappear?

Step 2 – Press the [**Shift**] and < keys together. How many lines disappeared? Remember, a bunch of lines drawn together without detaching (mouse button 3) are thought of as one "group." Using the [**Shift**] and < key together will erase the last group you have drawn.

Restoring

You can restore the last entity or group you erased!

Step 1 – Press the > key. Whatever you deleted last (group or single entity) will be restored. You will learn other ways to erase items during the following steps.

The EDIT and UTILITY menus

There are two main menus in DataCAD (See FIGS. 1-14, 1-15, and 1-16). They are:

- Edit – This menu contains menu options that allow you to create or change items, such as walls, windows, doors, etc.
- Utility – This menu contains menu options that allow you to define certain settings, defaults for your drawing, and other utility items such as drawing file control.

To change between the two main menus, all you have to do is press the mouse button **3**. (Of course, if you are drawing a line, the first time you press mouse button **3** it will detach your line. The second time you press mouse button **3**, you can switch menus.)

Step 1 – Look at the MESSAGE area at the bottom of the screen, as shown in FIG. 1-17 on page 13. Does it say Edit or Utility?

If it says **Edit**, then you are in the EDIT menu. You could switch to the UTILITY menu by pressing mouse button **3**.
    Notice that when you are in the EDIT menu, menu option S0 is "Utility." Pressing mouse button **3** will select S0 for you, and you will change to the UTILITY menu.

TWO MAIN DATACAD MENUS

ALL OTHER SUBMENUS ARE
ACCESSED THROUGH THESE
TWO MENUS.

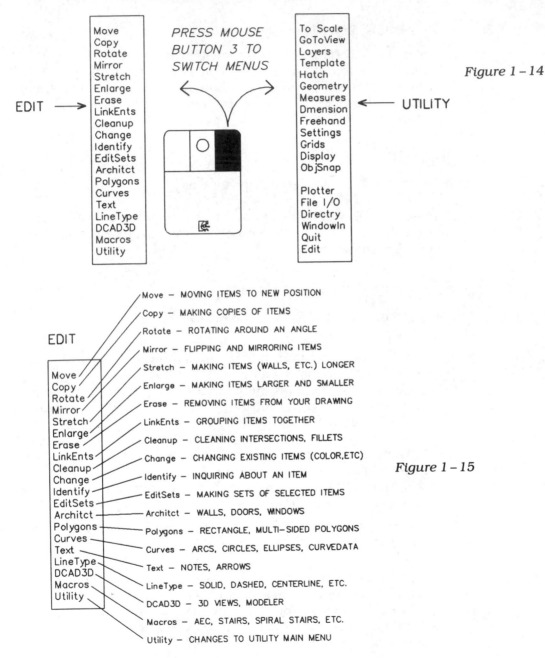

Figure 1 – 14

EDIT →

EDIT
Move
Copy
Rotate
Mirror
Stretch
Enlarge
Erase
LinkEnts
Cleanup
Change
Identify
EditSets
Architct
Polygons
Curves
Text
LineType
DCAD3D
Macros
Utility

*PRESS MOUSE
BUTTON 3 TO
SWITCH MENUS*

← UTILITY

UTILITY
To Scale
GoToView
Layers
Template
Hatch
Geometry
Measures
Dmension
Freehand
Settings
Grids
Display
ObjSnap
Plotter
File I/O
Directry
WindowIn
Quit
Edit

EDIT

Move – MOVING ITEMS TO NEW POSITION

Copy – MAKING COPIES OF ITEMS

Rotate – ROTATING AROUND AN ANGLE

Mirror – FLIPPING AND MIRRORING ITEMS

Stretch – MAKING ITEMS (WALLS, ETC.) LONGER

Enlarge – MAKING ITEMS LARGER AND SMALLER

Erase – REMOVING ITEMS FROM YOUR DRAWING

LinkEnts – GROUPING ITEMS TOGETHER

Cleanup – CLEANING INTERSECTIONS, FILLETS

Change – CHANGING EXISTING ITEMS (COLOR,ETC)

Identify – INQUIRING ABOUT AN ITEM

EditSets – MAKING SETS OF SELECTED ITEMS

Architct – WALLS, DOORS, WINDOWS

Polygons – RECTANGLE, MULTI–SIDED POLYGONS

Curves – ARCS, CIRCLES, ELLIPSES, CURVEDATA

Text – NOTES, ARROWS

LineType – SOLID, DASHED, CENTERLINE, ETC.

DCAD3D – 3D VIEWS, MODELER

Macros – AEC, STAIRS, SPIRAL STAIRS, ETC.

Utility – CHANGES TO UTILITY MAIN MENU

Figure 1 – 15

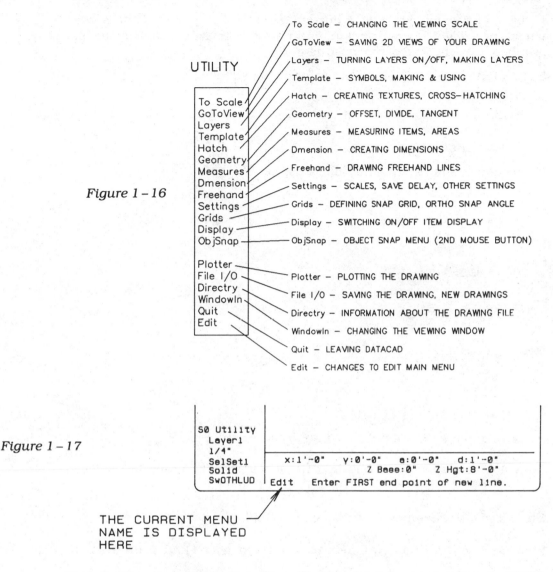

Figure 1 – 16

UTILITY

To Scale — CHANGING THE VIEWING SCALE
GoToView — SAVING 2D VIEWS OF YOUR DRAWING
Layers — TURNING LAYERS ON/OFF, MAKING LAYERS
Template — SYMBOLS, MAKING & USING
Hatch — CREATING TEXTURES, CROSS-HATCHING
Geometry — OFFSET, DIVIDE, TANGENT
Measures — MEASURING ITEMS, AREAS
Dmension — CREATING DIMENSIONS
Freehand — DRAWING FREEHAND LINES
Settings — SCALES, SAVE DELAY, OTHER SETTINGS
Grids — DEFINING SNAP GRID, ORTHO SNAP ANGLE
Display — SWITCHING ON/OFF ITEM DISPLAY
ObjSnap — OBJECT SNAP MENU (2ND MOUSE BUTTON)

Plotter — PLOTTING THE DRAWING
File I/O — SAVING THE DRAWING, NEW DRAWINGS
Directry — INFORMATION ABOUT THE DRAWING FILE
WindowIn — CHANGING THE VIEWING WINDOW
Quit — LEAVING DATACAD
Edit — CHANGES TO EDIT MAIN MENU

To Scale
GoToView
Layers
Template
Hatch
Geometry
Measures
Dmension
Freehand
Settings
Grids
Display
ObjSnap

Plotter
File I/O
Directry
WindowIn
Quit
Edit

Figure 1 – 17

```
S0 Utility
  Layer1
  1/4"
  SelSet1      x:1'-0"    y:0'-0"    a:0'-0"    d:1'-0"
  Solid                            Z Base:0"   Z Hgt:8'-0"
  SwOTHLUD  Edit    Enter FIRST end point of new line.
```

THE CURRENT MENU
NAME IS DISPLAYED
HERE

Step 2 – Press mouse button **3** until the main menu changes to EDIT. Notice the options that are displayed.

Step 3 – Press button **3** until it changes to UTILITY. This is called *toggling* between menus. Notice the options that are displayed in the UTILITY menu.

Object snap

As mentioned before, object snap allows you to grab onto items such as existing lines. You can grab an item by its endpoints, middle point, centerpoint, etc. Your object snap is currently set to "endpoint." That is why, when you picked close to an item and pressed mouse button **2**, your line grabbed onto the *end* of the existing line.

Suggested "common-use" settings for object snap are:

Endpoint
Midpoint
Center
Intersection

These object snap settings are illustrated in FIG. 1-18.

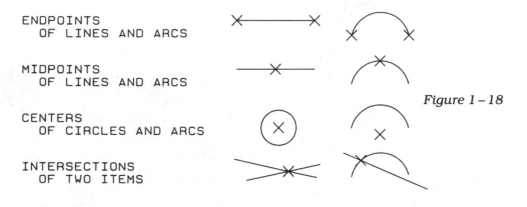

ENDPOINTS
   OF LINES AND ARCS

MIDPOINTS
   OF LINES AND ARCS

Figure 1 – 18

CENTERS
   OF CIRCLES AND ARCS

INTERSECTIONS
   OF TWO ITEMS

Setting your object snap

You can quickly set your object snap to these settings:

Step 1 – Press the mouse button **3** until the UTILITY menu is displayed (UTILITY appears in the MESSAGE area).

Step 2 – Pick the option displayed called **ObjSnap**.

Step 3 – The OBJECT SNAP menu is displayed, as in FIG. 1-19 on page 15.

Notice that some options might have a star * by them. This means that they have been set already, and they are *active*.

Step 4 – Pick the Center option until a * appears by it. Now it is active.

Step 5 – Pick the rest of the options you wish to have active.

    *Midpoint
    *Intrsect

Step 6 – If you pick an option by mistake, or wish to turn one off, just pick it again and the * will "toggle" off.

Figure 1 – 19

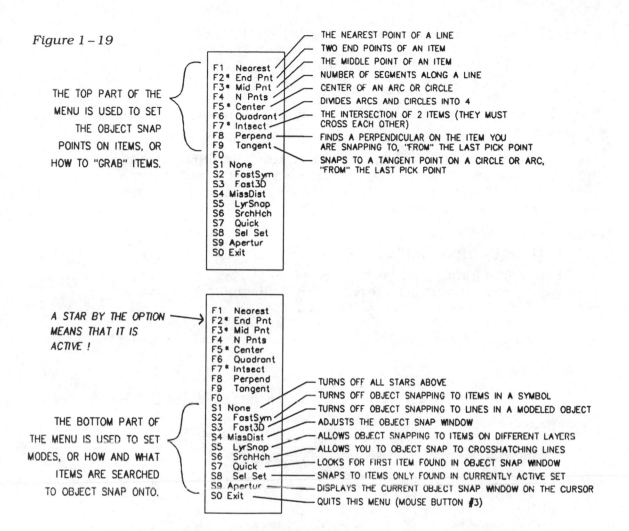

THE TOP PART OF THE MENU IS USED TO SET THE OBJECT SNAP POINTS ON ITEMS, OR HOW TO "GRAB" ITEMS.

F1 Nearest	THE NEAREST POINT OF A LINE
F2* End Pnt	TWO END POINTS OF AN ITEM
F3* Mid Pnt	THE MIDDLE POINT OF AN ITEM
F4 N Pnts	NUMBER OF SEGMENTS ALONG A LINE
F5* Center	CENTER OF AN ARC OR CIRCLE
F6 Quadrant	DIVIDES ARCS AND CIRCLES INTO 4
F7* Intsect	THE INTERSECTION OF 2 ITEMS (THEY MUST CROSS EACH OTHER)
F8 Perpend	FINDS A PERPENDICULAR ON THE ITEM YOU ARE SNAPPING TO, "FROM" THE LAST PICK POINT
F9 Tangent	SNAPS TO A TANGENT POINT ON A CIRCLE OR ARC, "FROM" THE LAST PICK POINT

F0
S1 None
S2 FastSym
S3 Fast3D
S4 MissDist
S5 LyrSnap
S6 SrchHch
S7 Quick
S8 Sel Set
S9 Apertur
S0 Exit

A STAR BY THE OPTION MEANS THAT IT IS ACTIVE !

F1 Nearest
F2* End Pnt
F3* Mid Pnt
F4 N Pnts
F5* Center
F6 Quadrant
F7* Intsect
F8 Perpend
F9 Tangent
F0

THE BOTTOM PART OF THE MENU IS USED TO SET MODES, OR HOW AND WHAT ITEMS ARE SEARCHED TO OBJECT SNAP ONTO.

S1 None	TURNS OFF ALL STARS ABOVE
S2 FastSym	TURNS OFF OBJECT SNAPPING TO ITEMS IN A SYMBOL
S3 Fast3D	TURNS OFF OBJECT SNAPPING TO LINES IN A MODELED OBJECT
S4 MissDist	ADJUSTS THE OBJECT SNAP WINDOW
S5 LyrSnap	ALLOWS OBJECT SNAPPING TO ITEMS ON DIFFERENT LAYERS
S6 SrchHch	ALLOWS YOU TO OBJECT SNAP TO CROSSHATCHING LINES
S7 Quick	LOOKS FOR FIRST ITEM FOUND IN OBJECT SNAP WINDOW
S8 Sel Set	SNAPS TO ITEMS ONLY FOUND IN CURRENTLY ACTIVE SET
S9 Apertur	DISPLAYS THE CURRENT OBJECT SNAP WINDOW ON THE CURSOR
S0 Exit	QUITS THIS MENU (MOUSE BUTTON #3)

Step 7 – When you are through, press the mouse button **3** to quit out of the OBJECT SNAP menu.

Step 8 – Check to see if you can object snap to the middle of a line, by holding your cursor at the midpoint of a line, and pressing the object snap button, mouse button **2**.

Did it work? If not, check your settings again.

Quick keys

Most of the options you can pick from menus also can be entered quickly by simply typing in a key, or a combination of keys, from the keyboard. These are called *quick keys*. You can use quick keys from within other menus, to access the next needed menu fast and easy.

You can use quick keys to enter the OBJECT SNAP menu.

Step 1 – Press the [**Shift**] and **X** keys simultaneously to type a capital X. (You can hold down the [**Shift**] key, then press **X**).

Step 2 – You will enter the OBJECT SNAP menu! Press mouse button **3** to quit.

User note – You can switch to the Object snap menu, using [**Shift**] **X**, anytime you are drawing lines or walls, or even from another menu. Once you quit the OBJECT SNAP menu, you will be returned to whatever menu you were doing or whatever menu you were in last.

Erasing items by picking

You already have learned how to "quick erase" as you are drawing lines. Because you will be starting a new project, you will want to know how to erase all of the lines at once from your screen.

Step 1 – Select the **Erase** option from the EDIT menu. The ERASE menu will be displayed (see FIG. 1-20).

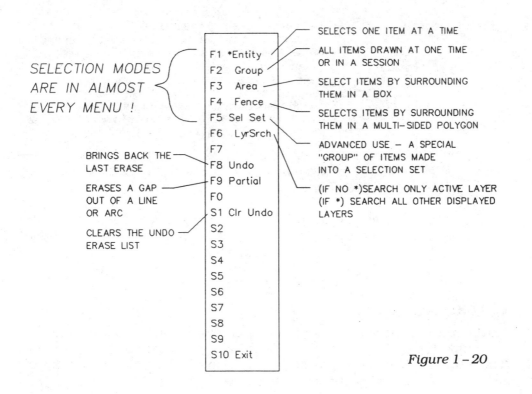

Figure 1 – 20

Step 2 – You will notice that the first 6 choices that appear in the ERASE menu are the "item selection modes." They are:

> Entity
> Group
> Area
> Fence
> SelSet
> LyrSrch

These selection modes are your options for defining how you will "pick" the items to erase. These same selection modes appear in almost every menu in DataCAD. You can erase an **Entity** (single item), a **Group** (all drawn together), an **Area** (items that can be enclosed by a box), or a **Fence** (items enclosed by a polygon). **SelSet** is for use with Selection sets, and you will not use it here. **LyrSrch** is used to pick items on other than the current layer. Because there is only one layer in this drawing, you do not need to use LyrSrch.

Pick the **Entity** option until it is active (***Entity**).

Step 3 – Pick a line to erase. It will be deleted!

Step 4 – Pick the **Area** option until it is active (***Area**).

Step 5 – Pick two points indicating a rectangle around the lines you wish to erase, as indicated in FIG. 1-21. Only the items **completely** enclosed in the box will be erased.

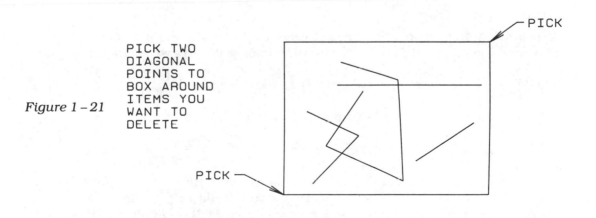

Figure 1 – 21

PICK TWO
DIAGONAL
POINTS TO
BOX AROUND
ITEMS YOU
WANT TO
DELETE

Step 6 – If you made a mistake, pick **Undo**, and all of the items would come back! Try it.

Refreshing your display screen

When you have erased items, you will see a little shadow on other lines the original item crossed. Some people complain that it looks like the item with the shadow "has a hole in it." You might see this happening where lines you erased crossed over lines that are still on your drawing.

What really has happened is the "pixels" have been turned off temporarily. This phenomenon occurs in all of the CAD packages I have used.

To eliminate these shadows, all you have to do is refresh the screen by pressing the [**Esc**] key.

Step 1 – Press the [**Esc**] on your keyboard. Your screen will be refreshed.

If you are using display list processing

Sometimes when you erase items, some of the pixels will remain ON, leaving behind a rather deceptive image of the original item. These images are also referred to as "shadows," but are more correctly known as "ghosts" or "ghost images."

After you erase items, then, it is a good idea to get rid of these ghosts, so that you know what is really happening to your drawing. To do that, you can usually just press the [**Esc**] key, and you should always try that first. However, if a ghost still remains, you can force a regeneration of the display list by pressing the **U** key. This type of regeneration will take longer in a large drawing than using the [**Esc**] key.

Step 1 – Press **U**. The ghosts will disappear.

Creating a fence

You can also draw a *polygon* fence around the items you want to erase. This way, you can stretch the fence around items you don't want erased.

Step 1 – Pick the **Fence** option until it is active (***Fence**).

Step 2 – Pick the first point of your fence.

Step 3 – Pick the second point of your fence.

Step 4 – Now pick a third point. Notice that a corner of the fence is always attached to your cursor. This is how you would "wrap" the polygon fence around items you want erased. See FIG. 1-22 on page 19.

Step 5 – The **Backup** option allows you to "re-pick" the last corner.

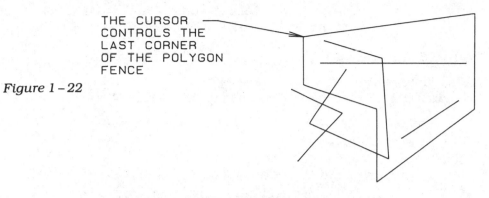

THE CURSOR
CONTROLS THE
LAST CORNER
OF THE POLYGON
FENCE

Figure 1 – 22

Step 6 – Notice that, after the third point of the Fence is created, S0 becomes "close." Press mouse button **3** to close the Fence, erasing the items you have drawn the fence around.

Step 7 – Continue playing with DataCAD for a few minutes, drawing and erasing lines. Get a good feel for using the mouse and pointing to objects. When you feel comfortable using the mouse, switching menus, and practicing what you learned during this lesson, continue to the next steps.

Exiting DataCAD

If you are going directly to the next lesson, you will not want to exit DataCAD. However, you can exit DataCAD and continue your lessons later. If you do want to exit DataCAD, follow these next steps. To ensure that your drawing is permanently saved when you leave DataCAD, make sure that you pick the yes option from the QUIT menu.

Step 1 – Select the **Quit** option from the UTILITY menu.

Step 2 – Notice you are given three options:

> **Abort** – This means you want to leave DataCAD, *without saving* the current drawing.
>
> **Yes** – This option allows you to leave DataCAD, and *save* the current drawing at the same time.
>
> **No** – Selecting this option means you do not want to leave DataCAD, and you will be returned back into the program, with your current drawing displayed.

Step 3 – Pick **Yes**, to *save your current drawing to your hard disk* before leaving the DataCAD program. Your drawing will be saved. The next time you enter DataCAD, all you will have to do is pick your drawing from the drawing list!

DataCAD exercise 1

Please complete the following exercise by reading each question carefully, then circling the letter that corresponds to the correct answer.

1. The first (left most) button on the mouse is used to:
    a. Pick on the screen.
    b. Object snap or to enter a typed value.
    c. Quit an operation or exit a menu.

2. The second (middle) button on the mouse is used to:
    a. Pick on the screen.
    b. Object snap or to enter a typed value.
    c. Quit an operation or exit a menu.

3. The third (right most) button on the mouse is used to:
    a. Pick on the screen.
    b. Object snap or to enter a typed value.
    c. Quit an operation or exit a menu.

4. The two main menus in 2D DataCAD are called:
    a. ERASE and EDIT.
    b. EDIT and UTILITY.
    c. EDIT and OBJECT SNAP.

5. The Mouse is called an:
    a. Processing device.
    b. Input device.
    c. Output device.

6. To make the selection of DataCAD options found in the different menus easy, you can use:
    a. The mouse to pick the menu options only. There is no quick way to enter menus.
    b. Either the mouse to pick options as you read them, press the correct function keys, or (preferably) use the "quick" keys, by pressing the correct key(s) on the keyboard.
    c. The mouse or function keys only. It is not recommended that you use the "Quick" keys from the keyboard.

7. The letters "SWOTHLUD" displayed on your screen:
    a. Mean nothing to you, and are only displayed for programmers.
    b. Help to let you know what your coordinates are.
    c. Are to help you know what the current status of certain settings are (e.g.; if you are drawing "W"alls or lines).

8. Object snapping means to:
   a. Grab onto an item.
   b. Pick anywhere on the screen.
   c. Snap to a grid dot.

9. To erase the last line you drew, you press the:
   a. / key.
   b. < key.
   c. > key.

10. To restore the last line you erased, you press the:
    a. / key.
    b. < key.
    c. > key.

11. To enter the ERASE menu quickly, you press the:
    a. **E** key.
    b. [**Alt**] **E** keys.
    c. < key.

12. To erase many items at one time by indicating a box around them, you use the ERASE option, then pick the:
    a. Box option.
    b. Area option.
    c. Group option.

13. To restore all of the items you erased by indicating a box around them, you use the:
    a. **Restore** option.
    b. [**Shift**] < keys.
    c. **Undo** option, before you leave the ERASE menu.

14. To save your drawing as you leave DataCAD, you select the QUIT option, then pick the:
    a. **Yes** option.
    b. **Save** option.
    c. **Abort** option.

Lesson 2
Initial drawing setup

What you will be doing

During this lesson, you will create a basic drawing setup. This setup will help make it easier to draw your projects during the following lessons. You only need to set up the drawing once. After that, you use the same setup over and over!

Drawing files that contain setup information are called *Default Drawings*. During this lesson you will create one type of Default Drawing—a ¼" scale drawing setup that you will use to complete your practice floor plans.

Later, you will again create default drawings in the lesson called: *Creating Default Drawings*. This advanced lesson covers what can be included in these drawing files in greater detail, and how to create the many different types you might need for your own drawings.

Objectives

Your lesson objectives are to:

- Define the Object Snap settings.
- Create, name, and add color to layers.
- Change the size of your text.
- Create a layout area for your drawing.
- Save your new drawing file to disk.
- Identify the drawing as your default drawing.

Default drawings

Default Drawings are simply drawing files that contain preset information, that you can use over and over again. Once you create a drawing file with the information you need, you can use it as a default drawing.

It only takes a few minutes to set up the settings for a default drawing, and it is one of the first things you will want to do for your own use.

A typical default drawing setup includes the following:

1. Layout area
2. Plotting settings, such as Scale and Paper size
3. Scale Type, Angle Type, and other options found in the SETTINGS menu predetermined
4. Dimension standards
5. Text font and size defined
6. Layers named and colors assigned
7. Display options set
8. Grids and Grid Snap defined
9. Linetype spacing
10. Object Snap settings

You will want to develop several Default Drawings for your personal, company, or school use—at least one for each size and type of drawing you create.

Note: If you are using a system that already has default drawings created on it, you might want to skip this section and use the existing default drawings. However, you can still study the steps that are involved for your own information, and you might choose to set up your own "training" defaults for practice.

Another note: the defaults created here result in a drawing file size of approximately 8,192 bytes in size. If you are using your own defaults that have drawing borders, logos, and other geometry as well as layers, the file size will be larger.

DataCAD 128 alert!

If you are using DataCAD 128, you will want to make sure your default drawings are small in file size. If you are sharing defaults from people who own the regular DataCAD software, check their file size before using them. The smallest a default drawing can be is 8,192 bytes, so the steps described here are quite satisfactory for your use.

How a default drawing is used

Once you have created your default drawings, you use them over and over again for all of your drawings.

When you start a new drawing, you first want to identify which default drawing you will be using. The default drawing serves as a basis for your drawing. Then you simply create your new drawing file, and all of the defaults you set appear! This flow is described in FIG. 2-1.

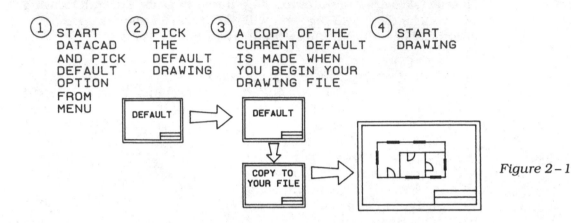

Figure 2-1

Your first Default Drawing you create during this lesson will be very basic, with only the minimum variables set. The reason for this is simple: With just the minimum settings, you can start drawing immediately. Later, during the lesson called *Creating Default Drawings*, you will learn more details about setting up your default drawings.

The default file directory

Just like the special drawer in the filing cabinet for the DataCAD software (MTEC), there is a special folder in the drawer for your default drawings. This folder is called DEFAULT. (FIG. 2-2.)

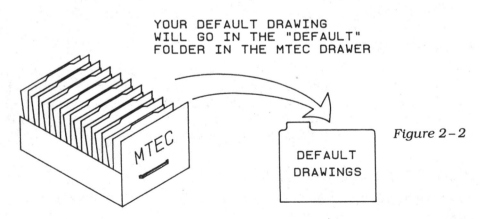

Figure 2-2

Creating your default directory

You create your default drawing as you would any DataCAD drawing. You just have to make sure you create this drawing in the correct directory.

Step 1 – Start DataCAD. If you are already in a DataCAD drawing, select **File I/O** (UTILITY menu), **New Dwg, Yes** to return to the opening screen.

Step 2 – Select the **New Path** option. This option allows you to tell Data-CAD to look in certain directories (or "file drawer and folder") for a drawing. (In this case, your Default Drawing.)

Step 3 – Type in the pathname for your default drawings. The easiest name for this directory is: **Default.**

Remember to press the [**Enter**] key after typing in the pathname.

Step 4 – If a file folder (directory) called "default" does not already exist in the MTEC drawer, you will be given an opportunity to create one, as in FIG. 2-3.

Figure 2–3

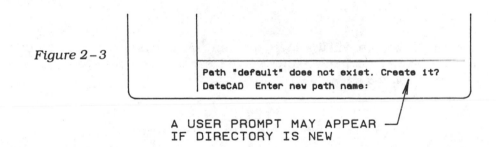

```
Path "default" does not exist. Create it?
DataCAD  Enter new path name:
```

A USER PROMPT MAY APPEAR
IF DIRECTORY IS NEW

Step 5 – If you are given a Yes/No choice to create this directory, select the **Yes** option.

Step 6 – Now you can create your Default drawing file. Type in the new name for your Default Drawing: **1-4PLAN**. This name will represent a drawing setup for a ¼ plan layout. Press the [**Enter**] key.

Note – Certain characters are illegal in directory and file names. This includes the **/, :, ?,** and any blank spaces. The \ character is also illegal in a name, because it delineates between directory names. Also, due to DOS format, the actual name is limited to eight (8) characters.

Step 7 – An empty drawing file will be displayed, which holds the Data-
CAD original settings. A grid pattern will be displayed on the
screen. DataCAD includes this predefined grid pattern in their
default settings. (See FIG. 2-4.)

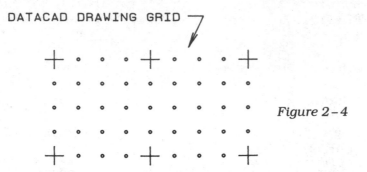

Figure 2–4

The grid settings

The grid in the DataCAD default drawing is displayed in the following settings:

Large Grid = 16 feet
Small Grid = 4 feet

This grid definition will work well for your first drawing setup. Later, during the Default Drawings lesson, you will learn to customize your grid settings. (See FIG. 2-5.)

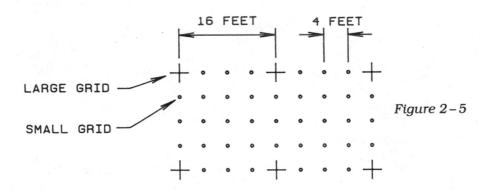

Figure 2–5

Snap setting

The *snap* definition for your cursor is set to four (4) inches. You can verify
this by moving your cursor into the drawing area. You will notice that the
cursor jumps to 4″ increments. If you look at your coordinate readout, you
will see that only 4″ coordinates are displayed. (See FIG. 2-6.)

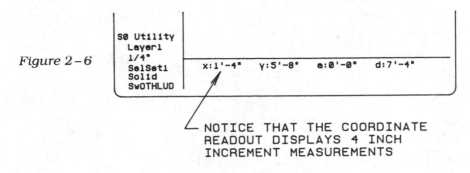

Figure 2-6

NOTICE THAT THE COORDINATE
READOUT DISPLAYS 4 INCH
INCREMENT MEASUREMENTS

This snap is designed to make it easier to place lines, walls, and other objects.

Setting the object snap

You will want to make sure the object snap defaults are set. This way, you will not have to set them each time.

Step 1 – Press the [**Shift**] and **X** keys together. The OBJECT SNAP menu will be displayed.

Step 2 – Pick the following options, until they have a "*****" in front of them:

> **End Pnt**
> **Mid Pnt**
> **Center**
> **LyrSnap**

(The "**LyrSnap**" option tells the system to search on all layers as you try to object snap onto an item.)

Step 3 – Press mouse button **3** to quit.

Creating layers

Each layer you define will hold a certain type of item. Your walls, for instance, will all be on their own layer. Your doors will be on their own layer too. Dimensions also are placed on a special layer. (FIG. 2-7.)

This type of item separation makes it possible to turn off and on the layers that contain the items you wish to view or plot. For example, you can turn off the furniture level and the reflected ceiling plan, in order to display only the floor plan and the electrical plan. (See FIG. 2-8.)

Step 1 – Press **L** to enter the LAYERS menu. This is the quick way to enter the LAYERS menu. Or, you can select the **Layers** option from the UTILITY menu.

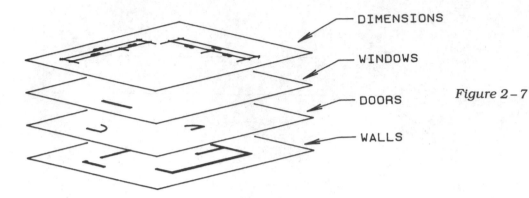

DIMENSIONS

WINDOWS

DOORS

WALLS

Figure 2–7

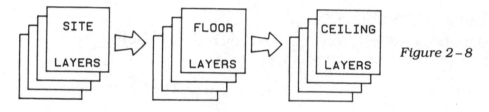

SITE LAYERS → FLOOR LAYERS → CEILING LAYERS

Figure 2–8

YOU CAN TURN OFF AND ON THE LAYERS
YOU NEED FOR YOUR FINISHED PLANS

Step 2 – Pick the **On/Off** option.

Step 3 – Notice that there is only 1 layer: Layer1. You will want to add 8 more layers, to make a total of 9 layers.

Step 4 – Press mouse button **3** once, to quit back to the LAYERS menu.

Step 5 – Pick the **NewLayer** option.

Step 6 – Pick the **8** option, and [**Enter**].

Step 7 – Pick the **Name** option, to name your layers.

Step 8 – Pick **Layer1**, as in FIG. 2-9.

Step 9 – Type in and the new name for this layer: **Walls** and press [**Enter**].

Step 10 – Pick **Layer2**.

Step 11 – Type in and the new name for this layer: **Doors** and press [**Enter**].

```
PICK THE ──────        ┌────────────────┐
LAYER          ╲──────▶│ F1   LAYER1    │
                       │ F2   LAYER2    │
                       │ F3   LAYER3    │
                       │ F4   LAYER4    │
                       │ F5   LAYER5    │
                       │ F6   LAYER6    │
                       │ F7   LAYER7    │
      Figure 2-9       │ F8   LAYER8    │
                       │ F9   LAYER9    │
                       │ F0             │
                       │ S1             │
                       │ S2             │
                       │ S3             │
                       └────────────────┘
```

Step 12 – Continue naming the layers for your default drawing, as indicated below and in FIG. 2-10.

> Layer 1 = **Walls**
> Layer 2 = **Doors**
> Layer 3 = **Windows**
> Layer 4 = **Cabinet**
> Layer 5 = **Furn**
> Layer 6 = **Plumb**
> Layer 7 = **Dims**
> Layer 8 = **Notes**
> Layer 9 = **Border**

Notice: Never name two layers alike!

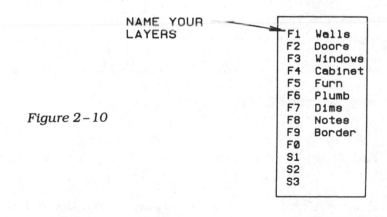

```
NAME YOUR ──────       ┌────────────────┐
LAYERS         ╲──────▶│ F1   Walls     │
                       │ F2   Doors     │
                       │ F3   Windows   │
                       │ F4   Cabinet   │
                       │ F5   Furn      │
                       │ F6   Plumb     │
                       │ F7   Dims      │
      Figure 2-10      │ F8   Notes     │
                       │ F9   Border    │
                       │ F0             │
                       │ S1             │
                       │ S2             │
                       │ S3             │
                       └────────────────┘
```

Step 13 – Press mouse button **3** to quit back to the LAYERS menu.

Setting the layer colors

When you define a color to a layer, items drawn on that layer will appear in that color. Later, you can identify colors to match certain pens in your plotter.

Step 1 – Pick the **Color** option, to give each layer a color.

Step 2 – The color you define will be set for the *active* layer. Notice that the current active layer is Walls, and the layer name is displayed in "white," as indicated in FIG. 2-11.

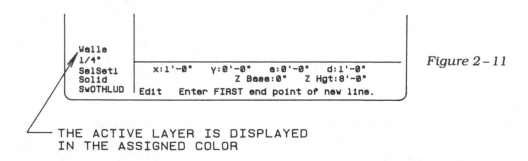

```
   Walls
   1/4"
   SelSet1      x:1'-0"    y:0'-0"    a:0'-0"    d:1'-0"
   Solid                        Z Base:0"    Z Hgt:8'-0"
   SwOTHLUD  | Edit    Enter FIRST end point of new line.
```
THE ACTIVE LAYER IS DISPLAYED
IN THE ASSIGNED COLOR

Figure 2 – 11

Step 3 – You will keep this layer white, to see the walls that you draw easily.

Step 4 – Change the active layer to **Doors**, by simply pressing the [**Tab**] key once. If you press the [**Tab**] key again, the active layer will turn to **Windows**, as indicated in FIG. 2-12.

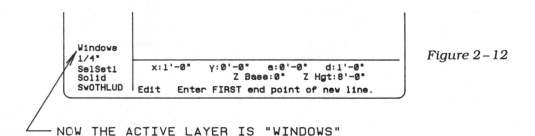

```
   Windows
   1/4"
   SelSet1      x:1'-0"    y:0'-0"    a:0'-0"    d:1'-0"
   Solid                        Z Base:0"    Z Hgt:8'-0"
   SwOTHLUD  | Edit    Enter FIRST end point of new line.
```
NOW THE ACTIVE LAYER IS "WINDOWS"

Figure 2 – 12

Step 5 – Continuing to press the [**Tab**] key will scroll you through the entire layer list. You can go backward through this list, by holding down the [**Shift**] key, then pressing [**Tab**].

Step 6 – Change the active layer until you are returned to the **Doors** layer. (FIG. 2-13.)

Step 7 – Pick the **Green** option.

Step 8 – Press the [**Tab**] key to change the active layer to **Windows**. (FIG. 2-14.)

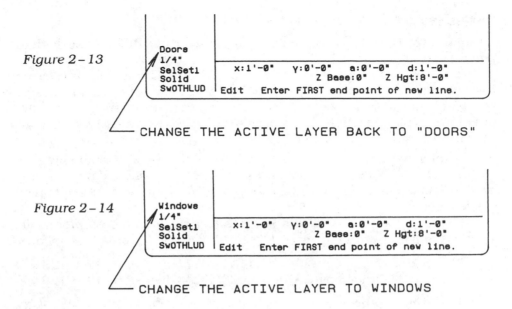

Figure 2–13

```
Doors
1/4"
SelSet1        x:1'-0"   y:0'-0"   a:0'-0"   d:1'-0"
Solid                              Z Base:0"   Z Hgt:8'-0"
SWOTHLUD  |Edit    Enter FIRST end point of new line.
```

CHANGE THE ACTIVE LAYER BACK TO "DOORS"

Figure 2–14

```
Windows
1/4"
SelSet1        x:1'-0"   y:0'-0"   a:0'-0"   d:1'-0"
Solid                              Z Base:0"   Z Hgt:8'-0"
SWOTHLUD  |Edit    Enter FIRST end point of new line.
```

CHANGE THE ACTIVE LAYER TO WINDOWS

Step 9 – Pick the **Color** option again.

Step 10 – Pick the **Cyan** option.

Step 11 – Now the **Windows** layer name displayed will appear in a cyan color.

Step 12 – Continue setting the colors for your layers, matching the settings listed below:

Walls	= **White**		Plumb	= **Lt. Blue**
Doors	= **Green**		Dims	= **Brown**
Windows	= **Cyan**		Notes	= **Green**
Cabinet	= **Lt Mgta**		Border	= **Yellow**
Furn	= **Lt Blue**			

Drawing boundary

As part of your setup, you will add a rectangle to help indicate your drawing area. When you plot your drawing, then, it will easily fit on a drawing sheet. For this default drawing setup, you will plan for a D size sheet.

The D size sheet is 24 inches by 36 inches. The actual drawing area is 23 by 32 inches, when you allow for a standard border. You will want your scaled plot to fit inside this area.

Plotted (scaled) size verses actual size

Using DataCAD, you are able to plot your drawing at a different scale than you drew it in.

Your CAD drawings should be drawn in FULL SCALE. This is referred to as *actual size*. When you plot your drawing, it will come out at a scaled size (such as 1/4" scale). DataCAD makes this easy to do, and you usually only have to plan for these differences when you are creating your default drawing setup.

Because you will be creating all of the elements of your drawings in full size (1" = 1"), you need to calculate the *actual size* of your drawing area. This calculation will be the size you create your "drawing area rectangle." See FIG. 2-15.

The formula for this calculation is: *sheet size divided by plot scale*. Because you are setting up for a 1/4" scaled plot, the formula is as follows:

23 × 32: 23 divided by .25/12 = 1104.0017" divided by 12 = 92 feet
32 divided by .25/12 = 1536.0024" divided by 12 = 128 feet

The actual size of the drawing area rectangle needs to be 92' × 128'. (FIG. 2-16.)

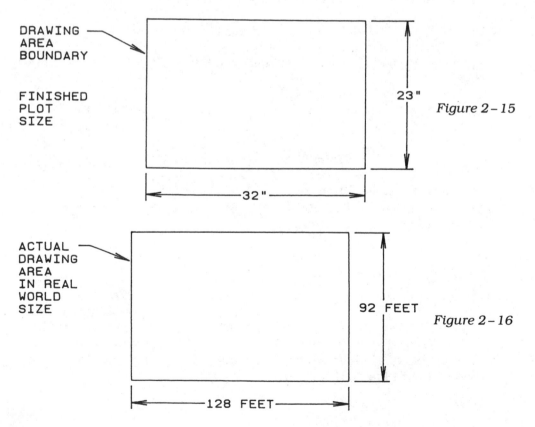

DRAWING
AREA
BOUNDARY

FINISHED
PLOT
SIZE

23"

32"

Figure 2-15

ACTUAL
DRAWING
AREA
IN REAL
WORLD
SIZE

92 FEET

128 FEET

Figure 2-16

Dimensions for this plot area and additional sizes for several plot scales are included in Appendix B *DataCAD Reference Guide*, Scales and Formulas section.

Creating a rectangle

You can define a rectangle by its two diagonal points. You will pick the first point with your cursor. Then you will type in the measurement for the second point. This is achieved by using relative cartesian coordinates.

Step 1 – Your **Border** layer should be displayed. This is the layer that is going to hold your rectangle. If it is not displayed as active in the status area, press the [**Tab**] key until it is. See FIG. 2-17.

Figure 2 – 17

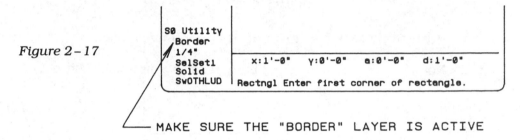

MAKE SURE THE "BORDER" LAYER IS ACTIVE

Step 2 – Pick the **Polygons** option from the EDIT menu.

Step 3 – Pick the **Rectngl** option.

Step 4 – Pick a grid point on your drawing, as indicated in FIG. 2-18. This will be the first corner of your rectangle.

Figure 2 – 18

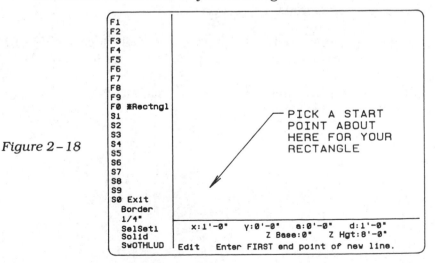

Step 5 – Press the [**Insert**] key. This key allows you to set the type of coordinate input you will use. Coordinate input modes allow you to type in the dimensions of items.

Keep pressing the [**Insert**] key until the user prompt reads: **The input mode is *relative cartesian***. This is illustrated in FIG. 2-19.

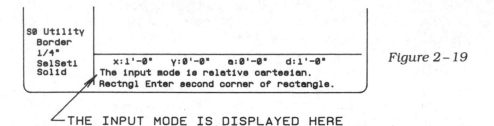

Figure 2 – 19

THE INPUT MODE IS DISPLAYED HERE

Step 6 – Press the [**Space bar**] to invoke the coordinate mode.

Step 7 – Notice you are prompted to "**Enter relative x distance**." (FIG. 2-20.)

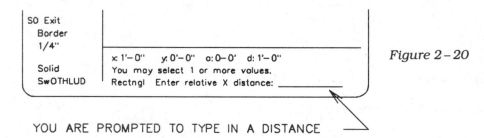

Figure 2 – 20

YOU ARE PROMPTED TO TYPE IN A DISTANCE

Step 8 – Type in **128** and press [**Enter**]. This will tell the system: 128 feet in the horizontal (X) direction.

Step 9 – Now you are prompted: **Enter relative Y distance**. Type in **92** and press [**Enter**]. This is the distance in the vertical direction.

Step 10 – Now your rectangle is displayed, as in FIG. 2-21.

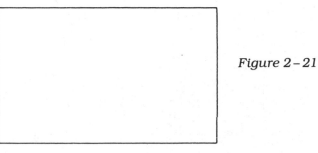

Figure 2 – 21

Step 11 – If your rectangle appears off the screen (FIG. 2-22), you can easily resize your viewing window.

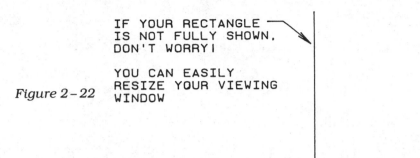

```
          IF YOUR RECTANGLE
          IS NOT FULLY SHOWN,
          DON'T WORRY!

          YOU CAN EASILY
          RESIZE YOUR VIEWING
Figure 2–22    WINDOW
```

Step 12 – Press the [/] key (forward slash—also has a ? on it).

Step 13 – Select the **Re-Calc** option. This option recalculates the extents of your viewing window. (FIG. 2-23.)

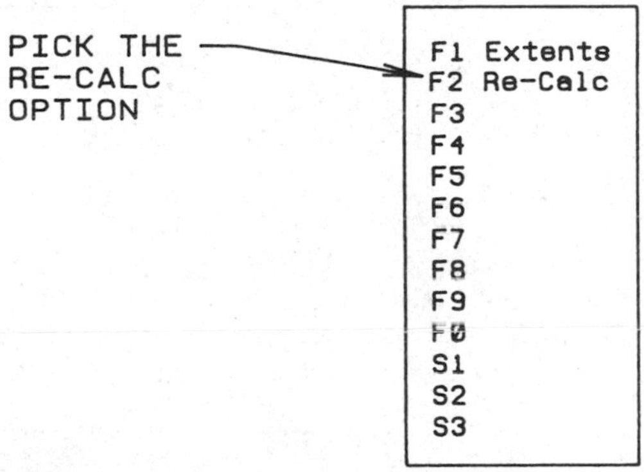

```
          PICK THE              F1 Extents
          RE-CALC               F2 Re-Calc
          OPTION                F3
                                F4
                                F5
                                F6
          Figure 2–23           F7
                                F8
                                F9
                                F0
                                S1
                                S2
                                S3
```

Presetting the plot specifications

You will want to set up the plot scale of your drawing.

Step 1 – Remember to press mouse button **3** to quit to the UTILITY menu.

Step 2 – Pick the **Plotter** option from the UTILITY menu.

Step 3 – Pick the **Scale** option.

Step 4 – Pick the **1/4″** option.

Step 5 – Pick the **PaperSiz** option.

Step 6 – Pick **Custom**.

Step 7 – Type in **32** for the width. (This menu assumes you are inputting inches.) Press [**Enter**].

Step 8 – Type in **23** for 23 inches in the height. Remember to press [**Enter**].

Step 9 – Press the mouse button **3** once, to return to the PLOTTER menu.

Step 10 – Pick the **Layout** option, to lay the *plotting area outline* on your rectangle.

Step 11 – Notice that a layout box is attached to your cursor, and that you are dragging it around by its centerpoint. (FIG. 2-24.)

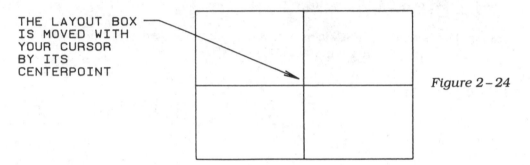

THE LAYOUT BOX
IS MOVED WITH
YOUR CURSOR
BY ITS
CENTERPOINT

Figure 2 – 24

Step 12 – Place the layout box over your rectangle, and object snap to the rectangle centerpoint by pressing mouse button **2**. (FIG. 2-25.)

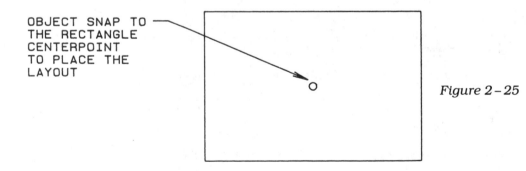

OBJECT SNAP TO
THE RECTANGLE
CENTERPOINT
TO PLACE THE
LAYOUT

Figure 2 – 25

Setting up your plotter pens

You can tell the plotter what pen it should pick up when it draws a line or other item. This is achieved by assigning pen numbers to colors. In other words, you can tell the system that everytime it plots an item that is colored cyan to use pen number 2, which happens to be a thicker pen than pen number 1.

You will define 4 pens for your setup. Number 1 will be the thinnest, and 4 the thickest.

Step 1 – Pick the **Set Pens** option from the PLOTTER menu, to define which pens will be used with which colors.

Step 2 – Pick **White**.

Step 3 – Enter the appropriate number for your pen: **4**.
This number will indicate the thickest pen for your walls.

Step 4 – Pick the next color you will be using: **Green**

Step 5 – Enter the number for this color: **2**
This number will indicate a thinner pen for your doors.

Step 6 – Continue defining pens for the colors you are using, as described here:

> White   = **4**   (walls)
> Green   = **2**   (doors, notes, and dimension text)
> Cyan   = **2**   (windows)
> Brown   = **1**   (dimension lines)
> Lt Blue = **2**   (furniture and plumbing)
> Lt Mgta = **3**   (cabinets)
> Yellow = **4**   (border)

These pen numbers later will be associated with appropriate pens in the plotter. The recommended pen widths that could be used with this type of numbering are (in point size for wet ink pens):

1 = .25
2 = .35
3 = .50
4 = .75

Step 7 – Once the numbers are defined, press mouse button **3** to quit back to the PLOTTER menu.

Step 8 – Check to make sure the following options have a star in front of the option name (*****). This means the option is active. If there is not a star, then pick the option until a star appears.

*ClrPlot
*PenSort

Step 9 – Press mouse button **3** to quit back to the UTILITY menu.

Dimension variables

You can set the variable once, in the LINEAR menu, and they will be set for all of the dimension types.

Step 1 – Press [**Alt**] **D** to quickly enter the UTILITY/Dmension/Linear menus.

Step 2 – Pick **TextStyl**.

Step 3 – Pick **TextSize**.

Step 4 – Because this drawing will be plotted at ¼″ scale (and the text also will be plotted at ¼″ scale), you must make sure the text is large enough to appear at ⅛″ on the finished plot. (See appendix B, The DataCAD Reference Guide, DataCAD Scales and Sizes.)

For a ¼″ scale plot, the text should be set at 6 inches. The formula for this is:

12 divided by drawing scale X desired text size.

- or -

12/.25 = 48
48 X .125 = 6 inches

Step 5 – Pick the 6″ option, or type in 0.6 for your text height. The system will read this as 6 inches. Press [**Enter**].

0.6

Step 6 – Pick **Color**. This will allow you to define a color for the text that will appear in your dimensions. This way you can have a wider pen for the text than for the dimension lines.

Step 7 – Pick **Green**.

Step 8 – Press mouse button **3** once to return to the Linear menu, then pick **Dim Styl**.

Step 9 – Pick ***FixdDis** until the star (*****) turns OFF. This option fixes the distance between the drawing and the dimension. To allow you to easily adjust this distance and place the dimension with the cursor, you want to turn it off. So, there should be no star by FixdDis.

Step 10 – Press mouse button **3** once, then pick the **ArroStyl** option.

Step 11 – Make the **TicMrks** option active.

Step 12 – Press mouse button **3** to quit to the EDIT menu.

Setting the text size for notes

You also need to adjust the text size you will be using to add your notes.

Step 1 – Pick the **Text** option, found in the EDIT menu.

Step 2 – Pick the **Size** option.

Step 3 – Change the size of your text to 6 inches again, which will be plotted at $1/8$ inch.

   0.6

Step 4 – Press mouse button **3** to quit to the UTILITY menu.

Saving your default drawing

Now you are ready to save your default drawing.

Step 1 – Pick the **File I/O** option, found in the UTILITY menu.

Step 2 – Pick **New Dwg**.

Step 3 – Pick **Yes** to save your default drawing.

User reminder – Do not pick **Abort**, or you will trash the settings you just created!

Step 4 – The Default Drawing list is displayed. Notice that your default drawing is added to this list. (FIG. 2-26.)

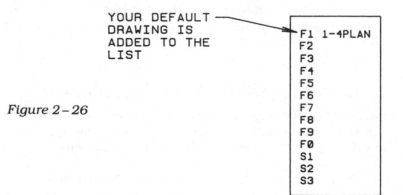

```
YOUR DEFAULT
DRAWING IS
ADDED TO THE
LIST
```

```
F1 1-4PLAN
F2
F3
F4
F5
F6
F7
F8
F9
F0
S1
S2
S3
```

Figure 2–26

Creating a 1:20 scale site default drawing

Follow the same steps that you did to create your $1/4''$ scale drawing, using the following variables:

1. Name of default drawing: **1-20SITE**
2. Add 6 new layers, to make a total of 7.
3. Name Layers:

    Layer 1 = **PROPLIN**
    Layer 2 = **STREET**
    Layer 3 = **BLDG**
    Layer 4 = **PARKING**
    Layer 5 = **TEXT**
    Layer 6 = **DIMS**
    Layer 7 = **BORDER**

4. Color Layers:

    PROPLIN = **Lt Mgta**
    STREET = **Lt Cyan**
    BLDG   = **Lt Cyan**
    PARKING = **Lt Grn**
    TEXT   = **Green**
    DIMS   = **Brown**
    BORDER = **Yellow**

5. Rectangle size (layout area):

    X = 640'
    Y = 460'

6. Plot Scale: **1:20**
7. Set Pens:

    Green   = 2
    Brown   = 1
    Lt Grn   = 2
    Lt Cyan = 3
    Lt Mgta = 4
    Yellow   = 4

8. Dimension Text and Note Text Size: **2.5 feet**
9. Remember to save your drawing, using the **File I/O, New Dwg, Yes** options.

Getting ready to draw using the default drawings

Once your default drawings are filed (using the **File I/O, New Dwg, Yes** options), you are ready to begin drawing. To do so, you will want to bring back the original drawing list. This is done by changing the pathname again.

Remember, the pathname is a way to describe to the system "what drawer to look in," or what directory, for your drawings. Currently, you set your pathname to the DEFAULT directory, which exists in the MTEC drawer. This means that only the default drawings are displayed.

Now you will change it back to DWG directory. This is the directory that came with DataCAD, and it contains some sample drawings.

Step 1 – At the DataCAD *drawing list* screen, pick the **New Path** option.

Step 2 – Type in **DWG** and press [**Enter**].

      -or-

      1. Pick **..** that appears in the [**F2**] option. This will take you out of the DEFAULT directory and into the MTEC directory.
      2. Pick **DWG**.
      3. Press mouse button **3** to quit back to the DWG drawing list.

Step 3 – Notice that the original drawing list appears on the left side of the screen.

DataCAD exercise 2

Please complete the following exercise by reading each question carefully, then circling the letter that corresponds to the correct answer.

1. You should create:
   a. 5 default drawings. This is as many as anyone would ever need.
   b. At least 1 for every different scale you will need, and for different layer naming schemes.
   c. 10 default drawings. This is the maximum you can create.

2. To change into another directory in order to access other drawing files (such as the DEFAULT directory), you use the:
   a. DIRECTORY menu, **New Dir** option.
   b. File I/O, **New Dwg** option to retrieve the Drawing List screen (or the first DataCAD menu if you are just starting DataCAD), then pick the **New Dir** option.
   c. File I/O, **New Dwg** option to retrieve the Drawing List screen (or the first DataCAD menu if you are just starting DataCAD), then pick the **New Path** option.

3. Default drawings are created in order to:
   a. Save many steps, increase productivity, help eliminate errors, and establish consistency in all of your CADD drawings.
   b. Increase the time-consuming steps in every drawing. Using Default drawings is not recommended.

4. Your default drawings should reside in the:
   a. MTEC/DEFAULT directory.

b. MTEC/DWG directory.
c. MTEC/SYM directory.

5. To create layers in your drawing, you use the LAYERS menus, then pick the:
   a. **AddLayer** option.
   b. **NewLayer** option.
   c. **On/Off** option.

6. Once you have added layers to your drawing, next you should:
   a. Use the **Snap** option found in the LAYERS menu, to define a snap setting for each layer.
   b. Name your layers.
   c. Leave the LAYERS menu. The layers will be automatically named.

7. The actual scale of the drawing:
   a. Is determined once you define a plot scale in your default drawing. All walls and lines are drawn full scale as you create them, then are plotted at the appropriate scale. Text, however, must be sized in accordance to the final plot scale.
   b. Effects the way you create walls and other lines. These type of entities must be scaled as you draw them.
   c. Doesn't effect the text size setting. No matter what your scale is, the text size stays the same.

8. To define the pens your plotter will use as the drawing is plotted, you use the:
   a. LAYER menu, **Color** and **Set Pens** options.
   b. PLOTTER menu, **Set Pens** option.
   c. PLOTTER menu, **Color** option.

9. Different pens are assigned to different entities in your drawing by associating pen numbers to:
   a. Linetypes.
   b. Colors.
   c. Line Widths.

10. When setting your Dimension variables, you:
    a. Have to define variables for all the different types of dimensions.
    b. Only have to define the variables for Linear and Angular dimensions.
    c. Only have to define the variables for Linear dimensions. These variables will then be set for all the dimension types.

11. The Text Size that you set in your default drawing is defined at:
   a. The appropriate size in relation to the plotting scale. (e.g.; If the drawing is to be plotted at $1/4''$, text created 6 inches high will be plotted at $1/8''$ high.)
   b. The size you want it plotted. It will always turn out the correct size, regardless of the plotted scale.

12. The text size must be set in:
   a. The TEXT menu only.
   b. Both the TEXT and DIMENSIONS menu.
   c. The TEXT, DIMENSION, and PLOTTER menus.

13. The most important thing to know about your drawings BEFORE you create your default drawings, is the:
   a. Text size.
   b. Paper size.
   c. Scale you will be plotting your drawing at.

Lesson 3
Basic drafting techniques

What you will be doing

You will use DataCAD to create a floor plan. You will add windows and doors, and use different kinds of snapping as well as coordinate input techniques. You will also organize the kinds of items you create (walls, doors, and windows) onto separate layers in your drawing.

Remember to refer to appendix A, *The DataCAD Operations Guide* when instructed. This section is your "quick" guide to DataCAD operations.

Objectives

Your lesson objectives are to:

- Select a default drawing.
- Create walls.
- Change the snap increment.
- Change layers.
- Add windows.
- Add doors.
- Define a reference point to help place items.
- Use coordinate input.

Walls

Look at the project shown in FIG. 3-1. This will be your first practice drawing. Walls are created easily using DataCAD. When you draw a wall, it looks like a double line. The space between the line is the wall *width*. This space is

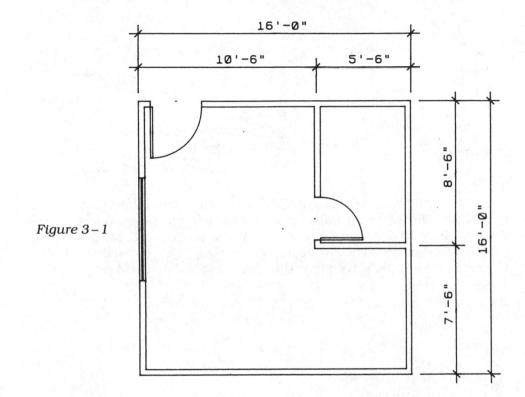

Figure 3–1

accurate to the actual width you define for your wall. In other words, an internal wall might be one width, while an external wall another width, and the difference is accurately represented on your screen. (FIG. 3-2.)

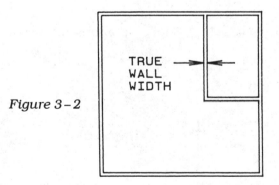

TRUE WALL WIDTH

Figure 3–2

What you don't see when you are drawing your wall is the "height" of your wall. Your wall is being drawn with the real floor, or "base" elevation, and the real ceiling, or "height" elevation. You are drawing a 3-dimensional wall! (FIG. 3-3.)

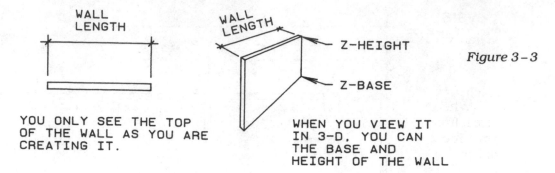

Figure 3 – 3

WALL LENGTH

WALL LENGTH

Z–HEIGHT

Z–BASE

YOU ONLY SEE THE TOP
OF THE WALL AS YOU ARE
CREATING IT.

WHEN YOU VIEW IT
IN 3–D, YOU CAN
THE BASE AND
HEIGHT OF THE WALL

This is all automatic in DataCAD. You can define different base and height elevations for your walls before you draw them. This is referred to as the "Z" base and height. The X and Y coordinates are parallel to the screen in ortho view. The Z coordinate is the height of your walls, which is perpendicular to the screen in ortho view. This is illustrated in FIG. 3-4.

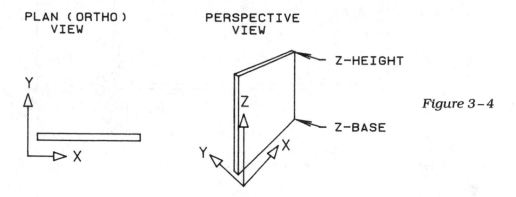

PLAN (ORTHO)
VIEW

PERSPECTIVE
VIEW

Z–HEIGHT

Z–BASE

Figure 3 – 4

The beginning base and height elevations, as shown in FIG. 3-5, are set to:

Z-base = 0.0
Z-height = 8.0

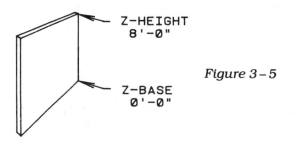

Z–HEIGHT
8'-0"

Z–BASE
0'-0"

Figure 3 – 5

Layers

When you examine a drawing, you naturally look at the entities (lines, arcs, etc.) as being certain types of items. These items might be walls, doors, windows, property lines, among other types of items that appear in your drawings.

When you create one type of item, such as walls, you will want to separate it from other types of items in your drawing. This is done by using "layers." You will put your walls on a layer called "Walls." When you create a different type of item, such as doors, you will separate that item onto another layer. Doors will reside on the "Doors" layer. When you create windows, you will put them on the "Windows" layer. This type of item layering helps you organize the entities in your drawing, as illustrated in FIG. 3-6.

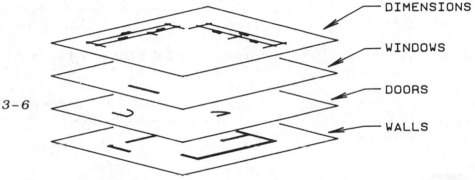

Figure 3-6

The concept of layering started with the pin graphics technique used in manual drafting, often called overlaying or overlay drafting. This technique permits items pertaining to certain disciplines to be divided onto separate sheets for many different reasons.

The same idea is used in your CADD drawings. When each type of entity is separated onto layers, then a series of layers can be viewed, plotted, and worked on independently or in conjunction with other entities in the drawing. (FIG. 3-7.)

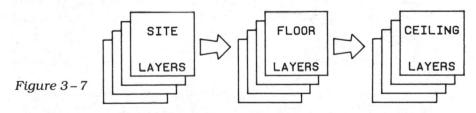

Figure 3-7

MANY DIFFERENT PLANS CAN BE WORKED ON USING THE SAME BASE LAYERS, AND TURNING ON AND OFF LAYERS FOR THAT DISCIPLINE

During this lesson, you will learn how easy it is to apply these techniques and to learn the essential skills for beginning drafting with DataCAD!

Starting the floor plan

To begin the floor plan (project 001), you will first want to create a drawing file. This drawing file will use the **1-4PLAN** default drawing you created during the **Initial Drawing Setup** in the previous lesson.

Step 1 – If you are not in the DataCAD program, type in: start DataCAD.

If you are presently in a DataCAD drawing, start a new drawing by selecting:

File I/O (UTILITY menu)
New Dwg
Yes

Step 2 – Before you begin a new drawing you will want to create a special drawing directory (special "folder") that will hold your personal drawings.

This "pathname" is where your lesson drawing projects will be stored on your computer (a special folder in the MTEC drawer of the file cabinet). See FIG. 3-8.

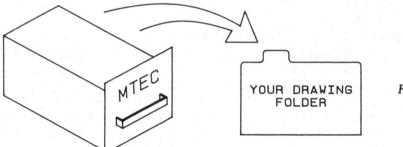

Figure 3–8

YOUR DRAWINGS WILL GO IN A SPECIAL DIRECTORY

Step 3 – Pick the **New Path** option.

Step 4 – Type in your first or last name for the directory name. This way, you will always be able to identify whose practice drawings are in this directory. Later, you will name your directories by project name instead of your name. (Only 8 alphanumeric characters are allowed.) Remember to press [**Enter**].

Step 5 – Since this is a new directory, a prompt will be displayed that informs you this directory does not exist, as in FIG. 3-9. If this directory already exists (perhaps you created it before), this prompt will not be displayed.

Figure 3 – 9

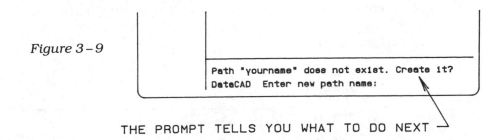

Path "yourname" does not exist. Create it?
DataCAD Enter new path name:

THE PROMPT TELLS YOU WHAT TO DO NEXT

Step 6 – Select the **Yes** option to create your new directory.

Step 7 – Now that you have defined the directory for your practice drawings, you do not have to go through these steps again. The directory will stay active until you tell the system you want to use another directory.

Of course, if you are sharing this computer with others that use the DataCAD program, they might want to switch the path to their own directory. In this case, you will have to reset your pathname before you work on your drawings again.

Step 8 – Now that you have created your new directory, you will choose the type of default drawing you will use. Select the **Default** option.

Step 9 – The Default Drawing list is displayed. Pick the default drawing you created for your 1/4 scale floor plans: **1-4PLAN**.

Notice: If the Default Drawing names do not appear:

1. Pick the **New Path** option.
2. Type in and [**Enter**]: **default**
3. Now pick the default you will use: **1-4PLAN**

Step 10 – Type in the name of your drawing project: **PLAN1**.

Step 11 – Your drawing file will be created, and you are ready to begin drawing!

Drawing walls

Refer to the project shown in FIG. 3-1. Notice that your project has exterior walls, interior walls, doors, and windows. First, you will make the exterior walls. This is easily done by using the "drawing walls" mode and either picking the placement of the wall with your cursor, or by using relative cartesian coordinates.

Step 1 – Make sure your **Walls** layer is active. If it is not, then press the [**Tab**] key until "Walls" appears in the "**Status area**" of your screen, as in FIG. 3-10.

```
                    S9 Macros
                    S0 Utility
"WALLS" ────────→ Walls
SHOULD              1/4"        x:9'-0"  y:12'-8"  a:54-36'-19"  d:15'-6 15/32       Figure 3-10
APPEAR
IN STATUS           Solid
AREA                SwOTHLUD | Edit    Enter first end point of new line.
```

Step 2 – Press the wall = key. This is the quick key to turn from the "drawing lines" mode, to "drawing walls."

Notice: The lines mode should have been active, and you should get a prompt that asks you to indicate a wall width. If you were set for walls already, you will be toggled to the lines mode ("**Now drawing lines**"). If you are not presented with a prompt to type in (enter) a wall width, just press the = key again.

Step 3 – The user prompt asks you to establish a wall thickness. Notice that it is already set to **4"**. You will accept this value by pressing [**Enter**].

Step 4 – You will draw the exterior walls first. Notice that these walls are dimensioned to the outside of the walls. You will want to use an option in DataCAD called **Sides** to draw your walls.

Press **A** to go to the **Architect** option, found in the EDIT menu.

Step 5 – Pick the **Sides** option, until a * appears in front of the option (***Sides**).

Step 6 – You can draw in this menu or press mouse button **3** to quit.

Step 7 – Pick the start point of your wall with your cursor, using mouse button **1**, as indicated in FIG. 3-11. Make sure the start point is inside the border rectangle.

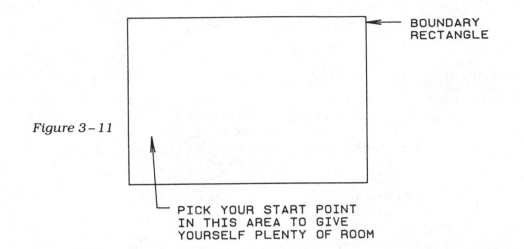

Figure 3 – 11

BOUNDARY
RECTANGLE

PICK YOUR START POINT
IN THIS AREA TO GIVE
YOURSELF PLENTY OF ROOM

Step 8 – Pick the second corner of your wall, using the grid as reference for measuring. You will notice that the coordinate readout displays the distance you are picking. "Picking" is one way to determine item placement (such as placing your wall). (FIG. 3-12.)

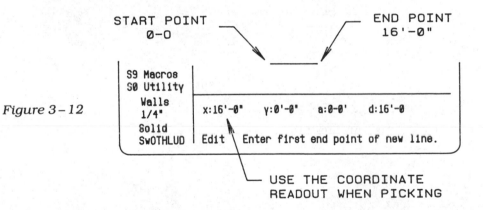

Figure 3 – 12

START POINT
0–0

END POINT
16'–0"

S9 Macros
S0 Utility
Walls
1/4"
Solid
SwOTHLUD

x:16'-0"   y:0'-0"   a:0-0'   d:16'-0

Edit   Enter first end point of new line.

USE THE COORDINATE
READOUT WHEN PICKING

Step 9 – Because you have set the "**Sides**" option, the system will not prompt you to pick the other side of the wall. This will be the undimensioned side of the wall, which in this case is the inside. Pick anywhere on the side you wish the inside wall should be drawn, as illustrated in FIG. 3-13.

PICK ON THE INSIDE
OF THE WALL

Figure 3 – 13

Notice: Do not press mouse button **3** before performing the next steps.

Zooming in

Step 10 – Notice that your first wall is drawn, but appears very small. You will want to "zoom in," or "Window in," to see the wall better. You do not have to quit drawing to zoom in, so don't press mouse button **3**. Press the **/** key. This is the same key that has the **?** on it.

Step 11 – Now pick two diagonal points around the wall that you drew, as indicated in FIG. 3-14.

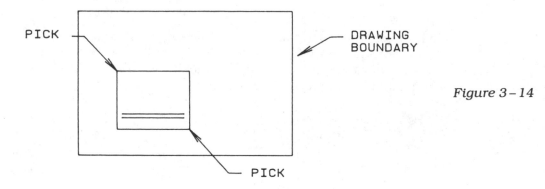

Figure 3 – 14

Step 12 – The wall appears bigger on your screen. Press mouse button **3** once, in order to quit out of the WINDOW IN menu, and return to drawing walls. Notice that the cursor is still connected to your wall, and you can continue drawing!

Coordinate input

Another, and usually more practical way of indicating a length for a wall is by using *coordinate input*. You have already used this type of input when you created the border rectangle in the previous lesson (Initial drawing set-up).

There are two major coordinate systems used by DataCAD. They are:

1. Cartesian
2. Polar

Cartesian coordinates are used for most of the simple X,Y movements. X is the axis that is horizontal, or "across" the screen. Y is the axis that is vertical, or "up and down" the screen. (FIG. 3-15.)

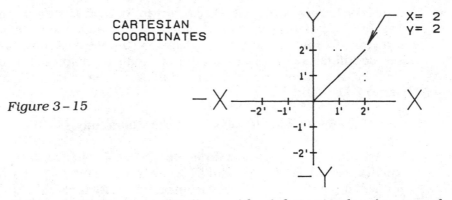

CARTESIAN
COORDINATES

Figure 3 – 15

Polar coordinates are typically used for defining angles. An example of polar coordinates is illustrated in FIG. 3-16.

Figure 3 – 16

To draw the rest of your walls, you can use the Relative Cartesian coordinates. This allows you to input a distance relative to the last point. In this case, the last point was the very last end of the wall, as indicated in FIG. 3-17.

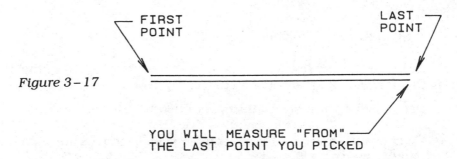

FIRST
POINT

LAST
POINT

Figure 3 – 17

YOU WILL MEASURE "FROM"
THE LAST POINT YOU PICKED

Note: You should still be drawing walls, with the wall line still connected to your cursor. If you "quit," or disconnected, this line by mistake, simply **Object Snap** back to the first line before continuing.

Step 1 – Your coordinates should already be set to **Relative Cartesian**, that was the last setting you used when you created your Default Drawing. To double check this, press the [**Insert**] key until **Relative Coordinates** appears as the input mode, as displayed in the MESSAGE area of your screen. (You might have to press the [**Insert**] key more than once.)

Step 2 – Press the [**Space bar**] to invoke the coordinate mode.

Step 3 – You will now be prompted to **Enter the relative X distance**. Because you are creating a vertical wall (X = horizontal and Y = vertical), you will not enter a relative X distance. Press [**Enter**] to accept O.

Step 4 – Next, you are prompted to **Enter a relative Y distance**. Type in **16** feet, and press [**Enter**].

Step 5 – Pick on the inside of the wall, for the "other side," as indicated in FIG. 3-18.

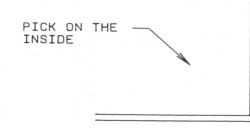

PICK ON THE
INSIDE

Figure 3 – 18

Step 6 – Press the [**Space bar**] again.

Step 7 – Type in the **– X** distance for the next wall: **– 16**.

    x = – 16
    y = 0

Step 8 – Pick on the inside for the other side of the wall.

Step 9 – To finish the exterior walls, place the cursor by the beginning of the first wall, and object snap to it using mouse button **2**.

Remember to pick on the inside for the other side of the wall.

Step 10 – When your exterior walls are complete, press mouse button **3** to quit drawing lines.

Step 11 – Your drawing should look like FIG. 3-19.

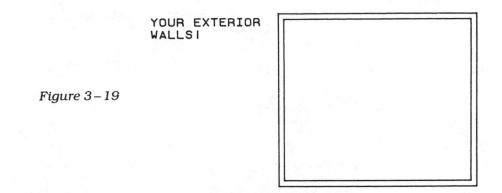

```
YOUR EXTERIOR
WALLS I
```

Figure 3–19

Drawing the interior walls

You are ready to add the interior walls for your project. Notice that the interior walls are dimensioned to the centers, unlike the exterior walls, which were dimensioned to the outside. See FIG. 3-20.

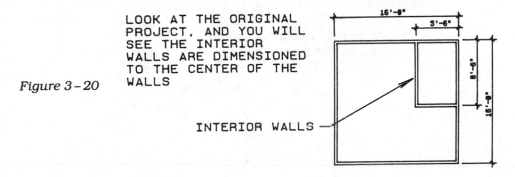

```
LOOK AT THE ORIGINAL
PROJECT, AND YOU WILL
SEE THE INTERIOR
WALLS ARE DIMENSIONED
TO THE CENTER OF THE
WALLS
```

Figure 3–20

```
INTERIOR WALLS —
```

This is easily accomplished by setting the **Center** option in the ARCHITCT menu. You will want to make the "Center" option active (instead of the **Sides** option), whenever your walls are dimensioned to centerlines.

Step 1 – Press **A** to go to the **Architct** option, found in the EDIT menu.

Step 2 – Pick the **Center** option until it is active (***Center**).

Step 3 – Remember to press mouse button **3** to quit.

Referencing a corner point

Now that the **Center** option is set, you are ready to begin drawing your interior walls. Notice that the interior wall (illustrated in FIG. 3-21) is dimen-

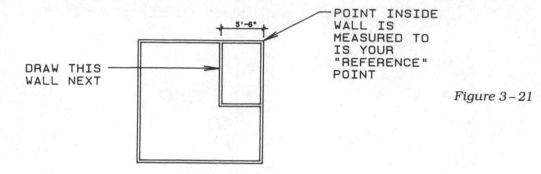

POINT INSIDE
WALL IS
MEASURED TO
IS YOUR
"REFERENCE"
POINT

5'-6"

DRAW THIS
WALL NEXT

Figure 3–21

sioned from a corner of your exterior wall. To make placement of this wall easier, DataCAD allows you to measure from this point, by defining the corner as a "reference point."

Step 4 – Press the ~ key. (*Do not* press the [**Shift**] key with the ~ key, as this would change the action of the key.) This is a quick key to establish a reference point.

Step 5 – Object snap to the outside upper right corner of the exterior wall, as illustrated in FIG. 3-22. Be sure to use the mouse button **2**!

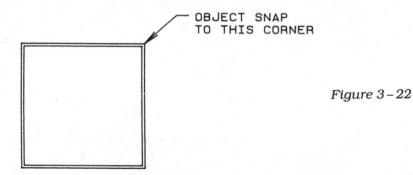

OBJECT SNAP
TO THIS CORNER

Figure 3–22

Step 6 – Move your cursor back to this corner again, and notice that it now reads out as the 0,0 coordinate location! (FIG. 3-23.)

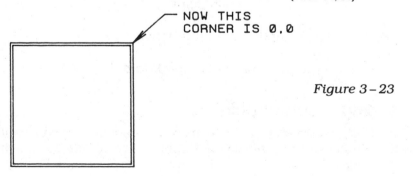

NOW THIS
CORNER IS 0,0

Figure 3–23

Step 7 – Press the [**Space bar**] to invoke the Relative Coordinate mode.

Step 8 – Type in **−5.6** in the **X** direction (5 feet 6 inches). This will define the start point of the interior wall.

x = −5.6
y = 0

Step 9 – Now type in the length of your wall, **−8.6** (8 feet 6 inches).

x = 0
y = −8.6

Step 10 – Finish your wall by picking the last endpoint using mouse button **1**, and using mouse button **3** to quit. Your drawing should look like FIG. 3-24.

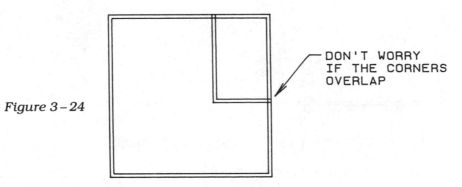

Figure 3 – 24

DON'T WORRY
IF THE CORNERS
OVERLAP

Saving your drawing file

While you are working on your drawing file, it is a good idea to periodically save it to a permanent hard disk file. This way if something happens to your drawing, or if you just goof it up entirely, you can get back a clean, saved version. It is easy to invoke a save, and you can do it at anytime.

Step 1 – Press [**Shift**] **F** to type in a capital **F**. You will get a message in the user prompt area that your file has been saved.

Refer to the DataCAD Operations Guide

Turn to the section called **WALLS** in appendix A, *The DataCAD Operation Guide*. It will be close to the end, because the sections are alphabetical. Notice that the names of the operations are listed on the left side of the page, while the "1,2,3" steps to follow are listed on the right side.

This is the page you might want to reference later, when you are creating walls in your own projects. Notice that the steps are written in a short, concise format. These instructions are designed to complement your lesson instructions and to remind you how each operation works.

Notice that one of the operations listed for WALLS is "Cleaning up wall intersections after they are created." These are the steps you will be following next. Examine them briefly before continuing.

Cleaning up intersections

Once you've created your interior walls, you will want to clean up the intersections noted in FIG. 3-25.

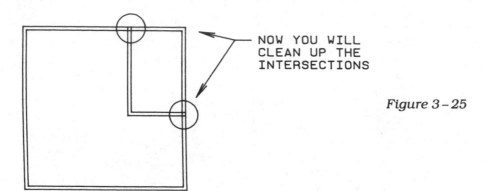

NOW YOU WILL
CLEAN UP THE
INTERSECTIONS

Figure 3 – 25

Step 1 – Pick the **Cleanup** option from the EDIT menu.

Step 2 – Pick the **T Intsct** option. (T-intersection.)

Step 3 – Pick two points indicating a rectangle around the first intersection you want to clean up, as indicated in FIG. 3-26.

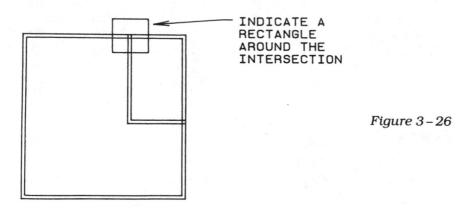

INDICATE A
RECTANGLE
AROUND THE
INTERSECTION

Figure 3 – 26

Step 4 – Pick the line of the wall you want the interior wall trimmed to, as indicated in FIG. 3-27.

Step 5 – Your wall will be trimmed, as in FIG. 3-28.

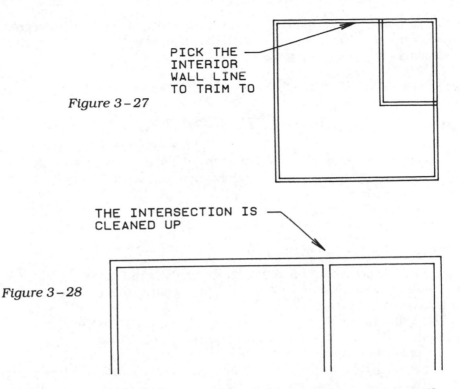

Figure 3-27

PICK THE
INTERIOR
WALL LINE
TO TRIM TO

THE INTERSECTION IS
CLEANED UP

Figure 3-28

Step 6 – If your wall is *not* trimmed, and you are given a message, the system is trying to tell you it found more than two endpoints or less than two endpoints. This could mean that you have a small segment of a line in this area. (Sometimes this happens because you are not used to using the mouse input device, and double pick as you are drawing.)

This is easy to correct, by using the **Erase** option, and erase by area, indicating a small area around the intersection you are trying to clean up. Only the fully surrounded lines will be erased.

If the message states that less than two endpoints were found, make sure you are enclosing both endpoints of the wall in your box.

Step 7 – Follow these same steps (Steps 1 through 5) to clean up the other intersection.

Step 8 – If necessary, use **L Intsct** to clean up the exterior wall corners.

Refreshing your display screen

Remember, if your drawing's walls appear to have little holes in them after cleaning up an intersection, it is because of the pixels being turned off temporarily. (A deleted entity "shadow.")

To eliminate these shadows, all you have to do is refresh the screen. You will find that once you get used to the shadows, you won't be inclined to refresh your screen as often.

Step 1 – Press the [**Esc**] key on your keyboard. Your screen will be refreshed.

If you are using display list processing

As a reminder, if you ever get the little "ghost images" left in your drawing, you can get rid of them by refreshing the screen using the [**Esc**] key also. However, if the [**Esc**] doesn't work, you can use the **U** key.

Step 1 – Press **U**. The ghosts will disappear.

Adding doors

When you add doors to your drawing, the walls automatically will be cut. You can set this so that they are not cut (by turning off the Cutout option) but this is usually not desired.

You will add the doors 3 inches from the inside corners of the walls. Again, this is achieved by using the "reference" key [~] and object snap to indicate a corner point.

Remember that your doors will be created on the DOORS layer.

Step 1 – Press the [**Tab**] key until the layer is changed to Doors. (FIG. 3-29.)
In a normal sequence of events, you will always add the walls first, then insert the doors into the walls. Because your coordinate mode is already set, and the correct layer is active, it is easy to put your doors exactly where you want them.

```
                    S9 Macros
                    S0 Utility
"DOORS" ─────────►  Doors
SHOULD              1/4"       x:9'-0"  y:12'-8"  a:54-36'-19"  d:15'-6 15/32      Figure 3-29
APPEAR
IN STATUS           Solid
AREA                SwOTHLUD   Edit   Enter first end point of new line.
```

Step 2 – Press the **A** key. This should put you in the ARCHITECT menu.

Step 3 – Pick the **DoorSwng** option.

Step 4 – Pick the **LyrSrch** option until the layer list is displayed. This option tells the system which layer contains the walls you want cut when you insert the doors on the active layer. (You can have many different layers with different kinds of walls if you wish. This option tells the system which one of those walls to cut.)

Step 5 – Pick **Walls**. This is now the layer you will be searching for your walls. You will not have to perform these steps again until you begin a new drawing, as DataCAD will remember that you have set the Walls layer as the layer to cut when you insert doors.

Step 6 – The prompt asks you to **Enter Hinge side of door**.
Because door jambs are measured off of the inside corner, you will want this as your reference point. Press the ˜ key, and **Object snap** to this corner, as indicated in FIG. 3-30.

Figure 3 – 30

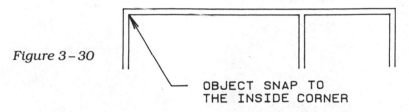

OBJECT SNAP TO
THE INSIDE CORNER

Step 7 – Once you have indicated this corner as your reference point, press the [**Space bar**].

Step 8 – The user prompt will ask you to **Enter relative x distance**. Type in **0.4** for 0 feet, 4 inches. (Remember that you should always press [**Enter**] after you type something in, or press mouse button **2** to enter.) You do not want to move in the Y direction this time.

$x = 0.4$
$y = 0$

Step 9 – Now the prompt asks you to **Enter strike side of door**. Press the [**Space bar**] again.

Step 10 – Type in the width of the door: **3** feet, for the relative X distance, and **0** feet for the Y direction.

$x = 3$
$y = 0$

Step 11 – Pick on the inside of the room for the **direction of swing**. (FIG. 3-31.)

Figure 3 – 31

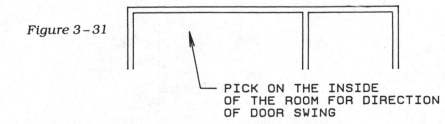

PICK ON THE INSIDE
OF THE ROOM FOR DIRECTION
OF DOOR SWING

Step 12 – Pick on the outside of the building for the **outside of the wall**, as in FIG. 3-32. This pick determines where the centerpoint (for dimensioning) will be placed.

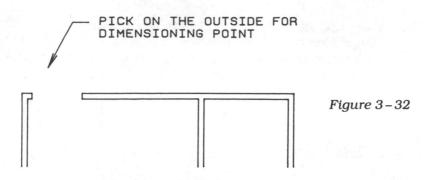

PICK ON THE OUTSIDE FOR
DIMENSIONING POINT

Figure 3 – 32

Step 13 – Your door is created, as in FIG. 3-33.

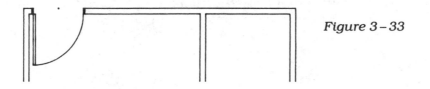

YOUR DOOR IS CREATED

Figure 3 – 33

Step 14 – Create the second door, **4″** from the inside corner, this time using the relative y distance. This door is 2′6″ in width. (FIG. 3-34.)

Remember to use the ~ key, object snap for the reference corner, and the [**Space bar**] to invoke coordinate mode.

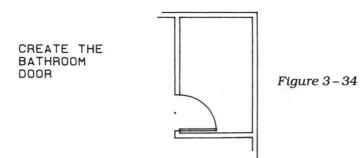

CREATE THE
BATHROOM
DOOR

Figure 3 – 34

Removing a door

If you make a mistake adding a door, don't worry, it is easy to remove! You might want to try out these steps even if you made your door correctly, just to see how it works.

Step 1 – Notice that there is a **"Remove"** option in the DOOR SWING menu. This option allows you to remove the door from the wall, and close up the wall at the same time. Let's try it!

Step 2 – Pick **Remove**.

Step 3 – Indicate two points to draw a box around the door you just created, being careful to enclose the entire door and just the adjoining wall, NOT the vertical wall. Do not include any other walls in your box.

Step 4 – The door is erased and the wall is "welded" close!

Step 5 – Make sure you add the door back in correctly, following the previous steps in ADDING DOORS, steps 1 through 14, before continuing.

Turning off and on the display of layers

Now that you have completed your walls and doors on two different layers, you might want to try turning them on and off to see how they work.

Step 1 – Press **L**. This is the quick way to enter the LAYERS option found in the UTILITY menu.

Step 2 – Pick the **On/Off** option, to turn the layers "on and off."

Step 3 – The layer names will be listed. Notice that most layers have a star * in front of the name. This means they are **displayed**.

The **Doors** layer will have a **$** in front of it (FIG. 3-35). This means the layer is *active*. In other words, if you created anything, it would reside and appear in this layer.

Step 4 – Press the [**Tab**] key. Did the **$** move to the next layer? Notice that this layer name now appears in the **STATUS area** of your display screen.

Step 5 – Pick the **Walls** layer with your cursor. The * will toggle off. The **Walls** layer will be turned off from displaying. (FIG. 3-36.)

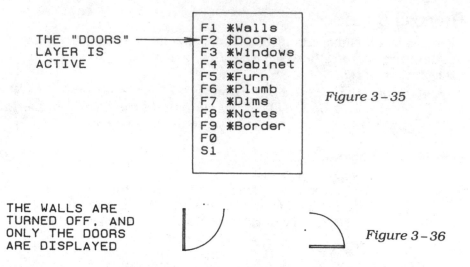

```
                          F1  *Walls
  THE "DOORS"           ─►F2  $Doors
  LAYER IS                F3  *Windows
  ACTIVE                  F4  *Cabinet
                          F5  *Furn
                          F6  *Plumb         Figure 3-35
                          F7  *Dims
                          F8  *Notes
                          F9  *Border
                          F0
                          S1
```

THE WALLS ARE
TURNED OFF, AND
ONLY THE DOORS   Figure 3-36
ARE DISPLAYED

Step 6 – Pick the **Walls** layer again. The walls will be displayed, and the *
will appear by the layer again.

Step 7 – When you are done turning the layers off and on, make sure they
are all on (*). Then press mouse button **3** to quit.

Creating windows

The window in your project is located in the center of the wall. You will set
the **center** option in windows, and object snap to the center of this wall for
window placement.

Step 1 – Make sure the **Windows** layer is active before you add the windows. Remember to press the [**Tab**] key until **Windows** appears as
the active layer.

Step 2 – Press **A** to enter the ARCHITECT menu.

Step 3 – Pick **Windows**.

Step 4 – Pick the **Sides** option until the * *is turned off*. This will allow you
to "create windows about a center," by defining a centerpoint.
The message line will say: **Windows defined by center and jamb**.

Step 5 – The user prompt now asks you to: **Enter center of window**. Object
snap to the center of the inside face of the wall, as indicated in
FIG. 3-37. Remember to use mouse button **2**. (Actually, you could
snap to either side of the wall in this case.)

Step 6 – Now the prompt asks you to: **Enter one jamb of window**. You will use coordinate input. Press the [**Space bar**].

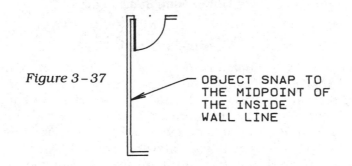

Figure 3 – 37

OBJECT SNAP TO
THE MIDPOINT OF
THE INSIDE
WALL LINE

Step 7 – Type in **a relative y** distance of **3** feet.

x = 0
y = 3

Step 8 – Now pick a point on the outside of the wall, shown in FIG. 3-38.

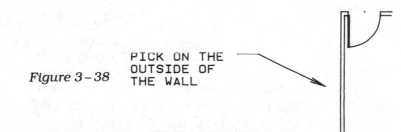

Figure 3 – 38

PICK ON THE
OUTSIDE OF
THE WALL

Step 9 – Your window is created, as illustrated in FIG. 3-39. Press mouse button **3** to quit.

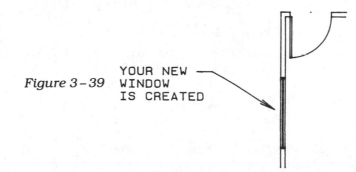

Figure 3 – 39

YOUR NEW
WINDOW
IS CREATED

Step 10 – Notice that this menu contains a "**Remove**" option just like **Door Swing** does. You can use this option to remove your window if you make a mistake or are modifying your project. You also can remove Doors with this option, and you can remove windows with the **Door Swing Remove** option!

Refer to the DataCAD Operations Guide

Turn to the section in appendix A, *DataCAD Operations Guide* called DOORS & WINDOWS. Because the operations are listed alphabetically, look for this section under "D." Notice that the steps you used to add these components to your drawing are found in this section. This section is your quick reference for adding doors and windows to your own drawings.

To manipulate the layers in your drawing, you will want to refer to the section called LAYERS. You will find that there are other kinds of operations that can be accomplished with your layers!

Automatic save

As you worked on your drawing, you might have noticed that every five minutes or so it was "automatically saved." This is a process that temporarily saves your current drawing, or *workfile* to a save file (ending with an .ASV extension).

This save file is "temporary." This means it is created only while you are working on your drawing. When you quit DataCAD normally, it is erased. If you experience a problem with DataCAD (such as a power failure), then DataCAD is not exited normally, and the save file still exists. You would be able to recover the last "auto save" of the drawing you were working on from this temporary save file when you restart DataCAD.

The Auto save file is not a replacement for permanently saving your drawing. You can only do this using the **File I/O, Save Dwg** options, or by pressing [**Shift**] **F**.

Notice: See "Retrieving the Automatic Save File," in appendix A.

Saving your drawing

As a reminder, every hour or so that you work on DataCAD, you should permanently save your drawing. It takes one step.

Step 1 – Press [**Shift**] **F** to type in a captial **F**. Your drawing will be saved.

DataCAD "quick keys"

You have used some quick keys to enter menus in DataCAD. Quick keys allow you to access menus without having to pick the options from the screen. There are many more quick keys on the *DataCAD Quick Key* chart.

Caution: The quick kcys might be updated and changed when the DataCAD software is updated. The DataCAD Quick Key chart is updated to the most recent 4.0 software. If you have an earlier version of DataCAD, a few of these keys will not apply. You could, however, test your keys and create your own Quick Key chart for your use.

Quitting DataCAD

If you are going directly to the next lesson, you will not want to exit Data-CAD. You can exit DataCAD and continue your lessons later, if you wish, by following these steps.

To assure that your drawing is permanently saved when you leave DataCAD, make sure that you pick the **Yes** option from the QUIT menu.

Step 1 – Press the [**Alt**] and **Q** keys, or pick **Quit** from the UTILITY menu. The QUIT menu will be displayed.

[**Alt**] **Q**

Step 2 – Pick **Yes**, and your file will be permanently saved, and you will leave DataCAD.

Yes

User reminder: Do not pick **Abort**. Remember that picking **Abort** will "trash" your drawing, and *not* save any changes or additions you made to it.

Additional assignments

Ready to practice your new drawing skills? If so, complete the following assignments, ASSIGNMENT 1 and ASSIGNMENT 2. (See FIGS. 3-40, 3-41, and 3-42.)

You will find the instructions for ASSIGNMENT 1 on the following page. however, ASSIGNMENT 2 allows you to think for yourself what your steps will be to complete it.

Good Luck!

DataCAD exercise 3

Please complete the exercise beginning on page 68 by reading each question carefully, then circling the letter that corresponds to the correct answer.

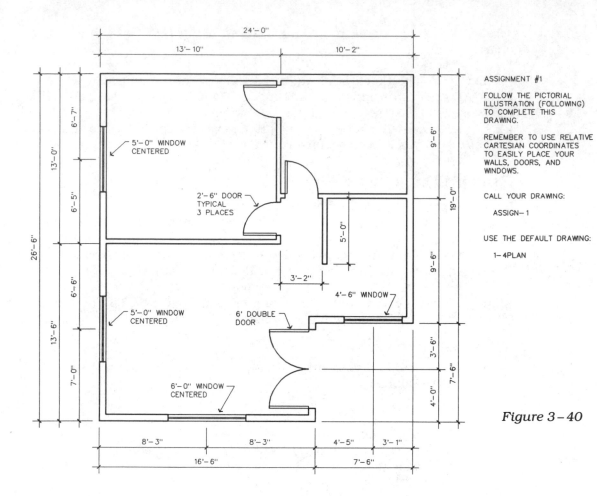

ASSIGNMENT #1

FOLLOW THE PICTORIAL
ILLUSTRATION (FOLLOWING)
TO COMPLETE THIS
DRAWING.

REMEMBER TO USE RELATIVE
CARTESIAN COORDINATES
TO EASILY PLACE YOUR
WALLS, DOORS, AND
WINDOWS.

CALL YOUR DRAWING:

   ASSIGN–1

USE THE DEFAULT DRAWING:

   1–4PLAN

Figure 3–40

Review of the mouse keys:

1. The first (left most) button on the mouse is used to:
   a. Pick an option or pick on the screen.
   b. Object snap or to enter a typed value.
   c. Quit an operation or exit a menu.

2. The second (middle) button on the mouse is used to:
   a. Pick an option or pick on the screen.
   b. Object snap or to enter a typed value.
   c. Quit an operation or exit a menu.

3. The third (right most) button on the mouse is used to:
   a. Pick an option or pick on the screen.
   b. Object snap or to enter a typed value.
   c. Quit an operation or exit a menu.

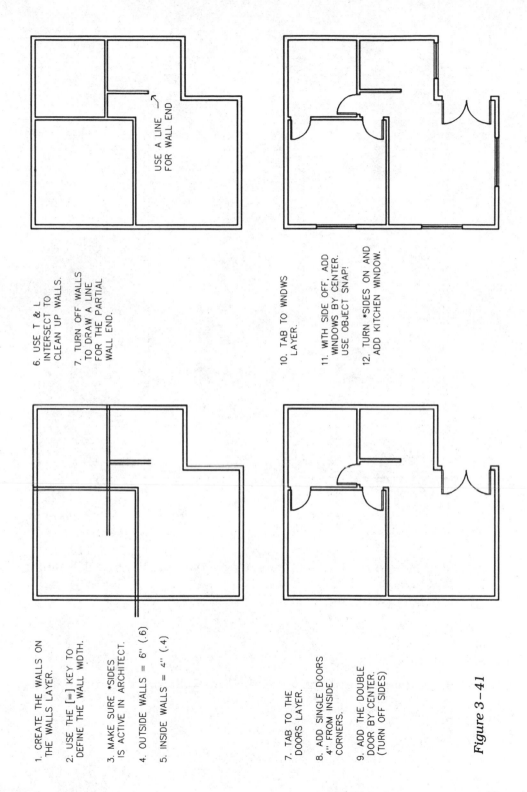

1. CREATE THE WALLS ON THE WALLS LAYER.

2. USE THE [=] KEY TO DEFINE THE WALL WIDTH.

3. MAKE SURE *SIDES IS ACTIVE IN ARCHITECT.

4. OUTSIDE WALLS = 6" (.6)

5. INSIDE WALLS = 4" (.4)

6. USE T & L INTERSECT TO CLEAN UP WALLS.

7. TURN OFF WALLS TO DRAW A LINE FOR THE PARTIAL WALL END.

USE A LINE FOR WALL END

7. TAB TO THE DOORS LAYER.

8. ADD SINGLE DOORS 4" FROM INSIDE CORNERS.

9. ADD THE DOUBLE DOOR BY CENTER. (TURN OFF SIDES)

10. TAB TO WNDWS LAYER.

11. WITH SIDE OFF, ADD WINDOWS BY CENTER. USE OBJECT SNAP!

12. TURN *SIDES ON AND ADD KITCHEN WINDOW.

Figure 3–41

Basic drafting techniques   **69**

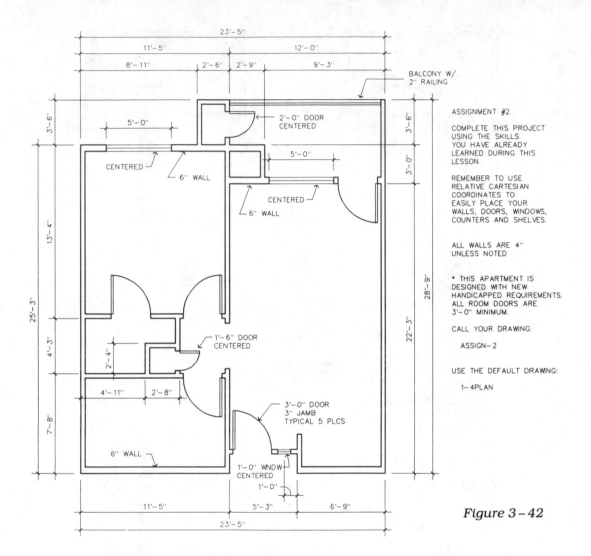

23'-5"
11'-5"
12'-0"
8'-11"
2'-6"
2'-9"
9'-3"

BALCONY W/
2" RAILING

3'-6"

5'-0"

2'-0" DOOR
CENTERED

CENTERED

6" WALL

5'-0"

CENTERED

6" WALL

13'-4"

25'-3"

4'-3"

1'-6" DOOR
CENTERED

2'-4"

4'-11"

2'-8"

7'-8"

3'-0" DOOR
3" JAMB
TYPICAL 5 PLCS

6" WALL

1'-0" WNDW
CENTERED

1'-0"

11'-5"

5'-3"

6'-9"

23'-5"

3'-6"

3'-0"

28'-9"

22'-3"

ASSIGNMENT #2

COMPLETE THIS PROJECT
USING THE SKILLS
YOU HAVE ALREADY
LEARNED DURING THIS
LESSON.

REMEMBER TO USE
RELATIVE CARTESIAN
COORDINATES TO
EASILY PLACE YOUR
WALLS, DOORS, WINDOWS,
COUNTERS AND SHELVES.

ALL WALLS ARE 4"
UNLESS NOTED

* THIS APARTMENT IS
DESIGNED WITH NEW
HANDICAPPED REQUIREMENTS.
ALL ROOM DOORS ARE
3'-0" MINIMUM.

CALL YOUR DRAWING:

  ASSIGN-2

USE THE DEFAULT DRAWING:

  1-4PLAN

Figure 3-42

4. To toggle to the UTILITY menu when you are in the EDIT menu, you press:

   a. Mouse button **3**.
   b. Mouse button **2**.
   c. = key.

Basic Drafting Review:

5. The quickest way to turn from lines to walls, or from walls to lines, is to use the:

   a. Menu option choices.
   b. < key.
   c. = key.

6. To draw the exterior walls in your project, which were dimensioned to the outside of the walls, you used the:
   a. **Sides** option.
   b. **Centers** option.
   c. **Exterior** option.

7. To draw the interior walls, which were dimensioned to the center of the walls, you used the:
   a. **Sides** option.
   b. **Centers** option.
   c. **Interior** option.

8. In order to define a reference point, you press the:
   a. [**Space bar**].
   b. ~ key while pressing the [**Shift**] key.
   c. ~ key.

9. The X,Y type of coordinates you used, is called:
   a. Relative polar.
   b. Absolute Cartesian.
   c. Relative Cartesian.

10. To set the coordinate input mode, you press the:
    a. [**Ins**] key.
    b. [**Tab**] key.
    c. [**Alt**] key.

11. To clean up wall intersections after you create them, you use the:
    a. CLEANUP menu.
    b. EDIT menu.
    c. ERASE menu.

12. To erase the last item you created, you use the:
    a. **Delete** option.
    b. < (less than) key.
    c. > (greater than) key.

13. To erase an entire area at one time by using a box you use the:
    a. ERASE menu, **Area** option.
    b. [**Shift**] < keys together.
    c. [**Shift**] > keys together.

14. To erase items in your drawing by picking them one-at-a-time, you use the:
    a. ERASE menu, make sure the **Any** option is active, then pick any item to erase.

b. ERASE menu, make sure the **Entity** option is active, then pick the items to erase.

c. CHANGE menu, **Delete** option, then pick the items to delete.

15. The Automatic-Save file is:

a. Really good for permanently saving your drawing file.

b. Only temporary. You would only retrieve it if DataCAD was halted abnormally (such as a power failure).

c. Retrievable even if you quit DataCAD normally.

16. To permanently save your drawing file, you:

a. Press [**Shift**] **F** every hour or before a major change in your drawing, or pick **Yes** to save your drawing as you quit DataCAD.

b. Let the Automatic-Save do it for you.

c. Quit DataCAD, then pick the **Abort** option.

Lesson 4
Windowing

What you will be doing

You will use the several windowing functions available to control the display of your drawing. These techniques will help you get in closer to your drawing, to see the littlest details, move around your drawing, and view your drawing in its entirety.

Objectives

Your lesson objectives are to:

- Window in to a small area of your drawing by defining an area to view.
- Window closer by using the **Page Down** key.
- Move away from your drawing using the **Page Up** key.
- Move across, up, and down your drawing using the arrows keys.
- Return your drawing to its full view.

Remember to refer to the *DataCAD Operations Guide* in appendix A when instructed. This section will be very useful when you are ready to learn more available windowing techniques.

Windowing

The term *windowing* means to manipulate the viewing window of your drawing. You are not changing the actual drawing in any way, and you are not "moving" the drawing. You are simply moving to another position to view it.

This might be a new concept to you, because you always have been able to look at the entire drawing you worked on when it was taped down to your board. On your computer, you are given two major ways to look at your drawing.

1. Window extends – A full window of your drawing. This is the easiest way to see everything, because the entire drawing is displayed on your screen. Detailed areas and text might be hard to examine, especially on large drawings.

2. Windowed in – An area is chosen to enlarge (magnify) for viewing. You will use this function often, in order to see the small details in your drawings. This is also called "zooming in."

Once you have defined the window you want to work in, you can quickly move it around your screen using quick keys!

Quick keys for windowing

There are 10 keys that are used to control your viewing window. They are illustrated in FIG. 4-1.

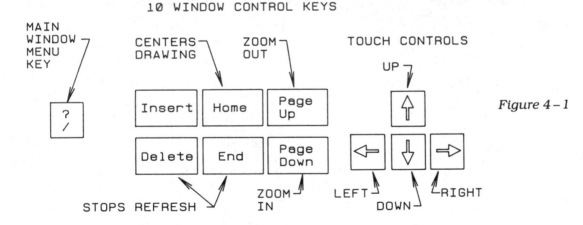

Figure 4 – 1

Practicing windowing techniques

Step 1 – Make sure you have entered DataCAD, and have the floor plan you created displayed on your screen, as in FIG. 4-2.

Windowing in

Step 2 – Press the / key, to enter the WINDOW menu. This is a special key that allows you to change your window without leaving the

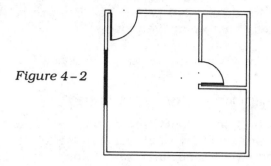

Figure 4 – 2

menu you are presently in. You can be performing almost any function, press /, window in, then go back to what you were doing.

Step 3 – Pick two points to indicate a rectangle around the items you would want to magnify for viewing, as indicated in FIG. 4-3.

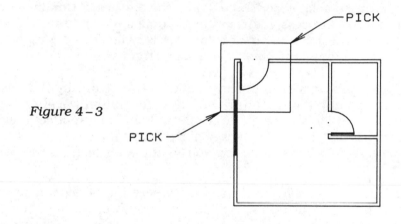

Figure 4 – 3

Step 4 – Your new window is displayed! (FIG. 4-4.)

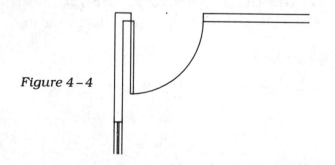

Figure 4 – 4

Step 5 – If you receive a message: "**This operation requires display regeneration,**" pick **Continue**. This message means that your system is set up for display list processing. Read the following section: If you are using display list processing.

Step 6 – Press mouse button **3** to quit from the WINDOW-IN menu.

If you are using display processing

A new addition to DataCAD, starting with the 4.0 release, is the ability to use display list processing with all supported graphics cards. Display list processing allows you to declare part of your expanded (preferable) or extended memory or hard disk for the processing of the graphics on your display screen. This really speeds up the zooming in of your drawing.

However, only so much of the display can fit into the memory. In other words, you can only "zoom-in" so much without the display list having to "rebuild" itself. This is referred to as "regenerating the display list." If you pick too little of a window when you zoom in, and the display list has to regenerate the graphics, then you might get a message that **"This operation requires a display regeneration"** and the choices of **Continue or Stop**. To continue the process you must pick **Continue**, or press **C**. You would pick **Stop**, or press **S**, if your drawing was very large and a regeneration would take too long, and you could pick a larger window not requiring a regeneration.

Because you are working with smaller drawings during the lessons in this book, you might want to turn off this regeneration warning. With the warning turned off, in a small drawing you really only notice a regeneration is occurring because it takes slightly longer than it normally would. As your drawings become larger, you might wish to turn this warning back on.

Note: The limitations of display list processing is dependent on how much memory you have, how big your drawings are, among other things.

Turning off the display list regeneration warning

Step 1 – Pick the **Display** option from the UTILITY menu.

Step 2 – Pick **DispList**.

Step 3 – Pick **RegenWrn** until it is OFF (no *).

Step 4 – Press mouse button **3** to quit. Now you can pan and zoom without the "Continue/Stop" options slowing you down.

> *Note*: You might want to set this warning to OFF in your default drawings.

Moving the window

Moving your viewing window is called *panning*. The term comes from photography, when the camera eye pans the landscape or subjects for the best frame.

Step 5 – Press the [**right arrow**] key. This is the key with the arrow pointing to the right. Your window will be moved to the right. Your drawing will appear to be shifted over to the left slightly.

If your arrow key doesn't work, press the [**NumLock**] key until the NumLock light is turned off.

Step 6 – Try pressing the [**left arrow**] key. The window will move to the left.

Step 7 – Now press the [**up arrow**] key. The window will move up.

Step 8 – The [**down arrow**] key moves your window down.

Centering the area you wish to see

Step 9 – The exact area you wish to view will appear over to the right side of your screen. To see it easily, you will want to center it. Place your cursor to the righthand corner of your drawing, as indicated in FIG. 4-5.

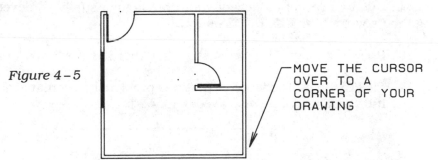

Figure 4 – 5

MOVE THE CURSOR
OVER TO A
CORNER OF YOUR
DRAWING

Step 10 – Press the [**Home**] key. Where your cursor appeared is now the center of your window! (FIG. 4-6.) Place the cursor on the area you want in the middle of the screen and press [**Home**].

Getting a closer look

Step 11 – Press the [**Page Down**] key. On some keyboards, this key appears as [**Pg Dn**]. Your window will move in closer to your

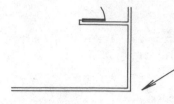

THE AREA INDICATED
BY YOUR CURSOR IS
NOW THE CENTER OF
YOUR DRAWING

Figure 4-6

drawing. You can move it until your viewing window reaches
its maximum limits. This might be 12″ scale.

You can remember to use [**Page down**], because you can think
of moving your camera "down" to view your drawing. This
would, of course, give you a magnified view of your drawing.

Taking a step back

Step 12 – Press the [**Page Up**] key. On some keyboards, this key appears
as [**Pg Up**]. Your window will move away from the drawing. You
can move out until the window reaches its limits. This might be
1:40 scale.

This is similar to moving your camera "up" and away from the
drawing, which would, of course, give you a fuller and less
detailed view.

Getting a full window

The fastest way to get a full view of your drawing is usually achieved by
using the / key, and the EXTENDS option.

Step 13 – Press the / key. This is the same key that has the ? mark on it.

Step 14 – Pick **Extends**. The window that was previously calculated as the
full window will be displayed. (FIG. 4-7.)

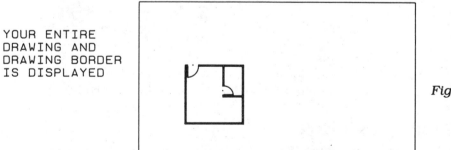

YOUR ENTIRE
DRAWING AND
DRAWING BORDER
IS DISPLAYED

Figure 4-7

Step 15 – If your drawing is not perfectly centered and fully displayed, you will want to recalculate the window extends. Pick the **Re-Calc** option.

Step 16 – Now your drawing is completely displayed. After recalculating the window extends, you can pick the **Extends** option, and it will remember this window. (This is important, because it takes more time to recalculate in big drawings.)

Step 17 – Practice windowing techniques to view different areas of your drawing.

Refer to the DataCAD Operations Guide

The section you will want to refer to in the *DataCAD Operations Guide* is called WINDOW VIEWS. This section describes other ways to control the window views that you will be using in your drawing when you become more experienced. A complete explanation is also available in the *Data-CAD Users Manual* that came with your DataCAD program.

DataCAD exercise 4

Please complete the following exercise by reading each question carefully, then circling the letter that corresponds to the correct answer.

1. To quickly enter the WINDOW menu, you press the:
    a. \ key.
    b. / key.
    c. [**Alt**] / keys.

2. Moving your viewing window across the drawing, is called:
    a. Panning.
    b. Paging.
    c. Windowing in.

3. To move the window in closer to your drawing, you can use the:
    a. [**PgUp**] key.
    b. [**PgDn**] key.
    c. [**right arrow**] key.

4. To move the window to the right of your drawing, you use the:
    a. [**left arrow**] key.
    b. [**PgUp**] key.
    c. [**right arrow**] key.

5. To get a precalculated full view of your drawing, you press the:

 a. / key, then pick the **Re-Calc** option.
 b. / key, then pick the **Extends** option.
 c. [**PgUp**] key.

6. The **Re-Calc** option:

 a. Recalculates the window extends for your drawing, and takes a little longer than using the **Extends** option.
 b. Should always be used because it is much faster than the **Extends** option.
 c. Works the same as the **Extends** option.

Some review questions:

7. The second (middle) button on the mouse is used to:

 a. Pick an option or pick on the screen.
 b. Object snap or to enter a typed value.
 c. Quit an operation or exit a menu.

8. In order to define a reference point, you press the:

 a. [**Space bar**].
 b. ~ key.
 c. **X** key.

9. The X,Y type of coordinates you used, is called:

 a. Relative polar.
 b. Absolute Cartesian.
 c. Relative Cartesian.

10. To set the coordinate input mode, you press the:

 a. [**Ins**] key.
 b. [**Tab**] key.
 c. [**Alt**] key.

11. To type in the actual coordinates, you press the:

 a. [**Ins**] key.
 b. [**Space bar**].
 c. [**Tab**] key.

Lesson 5
Adding symbols

What you will be doing

You will be using templates to add symbols to your drawing. You also will rotate symbols as you add them. During this lesson, you will be using some of the many symbols that are provided with the DataCAD Software. Later, during the Creating Templates and Symbols lesson, you will learn how to create your own symbols.

Objectives

Your lesson objectives are to:

- Define the correct directories for the templates you will use.
- Call up symbol templates.
- Retrieve symbols from the templates and place them on your drawing.
- Rotate the symbols into a new position as you place them.
- Adjust the height of the symbol.

Remember to refer to *The DataCAD Operations Guide* when instructed.

Templates and symbols

During this lesson, you will add the necessary furniture and plumbing to your floor plan. (See FIG. 5-1.)

The furniture and other items in your project are all precreated symbols. DataCAD symbols are attached to templates, as in FIG. 5-2, similar to

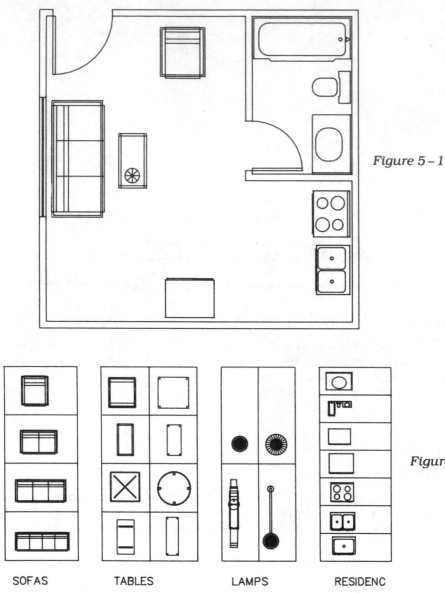

Figure 5 – 1

Figure 5 – 2

SOFAS   TABLES   LAMPS   RESIDENC

the plastic drafting templates you already use. Templates are a way to organize related symbols together for easy retrieval.

Template directories

When you install DataCAD 3.6, the templates that are supplied with the software are organized into a series of directories. The main directory for all the DataCAD software is **MTEC**. The main TEMPLATE directory resides in the MTEC directory, and is called **TPL**. The different types of templates are further organized into directories within the TPL directory. (See FIG. 5-3.)

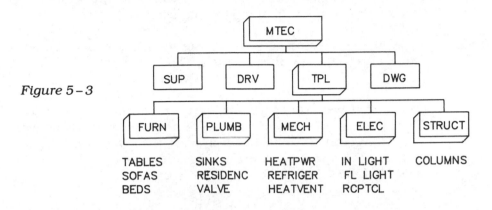

Figure 5 – 3

You can think of these directories as they relate to your filing cabinet. The file cabinet is your computer. A drawer of the cabinet is called MTEC, and the folder in the drawer for the templates is called TPL. Each section in the folder, which is organizing the types of templates, is labeled by that particular type. And within each section of the folder are the templates!

This is illustrated in FIG. 5-4.

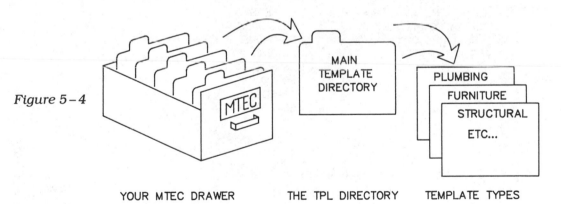

Figure 5 – 4

YOUR MTEC DRAWER　　　　THE TPL DIRECTORY　　　TEMPLATE TYPES

Getting a template

When you wish to add symbols, you first need to retrieve the template that hold the symbols you wish to use. For your living room, you will be using the template called SOFAS, which resides in the TPL/FURN directories.

Step 1 – Press [**Tab**] until the layer that will hold the furniture is active: **Furn**.

Step 2 – Press **T**. This is the quick way to enter the **Template** option, found in the UTILITY menu.

Step 3 – Pick the **New Path** option. This option will allow you to define the correct directory for the template you wish to use.

Step 4 – Type in the directory names for the template, separating each name with the \ key. Press [**Enter**].

tpl \ Furn

(Notice that you do not have to start the pathname with MTEC. This is because as you are using the program, you reside in the MTEC directory. Do not, however, start the directory pathname with a \. This would cause the program to look for the directory outside of the MTEC directory.)

-or-

After picking **New Path**, Pick the **..** that appears at the [**F2**] option. Pick **FURN**. Press mouse button **3** to quit.

Step 5 – The templates that reside in the FURN directory will be displayed as in FIG. 5-5.

ALL OF THE AVAILABLE ⟶ F1 BEDS
TEMPLATES IN THE   F2 CHAIRS
FURN DIRECTORY   F3 DESKS
ARE DISPLAYED   F4 DRESSERS   *Figure 5 – 5*
                        F5 FILES
                        F6 LAMPS
                        F7 SOFAS
                        F8 TABLES
                        F9

Step 6 – Pick the template called **Sofas**.

Step 7 – The symbols attached to the SOFAS template will be displayed, as indicated in FIG. 5-6.

Adding symbols to your drawing

Step 8 – Move your cursor over to the template symbols. Notice that, as the cursor is positioned over a symbol, the name of the symbol is displayed in the message area of your screen. (FIG. 5-7.)

THE SOFAS TEMPLATE
IS DISPLAYED

Figure 5 – 6

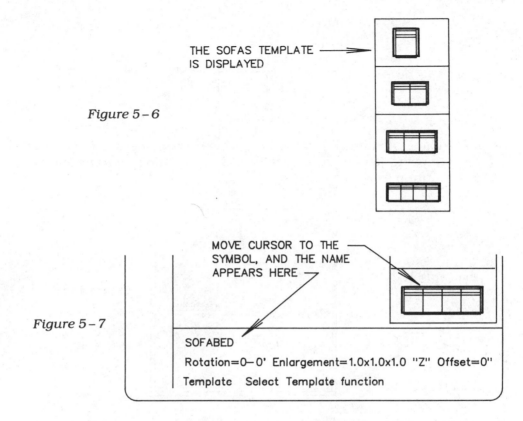

MOVE CURSOR TO THE
SYMBOL, AND THE NAME
APPEARS HERE

Figure 5 – 7

SOFABED

Rotation=0—0' Enlargement=1.0x1.0x1.0 "Z" Offset=0"

Template   Select Template function

Step 9 – Pick the symbol for the **lounge**, as indicated in FIG. 5-8, by pressing mouse button **1**.

PICK THE LOUNGE
SYMBOL

Figure 5 – 8

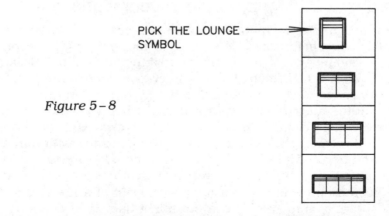

Step 10 – As you move your cursor back to the drawing area, you will notice a box indicating a copy of the symbol is now attached to your cursor. (See FIG. 5-9.)

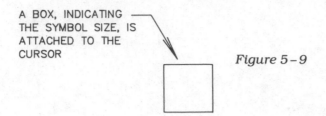

A BOX, INDICATING
THE SYMBOL SIZE, IS
ATTACHED TO THE
CURSOR

Figure 5 – 9

Step 11 – Place the lounge symbol in the living room, as in FIG. 5-10, by moving it into position with the cursor then pressing mouse button **1**.

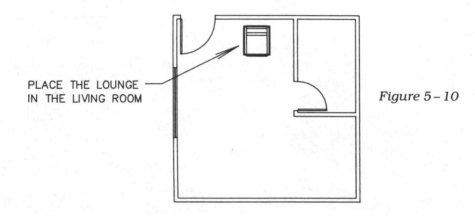

PLACE THE LOUNGE
IN THE LIVING ROOM

Figure 5 – 10

Step 12 – Press mouse button **3** to quit placing the symbol.

A note about adding symbols in your workfile

The first time you pick a symbol from your template, you will notice that it takes a little while before the box appears at your cursor. The second time you pick the same symbol, it appears almost instantly. Why? Because the first time you pick the symbol, before you even add it to your drawing, the symbol was added to your drawing database, called a "workfile."

After adding the symbol to your workfile, when you place the symbol, you are really just placing a "pointer." In other words, you add the symbol to your workfile, then you point to several positions and say "I want it here, and here and here." The advantage to this system is you can save a lot of file room in your drawing by using repeated symbols over and over.

One good example of this is a large site layout of a housing tract with repeated footprints of models. The layout might have A, B, C, and D models repeated 30 times each. If you use symbols for your models, it would save you time of course, but also it would result in a smaller file. Your drawing file might be only 120,000 bytes, versus 1,480,000 bytes if they were not symbols.

Another advantage is the immediate updating of symbols. If the B footprint changes in our example, you could easily use the **Redefine** option to update all of the 30 B symbols in one step. If you wanted to replace all of the C footprints with the D, you could simply use the **Replace** option to update them, again in one step. These procedures are explained in appendix A: *The DataCAD Operations Guide.*

Rotating symbols

The other furniture symbols in your living room will have to be rotated 90 degrees. You can set the rotation value once, then all symbols you bring in will be rotated until you reset the value back to 0.

Step 1 – Pick **DymnRot** from the TEMPLATE menu **twice** or until the ANGLE menu is displayed, to specify a rotation angle. (The first time you pick DymnRot the * will turn on. The second time the angle menu will be displayed.)

Step 2 – Pick the **90-0** option and press [**Enter**].

Step 3 – Pick the **sofa** symbol. Place it in the living room. Notice it is positioned at a 90 degree rotation angle, as in FIG. 5-11.

PLACE THE SOFA

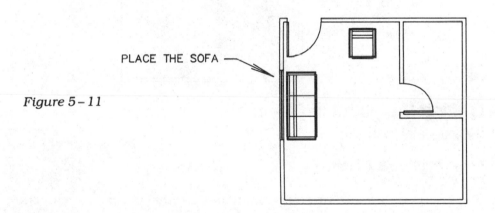

Figure 5 – 11

Getting a new template

Now you are done with the FURN template. You will want to get the template called TABLES.

Step 1 – Pick the **New File** option, found in the TEMPLATE menu.

Step 2 – Pick the **TABLES** template.

Step 3 – The Tables template is displayed, as in FIG. 5-12.

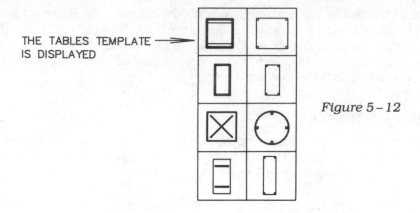

THE TABLES TEMPLATE ——→
IS DISPLAYED

Figure 5 – 12

Step 4 – Place the coffee table symbol in your drawing, as in FIG. 5-13.

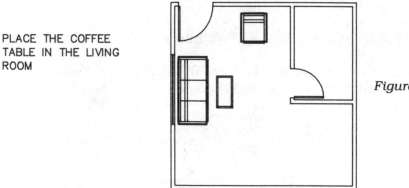

PLACE THE COFFEE
TABLE IN THE LIVING
ROOM

Figure 5 – 13

Getting the plumbing templates

Step 1 – Pick **New File**.

Step 2 – Pick **New Path**.

Step 3 – Type in the directory pathname for the plumbing templates. Press [**Enter**].

tpl \ plumb

-or-

After picking **New Path**, Pick the **..** that appears at the [**F2**] option. Pick **PLUMB**. Press mouse button **3** to quit.

Step 4 – Once the plumbing templates are displayed, pick the **RESIDENC** template.

RESIDENC

Step 5 – The **RESIDENC** template is displayed, as in FIG. 5-14.

THE RESIDENC TEMPLATE
IS DISPLAYED

Figure 5 – 14

Step 6 – Pick the **BathGrup** symbol. Notice that it comes in at the same 90 degree angle you set for the previous symbols, as illustrated in FIG. 5-15. This is because a rotation angle you define will stay set until you change it. Because this is the wrong angle for this symbol, you will need to change the rotation to either **270**, or **– 90**. Both angles will give the desired result.

THE BATHGROUP IS
IS STILL ROTATED
AT 90 DEGREES

Figure 5 – 15

YOU WILL CHANGE THIS

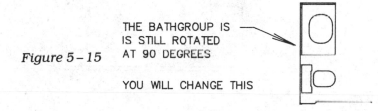

Step 7 – First, press mouse button **3** to drop the symbol.

Step 8 – Pick **DymnRot** twice. The first pick will turn on the Dynamic Rotation (allows you to drag the symbol "dynamically" into a rotation angle). The second pick will allow you to enter a specific angle.

Then, change the angle to **270**.

Step 9 – Pick the symbol again and place it in your drawing using object snap. Notice it is now positioned in the correct angle. (See FIG. 5-16 on page 90.)

Step 10 – Continue placing the symbols for your drawing that are found in this template, rotating as necessary. Use the second Wardrobe symbol as the double door refrigerator.

NOW THE BATHGRUP
SYMBOL FITS

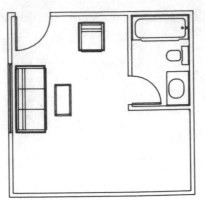

Figure 5 – 16

Your drawing should now look like FIG. 5-17.

ADD THE REFRIGERATOR,
STOVE, AND DOUBLE SINK
TO YOUR PLAN

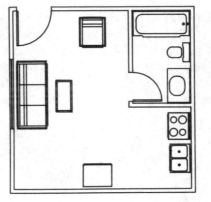

Figure 5 – 17

Renaming a symbol

Sometimes you may want to rename a symbol. This seems particularly true when it comes to using the Wardrobe symbol as a refrigerator. (Actually there are two Wardrobe symbols!) Because this template is in the plumbing directory, it is probably more accurate to rename these symbols.

Step 1 – From the TEMPLATE menu, pick, **EditFlds**. This option allows you to edit the template report fields that are connected with the symbols.

Step 2 – Pick the second **Wardrobe symbol** in the template window.

Step 3 – Pick the **Item Nam** option.

Step 4 – Type in the new name for this symbol, and press [**Enter**].

Large Refrigerator

Step 5 – Press mouse button **3** to quit.

Step 6 – Pick the first **Wardrobe symbol** in the template window.

Step 7 – Pick the **Item Nam** option.

Step 8 – Type in the new name for this symbol, and press [**Enter**].

> **Small Refrigerator**

Step 9 – Press mouse button **3** to quit.

Step 10 – If you place your cursor over to the template window you will notice the names for these symbols are still Wardrobe. You must reload the template (or individual symbol if you have used it in your drawing already). This is easy to do!

Step 11 – Pick the **Re-Load** option.

Step 12 – Pick **All**.

Step 13 – Pick **Yes**. The Symbols will be reloaded, as the new names will be displayed for the refrigerators.

Identifying a symbol

You can inquire about an object or symbol to find out certain information about it. This is called "Identifying," and the option you will use is called **Identify**. When you identify a symbol, you can find out the layer it is on, the color of the layer when the symbol was added (as specified by the handle point), and the lowest and highest points of the symbol (z-base and height). This is useful for a number of reasons, one being that knowing the height of the table symbol will allow you to add a lamp on it, as you will do in the following steps.

Step 1 – Press [**Shift**] **I** to enter the **Identify** option, found in the EDIT menu.

Step 2 – Pick the table symbol. It will become gray and dashed.

Step 3 – Notice the information displayed in the message area of your screen. It will tell you the **Z-Min** and **Z-Max** heights of your symbol. The minimum should be zero (unless someone has changed the table symbol), and the maximum could be about 1'-6", depending on the actual symbol you used.

Step 4 – Write down the maximum height for the next section: Adding the lamp at table height.

Identifying other items

Step 5 – Pick one of your walls while you are in the IDENTIFY menu. It will become gray and dashed also. Notice the type of information that is displayed.

The following is a brief explanation of the IDENTIFY menu:

[F1] – Item type (Line, arc, symbol, etc.)
[F2] – Layer the item resides on.
[F3] – Color of the item. If the item is a symbol, then color of the "handle point," which was the current color when the symbol was added.
[F4] – Linetype (Solid, Dashed, etc.) If the item is a symbol, then linetype of the "handle point," as above.
[F5] – Spacing for linetype, which is displayed in the MESSAGE area at the bottom of the screen.
[F6] – Line Weight, which is displayed in the MESSAGE area.
[F7] – Over Shoot factor, which is displayed in the MESSAGE area.
[F8] and [F9] – Z-base & height, which is displayed in the MESSAGE area.

Picking one of the options [F2-F9] will change the CURRENT SETTING to match the selected item. For instance, if [F2] is showing the layer for the selected item is **Walls**, picking [F2] will change the current layer to Walls, without having to [Tab] to it! To get back to FURN, you could pick the **sofa symbol**, which should be on FURN, and press [F2] again.

[S8] **Set All** – Picking this item will quickly change all of the current settings to match the selected item.

Step 6 – Press mouse button **3** to quit.

Adding the lamp at table height

There are times that you will want to adjust the Z-Height of your symbols. This is particularly true if you are working at multiple floor height, as in a two story building.

You have an occasion for changing the height of the symbol when you set your lamp on the top of the coffee table. The option to do this is called **Z Offset**. The **Z Offset** option is another option that remains set until you change it, so you will want to remember to do so after placing the lamp.

Step 1 – Pick **New File**, in the TEMPLATE menu.

Step 2 – Pick **New Path**.

Step 3 – Type in the directory pathname for the **Lamps** template.

Step 4 – Now pick the **Lamps** template.

Step 5 – The **Lamps** template will be displayed, as in FIG. 5-18.

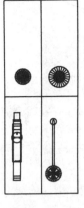

DISPLAY THE LAMPS
TEMPLATE

Figure 5 – 18

Step 6 – Pick the **Z Offset** option.

Step 7 – Type in the height of the table. This height will be 15 or 18 inches, depending on the table you used.

0.15 or 0.18

Step 8 – Pick the lamp called **Ceramic**, and place it on your table. This is illustrated in FIG. 5-19.

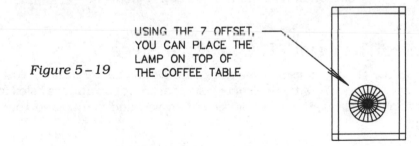

USING THE Z OFFSET,
YOU CAN PLACE THE
LAMP ON TOP OF
THE COFFEE TABLE

Figure 5 – 19

Step 9 – Pick the **Z Offset** option again.

Step 10 – Change the offset value back to **0**.

Step 11 – Your drawing should now look like FIG. 5-20.

Step 12 – File your drawing, using the **File I/O** menu, and the **Save Dwg** option, or press **[Shift] F**.

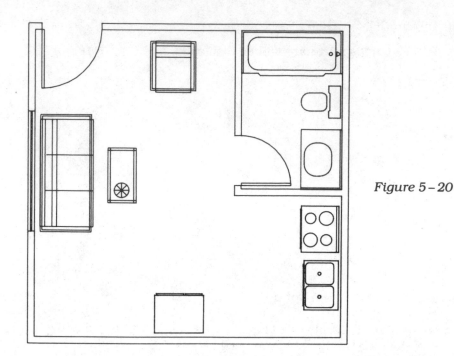

Figure 5–20

Turning off the template

Step 13 – To turn off the template when you are through working with it, pick the **TempOff** option, in the TEMPLATE menu.

Refer to The DataCAD Operations Guide

Turn to the Symbols section found in *The DataCAD Operations Guide* in appendix A. Notice how there are many symbol type of operations listed in this section. You will want to use this section as you add symbols to your own projects.

DataCAD 128 alert!

If you are using DataCAD 128, you will want to monitor the size of your drawing file. This is particularly true when adding symbols because some of the symbols provided to you with your DataCAD software can be very complex. (Many of these symbols are "modeled," meaning that they contained fully described geometry.)

However, don't be discouraged from using symbols. The overall use of symbology can save you space in your drawing, especially when geometry (such as door schedule bubbles) is repeated frequently.

Checking the size of your drawing

To check the size of your drawing, follow these steps.

Step 1 – Press [**Alt**] **Y** (UTILITY/DIRECTORY menus).

Step 2 – The information of the current drawing will be displayed.

Step 3 – Look for the "Current drawing size." The drawing at this point will probably be around 40K if you have followed the steps in this book. The maximum for Regular DataCAD is 6000K. The maximum for DataCAD 128 is 128K.

The maximum size a file can be to fit on a high density diskette is 1200K for 5¼" floppy, and 1400K for 3½" floppy. If your drawing becomes larger than this, you will have to use the BACKUP command to put it on more than 1 diskette, or a condensing program to store it. (See appendix A: *The DataCAD Operations Guide*.)

Additional assignments

Now you can practice adding symbols to your drawing ASSIGNMENTS 1 and 2. Follow the instructions found on the projects in FIGS. 5-21 and 5-22.

Exploding symbols

Notice that in ASSIGNMENT 2, you will need to "explode" the bath group symbol. Symbols are normally protected from changes, other than enlarging, mirroring, or erasing the entire symbol. This is because DataCAD looks at a symbol as one single entity. To manipulate a portion of a symbol, as necessary for the bath, you must "explode" it as you add it into your drawing.

Caution: Exploding symbols mean that they are no longer databased (connected with a report) or treated like a symbol. This also means they cannot be replaced or redefined in your drawing. These procedures are described in appendix A: *The DataCAD Operations Guide*.

Step 1 – From the TEMPLATE menu, pick **Explode** until it is active (***** = active).

* Explode

Step 2 – Now symbols you add to your drawing will be exploded, and can be manipulated.

Step 3 – Turn Explode OFF as soon as you are through using it.

Explode OFF

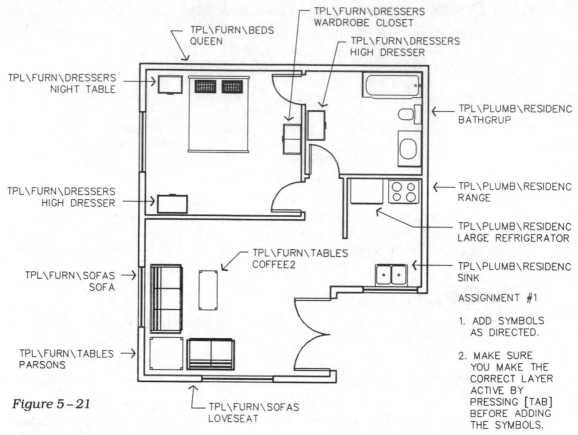

TPL\FURN\DRESSERS
WARDROBE CLOSET

TPL\FURN\BEDS
QUEEN

TPL\FURN\DRESSERS
HIGH DRESSER

TPL\FURN\DRESSERS
NIGHT TABLE

TPL\PLUMB\RESIDENC
BATHGRUP

TPL\PLUMB\RESIDENC
RANGE

TPL\FURN\DRESSERS
HIGH DRESSER

TPL\PLUMB\RESIDENC
LARGE REFRIGERATOR

TPL\FURN\TABLES
COFFEE2

TPL\PLUMB\RESIDENC
SINK

TPL\FURN\SOFAS
SOFA

ASSIGNMENT #1

1. ADD SYMBOLS
   AS DIRECTED.

2. MAKE SURE
   YOU MAKE THE
   CORRECT LAYER
   ACTIVE BY
   PRESSING [TAB]
   BEFORE ADDING
   THE SYMBOLS.

TPL\FURN\TABLES
PARSONS

Figure 5 – 21

TPL\FURN\SOFAS
LOVESEAT

DataCAD exercise 5

Please complete the following exercise by reading each question carefully,
then circling the letter that corresponds to the correct answer.

1. To quickly change layers, you press the:
   a. **[Tab]** key.
   b. **[Alt] L** keys.
   c. **L** key.

2. DataCAD symbols are attached to:
   a. Other symbols.
   b. Symbol libraries.
   c. Templates.

3. To change a template directory, you use the:
   a. **New Dir** option.
   b. **New Path** option.
   c. **Tem Dir** option.

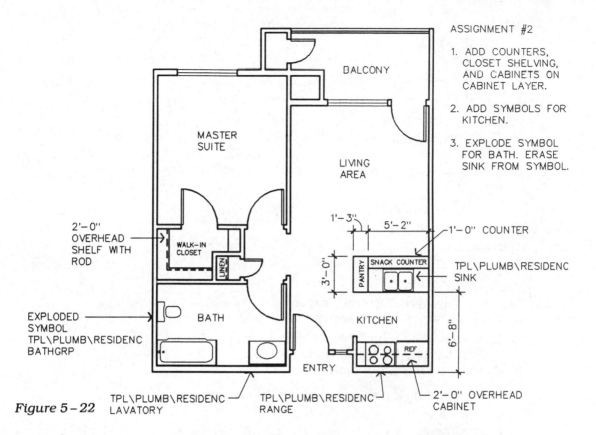

ASSIGNMENT #2

1. ADD COUNTERS, CLOSET SHELVING, AND CABINETS ON CABINET LAYER.

2. ADD SYMBOLS FOR KITCHEN.

3. EXPLODE SYMBOL FOR BATH. ERASE SINK FROM SYMBOL.

BALCONY

MASTER SUITE

LIVING AREA

2'-0" OVERHEAD SHELF WITH ROD

WALK-IN CLOSET

LINEN

1'-3"   5'-2"

1'-0" COUNTER

3'-0"   PANTRY   SNACK COUNTER

TPL\PLUMB\RESIDENC SINK

EXPLODED SYMBOL TPL\PLUMB\RESIDENC BATHGRP

BATH

KITCHEN

6'-8"

REF

ENTRY

TPL\PLUMB\RESIDENC LAVATORY

TPL\PLUMB\RESIDENC RANGE

2'-0" OVERHEAD CABINET

Figure 5-22

4. To use a symbol, you first have to:
   a. Pick a library.
   b. Pick a template.
   c. Call up a symbol file.

5. The quick way to enter the TEMPLATE menu is to press the:
   a. **A** key.
   b. **T** key.
   c. [**Alt**] **T** keys.

6. To pick a symbol off the template, you use mouse button:
   a. 1.
   b. 2.
   c. 3.

7. To quit placing the symbol, you use mouse button:
   a. 1.
   b. 2.
   c. 3.

8. To place a symbol at another angle, you use the:

   a. **Angle** option.
   b. **DymnRot** option.
   c. **NewAngl** option.

9. When you have set a rotation angle while placing a symbol, it:

   a. Automatically resets to 0 for the next symbol.
   b. Changes all of the rotation angles for the other symbols already placed in your drawing.
   c. Remains set for all new symbols you are adding, until you change it.

10. To open a new template, when you already have a template displayed, you pick:

    a. **New File**.
    b. **StrtFile**.
    c. **NewTempl**.

11. When you are working on the second floor of a building, before you pick a symbol you would want to set the:

    a. **Z Base** option in the **Template** menu.
    b. **X Offset** option in the **Template** menu.
    c. **Z Offset** option in the **Template** menu.

12. To use coordinate input, you press the:

    a. [**Space Bar**].
    b. [**Alt**] **C** keys.
    c. [**Tab**].

13. Exploding a symbol means:

    a. It is connected to a report and it is a single entity.
    b. It is no longer a single entity and you can change it.
    c. It is a single entity and you cannot change a portion of it.

14. After renaming a symbol:

    a. The new name appears immediately when you move the cursor to the template window.
    b. You can only see the new name in another drawing that doesn't contain the symbol with the old name.
    c. You can pick **Re-Load** to load the new symbol name in the drawing database.

15. Checking the size of your drawing is accomplished by using the:

    a. **File I/O** menu, **File size** option.
    b. **Directory** menu.
    c. **Display** menu, **File size** option.

16. Identifying a symbol is helpful to:

    a. Find out what layer it is on and what the Z-maximum and Z-minimum heights are.

    b. Identify what layer it should go on.

    c. Find out what items, such as lines and arcs, are in the symbol, along with the individual item colors.

17. The **Set All** option in the **Identify** menu allows you to:

    a. Change all of the current settings to match the identified item, such as layer, color, and Z-base and height.

    b. Set all of the selected items back onto their correct layer.

    c. Set all of the settings (layer, color, etc.) of the selected items to whatever you want with one pick.

Lesson 6
Adding dimensions and text

What you will be doing

You will add dimensions to your project. You also will add notes to describe your drawing components.

Objectives

Your lesson objectives are to:

- Create horizontal and vertical dimensions.
- Create stringline dimensions.
- Create an overall dimension.
- Add text to your drawing.
- Draw arrows.
- Change the size of the text.

Remember to refer to *The DataCAD Operations Guide* in appendix A when instructed. You will find many helpful sections that complement this lesson.

Adding dimensions and text to your drawing

Dimensioning your drawing is fast in DataCAD. The text in your dimensions is generated automatically. This is because the system already knows how big or what length you have created your items. All you do is tell the system what you want dimensioned, and where you want the dimension to appear. Figure 6-1 shows the dimensions you will be adding to your drawing.

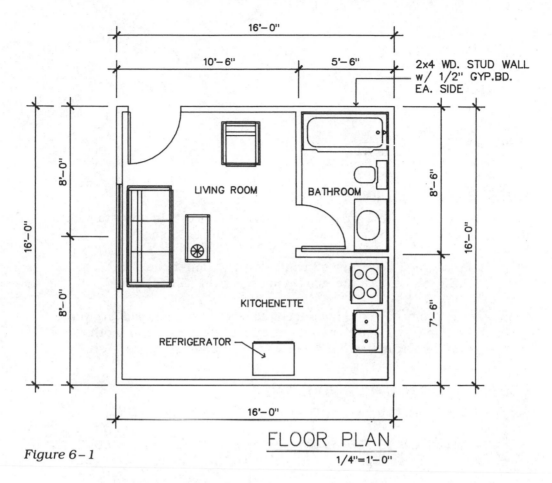

Figure 6-1

FLOOR PLAN

1/4"=1'-0"

When you tell the system what it is you want dimensioned, remember to use object snap! This is to make sure you are "grabbing" onto the object you are dimensioning.

There are certain times, however, when you will not want to object snap to a corner of a wall. In your project, the interior walls are dimensioned to the centers. Although this is not common practice in residential design, it is in commercial design. When you create a dimension to the center, there is not a corner of the wall to grab onto. You will learn, then, how to dimension to a pick point.

Four types of dimensions

There are four types of dimensioning available. They are shown in FIG. 6-2.

1. Linear
2. Angular
3. Diameter
4. Radius

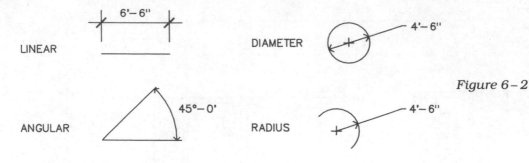

LINEAR

DIAMETER

4'–6"

Figure 6–2

ANGULAR 45°–0'

RADIUS

4'–6"

Setting the snap increments

Notice the current cursor snap increments are set to **4″**. In order to pick at the center of the wall, you will want to change the snap to **2″**.

Step 1 – Press the **S** key. This is the quick way to enter the GRIDS, GRID-SIZE, SET SNAP menus. Do not press the [**Shift**] key.

Step 2 – The prompt, in the message area of your screen, will ask you to type in the X and Y increment values. Type in 0.2 for both the X and Y coordinates. This will set the value to 2 inches.

Creating linear dimensions

Step 1 – Press the [**Tab**] key until the correct layer is active: **DIMS**.

Step 2 – Press [**Alt**] **D**. This is the quick way to enter the DIMENSION menu, **Linear** option, found in the UTILITY menu.

Step 3 – The LINEAR menu will be displayed, as described in FIG. 6-3.

Step 4 – Pick the **Horiznt** option until it is active (***Horiznt**).

*Horiznt.

Step 5 – Object snap to the first corner point of the wall to dimension, as illustrated in FIG. 6-4. Use mouse button **3**.

Step 6 – Press the **X** key until your grid snap is on. The message line will say: **Snapping is ON**, as shown in FIG. 6-5. This will allow you to easily pick at 6″ increments.

Step 7 – Now pick the centerpoint of the interior wall, as shown in FIG. 6-6 on page 104, using grid snap to help you pick. Use mouse button **1**.

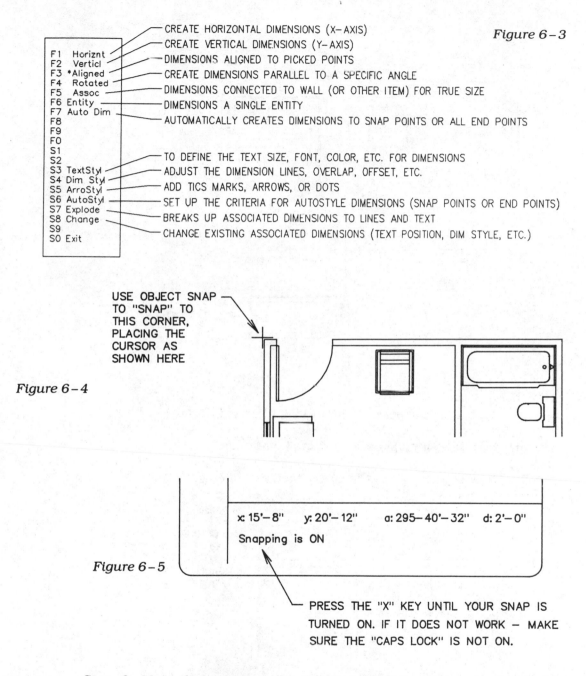

Figure 6-3

F1 Horizt ─── CREATE HORIZONTAL DIMENSIONS (X-AXIS)
F2 Verticl ─── CREATE VERTICAL DIMENSIONS (Y-AXIS)
F3 *Aligned ─── DIMENSIONS ALIGNED TO PICKED POINTS
F4 Rotated ─── CREATE DIMENSIONS PARALLEL TO A SPECIFIC ANGLE
F5 Assoc ─── DIMENSIONS CONNECTED TO WALL (OR OTHER ITEM) FOR TRUE SIZE
F6 Entity ─── DIMENSIONS A SINGLE ENTITY
F7 Auto Dim ─── AUTOMATICALLY CREATES DIMENSIONS TO SNAP POINTS OR ALL END POINTS
F8
F9
F0
S1
S2
S3 TextStyl ─── TO DEFINE THE TEXT SIZE, FONT, COLOR, ETC. FOR DIMENSIONS
S4 Dim Styl ─── ADJUST THE DIMENSION LINES, OVERLAP, OFFSET, ETC.
S5 ArroStyl ─── ADD TICS MARKS, ARROWS, OR DOTS
S6 AutoStyl ─── SET UP THE CRITERIA FOR AUTOSTYLE DIMENSIONS (SNAP POINTS OR END POINTS)
S7 Explode ─── BREAKS UP ASSOCIATED DIMENSIONS TO LINES AND TEXT
S8 Change ─── CHANGE EXISTING ASSOCIATED DIMENSIONS (TEXT POSITION, DIM STYLE, ETC.)
S9
SO Exit

USE OBJECT SNAP
TO "SNAP" TO
THIS CORNER,
PLACING THE
CURSOR AS
SHOWN HERE

Figure 6-4

x: 15'-8"   y: 20'-12"   a: 295-40'-32"   d: 2'-0"

Snapping is ON

Figure 6-5

PRESS THE "X" KEY UNTIL YOUR SNAP IS
TURNED ON. IF IT DOES NOT WORK — MAKE
SURE THE "CAPS LOCK" IS NOT ON.

Step 8 – Move the cursor to place the height of the dimension, and pick
with mouse button **1**. (See FIG. 6-7 on page 104.)

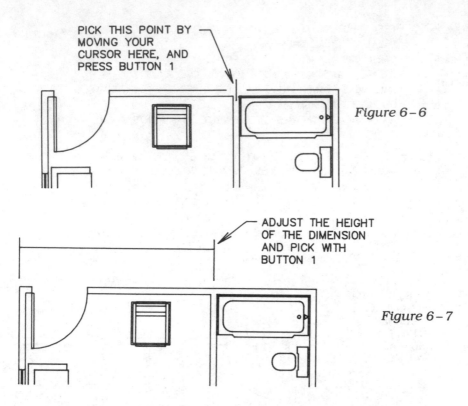

PICK THIS POINT BY
MOVING YOUR
CURSOR HERE, AND
PRESS BUTTON 1

Figure 6–6

ADJUST THE HEIGHT
OF THE DIMENSION
AND PICK WITH
BUTTON 1

Figure 6–7

Step 9 – The text will appear. (It might look like a small box.)

Step 10 – Pick the **StrngLin** option (**String Line**).

Step 11 – Now object snap to the last corner, as indicated in FIG. 6-8.

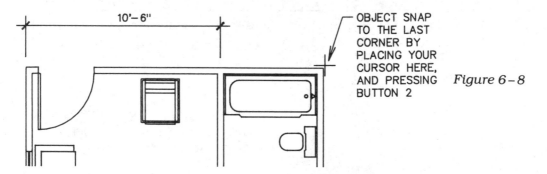

10'– 6"

OBJECT SNAP
TO THE LAST
CORNER BY
PLACING YOUR
CURSOR HERE,
AND PRESSING   *Figure 6–8*
BUTTON 2

Step 12 – The second dimension will pop up. (FIG. 6-9 on page 105.)

Step 13 – Now press mouse button **3** to quit. You will be returned to the
LINEAR DIMENSIONS menu.

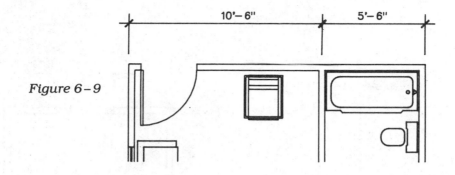

Figure 6–9

Step 14 – Pick the **OverAll** option.

Step 15 – The overall dimension will appear, as in FIG. 6-10.

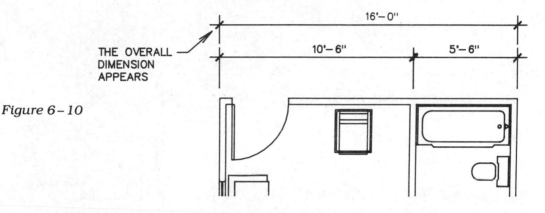

THE OVERALL
DIMENSION
APPEARS

Figure 6–10

Note on stacking dimensions

You might notice that using the **Overall** option leaves a small gap between the stacked dimension lines. This is impossible to avoid, because the overall dimension is "offset" from the first by the offset value set in the DIM STYLE menu. Going into this menu to reset the offset would take too many steps and the **Overall** option would disappear. So, if the gap bothers you, you will want to use this next technique.

To stack dimensions (see FIG. 6-11 on page 106), you can easily "object snap" to the tic marks of the first dimensions! This way, you can have many levels of dimensions, plus avoid the gap.

Step 1 – Press **E**, and use *Entity to Erase the OverAll dimension you created for the horizontal dimension. You can erase the dimension by picking it at the tic mark!

Step 2 – Press [**Alt**] **D** to return to Dimension/Linear.

YOU CAN EASILY STACK DIMENSIONS!

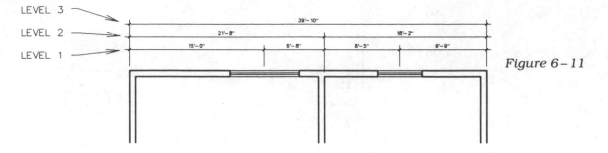

Figure 6 – 11

Step 3 – Using **Horizontal**, object snap to the two end "tic marks," as indicated by the example in FIG. 6-12.

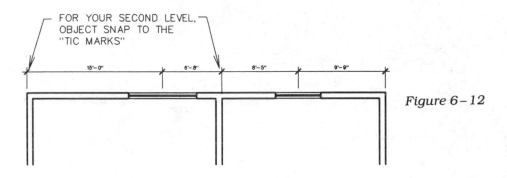

Figure 6 – 12

Step 4 – Now move the cursor out, and pick to place your dimension. No gaps! This technique can also be used to "add-on" to existing dimensions. (See FIG. 6-13.)

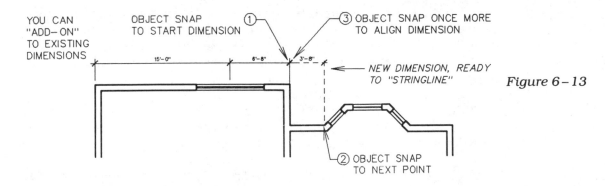

Figure 6 – 13

More dimensioning

Step 1 – To create the last horizontal dimension, you can use the **Entity** option. This option is useful for quickly dimensioning a wall that doesn't have windows or doors or other walls intersecting with it. In other words, the wall is "unbroken."

Pick **Entity**.

Step 2 – Pick the line to dimension, as indicated in FIG. 6-14.

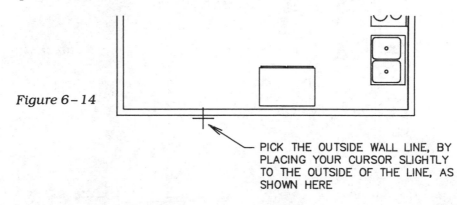

Figure 6 – 14

PICK THE OUTSIDE WALL LINE, BY
PLACING YOUR CURSOR SLIGHTLY
TO THE OUTSIDE OF THE LINE, AS
SHOWN HERE

Step 3 – Pick the height of the dimension line.

Step 4 – Your dimension is created! Your drawing should now look like FIG. 6-15.

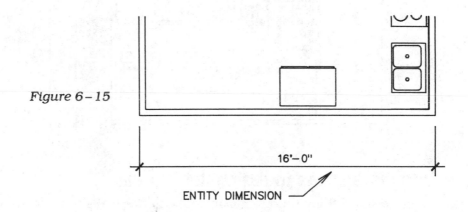

Figure 6 – 15

16'–0"

ENTITY DIMENSION

Step 5 – Pick the **Verticl** option until it is active. This option allows you to create the vertical dimensions in your drawing, as indicated in FIG. 6-16 on page 108.

Step 6 – Create the vertical dimensions for your project, shown in FIG. 6-17 on page 108. Follow the same steps for creating the horizontal dimensions. Be sure to object snap when applicable.

Step 7 – Be sure to save your drawing by pressing [**Shift**] **F**.

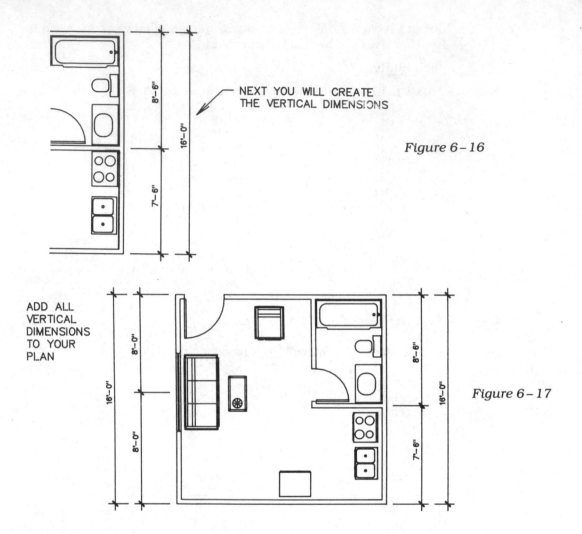

NEXT YOU WILL CREATE
THE VERTICAL DIMENSIONS
8'-6"
16'-0"
7'-6"

Figure 6-16

ADD ALL
VERTICAL
DIMENSIONS
TO YOUR
PLAN
16'-0"
8'-0"
8'-0"
8'-6"
16'-0"
7'-6"

Figure 6-17

Creating dimensions to the center of walls

Some offices require that you dimension your interior walls to the center. This is accomplished easily with just a few steps.

Step 1 – Press [**Alt**] **G** to quickly go to the GEOMETRY menu, found in the UTILITY menu.

Step 2 – Pick the **Divide** option. Divide allows you to add a number of snap points between two points or on an entity (arc, circle, or line).

Step 3 – Notice the message at the bottom should indicate: **Number of divisions = 2**. This means the points that you indicate will be divided

to two pieces, putting a snap point in the middle. If the number of divisions is NOT 2, you can pick the **Dvisions** option and type in **2**.

Step 4 – Object snap to the two inside corners of the wall you wish to dimension to the center of. This is indicated in FIG. 6-18. A snap point will be added. (You might want to Window-In slightly.)

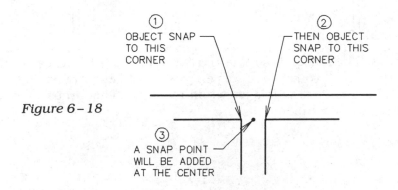

Figure 6 – 18

Step 5 – It is a good idea to add as many points as necessary in one step while you are in this option, instead of going back and forth. (FIG. 6-19.)

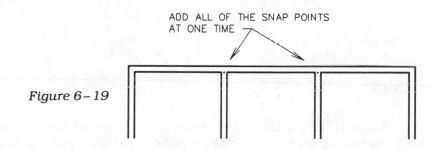

Figure 6 – 19

Step 6 – Now continue dimensioning as required, making sure you object snap to the new snap point you've added. (See FIG. 6-20 on page 110.) If you need a small centerline in your dimension (less seen now with CAD being used), you can use the snap point as the beginning point for your centerlines. Then you can simply dimension directly to the end of the centerlines.

Dimensioning against a wall (turning off extension lines)

When you are adding dimensions to the inside of a wall, against an outside wall, or against another item, you will want to turn off one or both exten-

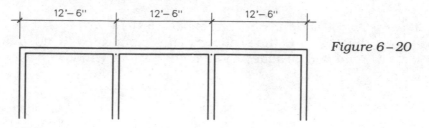

NOW YOUR CENTER DIMENSIONS
ARE EASY TO CREATE!

| 12'-6" | 12'-6" | 12'-6" |

Figure 6-20

sion lines. The reason is so that the extra line doesn't appear in the final plot, especially if you are using a pen plotter. The effect of having an extension line drawn in a wall is shown in FIG. 6-21. (This probably would not show up on a laser plot.)

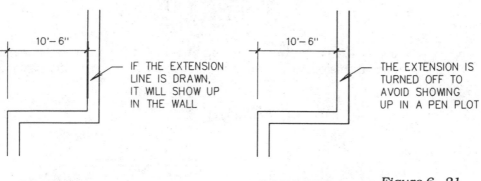

YOU CAN TURN OFF LINE 1 OR 2 TO DIMENSION AGAINST A WALL

10'-6"

IF THE EXTENSION
LINE IS DRAWN,
IT WILL SHOW UP
IN THE WALL

10'-6"

THE EXTENSION IS
TURNED OFF TO
AVOID SHOWING
UP IN A PEN PLOT

WRONG!

CORRECT!

Figure 6-21

The extension lines of the dimension are referred to as line 1 and line 2. Which extension line is 1 or 2 depends on the order you pick the points you want to dimension. The first pick becomes line 1, the second pick becomes line 2.

Although the project that you are dimensioning during this exercise doesn't require inside dimensioning, the additional assignments and of course some of your own projects will.

Step 1 – From the LINEAR menu, pick the **Dim Style** option. The DIMEN-SION STYLE menu will be displayed. This menu contains the two extension line options, as shown in FIG. 6-22.

Step 2 – Now pick either **Line1** or **Line2** until the * is turned off. (* = line will be drawn, no * = line will not be drawn.) If you want no extension lines drawn at all, you would turn off both lines.

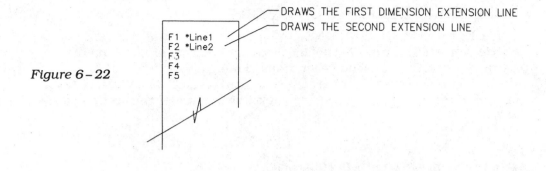

Figure 6-22

DRAWS THE FIRST DIMENSION EXTENSION LINE
DRAWS THE SECOND EXTENSION LINE

F1 *Line1
F2 *Line2
F3
F4
F5

DIMENSION STYLE MENU

Figure 6-23 shows an example of how the lines appear when Line2 has been turned off, based on the order of picked points.

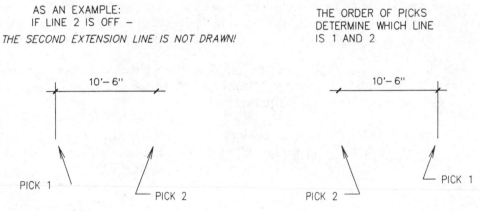

AS AN EXAMPLE:
IF LINE 2 IS OFF —
THE SECOND EXTENSION LINE IS NOT DRAWN!

THE ORDER OF PICKS
DETERMINE WHICH LINE
IS 1 AND 2

10'–6"   10'–6"

PICK 1   PICK 1
PICK 2   PICK 2

Figure 6-23

Step 3 – Press mouse button **3** to return to the LINEAR menu.

Step 4 – Create your new dimension. Remember that the order in which you pick the points to dimension determines which extension line is line1 and line2.

Step 5 – When you are through creating dimensions that require an extension line turned off, make sure you turn them back on again! Pick **Dim Styl** from the LINEAR menu.

Step 6 – Pick ***Line1** and ***Line2** until the stars appear again.

Step 7 – Press mouse button **3** to return to the LINEAR menu.

Refer to the DataCAD Operations Guide

If you turn to the DIMENSIONING section of *The DataCAD Operations Guide*, you will find easy to follow steps for creating single dimensions, string line dimensions, and other dimensioning operations.

To complement the last part of this lesson, you will also find additional operations for creating the notes in your drawing, under the section called Text.

Adding notes to your drawing

In DataCAD, notes are referred to as text, and are very easy to create. You just pick a spot to place the text, then type it in!

There are two ways to add text. The first is Dynamically. This means the text will show on your drawing as you type it in. The second way is to not use Dynamic. With Dynamic OFF, the text shows up at the message area of your screen. This is extremely helpful if you were zoomed out and could not read your text as you typed it in. Because you are close enough to read your text in your drawing, you will probably want to use Dynamic.

Step 1 – Press the [**Tab**] key to change the active layer to: Notes. (Reminder: If you use [**Shift**] and [**Tab**] together, you can scroll backwards through the layer list.)

Step 2 – Press [**Alt**] **T** to quickly enter the TEXT menu, found in the UTILITY menu. The TEXT menu will be displayed, as explained in FIG. 6-24.

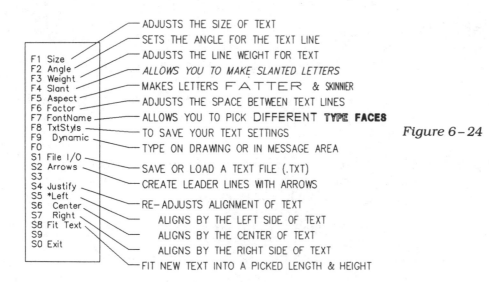

Figure 6 – 24

Step 3 – If **Dynamic** does NOT have a star by it (indicating that it is active), pick ***Dynamic** until the star comes on.

Step 4 – Pick the position for the Living room text, as indicated. Always make sure you pick the position for your text before you start typing. Notice that the shape of your cursor has changed. The new shape and size of the cursor now represents the size that your text is currently set to. (FIG. 6-25.)

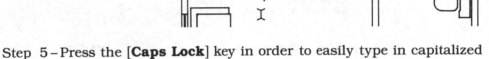

FIRST PICK A START POINT FOR YOUR
TEXT. NOTICE THE CURSOR NOW
INDICATES THE TEXT SIZE.

Figure 6 – 25

Step 5 – Press the [**Caps Lock**] key in order to easily type in capitalized letters.

Step 6 – Type in the text.

Living room

Step 7 – If you desired a second line of text, you would press the [**Enter**] key. Because you do not have a second line of text, press mouse button **3** to quit. The text is added to your drawing, as in FIG. 6-26.

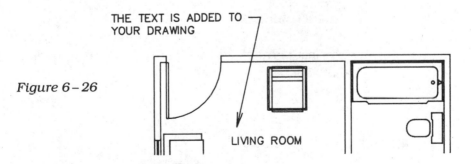

THE TEXT IS ADDED TO
YOUR DRAWING

Figure 6 – 26

LIVING ROOM

Step 8 – Notice the text for your REFRIGERATOR also has an arrow. This is easy to do. First, you add the text, then you add an arrow line.

Step 9 – Pick the starting position for the REFRIGERATOR text, and type it in.

Step 10 – Press mouse button **3** once, to quit back to the TEXT menu.

Step 11 – Pick the **Arrows** option. This option allows you to draw a line that ends with an arrow. The last line picked will be where the arrow appears.

Step 12 – Pick the start point of the leader line, as indicated in FIG. 6-27.

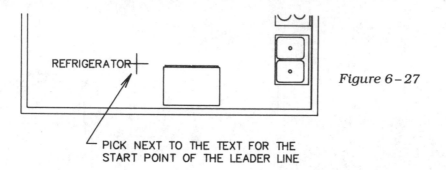

Figure 6 – 27

PICK NEXT TO THE TEXT FOR THE
START POINT OF THE LEADER LINE

Step 13 – Pick the point for the elbow of the line, as indicated in FIG. 6-28.

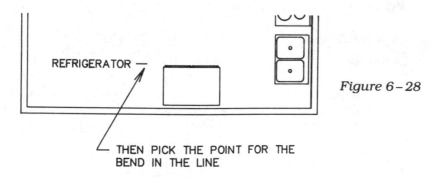

Figure 6 – 28

THEN PICK THE POINT FOR THE
BEND IN THE LINE

Step 14 – Now pick the last point of the line, in the position you wish the arrow to appear, as in FIG. 6-29.

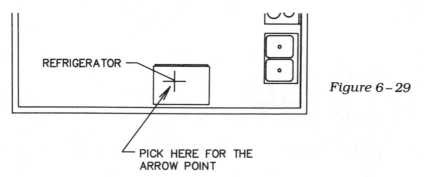

Figure 6 – 29

PICK HERE FOR THE
ARROW POINT

Step 15 – Press mouse button **3** to quit. The arrow will be drawn on the end of your line! (FIG. 6-30.)

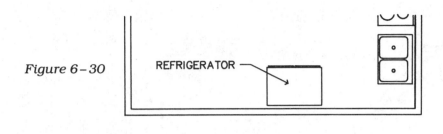

Figure 6 – 30

THE ARROW APPEARS AT
THE LAST PICK POINT

Step 16 – Continue adding the rest of the small text and necessary arrows for your drawing. This is indicated in FIG. 6-31.

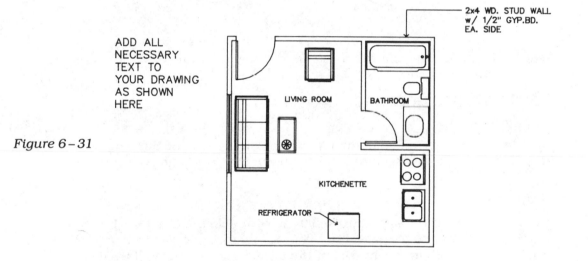

ADD ALL
NECESSARY
TEXT TO
YOUR DRAWING
AS SHOWN
HERE

Figure 6 – 31

Changing the size of your text

The drawing title: FLOOR PLAN is made in larger text than the rest of the sheet. You will want to change the text size in order to create it.

Because the drawing you are creating is in full scale, the text you are currently using is actually set to 6 inches. (This makes sense when you think about the perimeter of the building as a true 16 feet.) When you plot your drawing at 1/4″ scale, 6 inches will appear as 1/8″.

To make your text double in size, then, you will want to set the size of your text to 1 foot.

Step 1 – Pick the **Size** option from the TEXT menu.

Step 2 – Pick the **1'-0"** option. This setting will make your text appear at ¹/₄" high.

Step 3 – Finish adding the larger text to your drawing, and any other text that is necessary. (FIG. 6-32.)

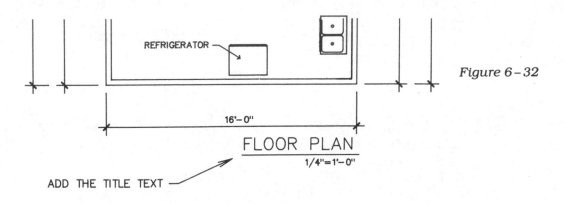

Figure 6–32

Step 4 – File your drawing when you are done by pressing [**Shift**] **F**.

Additional assignments

Add dimensions

Add dimensions to your additional drawing assignments: ASSIG-1, shown in FIG. 6-33, on page 117, and ASSIG-2, shown in FIG. 6-34 on page 118.

Something new

If you would like to try something different, complete the new assignment 3, shown in FIG. 6-35 on page 119. This floorplan is similar to ASSIG-2 drawing, but the living room part of the layout is 2 feet wider. To accomplish these changes, follow these steps:

Step 1 – Retrieve the drawing called **ASSIG-2** and modify it. DON'T SAVE IT using the [**Shift**] **F** technique!

Step 2 – To perform the **Stretch**, follow the instructions in appendix A: *The DataCAD Operations Guide*. Use the ***Fence** selection mode to select the area to stretch, as indicated in FIG. 6-36 on page 120.

Step 3 – Once the changes have been made, go to the FILE I/O menu (found in UTILITY).

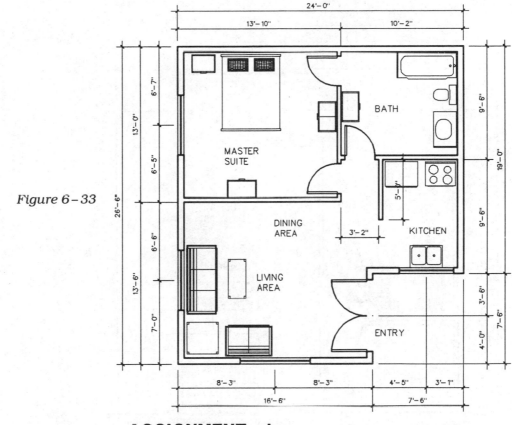

Figure 6-33

ASSIGNMENT #1

Step 4 – Pick **Save As** to save this version of your drawing under a new name.

Step 5 – Type in and [**Enter**] the new name of your drawing:

ASSIG-3

Step 6 – Now pick **New Dwg**.

Step 7 – Pick **Abort**.

Step 8 – Pick **Yes**. Now you have the original drawing (ASSIG-2) still intact, and a new drawing (ASSIG-3).

Defining another font

Different typefaces, or "fonts," are available with DataCAD. Many come with the basic package, and more can be purchased and added. The

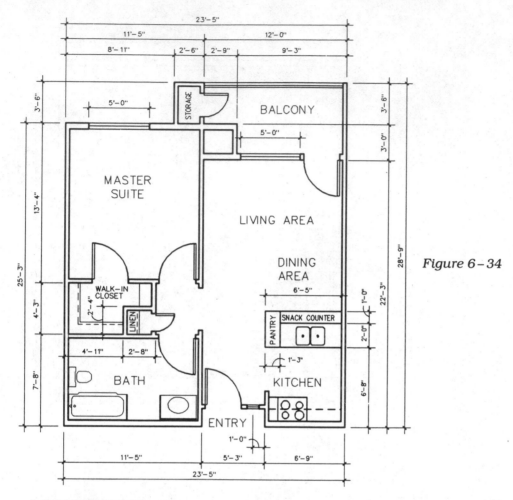

Figure 6 – 34

ASSIGNMENT #2

default font in your drawing is Roman. You can easily change the font to a bold helvetica for titles. There are also hand lettering fonts. A guide to the different fonts can be found in your DataCAD USERS Manual.

If you wish, you can erase the title you just made and replace it with a bold helvetica. Follow these steps to change your font.

Step 1 – In the TEXT menu, pick the **FontName** option. The font list will be displayed.

Step 2 – Look for the font called **HLV_BP**. This stands for ''Helvetica, Bold, Proportional.'' You might have to pick **SrclFwrd** if you don't see **HLV_BP** on the first page of the list. Once you find it, pick it.

Figure 6-35

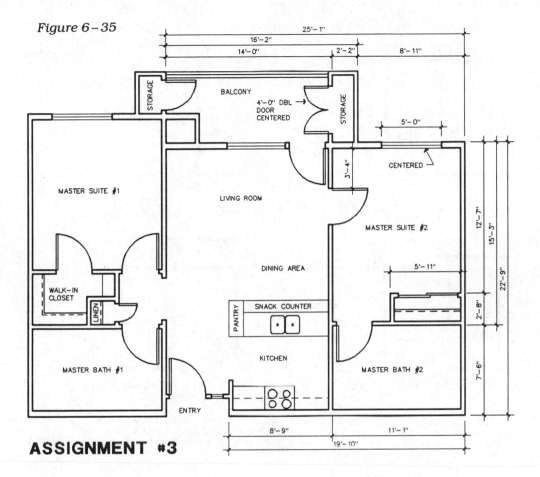

ASSIGNMENT #3

Step 3 – Now pick the starting point for your title, and type **in FLOOR PLAN**.

Saving your text settings

Once you have gone to all the trouble of defining your text settings (size, font, aspect, slant, angle, etc.), you can save the settings for future use. The option that allows you to do this is called "Text Styles."

Step 1 – From the TEXT menu, pick **TxtStyls**.

Step 2 – **Pick SaveCurr** (Save Current).

Step 3 – Type in an appropriate name for your new text style, and press [**Enter**].

   1FTHELV

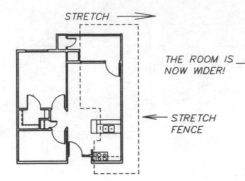
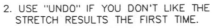

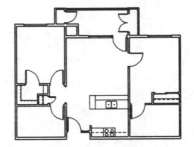

1. USE STRETCH, *FENCE, TO ADD 2 FEET TO THE WIDTH OF THE PLAN.

2. USE "UNDO" IF YOU DON'T LIKE THE STRETCH RESULTS THE FIRST TIME.

Figure 6–36

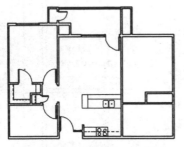

3. ADD THE NEW WALLS. CLEAN UP THE INTERSECTIONS

4. ADD THE WINDOWS AND DOORS. DIMENSION AND ADD ROOM LABELS.

5. USE "FILE I/O, SAVE AS" TO SAVE YOUR DRAWING, NAMING IT: ASSIGN–3

6. THEN USE "NEW DWG, ABORT, YES" SO THAT YOU DO NOT OVERWRITE THE ORIGNAL PLAN CALLED ASSIG–2.

Step 4 – Now when you want to use 1' helvetica font again, you can go into this option, **TxtStyls**, pick **Load**, and pick the **1FTHELV** style you just created, even if you are in another drawing!

DataCAD exercise 6

Please complete the following exercise by reading each question carefully, then circling the letter that corresponds to the correct answer.

1. To quickly change layers, you press the:
   a. [**Tab**] key.
   b. [**Alt**] **L** keys.
   c. **L** key.

2. To put the items (walls, dimensions, text, etc.) you are creating onto the right layer, you should:

a. Change to the correct layer BEFORE you create the item.
b. Change to the correct layer AFTER you create the item.
c. Just create the item. It automatically goes to the correct layer.

3. To make a horizontal or vertical straight dimension, you would use the:
   a. **Angular** option.
   b. **Radius** option.
   c. **Linear** option.

4. If you are dimensioning a line that is the Y axis, you would pick the:
   a. **Horizontal** option.
   b. **Vertical** option.
   c. **Baseline** option.

5. To string a series of chained dimensions, you pick the:
   a. **Chain** option.
   b. **Strnglin** option.
   c. **Series** option.

6. To get the total length of the wall dimensioned after you have defined string line dimensions, you use the:
   a. **Total** option.
   b. **Length** option.
   c. **OverAll** option.

7. To dimension an unbroken wall (has no windows or doors) quickly, you use the:
   a. **Entity** option.
   b. **Wall** option.
   c. **Length** option.

8. To create text, you:
   a. Type in the text, then position it on your drawing.
   b. Pick a start point, then type in your text.
   c. Pick a start point, type in your text, then drag the text to a new position.

9. To have text that is plotted at $1/8$ inch when you are plotting at a $1/4$ inch scale, you create your text at the size of:
   a. $1/8$ inch.
   b. 1 foot.
   c. 6 inches.

10. To permanently save a drawing to your hard disk, you must:
    a. Save the file using **File I/O**, and **Save Dwg**, or pick **Yes** to save when quitting DataCAD.

b. Not do anything. The file is automatically saved.

c. Exit the system, and pick **Abort**.

11. When "stacking" dimensions or to avoid a gap from using "Overall," you can object snap to the:

    a. Wall corners again, because you cannot stack dimensions.

    b. Tic Marks of the first dimension.

    c. Text in the first dimension.

12. To make your text skinnier, you can adjust the:

    a. **Factor** option.

    b. **Justify** option.

    c. **Aspect** option.

13. To give your text a slight italicized look, you can use the:

    a. **Angle** option.

    b. **Slant** option.

    c. **Factor** option.

14. In order to add more space between text lines, you can use the:

    a. **Aspect** option.

    b. **Factor** option.

    c. **NextLine** option.

15. If you need to dimension to the center of your walls, it is a good idea to first create the center snap points, using:

    a. **Divide**, found in the GEOMETRY menu.

    b. **CntrSnap**, found in the ARCHITECT menu.

    c. **CntrPnt**, found in the ARCHITECT menu.

16. When you are adding text, in order for the text to appear at the MESSAGE area of your screen (in contrast to appearing on the drawing), you:

    a. Turn OFF the **Dynamic** option.

    b. Turn ON the *__Dynamic__ option.

    c. Turn OFF the **On Dwg** option.

17. To define another type face for your text, you use the:

    a. **FontName** option.

    b. **TypeFace** option.

    c. **Charctr** option.

18. If you wish to save the current text settings, you would use the:

    a. **SaveSets** option.

    b. **SaveText** option.

    c. **TxtStyls** option.

Lesson 7
Viewing your drawing in 3-D

What you will be doing

You will create a 3-D perspective view of your drawing. You will use the hidden line removal function to enhance your 3-D view. Then you will add the 3-D view image to your drawing, and scale it down to fit in your drawing border.

Objectives

Your lesson objectives are to:

- Create a 3-dimensional perspective view.
- Save the view as an image.
- Add the image to the drawing.
- Scale the size of the image to make it fit within the drawing boundary.
- Create a perspective image with hidden lines removed.

Remember to refer to *The DataCAD Operations Guide* when instructed.

3-D views

You can create 3-D views for presentations, spatial studies, and illustration purposes, directly from your plan view drawings. You can create three types of 3-D views:

1. Parallel
2. Perspective
3. Oblique

During this lesson, you will create Perspective views as shown in FIG. 7-1.

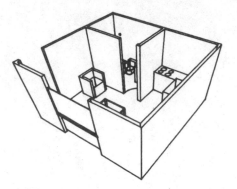

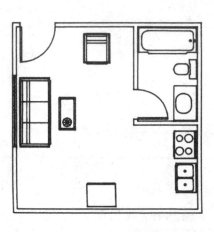

Figure 7 – 1

NOTE: PARTS OF DRAWING HAVE
BEEN SIMPLIFIED FOR
ILLUSTRATION PURPOSES

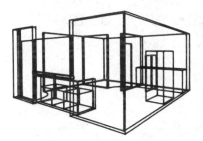

Turning off unnecessary layers

Before you create a 3-D image, you will want to turn off the layers that hold
graphics you do not want to see in 3-D.

Step 1 – Press **L**, to enter the LAYERS menu.

Step 2 – Pick the **On/Off** option.

Step 3 – Pick the layers called: **Notes, Dims,** and **Border**, to turn them off.

DataCad 128 alert!

If you are using DataCAD 128, you will have to be careful when creating a
3-D image. At this point in your drawing, your file size is approximately
40,000 bytes. Because creating an image duplicates the items in your
drawing, it will increase your file size. Once an image is saved, the geometry is flattened out to 2-D. This means all the symbols are exploded and

broken down into lines. **Curves, circles, and arcs are broken into very small lines**, adding even more size to the file.

To avoid going over your file size limit, simply turn off the layers that your furniture and plumbing symbols are on BEFORE creating your image. This step will keep your file size down to 68K or so, even after your two images are added to your drawing.

Step 4 – Quit by pressing mouse button **3**.

Step 5 – Now, only the plan view is displayed, as illustrated in FIG. 7-2.

MAKE SURE THE
PLAN DRAWING IS
DISPLAYED

Figure 7 – 2

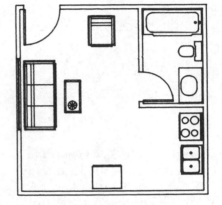

Creating the perspective view

Step 6 – Press [**Shift**] **V** to quickly go to the 3-D VIEWS menu, found in the DCAD 3D menu. The 3-D VIEWS menu will be displayed, as explained in FIG. 7-3.

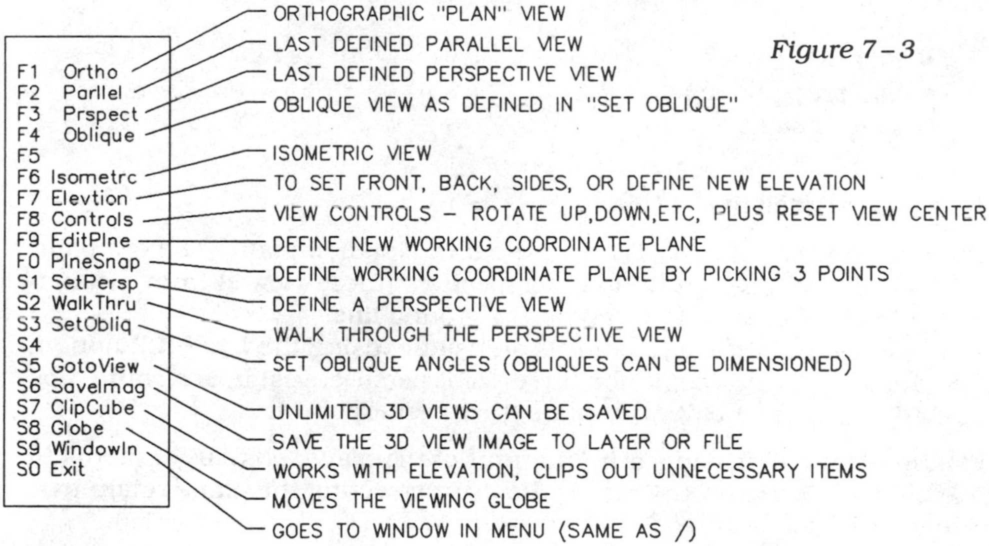

Figure 7 – 3

Key	Label	Description
		ORTHOGRAPHIC "PLAN" VIEW
F1	Ortho	LAST DEFINED PARALLEL VIEW
F2	Parllel	LAST DEFINED PERSPECTIVE VIEW
F3	Prspect	OBLIQUE VIEW AS DEFINED IN "SET OBLIQUE"
F4	Oblique	
F5		ISOMETRIC VIEW
F6	Isometrc	TO SET FRONT, BACK, SIDES, OR DEFINE NEW ELEVATION
F7	Elevtion	VIEW CONTROLS – ROTATE UP,DOWN,ETC, PLUS RESET VIEW CENTER
F8	Controls	DEFINE NEW WORKING COORDINATE PLANE
F9	EditPlne	DEFINE WORKING COORDINATE PLANE BY PICKING 3 POINTS
F0	PlneSnap	DEFINE A PERSPECTIVE VIEW
S1	SetPersp	WALK THROUGH THE PERSPECTIVE VIEW
S2	WalkThru	SET OBLIQUE ANGLES (OBLIQUES CAN BE DIMENSIONED)
S3	SetObliq	
S4		
S5	GotoView	UNLIMITED 3D VIEWS CAN BE SAVED
S6	SaveImag	SAVE THE 3D VIEW IMAGE TO LAYER OR FILE
S7	ClipCube	WORKS WITH ELEVATION, CLIPS OUT UNNECESSARY ITEMS
S8	Globe	MOVES THE VIEWING GLOBE
S9	WindowIn	GOES TO WINDOW IN MENU (SAME AS /)
S0	Exit	

Step 7 – Pick the **SetPersp** option (**Set Perspective View**).

Step 8 – Now the CONE OF VISION might be displayed (as dashed) somewhere on your drawing, as in FIG. 7-4. (If the cone is not displayed, don't worry.) This cone graphically represents the formula for your perspective.

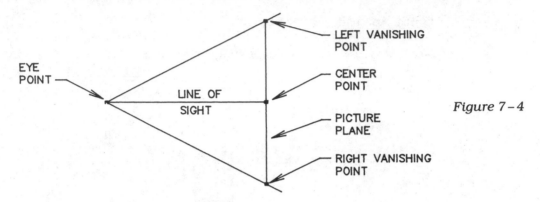

Figure 7 – 4

Step 9 – If the cone of vision is not displayed—The default cone of vision placement might not be by your building, and is located off your screen. That's okay, because as soon as you pick your eye point, the cone will show up! Just keep reading to find out how it all works.

What is the cone of vision?

The cone defines:

- Eye point
- Picture plane
- Vanishing points
- Line of sight
- Centerpoint

This is illustrated in FIG. 7-5.

Eye point   Your point of vision, also called a station point. The eye point height (horizon line), in normal perspectives (those viewed from a standing position) is located 5'-0" above the ground line.

The height of the Eye point is adjustable using the **EyePnt Z** option. The angle of the eye point (for three point perspectives) is determined by also adjusting the **CentPnt Z** option. (See Centerpoint.)

Picture plane   Items appearing in front of the plane look larger, items in back of the plane appear smaller. Items intersecting the plane retain true size.

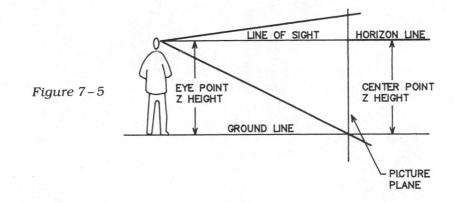

Figure 7–5

LINE OF SIGHT   HORIZON LINE

EYE POINT Z HEIGHT

CENTER POINT Z HEIGHT

GROUND LINE

PICTURE PLANE

Vanishing points These are the vanishing points for your perspective, which are projected to the horizon line.

Line of sight This is the line drawn from the eye point to the picture plane. Where it intersects the plane is the centerpoint. The angle of the line of sight is adjustable by using the **EyePnt Z** and **CentPntZ** options.

Centerpoint This is the point where the line of sight meets the picture plane. The result is the horizon line. The height of the centerpoint (and resulting horizon line) is adjustable using the **CentPntZ** option.

For a normal two point perspective (horizon line height is the same as eye level) the centerpoint height is 5'-0", or the same as the eye point setting. This provides you a level line of sight.

For a three-point perspective (horizon line is at a different level than the eye level), you would adjust the centerpoint and the eye point heights to provide you an angled line of sight. This is the case when the desired effect is looking down at a building, or looking up.

Setting the cone of vision

Step 10 – Press the [**left arrow**] key until your plan view is moved over to the righthand side. This will give you a better area to work with for positioning your cone of vision. (If it doesn't work, make sure your [**Num Lock**] is off.)

Step 11 – Press your [**down arrow**] key until the view is moved into the upper righthand corner.

Step 12 – Pick a point in the lower left of your drawing, as indicated in FIG. 7-6 on page 128. This will be your new eye point. (The height for your eye point is preset to 5'-0".)

Step 13 – Move your cursor around. Notice that the length of the cone

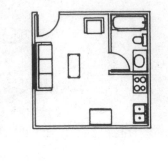

Figure 7 – 6

PICK HERE —
FOR EYE
POINT

does not change as you move your cursor. This is because the **FixCone** option is active. If **FixCone** is NOT active, pick it until the * appears by it. This will keep your vanishing angle set to 30 degrees for each half of the cone (60 degrees total).

*FixCone

Step 14 – Now move your cursor all the way over to your building. **Object snap** to the lower left corner of the building, as indicated in FIG. 7-7.

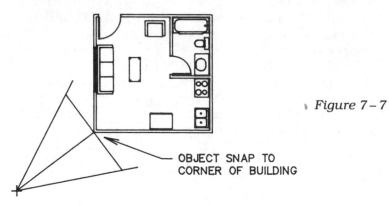

Figure 7 – 7

OBJECT SNAP TO
CORNER OF BUILDING

Step 15 – A text-book perspective will be displayed, and should look similar to FIG. 7-8.

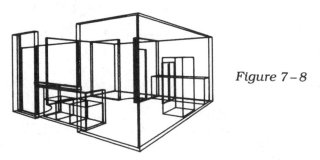

Figure 7 – 8

The globe

When you use any of the **view** options (**perspective, parallel, oblique**) except for orthographic, the "globe" will appear on the screen. What the globe is representing is a flattened out world. The middle is the top of the world, and the bottom is spread out around the top, making a flat world. The idea is that you can change your viewing position by picking somewhere on the globe.

The specific regions of the globe are explained in FIG. 7-9. This illustration shows the world and its relationship to a round world.

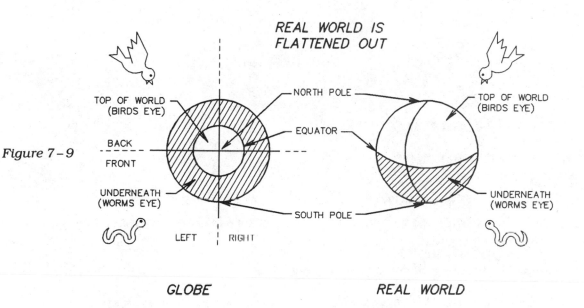

Figure 7-9

REAL WORLD IS FLATTENED OUT

GLOBE   REAL WORLD

Although the globe is very helpful when using a parallel view definition (as you will see in a later lesson), it is clumsy for perspectives. This is because the original eye point and center point calculated the appropriate vanishing points. Moving about your building by picking on the globe is changing your view position, but the building is still true to the original vanishing point calculations. You might want to try several picking points to see how this looks.

Step 1 – Move your cursor up to the inside of the globe.

Step 2 – Press mouse button **1** to pick a globe position. You must pick inside the globe, and you cannot use object snap.

After trying globe pick points, you can get close to your original view by picking in the bottom of the inside circle. The reason is, when you first defined your perspective, this is where your building was, as indicated in FIG. 7-10. (Although you didn't see your house dangling on the globe, it was there theoretically.)

Picking on the globe will get you close to the original perspective, but to get back to the true original perspective, you will want to "**Reset**" it.

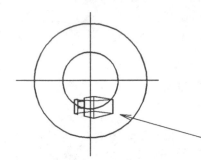

Figure 7–10

YOUR PERSPECTIVE IS
LOCATED ABOUT HERE
ON THE GLOBE

Step 3 – Pick **SetPersp**.

Step 4 – Pick **Reset**.

Saving the 3-D view

Once you are satisfied with your view, you can save in onto a layer, and add it to your plan view.

Step 1 – Pick the **SaveImag** option (**Save Image**).

Step 2 – Pick the **NewLayer** option. This will allow you to name a special layer for your 3-D view.

Step 3 – Type in the name for your new layer: **PERSP1**. (**Perspective 1**.)

Step 4 – Pick **On**, to keep this new layer displayed.

Step 5 – Once you are returned to the 3-D VIEW menu, **pick** the **Ortho** option. This will return you to the original plan view, and display the new image as well. If you forget to pick Ortho, don't worry. As soon as you return to 2-D and pick Move, Copy, Rotate, or other 2-D Edit options, your plan view would return.

Step 6 – Press mouse button **3** and you should return to 2D DataCAD. [**Shift**] **V** is an "interrupt key," and when you quit with mouse button **3**, you will be returned to whatever menu you were in previously.

If you did not use [**Shift**] **V**, but picked the options to enter **3D Views**, you can quickly return to 2D DataCAD by pressing the [;] key. (Otherwise, pressing mouse button three will switch you back and forth from 3D Edit and 3D Entity, which are the SO selecitons in DCAD 3D.)

Notice that your perspective view might not be located exactly where you would like it to be. You will want to move it to a better location. You might also want to change the size of your perspective to better fit in the border area. (FIG. 7-11.)

THE PERSPECTIVE VIEW ———▶
MAY NOT BE LOCATED
IN THE CORRECT
POSITION

Figure 7–11

NOTE: DRAWINGS ARE
SIMPLIFIED FOR
ILLUSTRATION
PURPOSES

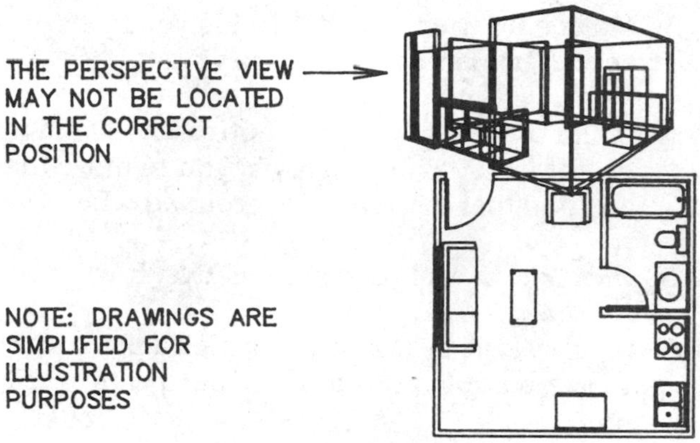

Step 7 – Display all of your layers, by using the **L** key, and the **On/Off** option. This will allow you to see all of the objects in your drawing to adjust the perspective view to fit.

Step 8 – You might want to center your drawing again, using the [**arrows**] keys.

User hint: You also can instantly center your drawing by placing the cursor where you desire the center to be, then pressing the [**Home**] key.

Moving items in your drawing

When an item or items are created in the wrong place, it is an easy task to move them. You will want to move the perspective image to a new location in your drawing.

Note: As you make your perspectives, you will notice that they are created at all different sizes, some very large and some closer to correct size. This seems to be relative to the original viewing size of the building BEFORE you defined your perspective.

If your perspective is overly large at this point, and you cannot easily move it, you may want to shrink it first. If so, see the next section "Enlarging and shrinking items in your drawing,'' and come back to this section to move the perspective once it is an appropriate size.

Step 1 – Press **M** to quickly enter the **Move** option, found in the EDIT menu. (If you had forgotten to pick **Ortho**, and your drawing view was still perspective, picking **move** would immediately return your view to plan view!)

   M

Step 2 – Pick the **Drag** option.

Step 3 – Make sure the layer that holds your perspective view: **PERSP1**, is active, by using the [**Tab**] key.

Step 4 – Make the ***Group** option active, by picking it until there is a star in front of it. This will allow you to move the entire perspective as a group (perspectives are grouped when they are created).

Step 5 – Pick a corner of your perspective. It will become **gray and dashed**.

Step 6 – Now you will be prompted to pick a point to move the perspective by. Pick a point to the left of the perspective, as indicated in FIG. 7-12.

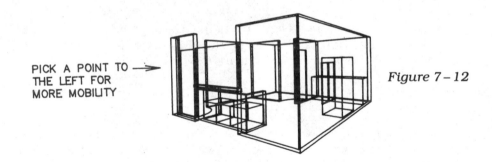

PICK A POINT TO →
THE LEFT FOR
MORE MOBILITY

Figure 7 – 12

Step 7 – Now a box outline will appear, and you will be able to drag it to a new location. Pick a spot over to the lower right of the original floor plan, as indicated in FIG. 7-13.

Enlarging and shrinking items in your drawing

You use the same function to enlarge items in your drawing as you do to shrink it.

Step 1 – Press mouse button **3** to quit the MOVE menus.

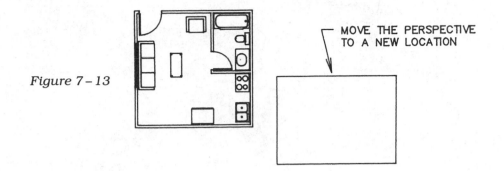

Figure 7–13

MOVE THE PERSPECTIVE
TO A NEW LOCATION

Step 2 – Pick the **Enlarge** option, found in the EDIT menu. (Or press [**Alt**] **E**.)

Step 3 – Pick in the center of your perspective to establish a center of enlargement, as indicated in FIG. 7-14. This is the point that will stay stationary as the group is enlarged or shrunk.

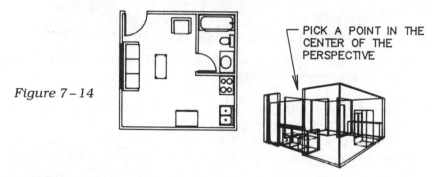

Figure 7–14

PICK A POINT IN THE
CENTER OF THE
PERSPECTIVE

Step 4 – Pick the **Enlrgmnt** option, to enter an enlargement factor, then pick **Set All**.

Step 5 – Pick an enlargement factor that you want to change the size of the perspective by. For example, .5 will shrink your items to half the present size. An enlargement factor of 2 will make items twice the present size.

You might want to pick **.75**.

Step 6 – Now press mouse button **2** to enter this factor. (You could also use the [**Enter**] key if you wish.) Press mouse button **3** to return to the ENLARGE menu.

Step 7 – Notice that the ***Group** option is still active. Pick a corner of your perspective and it will become smaller. (FIG. 7-15.)

Step 8 – Once the size of the perspective image is reduced, you might want to "Move" it in your border again.

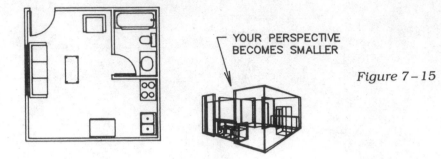

YOUR PERSPECTIVE
BECOMES SMALLER

Figure 7–15

User note: The **Inverse** option will change the enlargement to the opposite of the set value. Example: If the value was set to 2, for twice the size, the inverse of that would be 0.50, or half the size. You can use this if you want your items back to their previous size.

Creating a second perspective with hidden lines

Now you will create another perspective view. This time, you will change your eye level and remove the hidden lines.

Step 1 – Use the **Layers** menu to turn off your new layer called **PERSP1** and all other layers except the layers called **Walls, Doors, Windows, Furn,** and **Plumb.** Your drawing will now be ready for your next perspective.

Note: If you wish to make the hidden line removal process faster (this could take 10 or 15 minutes on a 386 20mHz machine) or have DataCAD 128 software—turn OFF your **Furn** and **Plumb** layer also! Now the hide process will only take a few minutes (maybe less) and it will not take up as much space.

Step 2 – Press **Y**.

Step 3 – Pick **Prspect**. Your original perspective view is displayed.

Step 4 – Pick **SetPersp**. This option allows you to redefine your viewing orientation.

Step 5 – Pick **EyePntZ**, to change your eye point height.

Step 6 – Pick **Custom**.

Step 7 – Type in **30**. This will change your eye point height to 30 feet. Now you will be able to look over the walls and into the room when you create your perspective.

Step 8 – Pick the points for your cone again, following the original cone displayed, but this time pick **INSIDE** your building for the center-point. This way, the inside of your building will become your "focal point."

Remember, you MUST move your cursor inside the building, NOT JUST make the cone look like it is pointing inside the building!

Your new perspective will be displayed, and you will have a bird's-eye view of the building, as shown in FIG. 7-16.

Figure 7 – 16

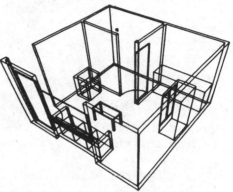

NOTE: DRAWING
IS SIMPLIFIED FOR
ILLUSTRATION
PURPOSES

Step 9 – As a reminder, you can change your viewing point using the small globe, but it can be difficult to get the desired result. (See FIG. 7-17.) If you wish, you can also pick **SetPersp** to change your settings and viewing position.

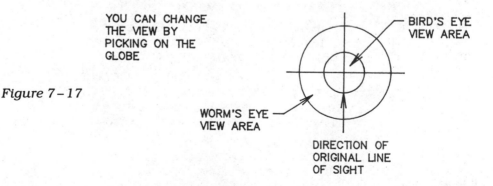

YOU CAN CHANGE
THE VIEW BY
PICKING ON THE
GLOBE

BIRD'S EYE
VIEW AREA

Figure 7 – 17

WORM'S EYE
VIEW AREA

DIRECTION OF
ORIGINAL LINE
OF SIGHT

Step 10 – After you have picked different positions on the globe, if you would like to return quickly to your original bird's-eye view, you can pick the **SetPersp** option.

Step 11 – Now pick the **Reset** option. Your original view is returned, as in FIG. 7-18.

THE RESET OPTION
RETURNS YOU TO
THE FIRST VIEW
YOU DEFINED

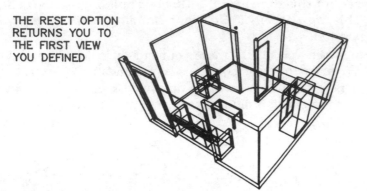

Figure 7 – 18

Hidden line removal

Once you have achieved the desired view, you will want to remove the hidden lines from your view.

Step 1 – Press [**Shift**] **Y** to enter the HIDE menu, found in the DCAD 3D, 3D EDIT menus.

Step 2 – The HIDE menu is displayed, as explained in FIG. 7-19.

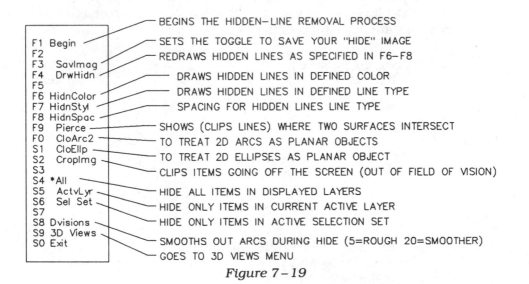

F1 Begin	BEGINS THE HIDDEN-LINE REMOVAL PROCESS
F2	SETS THE TOGGLE TO SAVE YOUR "HIDE" IMAGE
F3 SavImag	REDRAWS HIDDEN LINES AS SPECIFIED IN F6-F8
F4 DrwHidn	DRAWS HIDDEN LINES IN DEFINED COLOR
F5	DRAWS HIDDEN LINES IN DEFINED LINE TYPE
F6 HidnColor	SPACING FOR HIDDEN LINES LINE TYPE
F7 HidnStyl	
F8 HidnSpac	
F9 Pierce	SHOWS (CLIPS LINES) WHERE TWO SURFACES INTERSECT
FO CloArc2	TO TREAT 2D ARCS AS PLANAR OBJECTS
S1 CloEllp	TO TREAT 2D ELLIPSES AS PLANAR OBJECT
S2 CropImg	CLIPS ITEMS GOING OFF THE SCREEN (OUT OF FIELD OF VISION)
S3	
S4 *All	HIDE ALL ITEMS IN DISPLAYED LAYERS
S5 ActvLyr	HIDE ONLY ITEMS IN CURRENT ACTIVE LAYER
S6 Sel Set	HIDE ONLY ITEMS IN ACTIVE SELECTION SET
S7	
S8 Dvisions	SMOOTHS OUT ARCS DURING HIDE (5=ROUGH 20=SMOOTHER)
S9 3D Views	GOES TO 3D VIEWS MENU
SO Exit	

Figure 7 – 19

Step 3 – Pick **SavImag** until it is active (***SavImag**), to save the image you will be creating. You always will want to do this *before* you create the hidden line view.

Step 4 – Pick the **Begin** option.

Step 5 – After the hidden line removal process is complete, pick the **New-Layer** option.

Step 6 – Name this layer: **PERSP2**.

Step 7 – Pick **On**, to keep this layer active.

Step 8 – Press the [**;**] to return to the 2D DCAD.

Step 9 – Pick [**Alt**] **O** (zero!) to quickly return to the orthographic view of your drawing. (DO NOT press [**Alt**] **o**, because this sets Perpendicular in the OBJECT SNAP menu.)

Step 10 – Press **L** and use **All On, Yes** to turn on the other layers in your drawing.

Step 11 – Use the [**Tab**] key to make the new layer that holds your perspective view active: **PERSP2**.

Step 12 – Finish your drawing by **Moving** your new perspective view, Dragging it as a **Group** to a new location, then **Enlarge** it to a reduced size. Follow the same steps described earlier.

Step 13 – Your drawing should now look like FIG. 7-20.

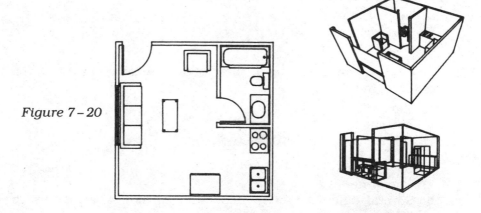

Figure 7 – 20

Step 14 – Remember to press [**Shift**] **F** to quickly file your drawing.

DataCAD exercise 7

Please complete the following exercise by reading each question carefully, then circling the letter that corresponds to the correct answer.

1. Before creating a 3-D view, you should:
   a. Make sure all of the layers are displayed.
   b. Turn off the layers that you do not want to view in 3-D.
   c. Make sure the dimensions layer is displayed.

2. To help you create the perspective, DataCAD displays a:
   a. Cone of Vision.
   b. Option called Line of sight.
   c. View of Vision.

3. To create a new perspective, you use the:
   a. **MakePersp** option.
   b. **SetPersp** option.
   c. **Prspect** option.

4. To create a bird's-eye view, you need to adjust the:
   a. **CntrPntZ** option.
   b. **BirdsView** option.
   c. **EyePntZ** option.

5. The globe that is displayed when you are in perspective view, is:
   a. Really useful for redefining the perspective.
   b. Not really correct for defining a perspective view, because the vanishing points are still being calculated by the original center point locations.
   c. Shows you where your building is located.

6. The middle of the globe is really the:
   a. Top of the world.
   b. Bottom of the world.
   c. Worm's eye view.

7. Picking on the outer ring of the globe will display a view of your building from the:
   a. Top.
   b. Bottom.
   c. Side.

8. The 3-D image is saved as:
   a. One group.
   b. Several different groups, depending on how many layers the items were on.
   c. The same amount of groups that were in the original building.

9. To "Move" objects by pulling them with your cursor dynamically, pick the:
   a. **Pull** option.
   b. **Drag** option.
   c. **Dynamic** option.

10. To save the 3-D view, you use the:
    a. **SaveView** option.
    b. **NewView** option.
    c. **SaveImag** option.

11. When sving the 3-D view, you:
    a. Must have a predefined layer to hold your views on.
    b. Are given the option to create a new layer for your view.
    c. Cannot save in on any layer but the active one.

12. The saved perspective image:
    a. Usually will have to be moved to a better location.
    b. Pops into your drawing in the exact location you want it to be.
    c. Automatically moves to an upper righthand corner.

13. The **Enlarge** option:
    a. Enlarges items only.
    b. Allows you ot enter a new plot scale for your drawing.
    c. Lets you enlarge or shrink items.

14. To increase the eye level height for viewing the perspective, you use the:
    a. **BirdsEye** option.
    b. **EyePntZ** option.
    c. **EyeLevel** option.

15. If you want to save the view with hidden lines removed, you must:
    a. First set the **SavImag** option.
    b. Remove the lines, then pick the **SavImag** option.
    c. Remove the lines, then pick the **SaveView** option.

16. To display the plan view of your drawing after creating a perspective, you use the:
    a. **Ortho** option.
    b. **PlanView** option.
    c. Mouse button **3**. The plan view is automatically displayed.

17. To have text that is plotted at $1/2$ inch when you are plotting at a $1/4$ inch scale, you create your text at the size of:
    a. $1/8$ inch.
    b. 1 foot.
    c. 2 feet.

18. To permanently save a drawing to your hard disk, you must:
    a. Press [**Shift**] **F**, or use **File I/O** and pick **Save Drawing**. Or, pick **Yes** when quitting DataCAD or starting a **New Dwg**.
    b. Not do anything. The file is automatically saved.
    c. Quit DataCAD, and pick **Abort**.

Lesson 8
Plotting your drawing

What you will be doing

You will create a finished plot of your drawing. You will create this plot at a $1/4''$ scale. Your drawing will be plotted on a D size sheet, 24 × 36. It is assumed that you have a plotter, it is properly set up according to the owner's manual and DataCAD, and it is capable of plotting a D size drawing.

Objectives

Your lesson objectives are to:

- Check the plot scale of the drawing.
- Check the location of the plot area (layout).
- Check the colors are set to the proper pen numbers.
- Prepare the plotter.
- Run the plot.

Remember to refer to the Plotting section of *The DataCAD Operations Guide*.

Plotting

The final plot is the ultimate goal of creating your CAD drawing! Figure 8-1 shows a final plot on a standard architectural sheet. The border can be added as part of your drawing or you can plot on a preprinted sheet.

Preset plot specifications

As mentioned earlier, the *Standard Default Drawing* that you have been using (1-4PLAN) contains preset defaults and standards (such as

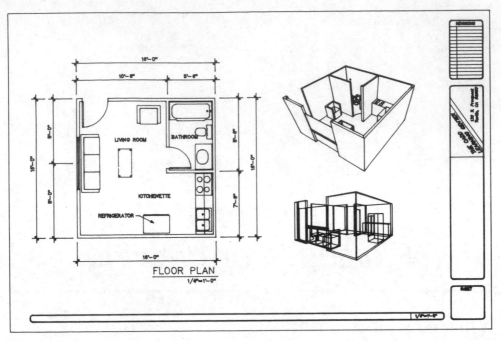

Figure 8 – 1

drawing boundaries, text size, layers, etc.). This drawing also contains information for your plot.

If you created your own default drawing, during the Drawing set-up lesson, you already know what goes into setting up the drawing for plotting. Having the plotting information preset makes plotting a one step process. This means you simply pick the **Plot** option and go!

When <u>first</u> defining these specifications, for the standard default drawing, you follow 4 basic steps:

1. Defining the scale of the plot.
2. Identifying the actual plotting area of your paper.
3. Defining the layout, or the plotting area of your drawing.
4. If you are using different pens, then setting the pens for your plot.

When your default drawing has this information in it already, then you will follow these 4 steps:

1. Put the correct pens in the plotter.
2. Put the paper in the plotter.
3. Turn the plotter on.
4. Pick **PLOT** in DataCAD.

During this lesson, to reinforce the process involved in setting up the plot specifications, you will check these settings before you send your drawing to plot. If you find an incorrect setting, you will want to change it as you proceed through the following steps.

Step 1 – Start DataCAD.

Step 2 – Retrieve the drawing you wish to plot.

Step 3 – Once the drawing you wish to plot is displayed, pick the **Plotter** option from the UTILITY menu. The PLOTTER menu is displayed, as explained in FIG. 8-2.

Figure 8–2

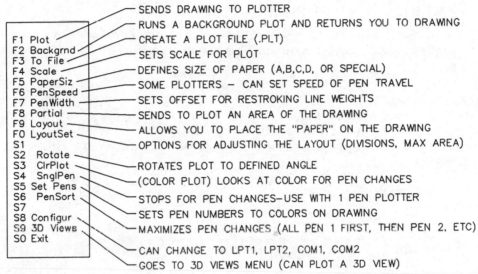

```
F1 Plot          ──────── SENDS DRAWING TO PLOTTER
F2 Backgrnd      ──────── RUNS A BACKGROUND PLOT AND RETURNS YOU TO DRAWING
F3 To File       ──────── CREATE A PLOT FILE (.PLT)
F4 Scale         ──────── SETS SCALE FOR PLOT
F5 PaperSiz      ──────── DEFINES SIZE OF PAPER (A,B,C,D, OR SPECIAL)
F6 PenSpeed      ──────── SOME PLOTTERS – CAN SET SPEED OF PEN TRAVEL
F7 PenWidth      ──────── SETS OFFSET FOR RESTROKING LINE WEIGHTS
F8 Partial       ──────── SENDS TO PLOT AN AREA OF THE DRAWING
F9 Layout        ──────── ALLOWS YOU TO PLACE THE "PAPER" ON THE DRAWING
F0 LyoutSet      ──────── OPTIONS FOR ADJUSTING THE LAYOUT (DIVISIONS, MAX AREA)
S1
S2  Rotate       ──────── ROTATES PLOT TO DEFINED ANGLE
S3  ClrPlot      ──────── (COLOR PLOT) LOOKS AT COLOR FOR PEN CHANGES
S4  SnglPen      ──────── STOPS FOR PEN CHANGES–USE WITH 1 PEN PLOTTER
S5 Set Pens      ──────── SETS PEN NUMBERS TO COLORS ON DRAWING
S6  PenSort      ──────── MAXIMIZES PEN CHANGES (ALL PEN 1 FIRST, THEN PEN 2, ETC)
S7
S8 Configur      ──────── CAN CHANGE TO LPT1, LPT2, COM1, COM2
S9 3D Views      ──────── GOES TO 3D VIEWS MENU (CAN PLOT A 3D VIEW)
S0 Exit
```

Checking the plot scale

Step 4 – Pick the **Scale** option.

Step 5 – Check that the current scale is set to $1/4''$. If it is, quit back to the PLOTTER menu. If it isn't, select this setting from the menu.

Checking the paper size

Step 6 – Pick the **PaperSiz** option.

Step 7 – Make sure the paper size is set to 23×32. If it is, quit back to the Plotter menu. If it isn't, pick **Custom** from the menu, and set the correct size.

23×32 (X = 32, Y = 23)

Checking the layout

Next, you will want to check the layout, to make sure the drawing is positioned correctly on the sheet.

Step 8 – Pick the **Layout** option. The current sheet layout will be displayed. It should line up exactly on your rectangle boundary. If it does, quit back to the PLOTTER menu. If it doesn't, object snap to the centerpoint of the rectangle to reposition the layout.

Using the layout setting: extents

You can make adjusting the layout of your drawing a lot faster by using a new option called **Layout Extents**. This option is found in the LYOUTSET menu.

The "Extents mode" is used during the layout procedure, and it turns your drawing into a box, showing the maximum area your drawing takes up. (See FIG. 8-3.) This makes Layout faster because the entire drawing does not have to be redrawn on the screen. (However, sometimes you don't want to use it because you cannot see details in your drawing with which to line up your layout.)

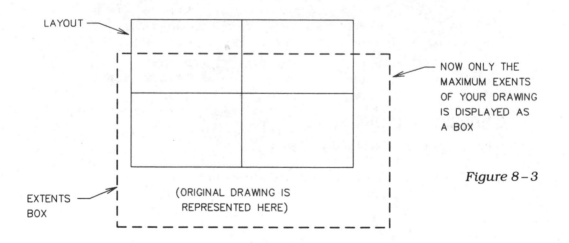

LAYOUT

NOW ONLY THE MAXIMUM EXENTS OF YOUR DRAWING IS DISPLAYED AS A BOX

Figure 8 – 3

EXTENTS BOX

(ORIGINAL DRAWING IS REPRESENTED HERE)

Step 9 – Pick **LyoutSet**.

Step 10 – Pick ***Extents** until a star is displayed.

Step 11 – Press mouse button **3** to quit. Now the drawing is displayed as a dashed box. You can either quit again to except the present layout position, or place it using your cursor and picking.

Checking the pen settings

Step 12 – Pick the **Set Pens** option.

Step 13 – Notice that the names of colors are displayed in the menu area. The colors listed represent the colors that can be displayed on your screen. As mentioned in the earlier lesson, Drawing setup, you can connect a certain pen number to each color. This pen number is used by your plotter, in order to pick up a certain pen to draw with.

Pen tables

It is essential that you standardize color use in your office. This is done by defining a Pen table. Pen tables are used to graphically connect colors and pen numbers to pen widths. This way, you can be confident that a certain color will be plotted with the correct pen.

The following pen table, shown in FIG. 8-4, is currently set for your drawings. This is a good example of a pen table used for training purposes.

Figure 8 – 4

PEN TABLE FOR TRAINING PURPOSES			
LINE	PEN SIZE	NUMBER	COLOR
————	.70	4	WHITE YELLOW
————	.50	3	LT MGTA
————	.35	2	GREEN CYAN LT BLUE
————	.25	1	BROWN

Step 14 – If you wish to check that these settings are correct in your SET PENS menu, pick the **White** option.

Step 15 – White should be set to pen number **4**. If necessary, enter this number.

Step 16 – The rest of the colors should be set to:

Green = **2**
Cyan = **2**
Brown = **1**
Lt Blue = **2**
Lt Mgta = **3**
Yellow = **4**

Note: DO NOT use 0 (zero) as a pen number. In most plotters this would be okay if you didn't want items in the color defined as pen 0 drawn. But on some new raster type plotters (such as the new large scale lasers) this could cause the plotter to halt, and your drawing would not continue being plotted.

Step 17 – Press mouse button **3** to quit back to the PLOTTER menu.

Setting up the plotter

Before you send your drawing to the plotter, make sure that your plotter is ready to draw. This means the paper is properly installed, the pens are wet and in the proper order (see the next step), and the plotter is on-line.

Step 18 – If you have a multiple pen plotter, check that your pens are set in the following order:

1 = Smallest of pen widths.   Recommended - **.25**
2 = Next size larger.   Recommended - **.35**
3 = Next size larger.   Recommended - **.50**
4 = Largest of pen widths.   Recommended - **.70**

Step 19 – If you have a single pen plotter, make sure the ***Snglpen** option is active. Check that the smallest of your pen is inserted in the pen holder. The plotter will stop when it is time to insert the second pen.

Step 20 – Place a **D** size paper in your plotter (24 × 36). Make sure it is aligned properly, and the paper holder (clamp) is firmly on the paper.

Step 21 – Turn the plotter on. It will probably view the paper and test the pens, depending on the type of plotter you have.

Step 22 – If you have made any changes to your drawing, make sure you file it by pressing [**Shift**] **F**.

Step 23 – Pick the **Plot** option. Your plotter should start drawing!

If your plotter doesn't plot – This might be due to several problems:

• Your DataCAD is not configured to the correct plotter.
• Your plotter is plugged into the wrong port.
• You have not prepared your plotter properly.

Check with the owner's manual, and the *DataCAD User Man-*

ual to assure that you have installed your plotter correctly, and for the procedures you should follow.

Step 24 – If you have made any changes to your drawing, make sure you file it, using the **File I/O** option, then picking **Save Dwg**.

Step 25 – Or, if you are quitting DataCAD, press [**Alt**] **Q**.

Step 26 – Pick **Yes**.

Additional assignments

Plot ASSIG-1, ASSIG-2, and ASSIG-3.

DataCAD exercise 8

Please complete the following exercise by reading each question carefully, then circling the letter that corresponds to the correct answer.

1. To make plotting an easy, one step process, you:
   a. Change the colors you use for different items, instead of standardizing the colors used for all of your drawings.
   b. Change the pen numbers every time you plot.
   c. Should have all of the information preset in your standard default drawing, and never vary your color standards.

2. To set the factor by which your drawing will be plotted, you pick:
   a. The **Factor** option.
   b. The **Scale** option.
   c. None of the options. You should always plot full size.

3. To pick the sheet size you will plot your drawing on, you pick the:
   a. **Sheet** option.
   b. **Layout** option.
   c. **PaperSiz** option.

4. To adjust the position of the plotting area on the drawing, you pick the:
   a. **Layout** option.
   b. **Sheet** option.
   c. **Adjust** option.

5. If you want to make the layout step of your drawing faster, you could set a mode that turns your drawing into a box. To do this, you use the:
   a. **BoxLyout** option.
   b. **LyoutSet, Fast** option.
   c. **LyoutSet, Extents** option.

6. If you wish to turn your plot 90 degrees counterclockwise, in the PLOTTER menu you use the:

   a. **Rotate** option.
   b. **LyoutSet** option.
   c. **Angle** option.

7. If you want the plotter to make pen changes, you must have on:

   a. ***ClrPlot**.
   b. ***MkeChan**.
   c. ***MultPen**.

8. When you are using line weights, it would be a good idea to adjust the:

   a. **PenSpeed** option.
   b. **Offset** option.
   c. **PenWidth** option.

9. When you are using multiple pens for your plots, it is important that you:

   a. Set your pen numbers for the colors you have used, and have a defined pen table for plotting purposes.
   b. Have all of your colors set to pen 1.
   c. Do not set pen numbers.

10. The final step in plotting your drawing, is:

    a. Setting the scale.
    b. Adjusting the layout.
    c. Picking the **Plot** option from the PLOTTER menu.

Some review questions

11. To change from creating "walls" to creating "lines," and back again, you press the:

    a. Mouse button **3**.
    b. **=** key.
    c. **L** key.

12. To draw walls that are dimensioned to the centers, you use the:

    a. **Center** option.
    b. **Sides** option.
    c. **Midpt** option.

13. If your walls are dimensioned to the corners, you use the:

    a. **Exterior** option.
    b. **Outside** option.
    c. **Sides** option.

14. To set your coordinate input mode, you press the:
    a. [**Space bar**].
    b. [**Ins**] key.
    c. [**Del**] key.

15. To use coordinate input, you press the:
    a. [**Space bar**].
    b. [**Ins**] key.
    c. [**Del**] key.

16. If you pick a symbol from a template, and it comes in at a different angle than it should, you:
    a. Have a problem with your symbol.
    b. Probably have a rotated value set. Simply set it back to 0, or to the proper angle, before you place your symbol.
    c. Should place it, then rotate it after it has been placed in your drawing.

17. If you are picking the position for your linear dimension, and it seems locked on the item you are dimensioning so that you cannot drag it away from the item to place it, you should:
    a. Quit to the LINEAR DIMENSION menu, and check the vertical or horizontal setting.
    b. Quit, and call someone for help.
    c. Stop creating dimensions. Your drawing has too many already.

18. To have text that is plotted at $1/8$ inch when you are plotting at $1/4$ inch scale, you need to create your text at the size of:
    a. $1/8$ inch.
    b. 1 foot.
    c. 6 inches.

19. When you create a 3-D view, you want to:
    a. Make sure all of the layers are displayed.
    b. Turn off all layers that you do not want to view in 3-D.
    c. Make sure the dimensions layer is displayed.

20. When you create a 3-D view, it:
    a. Usually will have to be moved to a better location.
    b. Pops into your drawing in the exact location you want it to be.
    c. Automatically moves to an upper righthand corner.

21. The **Enlarge** option:
    a. Enlarges items only.
    b. Allows you to enter a new plot scale for your drawing.
    c. Lets you enlarge or shrink items.

22. To permanently save a drawing to your hard disk, you can:

    a. Save the file by pressing [**Shift**] **F**, or use **File I/O** and the **Save Dwg** option, or pick **Yes** when you are Quitting DataCAD.

    b. Only save it using **File I/O** and picking **Save Dwg**. Quitting Data-CAD does not allow you to save your drawing.

    c. Quit DataCAD, and pick **Abort**.

Lesson 9
Creating initial site plans

What you will be doing

You will be transferring survey information to your initial site plan drawing. To do so, you will use the **Bearings** type of coordinate input, and the CURVE DATA menu to create survey radii.

Your site plan will be plotted at a 1:20 inch scale. You will use the special standard Default Drawing for your project you created in the earlier lesson, Drawing setup, which is designed for site drawings.

Objectives

Your lesson objectives are to:

- Set the correct Default Drawing.
- Change the angle type to bearings and check that the scale type is set to Decimal.
- Use survey information to enter coordinates when drawing property lines.

Remember to refer to *The DataCAD Operations Guide* when instructed.

Site default drawing

When you change the type of drawing you are using, or changing the scale you will be plotting in, you will want to change the default drawing. This is because these settings are already defined in the default drawing, along with the appropriate border and plot scale ratio.

As an example, when you created your plan layout, it was plotted at ¼" scale. You used the default drawing that was set up, called 1-4PLAN. The boundary rectangle and text in your drawing was preset to be the exact size needed when it was plotted at a ¼" scale.

Now that you will be creating a drawing that is to be plotted at a 1:20 scale (FIG. 9-1), or 1" = 20 feet, you will need to call up the default drawing called 1-20SITE. You might have created this default drawing during the lesson called Drawing setup, or someone might have created it for you. This Default Drawing contains a boundary that is designed for this scale, along with settings adjusted for scale and site work considerations.

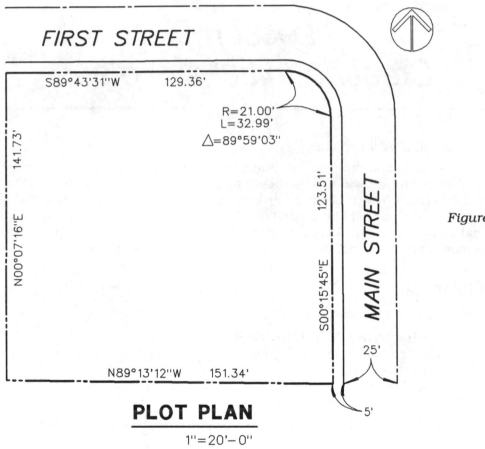

Figure 9–1

Changing the default drawing

Step 1 – Start DataCAD. If you are currently using DataCAD, press [**Alt**] **N** to start a new drawing. Pick **Yes** to save your drawing and return to the drawing list.

Step 2 – When the drawing list is displayed, pick the **Default** option.

Step 3 – The Default Drawing list should be displayed. If it is not, check that the New Pathname is set to DEFAULT.

Step 4 – Once the list is displayed, pick the drawing called **1-20SITE**.

Step 5 – If there is not a default drawing named **1-20SITE**, and you did not make one earlier, go back to the lesson called Drawing setup and follow the steps to create this Default Drawing.

Step 6 – Once the Default Drawing is picked, the drawing list will be displayed again. Make sure you are in your own special drawing directory by checking the pathname for the drawing list. Pick the **New Path** option, and check that it is set to your name. Press [**Enter**].

Step 7 – Now you can type the new name for your drawing: **SITE1**.

Property linetype

You will create the property line using the *propline* linetype. This is a line that is made up of the typical property line pattern, as indicated in FIG. 9-2. The exact size of the spacing is adjusted in accordance with the final plot scale.

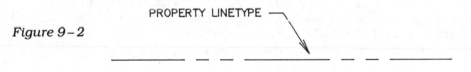

Figure 9 – 2

Like text, that is sized with the final scale in mind, you also want to adjust the size of the spacing for the pattern. Linetypes, like ''propline,'' and text are both *descriptive* items in your drawing. (FIG. 9-3.)

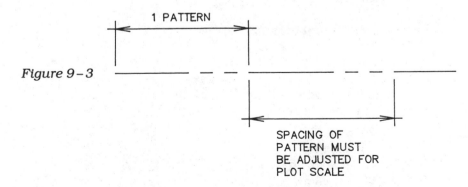

Figure 9 – 3

Descriptive items vs real items

As you draw and design with DataCAD, you will find that there are items that describe things, and things that are real items.

Descriptive items are things that are sized in relation to the final plot scale. Examples of this are:

- Text
- Material description (earth, concrete, steel, etc.)
- Linetype spacing (dashed, dot-dash, etc.)
- Drawing boundaries
- Hatch pattern spacing
- Details and detail boxes (drawn in true size, then reduced to scale)

Real items are drawn in true size, and remain in true size. Examples of this are:

- Walls
- Doors and windows
- Furniture
- Plumbing
- HVAC
- Streets
- Parking lots
- Anything that represents something you can touch in the "real" world

Of course, the property line represents something in the real world, and will represent the true perimeter in full size. But the particular linetype that you are going to draw it with is "descriptive." (You can't go to the real world site and see a line-dash-dash-line pattern drawn on its perimeter.)

Setting the linetype spacing

Step 1 – Press [**Alt**] **L** to quickly go to the LINETYPE menu, found in the EDIT menu.

Step 2 – Pick the **Spacing** option.

Step 3 – The plot scale for this drawing is 1:20, or 20 feet = 1 inch in the final plot. A 20 foot line spacing would result in a 1″ repeat in the final plot. Some people prefer a 2″, 2¹/₂″, or 3″ repeat. So, you can pick your own spacing:

> **1″ = 20′ spacing**
> **2″ = 40′ spacing**
> **2¹/₂″ = 50′ spacing**
> **3″ = 60′ spacing**

If you wanted a 2½″ repeat of the property linetype, change the spacing to **50**, and press [**Enter**].

Step 4 – When you are returned to the LINETYPE menu, pick the **Propline** option. The current linetype will be set to "property line," and will appear as the active linetype in the status area of the screen, as in FIG. 9-4.

Figure 9 – 4

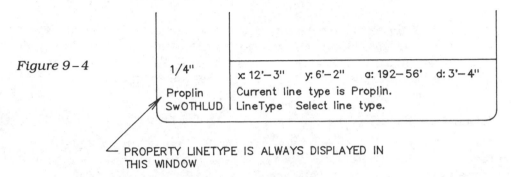

PROPERTY LINETYPE IS ALWAYS DISPLAYED IN THIS WINDOW

Using the DataCAD Reference Guide

Turn to the appendix B, *DataCAD Reference Guide*. Find the DataCAD Linetypes chart. This chart illustrates the various linetype you can use, and the formula for the correct spacing.

Site plans and survey drawings

Site plans are developed from information supplied by the civil engineer, in the form of a survey drawing. Although these types of drawings are routinely traced for site layouts when manually drafting, DataCAD has developed special options to allow the correct input of this information to your drawing.

Correctly drawing the site is especially important when using a computer, because all subsequent plans will be developed from this information, in true scale and accuracy.

Using the exact information supplied by the survey drawing also helps you to screen inaccuracies during the initial site development. In manual drafting, when site information is traced, "fudged" areas in error are often transferred to all of the proceeding drawings without being caught until correction of these errors causes major impact to the original investment. Using DataCAD properly helps to eliminate such problems.

Survey drawings are supplied with *bearings* information calling out the length and direction of lines, in a North/East/South/West type of format. Radii in the drawings are notated with curve data information (length, bearings in, bearings out, radius, etc.) This is illustrated in FIG. 9-5.

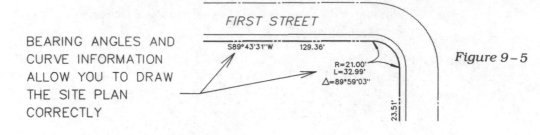

BEARING ANGLES AND
CURVE INFORMATION
ALLOW YOU TO DRAW
THE SITE PLAN
CORRECTLY

Figure 9 – 5

As you refer to the survey drawing that will be used for the site layout project during this lesson, you will notice the bearings and radius notations are similar to the survey information you usually find in your civil drawings. You will use this data to create your site layout!

Bearing angle type

"Bearings" is a type of angle you can use for "polar" input (Polar = distance + angle). There are 6 types of angles you can choose from, as indicated in FIGS. 9-6 and 9-7. They are:

1. Normal - used in daily use for typing in measurements of lines, walls, doors, windows, etc., when there are angles in the drawing.
2. Compass - sometimes used in site plans, as seen in some overseas and European survey drawings.
3. Bearing - used by architects in U.S. to transfer the plot information given by the civil engineer into DataCAD, if given in bearings.
4. Decimal Degrees - helpful when using DataCAD for drawing mechanical details, because some are in decimal measurements. Also helpful if the main scale setting is a metric unit.
5. Radians - used by civil engineers in developing site calculations using DataCAD.

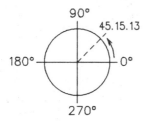

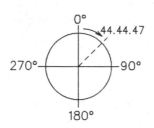

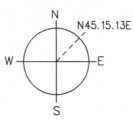

Figure 9 – 6

NORMAL	COMPASS	BEARINGS
BASED ON A RIGHT– NORMAL (90°) ANGLE	CLOCKWISE 360° ANGLE DEFINITION	NORTH–EAST– SOUTH–WEST ANGLE
FORMAT:	FORMAT:	FORMAT:
ANGLE–MINUTES–SECONDS INPUT: 45.15.13	ANGLE–MINUTES–SECONDS INPUT: 44.44.47	ANGLE–MINUTES–SECONDS INPUT: N45.15.13E

Figure 9-7

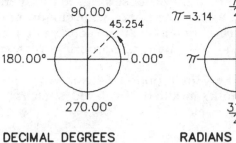 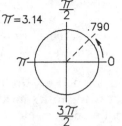 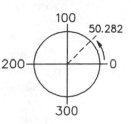

DECIMAL DEGREES	RADIANS	GRADIANS
BASED ON A RIGHT-NORMAL (90°) ANGLE	COUNTER-CLOCKWISE ANGLE DEFINITION	COUNTER-CLOCKWISE 400 GRAD INCREMENTS
FORMAT:	FORMAT:	FORMAT:
ANGLE-DECIMAL	RADIAN-DECIMAL	GRAD-DECIMAL
INPUT: 45.254	INPUT: .790	INPUT: 50.282

6. Gradians - another engineering angle, a grad is $1/100$ of a right angle.

For replicating survey north-south information, you will use the bearings angle type.

Setting the angle type

The polar, or "angle" input type should be set to "bearings." You can check this by using the **Angle Type** option.

Step 1 – Pick the **Settings** option from the UTILITY menu.

Step 2 – Pick the **AngleTyp** option.

Step 3 – The three angle types are displayed. The current angle is probably set to ***Normal**. Pick the **Bearings** option until a star appears in front of it.

Step 4 – Press mouse button **3** to quit.

Checking the scale type

In the original default drawing the **Scale Type** was set to **Decimal**. To check this, use the **Scale Type** option.

Step 1 – Pick the **ScalType** option, found in the SETTING menu.

Step 2 – The Decimal option should have a star in front of it. If not, pick ***Decimal** to make it active. Press mouse button **3** to quit back to the EDIT menu.

Note: If you are curious about the other settings in this menu, simply pick one to make it active, then drag your cursor out to the drawing area of the screen, then look at the coordinate read-out. You will see the coordinates change appropriately as you change the scale type.

Make sure you keep the ***Units** option active. This option allows the type of drawing unit mark to be displayed, such as " for inches, ' for feet, **m** for meters, etc.

Changing the input mode and layer

The input mode you will learn to use for site plans is *relative polar*. This setting will allow you to input distances and bearing angles.

Step 1 – Set the input mode, press the [**Ins**] key until **Current input mode is relative polar** is displayed.

Step 2 – Make sure the correct layer is displayed that will hold your property line: **PROPLIN**. Press [**Tab**] until the Proplin layer is active.

Setting the Z-base and height

Because you will want the property line to be at the 0 elevation only, you must set the Z-base and height to 0.

Step 1 – Press the **Z** key.

Step 2 – Change both the base and height to **0**.

Typing in bearing angles

Before you type in the bearing angle, you should notice which quadrant the line will fall in. In other words, is the line going north-east, south-east, north-west or south-west? The quadrant the line is angled into determines the actual direction. (See FIG. 9-8.)

If the line is going north-east, the line will be drawn to the right, as shown in FIG. 9-9. If the line is going south-west, it will be drawn to the left. If you have a line that is angled to the right, but you wish it drawn to the left, you just change the major and minor axes. This way, you have drawn the same line, but in the direction you desire.

The technique of reversing a line angle is necessary when inputting site plans, because you have to start in one place and work around the site in a single direction (clockwise or counter-clockwise). The lines are seldom angled true to one direction because the plot is usually derived from subdivisions.

You will get the opportunity to reverse the direction of a line in your first project!

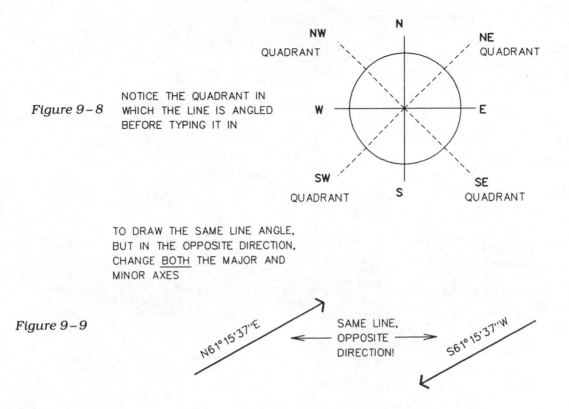

Figure 9–8

NOTICE THE QUADRANT IN WHICH THE LINE IS ANGLED BEFORE TYPING IT IN

TO DRAW THE SAME LINE ANGLE, BUT IN THE OPPOSITE DIRECTION, CHANGE <u>BOTH</u> THE MAJOR AND MINOR AXES

Figure 9–9

When you type in a bearing angle, you will follow the format described in FIG. 9-10. For example, an angle given as North 47 (degrees) 15′ (minutes) 35″ (seconds) West will be typed in as **n47.15.35w**. The N,E,S, or W can be typed in lower- or uppercase letters and the angles, minutes, and seconds are separated by periods. Do not include spaces.

Bearings are very easy to use, as you will see. As a reminder, the 4 important bearing input facts are shown in FIG. 9-11.

Using bearings input mode

Step 1 – Pick a start point for your line, as shown in FIG. 9-12. Always pick a start point before you use relative input.

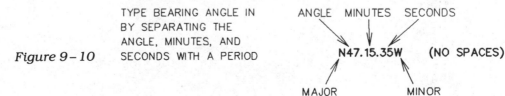

Figure 9–10

TYPE BEARING ANGLE IN BY SEPARATING THE ANGLE, MINUTES, AND SECONDS WITH A PERIOD

ANGLE MINUTES SECONDS

N47.15.35W   (NO SPACES)

MAJOR AXIS

MINOR AXIS

IMPORTANT BEARING INPUT FACTS:

1. IN SETTINGS MENU, ANGLE TYPE = BEARING
   AND SCALE TYPE = DECIMAL.

2. THE INPUT MODE = RELATIVE POLAR.

3. ANGLES SHOULD BE TYPED IN AS:
   n45.15.13e

Figure 9 – 11

4. TO CHANGE DIRECTION OF THE LINE,
   CHANGE <u>BOTH</u> THE MAJOR AND MINOR
   AXES! (FOR THE INVERTED SUPPLEMENTARY
   ANGLE).

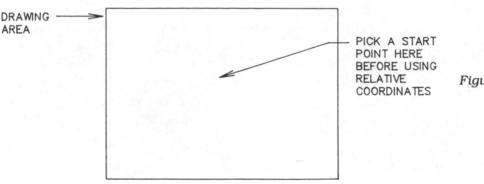

DRAWING
AREA

PICK A START
POINT HERE
BEFORE USING
RELATIVE
COORDINATES

Figure 9 – 12

Step 2 – Press the [**Space bar**].

Step 3 – You will be asked to: **Enter relative distance**. This is the length of
the line, at a distance relative to the starting point you picked.
Type in the desired length of the first line.

    123.51

Step 4 – Press [**Enter**].

Step 5 – Now you will be prompted to: **Enter relative angle:** A default of
North might appear at the cursor area. Type in the following:

    S0.15.45E

Step 6 – Press [**Enter**].

Step 7 – Press the [**Space bar**] again, and type in the length for the next
line. Remember to press [**Enter**].

    151.34

Step 8 – Enter the angle, and press [**Enter**].

N89.13.12W

Step 9 – Press the [**Space bar**] and type in and [**Enter**] the length for the next line. Make the direction of this line N0.7.16E.

Distance = **141.73**

Direction = **N0.7.16E**

Step 10 – Notice that the direction of the last line is "south-west" (S89.43.31W). This means that it will be drawn to the left, when the desired direction is to the right. To change the direction of the line, simply change both the major and minor axis. This will result in a north-east line, drawn to the right. Create this line.

Distance = **129.36**

Direction = **N89.43.31E**

Step 11 – Your drawing should look like FIG. 9-13. You are now ready to create the curve in your drawing.

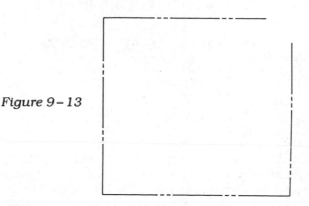

Figure 9–13

Creating a curve using curve data

When you are given a drawing from the surveyor, the curves are dimensioned with data that can be used to recreate the curve using the option called **Curve Data**.

Curve Data will create a curve using such survey information (typical on these types of drawings), as:

- Radius
- Cord length
- Arc length
- Delta angle (included angle)
- Bearings in
- Bearings out, etc.

Step 1 – Pick the **Curve** option, from the EDIT menu.

Step 2 – Pick the **CurvData** option from the menu.

Step 3 – The CURVE DATA menu is displayed, as shown in FIG. 9-14. Notice that the figure illustrates how the menu is divided into three parts: "Point" placement, "Arc" definition, and "Bearing" definition. You will only need four options defined in this menu to create your arc, one from the point section, two from the arc section, and one from the bearing section.

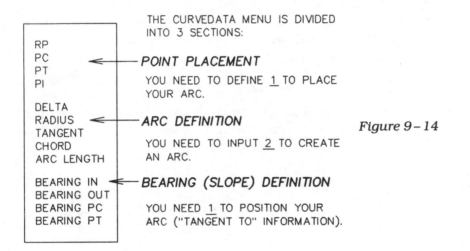

Figure 9 – 14

Definitions of options

RP	(Radius Point) The center of the radius, or "arc" to be defined.
PC	(Point of Curve) The starting point of the arc. Remember – curve is created in a clockwise direction!
PT	(Point of Tangency) The ending point of the arc.
PI	(Point of Intersection) The point where the tangent lines through PC and PT intersect. (Lines are tangent to the resulting arc.) See FIG. 9-15.
Delta	Once you have defined the point for your curve, it is like nailing it into place by that point. Now the arc has to be defined.
Radius	The radius of the arc.
Tangent	The distance from the start point of the arc, to the PI. This distance will be identical to the distance from the endpoint to the PI.
Chord	The straight line from the starting point to the ending point of the arc.
ArcLnth	(Arc Length) The distance along the arc from the starting point to the ending point.

Figure 9-15

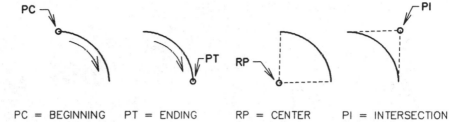

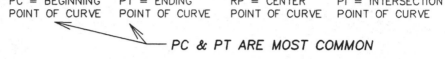

PC = BEGINNING   PT = ENDING   RP = CENTER   PI = INTERSECTION
POINT OF CURVE   POINT OF CURVE   POINT OF CURVE   POINT OF CURVE

PC & PT ARE MOST COMMON

ArcLnth   (Arc Length) The distance along the arc from the starting point to the ending point.

The most common arc annotations you will find in the site plan are the arc radius, length, and delta (included angle). Since you only need 2 options to describe an arc, which of the three should you use?

Use Radius and Delta! The arc radius is usually a well rounded figure and all other calculations are derived from it. The delta includes an angle, minutes, and seconds. This calculation is equivalent to 3 decimal places, where all other dimensions (including the arc length) have been rounded to 2 places. See FIG. 9-16 on page 164.

Now you have the arc defined and nailed into place by one point. Next, the "Tangency," or bearing information, must be supplied. The following illustration, FIG. 9-17, shows how the arc is swiveling around the point. Once a tangent slope (bearing in or bearing out), or a slope defining the cross tangency (bearing PC or bearing PT) is defined, then the arc can be placed!

Brng In   (Bearing In) The tangent line going into the start of the arc.
Brng Out   (Bearing Out) The tangent line coming out of the end of the arc.
Brng PC   (Bearing Point of Curve) The line created from the centerpoint of the start point of the arc.
Brng PT   (Bearing Point of Tangency) The line created from the centerpoint to the endpoint of the arc.

The following illustrations (FIG. 9-18), show how to identify the correct bearing choice to describe your curve. The bearing description will appear in your drawing on a dashed line pointing into the start or end of the curve, and will have a "RAD" identifier along with an angle described. If there is not a dashed line, then it may be that the curve is assumed tangent, as it is in your first site project. Then you use the actual property line as a bearing in or out angle.

EXAMPLES OF ARCS DEFINED WITH RADIUS

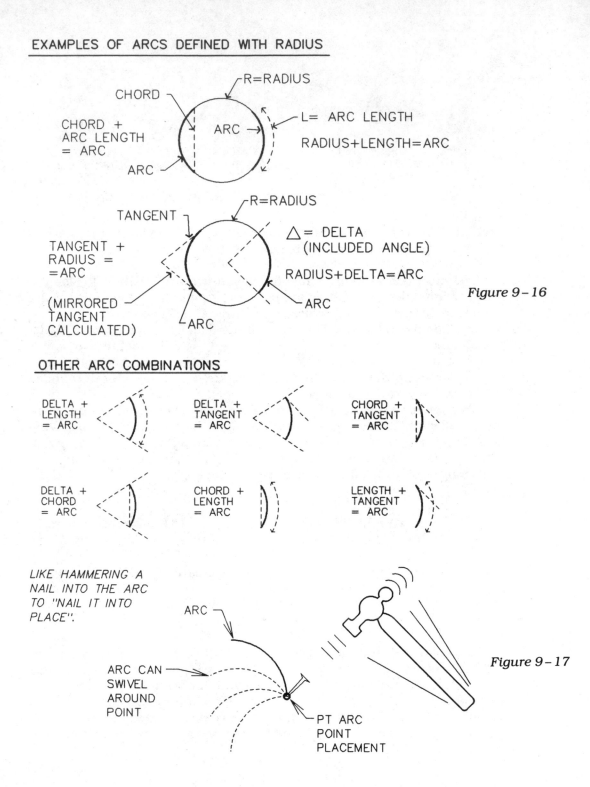

CHORD

CHORD +
ARC LENGTH
= ARC

ARC

R=RADIUS

ARC

L= ARC LENGTH

RADIUS+LENGTH=ARC

TANGENT

TANGENT +
RADIUS =
=ARC

(MIRRORED
TANGENT
CALCULATED)

ARC

R=RADIUS

△ = DELTA
(INCLUDED ANGLE)

RADIUS+DELTA=ARC

ARC

Figure 9–16

OTHER ARC COMBINATIONS

DELTA +
LENGTH
= ARC

DELTA +
TANGENT
= ARC

CHORD +
TANGENT
= ARC

DELTA +
CHORD
= ARC

CHORD +
LENGTH
= ARC

LENGTH +
TANGENT
= ARC

*LIKE HAMMERING A
NAIL INTO THE ARC
TO "NAIL IT INTO
PLACE".*

ARC

ARC CAN
SWIVEL
AROUND
POINT

PT ARC
POINT
PLACEMENT

Figure 9–17

4 EXAMPLES OF CURVE BEARINGS

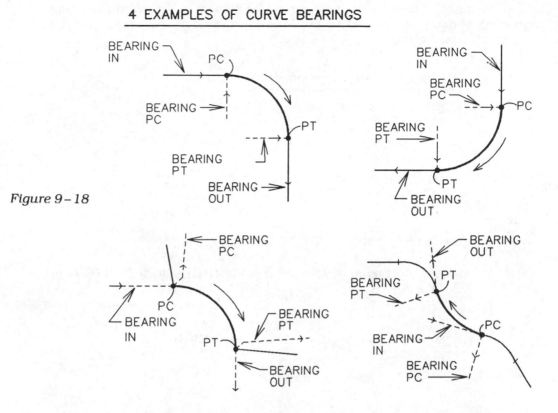

Figure 9-18

As you supply some of the answers to these questions, DataCAD will answer any options it can figure out from the data you have supplied! When all options are answered (all have a "*" in front of their name), you will be able to "Add" the curve.

The following illustration, FIG. 9-19, shows how all of the choices in the CURVE DATA menu are related to your curve.

Figure 9-19   ARCS CREATED IN CURVE DATA ARE ALWAYS DRAWN IN A CLOCKWISE DIRECTION

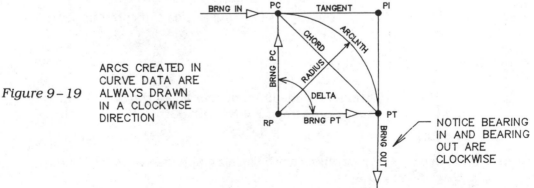

The rules shown in FIG. 9-20 should be remembered when inputting your curve data, with particular attention being paid to the direction of the angle you use for the bearing options.

CURVE BEARING DEFINITION RULES:

— MAKE SURE BEARING INPUT IS
  GOING THE <u>CORRECT DIRECTION</u>

Figure 9–20

— ARC DESCRIPTIONS GENERALLY
  APPEAR ON <u>DASHED LINES</u> IN DRAWING.

— IF NO BEARING LINES APPEAR, ARC
  MAY BE ASSUMED TANGENT TO EXISTING
  LINES OR ARCS.

Step 4 – Pick the **PC** option.

Step 5 – Pick the start point of your arc, as indicated in FIG. 9-21. Be sure to OBJECT SNAP.

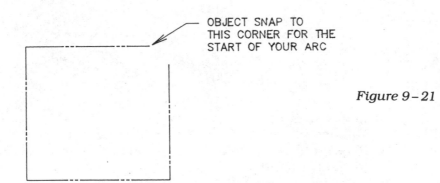

OBJECT SNAP TO
THIS CORNER FOR THE
START OF YOUR ARC

Figure 9–21

Step 6 – Pick the **Radius** option.

Step 7 – Type in and [**Enter**] the radius for your arc, as indicated in your survey drawing. (R = 21'-0").

Step 8 – Pick the **Delta** option.

Step 9 – Type in and [**Enter**] the delta (included angle) of the arc, as indicated on your survey drawing. (Δ = 89° 59' 03")

89.59.03

Step 10 – Notice that other options are beginning to be answered by Data-CAD, as in FIG. 9-22.

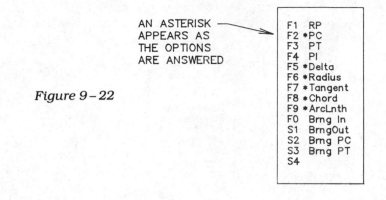

AN ASTERISK
APPEARS AS
THE OPTIONS
ARE ANSWERED

F1 RP
F2 *PC
F3 PT
F4 PI
F5 *Delta
F6 *Radius
F7 *Tangent
F8 *Chord
F9 *ArcLnth
F0 Brng In
S1 BrngOut
S2 Brng PC
S3 Brng PT
S4

Figure 9 – 22

Step 11 – Pick the **BrngIn** option.

Step 12 – Type in the angle for the bearing in of your arc. This angle is supplied by the top line, as indicated by FIG. 9-23. Make sure you use the correct north-east direction! Once you have typed it in, press [**Enter**].

N89.43.31E

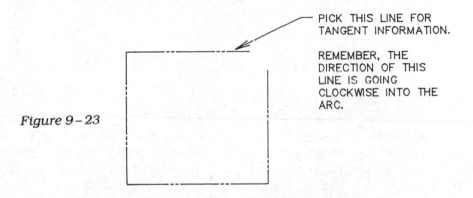

PICK THIS LINE FOR
TANGENT INFORMATION.

REMEMBER, THE
DIRECTION OF THIS
LINE IS GOING
CLOCKWISE INTO THE
ARC.

Figure 9 – 23

Step 13 – Notice now that all of the options have a star by them, as shown in FIG. 9-24 on page 168. This means that all necessary data is supplied to create the arc. Now the **Add** option appears. This option allows you to add the arc to your drawing.

Step 14 – Pick the **Add** option. The arc is added; see FIG. 9-25 on page 168.

Add

Step 15 – Use the **File I/O, Save Dwg** option to save your drawing to hard disk.

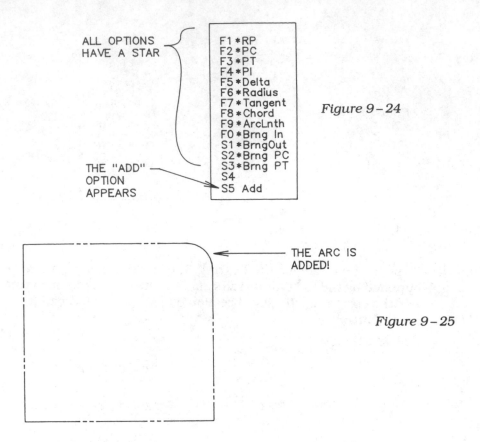

ALL OPTIONS
HAVE A STAR

```
F1 *RP
F2 *PC
F3 *PT
F4 *PI
F5 *Delta
F6 *Radius
F7 *Tangent
F8 *Chord
F9 *ArcLnth
F0 *Brng In
S1 *BrngOut
S2 *Brng PC
S3 *Brng PT
S4
S5  Add
```

THE "ADD"
OPTION
APPEARS

Figure 9–24

THE ARC IS
ADDED!

Figure 9–25

Validating the closing point of your site

The point where you started drawing the property line and where you ended is called the "closing point." The end point of the first line and the end point of the last line, or arc, will never actually touch each other. They will be slightly off. This is because of the decimal round off to 2 decimal places in the dimensions of the site plan. Because .083 (three decimal places) equals 1 inch, it is easy to see how the site plan's final closing points can be off. How far off they are is very important.

The civil engineer is limited to a .01 tolerance on calculations. This is around 1/8″, which of course would not show up in any drawing after being plotted, and might not show up on the screen unless you zoom in.

Sometimes, through mistakes in calculations, the closing point might have a large discrepancy easily seen. One site was 27 feet off once it was checked with DataCAD! (The civil engineer quickly corrected it.)

To check the closing point, you can use "Measures."

Step 1 – Press [**Alt**] **X** to quickly go to the MEASURES menu, found in the UTILITY menu.

Step 2 – Pick the **PntToPnt** option.

Step 3 – Object snap to the end point of the arc (right side), indicating the final end point of your property line, as in FIG. 9-26. You might want to "window in."

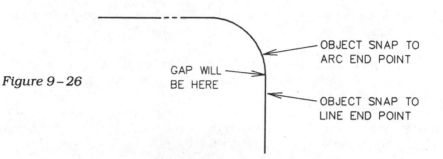

Figure 9 – 26

GAP WILL
BE HERE

OBJECT SNAP TO
ARC END POINT

OBJECT SNAP TO
LINE END POINT

Step 4 – Now object snap to the end point of the line, indicating the starting point of the property line.

Step 5 – The distance between the two points will be displayed at the bottom of the screen. If you have done everything correctly, the distance will be around .008.

When you perform this check on your own drawings, you might find that a .01 or .009 is common for a closing point distance. If you get a .08 or .1, remember that this is still a very close distance and you could start your working drawings.

If you get a distance reading any larger than this, you might want to make it a rule to check back with your civil engineer with your findings. Of course, anymore than a few inches will indicate that the drawing must be returned for recalculating.

If a line is in error

If you find that a line or arc might be drawn wrong, and wish to check it, you can use the **Measures** option to do this.

Step 1 – Press [**Alt**] **X** to quickly go to the MEASURES menu, found in the UTILITY menu.

Step 2 – Pick the **LineAngl** option.

Step 3 – Pick the line. The angle will be displayed at the bottom of the screen. Continue picking the lines you want to check. When you are done, you can return to the MEASURES menu by pressing mouse button **3** once.

Step 4 – If you want to check the length of the line, you can use the **Line** option and pick the lines you want to check.

Step 5 – To check the arcs in your drawing, you can use the **Radius, Chord,** and **ArcLnth** options.

Step 6 – Another way to check the line lengths and angles is to use the **Identify** option. Press [**Shift**] **I** (capital I).

Step 7 – Pick the line you wish to check. The length and angle will appear at the bottom of the screen. Identify will only give you the radius for arcs.

Step 8 – When you quit from **Identify** (press mouse button **3**), you will be returned to the MEASURES menu.

Dimensioning the property lines

You can use the MEASURES menu to add dimensions to your plot drawing.

Step 1 – Pick the **LineAngl** option in the MEASURES menu.

Step 2 – Pick the line that you wish to dimension. The measurement appears at the bottom of the screen.

Step 3 – This measurement can be added to the drawing by picking the **ToDrwing** option.

Step 4 – A text menu will be displayed, and the cursor will now appear as a text cursor. If you pick on the drawing, the measurement will be added, as in FIG. 9-27.

Step 5 – To align the text cursor to the line you are dimensioning (which will in turn align the dimension), you can pick the **Angle** option.

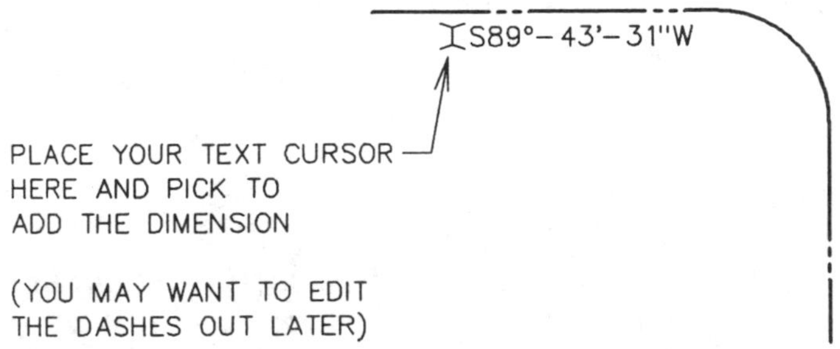

PLACE YOUR TEXT CURSOR —
HERE AND PICK TO
ADD THE DIMENSION

(YOU MAY WANT TO EDIT
THE DASHES OUT LATER)

Figure 9–27

Step 6 – Pick **Match**.

Step 7 – Pick the line you are dimensioning. The angle of the line will appear at the bottom of the screen, as shown in FIG. 9-28.

Figure 9 – 28

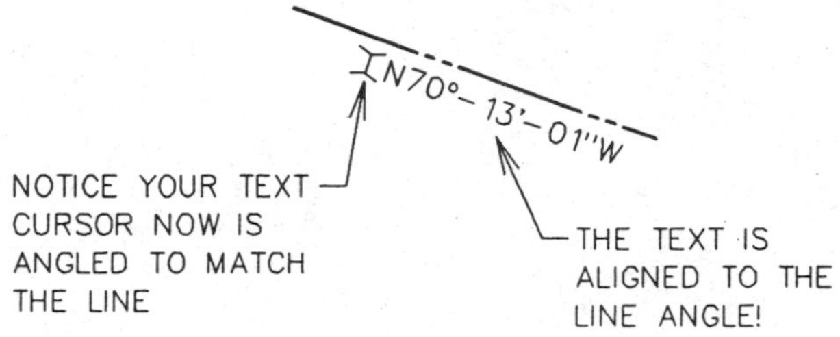

NOTICE YOUR TEXT
CURSOR NOW IS
ANGLED TO MATCH
THE LINE

THE TEXT IS
ALIGNED TO THE
LINE ANGLE!

N70°– 13'– 01"W

Step 8 – Quit back to the "TODRWING" text menu by pressing mouse button **3** twice. Notice that the text cursor now appears aligned with the line you are dimensioning.

Step 9 – Pick near the line to place your text. It will be aligned to the line's angle.

Step 10 – Quit by pressing mouse button **3** once, then pick another line you want dimensioned.

Step 11 – Follow steps 3 through 10 again.

Validating the lines

The final step in validating the property lines is to double check them against the original lines of the civil engineering drawing. This is easy to do.

Simply plot out your DataCAD drawing to the same scale as the engineering drawing you were working from. Then, hold the DataCAD drawing over the original drawing so that the lines can be seen through the paper. Of course, it is easier to see through the paper if you used vellum or have a light source to backlight the drawings.

Look closely at the lines. If there is a discrepancy you might also want to contact your civil engineer. The question becomes: which is correct, the calculations or the line?

Additional assignments

Complete the following projects, ASSIGNMENTS 4 and 5 shown in FIGS. 9-29 and 9-30.

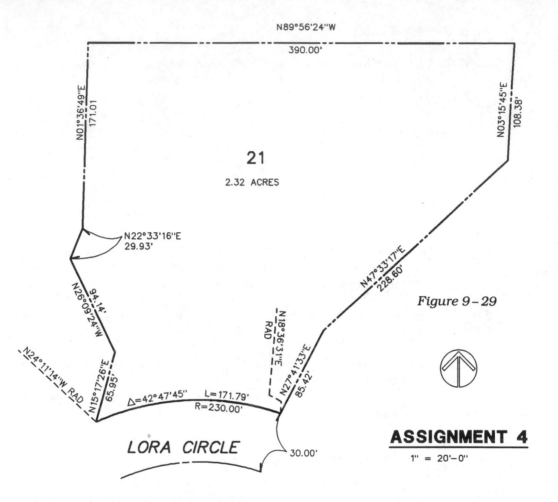

Figure 9-29

ASSIGNMENT 4

1" = 20'-0"

DataCAD exercise 9

Please complete the following exercise by reading each question carefully, then circling the letter that corresponds to the correct answer.

1. Default drawings allow you to:

   a. Change the type of drawing you are going to create, but not the scale or drawing borders.

   b. Preset several different "drawing formats" (blank drawing sheets) for the types and scales of drawings you will be creating. This includes setting up special layers for your drawings also.

   c. Have the correct title block already set in your drawing only. The layers and scale cannot be preset in the default drawing.

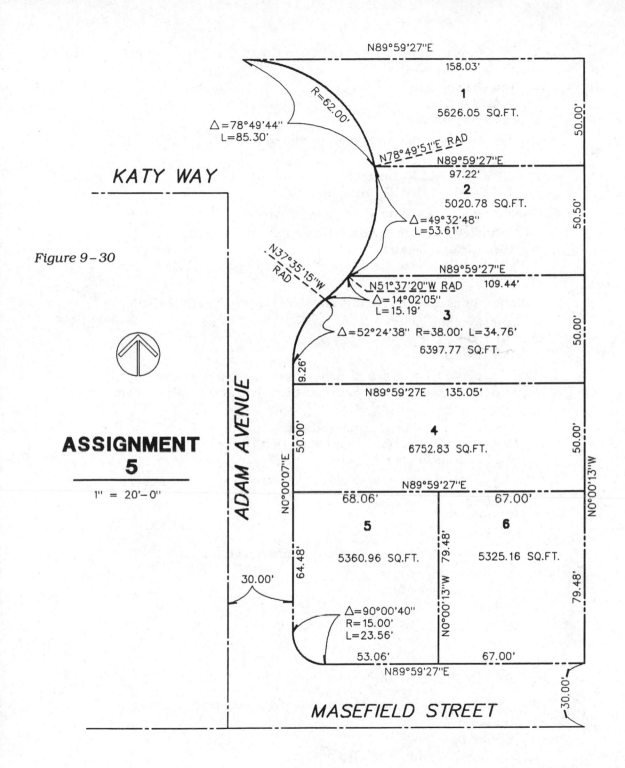

N89°59'27"E
158.03'

1
5626.05 SQ.FT.

50.00'

R=62.00'

△=78°49'44"
L=85.30'

N78°49'51"E RAD
N89°59'27"E
97.22'

2
5020.78 SQ.FT.

50.50'

△=49°32'48"
L=53.61'

KATY WAY

N37°35'15"W RAD

N89°59'27"E
109.44'

N51°37'20"W RAD
△=14°02'05"
L=15.19'

3
△=52°24'38" R=38.00' L=34.76'
6397.77 SQ.FT.

50.00'

Figure 9-30

9.26'

N89°59'27E   135.05'

4
6752.83 SQ.FT.

50.00'

ADAM AVENUE

N89°59'27"E
68.06'   67.00'

5
5360.96 SQ.FT.

6
5325.16 SQ.FT.

**ASSIGNMENT
5**

1" = 20'-0"

N0°00'07"E
50.00'

N0°00'13"W
79.48'

N0°00'13"W
79.48'

N0°00'13"W

30.00'

64.48'

△=90°00'40"
R=15.00'
L=23.56'

53.06'   67.00'

N89°59'27"E

30.00'

MASEFIELD STREET

2. To change your default drawing, when the original drawing list is displayed, you pick the:
   a. **New Path** option.
   b. **Default** option.
   c. **Set Deflt** option.

3. Your default drawings should all be stored in the:
   a. MTEC/DWG directory.
   b. MTEC/DEFAULT directory.
   c. MTEC/DWG/DEFAULT directory.

4. The different types of polar angle types are:
   a. Normal, Cartesian, Relative, Radians, and Gradians.
   b. Absolute and Relative.
   c. Normal, Compass, Bearings, Decimal Degrees, Radians, and Gradians.

5. Different lines (such as solid, dashed, dot-dash, etc.) are called:
   a. Line Weights.
   b. Linetypes.
   c. Line Scales.

6. There are two basic types of items on your drawings. One represents true life objects, and is called the "real world." The second type:
   a. Are the things that are not built yet.
   b. Describes the objects, and is called Descriptive.
   c. Are the walls in your drawing.

7. When you are drawing real world objects, they are always drawn in:
   a. Relation to the plot scale.
   b. White.
   c. Full size.

8. When you add descriptive items, they are drawn in:
   a. Relation to the plot scale.
   b. Another drawing file.
   c. Full size.

9. To set the angle mode to Bearings, you use the:
   a. [**Insert**] key.
   b. [**Space bar**].
   c. SETTINGS menu, **AngleTyp** option.

10. To set the input mode to Relative Polar, you use the:
    a. [**Insert**] key.
    b. [**Space bar**].
    c. SETTINGS menu, **AngleTyp** option.

11. Before you use a relative input mode, you should:

    a. ALWAYS pick a start point.
    b. NEVER pick a start point.
    c. Only pick a start point if the drawing tells you to.

12. When you use Bearings, the following angle could be entered:

    a. 90-0
    b. N90W
    c. 90W

13. The Bearings input mode in DataCAD is usually used:

    a. By Civil Engineers only, to create survey drawings. The Architect will never use it.
    b. To quickly input survey information supplied by Civil Engineers, to correctly create the site plan.
    c. When first creating the survey drawing only. It is never used while drawing site plans, since you only have to trace the survey drawing on the computer.

14. To recreate Radii found in the survey drawing, you can use the:

    a. SURVEY menu, **Curve** option.
    b. CURVE menu, **Radius** option.
    c. CURVES menu, **CurvData** option.

15. To draw site plans using bearing angles, the Scale Type of your drawing should be set to:

    a. Engineering.
    b. Decimal.
    c. Civil.

16. If a line's bearing direction is to the right, and you wish to draw the same line but to the left direction, you must:

    a. Change just the minor axis from east to west.
    b. Change both the major and minor axis in order to draw the same angle.
    c. Draw the line going to the right, then move it later.

17. When using the CURVE DATA menu, you need to describe:

    a. 1 point, 2 arc definitions, and 1 bearing angle.
    b. Every option in the menu.
    c. 2 points, 2 arc definitions, and 2 bearing angles.

18. To measure the line angle, you can use the:

    a. **Measures, LineAngl** options.
    b. **Dimension, Linear, and LineAngl** options.
    c. **Measures, PntToPnt** options.

19. To validate your site plan, you should:

    a. Run the **SiteChk** option, which will check the site for you.
    b. Check the closing points for a large gap and the final plotted lines against the original drawing.
    c. Not worry about it, since civil drawings are always correct.

20. The site plan will:

    a. Never have a gap. If it does, just use **CleanUp** to correct it.
    b. Sometimes have a gap, but will usually close completely.
    c. Always have a gap at the closing point, due to the round off of the decimal places.

Some more review questions:

21. The quickest way to turn from lines to walls, or from walls to lines, is to use the:

    a. Menu option choices.
    b. [<] "less than" key.
    c. [=] "equal" key.

22. In order to define a reference point, you press the:

    a. [**Space bar**].
    b. ~ key.
    c. **X** key.

23. To clean up wall intersections after you create them, you pick the:

    a. **Cleanup** option, then pick **T** or **L Intsect**.
    b. **Cleanup** option, then pick **Corner**.
    c. **Architect** option, then pick the **Clean** option.

24. To erase the last item you created, you use the:

    a. **Delete** option.
    b. < less than key.
    c. > greater than key.

Lesson 10
Creating 3-dimensional lines

What you will be doing

You will be creating lines in your drawing that angle through all 3 axes (X,Y,Z). Up until now, your lines have been drawn parallel to the XY axes plane. During the first lessons, you drew wall lines that also were duplicated in the Z depth (Z-Base and Z-Height). You were able to see these lines when you viewed your drawing in 3-D View.

When you created your initial site layout, you used a single line located in the Z base of zero, again parallel to the XY axes plane. During this lesson, you will learn how to create lines that are not parallel to the XY axes plane.

Objectives

Your lesson objectives are to:

- Draw a building with temporary ridge and hip lines
- Create a Parallel view
- Use the 3-D Cursor to draw 3-D lines

Remember to refer to *The DataCAD Operators Guide* and *DataCAD Reference Guide* when instructed.

3-dimensional lines

Three-dimensional lines are drawn as single lines. During this lesson, you will use the 3-D lines task to connect two lines that have different heights. This is easy, because the 3-D line function allows you to object snap to these line endpoints, overruling any currently active Z-height or base settings.

One thing to remember about 3-D lines, is that they represent single lines, and not a wall. This means that you cannot "hide" hidden lines behind them, as you do with walls using the **"3-D View, Hide"** options. (You can still use the Hide function, but lines will not be hidden behind any of your 3-D lines!) You will have to erase any lines you want hidden manually.

Step 1 – You will be adding a building to the site plan you created earlier. See FIG. 10-1. Make sure DataCAD is running, and the SITE1 drawing is displayed on your screen before continuing, as illustrated in FIG. 10-2.

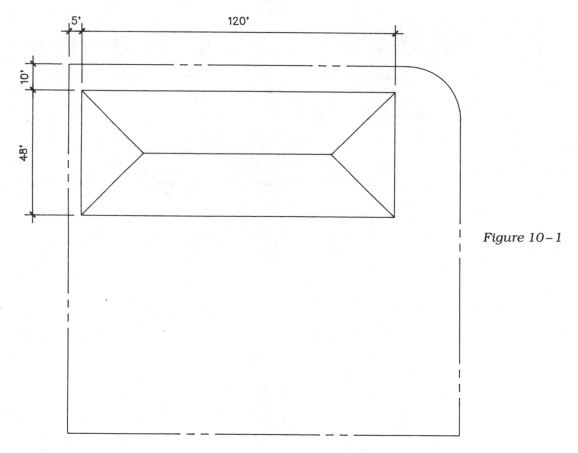

Figure 10–1

Adjusting your settings

When you draw the building, you will want to change some of the current settings. This includes the linetype, layer, and Z-height and base for your line, and the angle type.

YOU WILL BE ADDING
A BUILDING TO YOUR
SITE PLAN

Figure 10-2

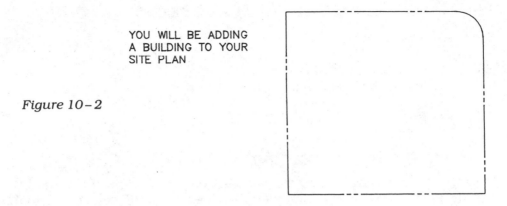

Changing the linetype

The first thing you will want to do is to change to a solid line.

Step 1 – Press **Q** until the linetype displayed is Solid. (Hint: Pressing the [**Shift**] key simultaneously with the **Q** key scrolls the linetype list backward.)

Changing the layer

Step 2 – Press [**Tab**] until the BLDG layer is active. (Again, pressing the [**Shift**] key along with [**Tab**] scrolls backward through the layer list.)

Changing the z-base and height

Step 3 – Press **Z**.

Step 4 – Type in **0** for the Z-base elevation, then press [**Enter**].

Step 5 – Type in **26** for the Z-height elevation, then press [**Enter**].

Setting angle type and scale type

You no longer need to use the Bearings angle type. You can set it back to the normal polar setting and can change from Decimal units back to Architectural.

Step 6 – From the UTILITY menu, pick the **Settings** option.

Step 7 – Pick **AngleTyp**.

Step 8 – Pick **Normal**.

Step 9 – Press mouse button **3** to quit back to SETTINGS.

Step 10 – Pick **ScaleTyp**.

Step 11 – Pick **Arch** until it is active, to change your input units back to feet-inches-fractions.

Step 12 – Press mouse button **3** to quit.

Drawing the building outline

Now that your settings are ready, you will draw the outline of your building. To make it easier in adding your 3-D line, you will complete the roof last.

Step 1 – Notice that the building shape is a simple rectangle, as in FIG. 10-3. This is very common when making building layouts. You will learn how to make rectangles easily with DataCAD.

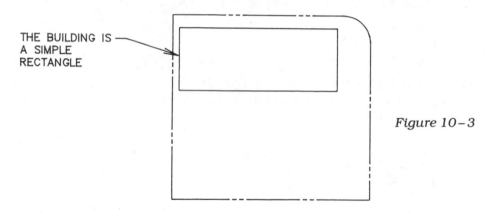

THE BUILDING IS
A SIMPLE
RECTANGLE

Figure 10 – 3

Step 2 – Pick the **Polygon** option, found in the EDIT menu.

Step 3 – Pick the **CentrPt** option until the * turns off. This will eliminate the little "belly button" center snap point of the rectangle.

Step 4 – Because this building is located from the upper left corner of the property line, you will reference this corner to define the dimensions of your building. See FIG. 10-4.

Step 5 – Press the ~ key.

Step 6 – Object snap to the upper left corner of the property line, as indicated in FIG. 10-5. (Layer Snap should be active. If it isn't, you

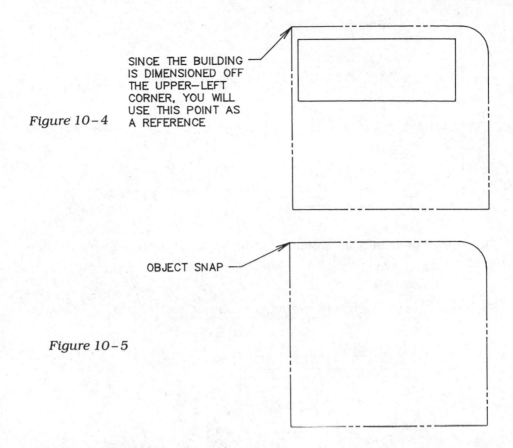

Figure 10-4   SINCE THE BUILDING IS DIMENSIONED OFF THE UPPER–LEFT CORNER, YOU WILL USE THIS POINT AS A REFERENCE

OBJECT SNAP

Figure 10-5

won't be able to snap to the lines on the Propline layer unless it is active.)

User hint: You can set Layer Snap using your OBJECT SNAP menu. (Press [**Shift**] **X**.)

Step 7 – Press the [**Insert**] key until the Relative Cartesian coordinate mode is active.

Step 8 – Press the [**Space bar**].

Step 9 – Type in the X distance from the reference corner (**5**) and press [**Enter**].

Step 10 – Type in the Y distance from the reference corner (**– 10**) and press [**Enter**]. You have defined the first corner of your building. The rectangle is connected to your cursor (FIG. 10-6, page 182).

Step 11 – Press the [**Space bar**] again.

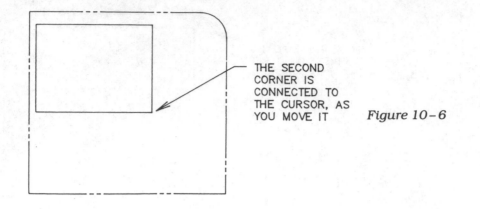

THE SECOND
CORNER IS
CONNECTED TO
THE CURSOR, AS
YOU MOVE IT

Figure 10–6

Step 12 – Type in the coordinates for the opposite corner of your building.

X = 120
Y = –48

Step 13 – Your rectangle is created, and should look like FIG. 10-7.

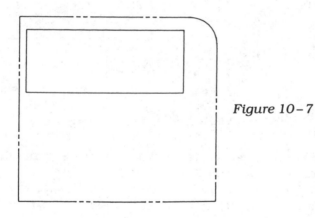

Figure 10–7

Moving the building

DataCAD is an excellent design tool for this stage of project development. You can easily drag your buildings around until you are happy with their locations.

Step 1 – Press **M** to enter the MOVE menu.

Step 2 – Pick the **Drag** option.

Step 3 – Make sure the **Group** option is active. (***Group**.)

Step 4 – Pick any line of the building rectangle. The building will become gray and dashed.

Step 5 – Object snap to the upper left corner of your building, as indicated in FIG. 10-8. This point will become your moving "handle point."

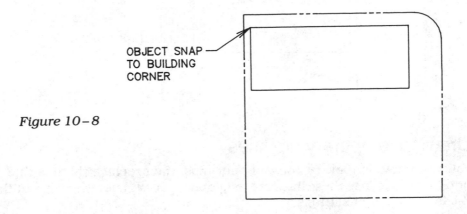

OBJECT SNAP —
TO BUILDING
CORNER

Figure 10–8

Step 6 – Notice that you can now drag the building with your cursor!

Step 7 – Press the ~ key.

Step 8 – Object snap to the upper left corner of your property line again, as in FIG. 10-9.

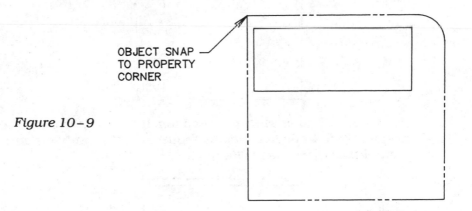

OBJECT SNAP —
TO PROPERTY
CORNER

Figure 10–9

Step 9 – Press the [**Space bar**], and enter new coordinates to move your building 5 feet in the X and the – Y direction from the corner of your property line.

X = 5
Y = –5

Step 10 – Your building should now be located as dimensioned in FIG. 10-10. Remember to press mouse button **3** to quit.

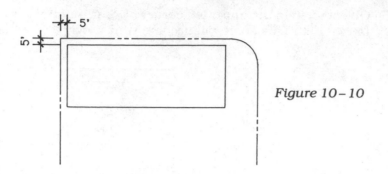

Figure 10–10

Drawing temporary hip lines

You will draw temporary lines for your hips, then replace them with 3-D lines later. Because these lines are temporary, you will not worry about the Z-base and height settings.

Step 1 – **Object snap** to the first corner of your building, as indicated in FIG. 10-11.

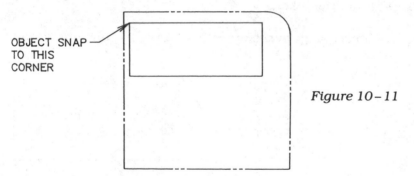

OBJECT SNAP TO THIS CORNER

Figure 10–11

Step 2 – Drag your line out in the right direction. It should lock onto a horizontal, then 45 degree axis rotations as you move your cursor around the screen, as in FIG. 10-12.

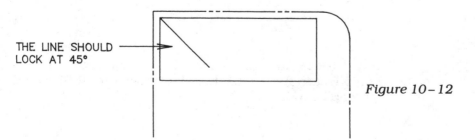

THE LINE SHOULD LOCK AT 45°

Figure 10–12

Step 3 – If your lines do not lock into 45 degree axis, you will want to turn Ortho Lock On. To do so, press the **O** key until the message is displayed: **Ortho mode is ON**.

Step 4 – Create a 45 degree line, as indicated in FIG. 10-13. Make sure that it is long enough to overlap the opposing temporary hip line you will draw next.

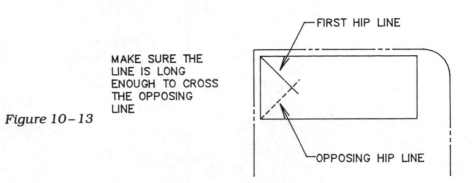

MAKE SURE THE LINE IS LONG ENOUGH TO CROSS THE OPPOSING LINE

Figure 10 – 13

FIRST HIP LINE

OPPOSING HIP LINE

Step 5 – Quit this line, and **object snap** to the next corner. See FIG. 10-14.

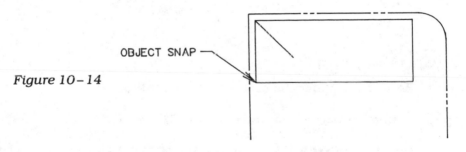

OBJECT SNAP

Figure 10 – 14

Step 6 – Draw a 45 degree line again, as in FIG. 10-15.

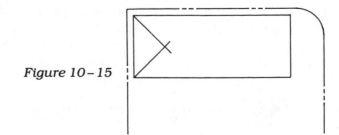

Figure 10 – 15

Step 7 – Create the other two lines for your hips, as indicated in FIG. 10-16.

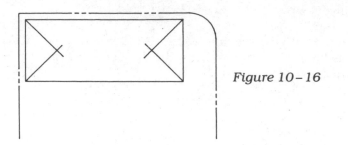

Figure 10 – 16

Step 8 – Now you are ready to draw your ridge line. (FIG. 10-17.)

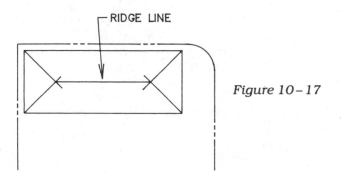

Figure 10 – 17

Drawing the ridge line

Step 1 – Press **Z** to change the base and height of the line.

Step 2 – Change both the base and height to **38** feet.

Step 3 – Use the [**Shift**] **X** keys to enter the OBJECT SNAP menu. Pick **Intsect** until it is Active (***Intsect**).

Step 4 – Turn OFF **Mid Pnt** and **End Pnt** by picking the options until the star (*) disappears. This will help to make sure that you correctly snap to an intersection point of two lines, and not the midpoint or endpoint of one of the lines.

Step 5 – Press mouse button **3** to quit, then **object snap** to the intersection of the temporary hip lines, as indicated in FIG. 10-18.

Step 6 – Draw the ridge by object snapping to the opposite hip lines intersection. (FIG. 10-19.)

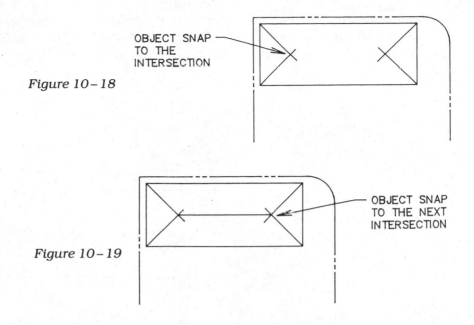

OBJECT SNAP
TO THE
INTERSECTION

Figure 10–18

OBJECT SNAP
TO THE NEXT
INTERSECTION

Figure 10–19

Step 7 – Erase the temporary hip lines, as shown in FIG. 10-20.

User hint: Use the **E** key to enter the ERASE menu, then use the ***Entity** setting to erase the individual lines.

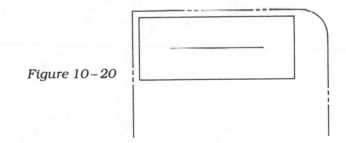

Figure 10–20

Step 8 – You are ready to draw your 3-D lines!

Changing to a parallel view

You will draw your 3-D lines while viewing in a 3-D angle (3-D view). The first thing you will do, then, is change your view to PARALLEL.

Step 1 – Press **Y**.

Step 2 – Pick **Parllel**.

Step 3 – Pick a viewing location on the globe that appears on the screen. (You might have to try different areas on the globe for better viewing.) See FIG. 10-21.

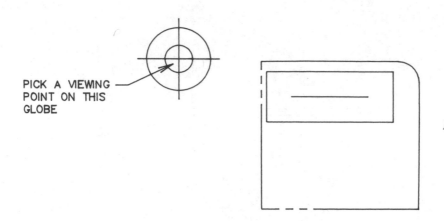

PICK A VIEWING POINT ON THIS GLOBE

Figure 10–21

Step 4 – Your view should expose all four upper corners of the building, AND the two endpoints of the ridge line, as in FIG. 10-22. This is important because you will be picking these endpoints to attach your 3-D lines.

THE VIEW SHOULD EXPOSE ALL FOUR CORNERS OF THE BUILDING, TO MAKE PICKING EASIER

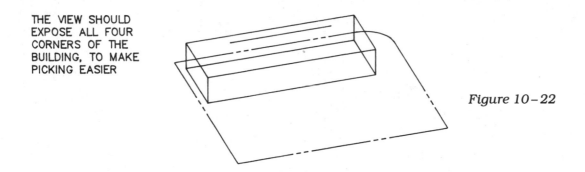

Figure 10–22

Step 5 – Press mouse button **3** until you are in the 3-D ENTITY menu.

Drawing the 3-D line

Step 6 – Pick the **3-D Line** option.

Step 7 – Pick the **3-D Cursr** option until it is active (***3-D Cursr**).

Step 8 – Notice that your cursor is now displayed as an XYZ axis. This option enables the ability to object snap in 3-D. (FIG. 10-23.)

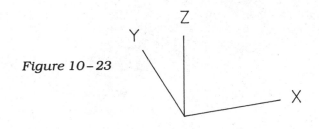

Figure 10–23

Step 9 – The axis point is the pick point of your cursor, as indicated in FIG. 10-24.

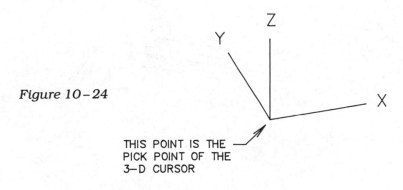

Figure 10–24

THIS POINT IS THE
PICK POINT OF THE
3–D CURSOR

Step 10 – **Object snap** to the first corner of the building for the hip, as indicated in FIG. 10-25.

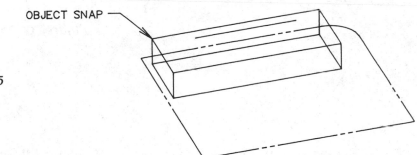

OBJECT SNAP

Figure 10–25

Step 11 – **Object snap** to the ridge line endpoint; see FIG. 10-26 on page 190.

Step 12 – Your 3-D line will be drawn! Your drawing should now look like FIG. 10-27 on page 190.

Step 13 – Connect the endpoints of the other corners to the ridge line, as indicated in FIG. 10-28 on page 190.

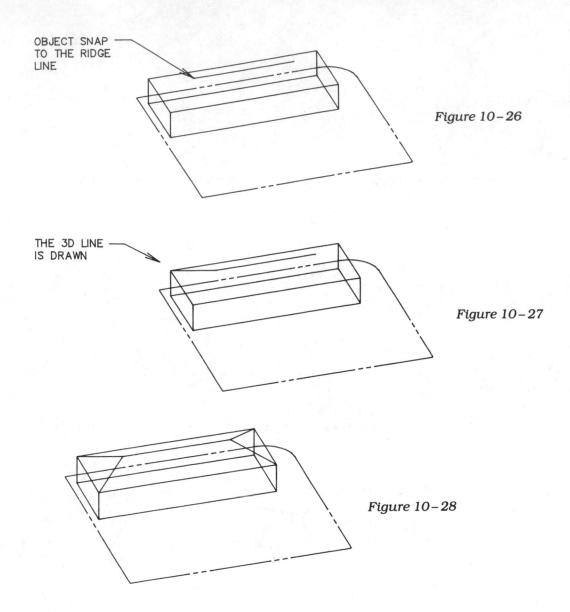

OBJECT SNAP
TO THE RIDGE
LINE

Figure 10–26

THE 3D LINE
IS DRAWN

Figure 10–27

Figure 10–28

Step 14 – Return to the plan view of your site, by using the 3-D VIEW menu, then selecting the **Ortho** option.

Step 15 – Your building is done! See FIG. 10-29. Remember, if you use Hide to remove hidden lines from the 3-D view, your "3-D lines" will not hide lines like a wall.

Step 16 – Save your drawingby pressing [**Shift**] **F**, or by using the **File I/O, Save Dwg** options.

THE BUILDING
IS DONE!

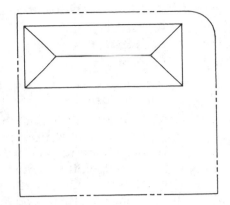

Figure 10–29

DataCAD exercise 10

Please complete the following exercise by reading each question carefully, then circling the letter that corresponds to the correct answer.

1. To draw a line angled through all three axis (X,Y,Z) you use:
   a. Z-height and base settings.
   b. 3-D Line
   c. AngLine.

2. When you use 3-D Lines in your drawing, you:
   a. Cannot remove hidden lines behind them automatically when using the "Hide" function. You simply erase them manually.
   b. Can remove hidden lines behind them automatically when using the "Hide" function.

3. When drawing a building that is a simple rectangle, you can use the:
   a. **Polygon, Rectangle** options.
   b. **Rectangle, 4Corners** options.
   c. **3-D Line, Rectangle** options.

4. Before picking a reference point to measure from, you press the:
   a. **R** key.
   b. > key.
   c. ~ key.

5. In order to object snap to items not on the current active layer, you use the:
   a. Middle button on the mouse. It does not matter if Layer Snap is on or not.
   b. The OBJECT SNAP menu to turn on Layer Snap, then use the middle mouse button.

6. The quick way to enter the OBJECT SNAP menu, is to press the:
   a. [**Shift**] **X** keys.
   b. [**Shift**] **O** keys.
   c. **X** key.

7. When you want to move a rectangle by dragging it with your cursor, you use the:
   a. MOVE menu, make the **Entity** option active, pick the rectangle, then drag it to the new location.
   b. MOVE menu, pick **Drag**, make the **Entity** option active, pick the rectangle, then drag it to the new location.
   c. MOVE menu, pick **Drag**, make the **Group** option active, pick the rectangle, then drag it to the new location.

8. To enter the MOVE menu quickly, you press the:
   a. **D** key.
   b. **M** key.
   c. [**Alt**] **M** keys.

9. To turn on the mode that locks your line in 45 degree angles as you draw it, you press the:
   a. **O** key until the message says: **Ortho mode is on.**
   b. **A** key until the message says: **Angle lock is on.**
   c. **L** key until the message says: **Ortho lock is on.**

10. When you wish to easily snap to the intersection point of two lines, in the OBJECT SNAP menu, you should make the option **Intsect** active, and:
    a. The **Mid Pnt** option active also.
    b. Turn **Mid Pnt** and **End Pnt** off.
    c. The **End Pnt** and **Mid Pnt** options active.

11. In order to object snap to entities in different Z elevations, in 3-D Line you use the:
    a. **3-D Cursr** option.
    b. **Entity** option.
    c. **Z Off** option.

12. The 3-D Line option is found in the:
    a. ARCHITECT menu.
    b. PARALLEL menu.
    c. 3-D ENTITY menu.

13. Before creating your 3-D line, you should:
    a. Window in for better viewing.
    b. Create a 3-D view in order to see all of the line endpoints you will be connecting.
    c. Make sure you are in Ortho view.

14. To return to the plan view of your drawing, you use the:
    a. 3-D View, **Ortho** option.
    b. 2-D View, **Ortho** option.
    c. 3-D View, **Plan** option.

Lesson 11
Copying techniques

What you will be doing

You will use copying techniques to create new entities in your drawing. You will copy lines in a repeated pattern, mirroring this pattern, offset lines, and changing lines to a linestyle.

Objectives

Your lesson objectives are to:

- Offset copies of existing lines
- Offset copies of arcs
- Change attributes of items
- Copy in a rectangular pattern
- Mirror copies of items
- Trim lines
- Extend lines
- Add fillets to round the corners of existing lines

Remember to refer to *The DataCAD Operations Guide* when instructed.

Copying techniques

Whenever possible, you should always copy! Why? Because copying existing geometry saves time, eliminates steps, increases accuracy, and reduces error. Notice the parking lot in FIG. 11-1 is made up of repeated lines (parking stripes). One line is drawn and copied many times.

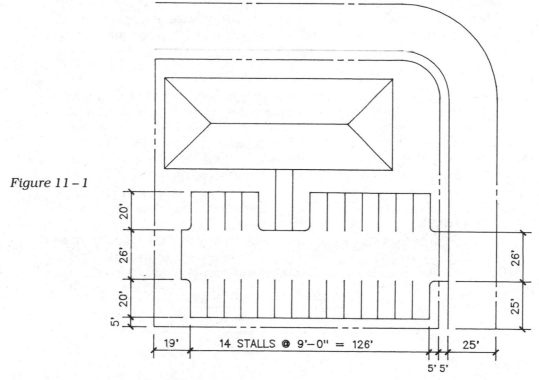

Figure 11 – 1

20'

26'

20'

5'

26'

25'

19'   14 STALLS @ 9'–0" = 126'   25'

5' 5'

Copying techniques includes such things as:

- Copying in a rectangular pattern
- Copying in a circular pattern
- Moving and copying
- Mirroring and copying
- Offsetting copies

Copying techniques might even include making symbols of items or a part of a building, and using the symbol in several drawings!

How copying saves time and steps

Copying reduces the amount of time it would take to recreate duplicate geometry. You might even want to copy when geometry is not exactly duplicated, but instead would require minor changes. Copying from "look alike" sets of entities would be better than starting from scratch.

How copying increases accuracy and reduces errors

Once you have created an item or a set of items correctly, then every time you copy it, it is correct! There will be no errors in subsequent copies, if there are none in the original.

Also, in the case of a copied pattern, you will find that it is much easier and more accurate to define the repeat of the pattern and the spacing, and let the computer do your work, than if you created each piece manually.

Preplanning your drawing

If you spend a few minutes organizing your steps prior to starting your drawings, you will be able to scan the items for repeated patterns and the "best" way to create the drawing. This technique is called "preplanning."

Good users of CAD systems always preplan their drawings. How long it takes depends on the experience of the user, and the complexity of the project. Some users have found it very effective to rough out a "quick and dirty" sketch of the drawing, only penciling the major steps of the drawing creation. Later, when the user is more experienced, sketches only have to be made mentally.

All of the drawings you are guided through in your lessons have been preplanned for you. It is good, though, to take a minute to look at your project for this lesson, and analyze how it was preplanned, as in FIG. 11-2.

SOMETIMES A
QUICK SKETCH
HELPS YOU TO
PREPLAN YOUR
DRAWING

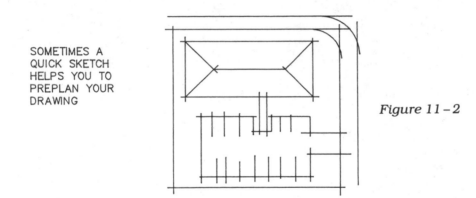

Figure 11 – 2

Step 1 – Examine your project for repeated geometry.

In this case, the street lines are lines and an arc moved a certain constant distance from the property lines. This can be achieved by "copying" the property lines, "offset" at an equal distance.

Although the linetypes are not the same, it becomes an easy task to simply change the linetype of the copied lines. See FIG. 11-3.

Step 2 – Look for repeated patterns in your drawings.

Notice that the parking lot is a very good example of a repeated pattern. (FIG. 11-4.)

Step 3 – Look for ways of eliminating steps.

For instance, although the entire parking could be made by two

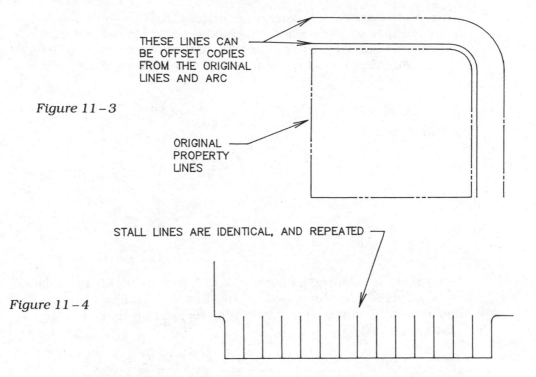

THESE LINES CAN
BE OFFSET COPIES
FROM THE ORIGINAL
LINES AND ARC

Figure 11 – 3

ORIGINAL
PROPERTY
LINES

STALL LINES ARE IDENTICAL, AND REPEATED

Figure 11 – 4

repeat patterns, establishing the second repeat pattern items, then creating the pattern consumes many more steps than involved in just mirroring the first pattern over to the other side. This is shown in FIG. 11-5.

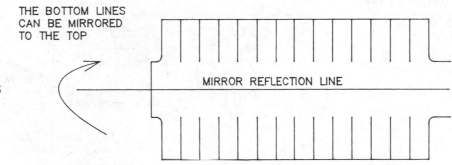

THE BOTTOM LINES
CAN BE MIRRORED
TO THE TOP

MIRROR REFLECTION LINE

Figure 11 – 5

Step 4 – Figure how you will start, and what the progression will be in creating the geometry. What is your first step? What will you do next? Can you lump together some related steps to perform at one time, without having to change back and forth through menus?

It would be faster, for instance, to offset all of the street lines in one step. Then the second step would be to change the offset copies to the correct linetype all at one time, as in FIG. 11-6. This avoids needless changes of menus and unnecessary steps.

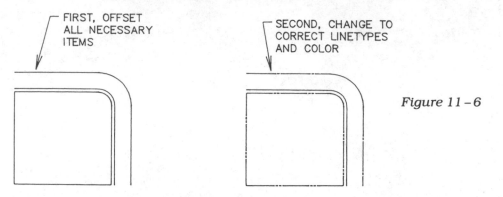

FIRST, OFFSET
ALL NECESSARY
ITEMS

SECOND, CHANGE TO
CORRECT LINETYPES
AND COLOR

Figure 11 – 6

Examine the following pictorial, FIG. 11-7, which graphically illustrates the creation steps used for this drawing. Each step is storyboarded to help you understand the preplanning that went into the drawing.

1. CREATE PROPERTY
   LINES AND ARC

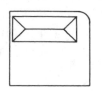

2. LAYOUT
   BUILDING

3. OFFSET
   COPIES

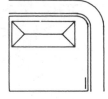

4. CREATE FIRST
   LINE FOR PATTERN

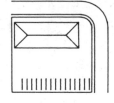

5. MAKE COPIES

Figure 11 – 7

6. READY TO
   MIRROR

7. MIRROR COPY

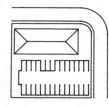

8. CLEANUP

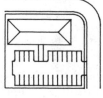

9. FINISHING
   TOUCHES

Offsetting the property lines

The Offset function is found in the GEOMETRY menu. Offset allows you to make a copy of an item at a defined distance. You will use Offset to create copies of the property lines to draw lines for your sidewalk and street. You will not have to draw these lines from scratch with input coordinates, or figure out the correct radius for the arc. DataCAD does it for you!

Step 1 – Make the **Street** layer active.

Step 2 – Pick the **Geometry** option found in the UTILITY menu.

Step 3 – Pick the **Offset** option.

Step 4 – Make sure the ***LyrSrch** option is active.

Step 5 – Make sure the **Dynamic** option is inactive (no star *****).

Step 6 – Pick the **PerpDist** option. (This option is only displayed if the Dynamic option is turned off.)

Step 7 – Type in and [**Enter**] the distance for the sidewalk lines.

Step 8 – Pick the first line you will offset, as indicated in FIG. 11-8.

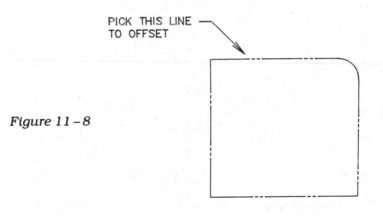

PICK THIS LINE
TO OFFSET

Figure 11 – 8

Step 9 – Pick anywhere on the side of the line you wish the offset copy to appear, as in FIG. 11-9 on page 200.

Step 10 – The copy will be created! (FIG. 11-10 on page 200.)

Step 11 – Offset copies for the arc and other line; see FIG. 11-11 on page 200.

Step 12 – Once the sidewalk is completed, pick the **New Dist** option.

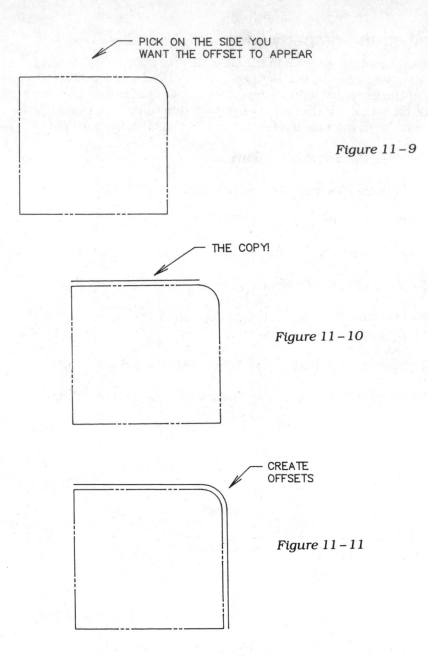

PICK ON THE SIDE YOU
WANT THE OFFSET TO APPEAR

Figure 11 – 9

THE COPY!

Figure 11 – 10

CREATE
OFFSETS

Figure 11 – 11

Step 13 – Pick **PerpDist** again.

Step 14 – Type in and [**Enter**] the offset distance for the street.

25

Step 15 – Offset all the geometry for the street, as shown in FIG. 11-12.

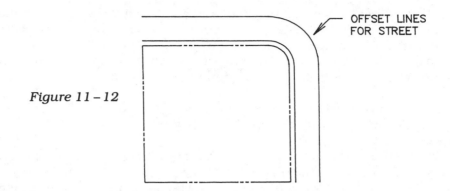

OFFSET LINES
FOR STREET

Figure 11 – 12

Changing the attributes of existing items

Step 1 – Pick the **Change** option, found in the EDIT menu.

Step 2 – Pick **LineTyp**.

Step 3 – Set the linetype to **CentrLn**.

Step 4 – Pick **Color**.

Step 5 – Set the color to **Lt Cyan**.

Step 6 – Make sure **Entity** or **Group** is active (either will work).

Step 7 – Pick all of the items you want changed to the new color and line-type, indicated in FIG. 11-13. Follow these steps to change the curb lines to solid.

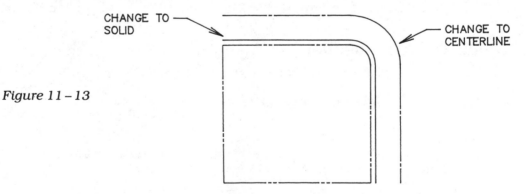

CHANGE TO
SOLID

CHANGE TO
CENTERLINE

Figure 11 – 13

Moving items to a layer

Because the **Offset** option creates copies of the original line or arc, the new lines and arcs in your street had the same color and linetype as the originals. This was easy to see, as the color and linetype are displayed on the screen. What is not easy to see is that the new items are also on the same LAYER as the original items.

Because the original items were on the PROPLIN layer, and you want them on the STREET layer, you will want to "Move" them.

Step 1 – To confirm what layer the street lines are on, you can use the interrupt mode of Identify. Press [**Shift**] **I**.

Step 2 – Pick one of the lines or arcs in the street. It will become gray and dashed. Look at the [**F2**] option in the menu, which tells you what layer the item is on. If you have drawn your site correctly, it will still be on the PROPLIN layer.

Step 3 – Press **M** to quickly enter the **Move** option, found in the EDIT menu.

Step 4 – Pick the **To Layer** option.

Step 5 – Now pick the layer you want the items MOVED TO. In this case, you want to pick the **Street** layer.

Step 6 – Using the ***Entity** setting, pick all of the lines and arcs that should be on the street layer. Usually you can see them blink a little when you pick them, but the real indicator is in the message area of the screen. It should read "**1 entity selected**" as you pick the items.

Step 7 – When you have picked all of the street lines and arcs, press mouse button **3** to quit.

Creating the parking lot

Step 1 – Press the [**Tab**] key to change the active layer to Parking.

Step 2 – Press **Z**, and set the **Z base and height** to **0**.

    Z

Step 3 – Make sure the coordinate input mode is set to **Relative Cartesian** coordinates. (Use the [**Insert**] key.)

Step 4 – The parking lot outline is dimensioned off the lower right corner of the property line, indicated in FIG. 11-14. You will use this corner as your reference point.

Step 5 – Press the ⁓ key.

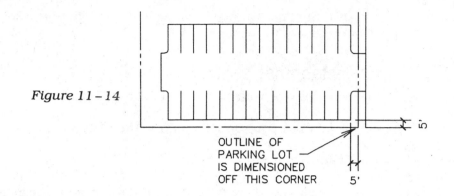

Figure 11 – 14

OUTLINE OF
PARKING LOT
IS DIMENSIONED
OFF THIS CORNER

5'

5'

Step 6 – Pick the reference corner. (FIG. 11-15.)

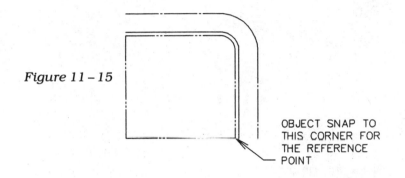

Figure 11 – 15

OBJECT SNAP TO
THIS CORNER FOR
THE REFERENCE
POINT

Step 7 – Press the [**Space bar**] to use Relative coordinates.

Step 8 – Type in the coordinates for the distance from your reference corner.

(See project for dimensions.)

Step 9 – Press the [**Space bar**] again, and type in the coordinates for the length of the line indicated in FIG. 11-16.

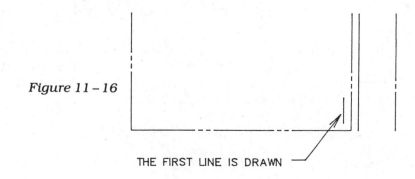

Figure 11 – 16

THE FIRST LINE IS DRAWN

Step 10 – This is the only line you need to create for your pattern. Press mouse button **3** to quit.

Copying in a rectangular array

You can copy all the stripes for your parking lot from this single line.

Step 1 – Press **C** to enter the **Copy** option found in the EDIT menu.

Step 2 – Pick the **RectArry** option.

Step 3 – Pick a start point anywhere (FIG. 11-17). It doesn't matter exactly where you pick, because the distance you define will be the important factor.

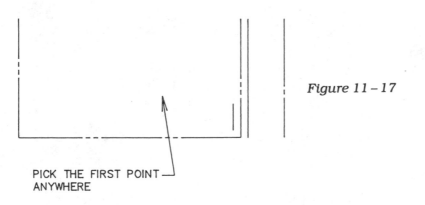

Figure 11 – 17

PICK THE FIRST POINT
ANYWHERE

Step 4 – Press the [**Space bar**], and type in the coordinates defining the distance for the first copy. This will be the distance between the stripes.

X = −9
Y = 0

Step 5 – Now type in the number of repetitions for the X direction. This is the *total* number of stripes you will want created, including the original.

Because it is often hard to predetermine the real number of stripes for your parking lot, you will usually define more than enough, then delete the stripes you don't need. In this case, try the number **20** to see how they fit.

Step 6 – Now press [**Enter**] to accept the **Y** default of **1**.

Step 7 – Pick the line you will want to copy, as shown in FIG. 11-18.

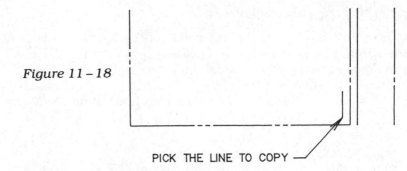

Figure 11 – 18

PICK THE LINE TO COPY —

Step 8 – The new lines will appear! (FIG. 11-19.) Be sure to press mouse button **3** to quit out of COPY menu.

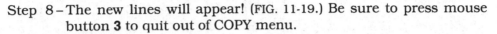

Figure 11 – 19

Step 9 – Press the < key to erase any extra lines.

Step 10 – Create a line to close the bottom of the lot outline, as shown in FIG. 11-20, by object snapping to the bottom of the two end lines.

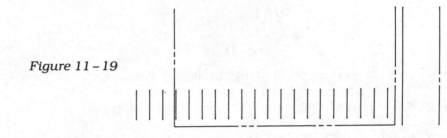

Figure 11 – 20

Step 11 – Use object snap and relative cartesian coordinates to create the 5 foot line and the 26 foot line, as indicated in FIG. 11-21.

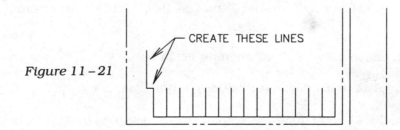

CREATE THESE LINES

Figure 11 – 21

Mirroring the parking stripes

You can mirror the stripes to the other side of the lot. When you mirror, you need to define a mirror axis line. The items you mirror will be reflected to the other side of this line, as though you were holding a mirror there.

You can use the midpoint of the line indicated in FIG. 11-22, as the beginning point for your reflection line, then drag your line out on the X axis.

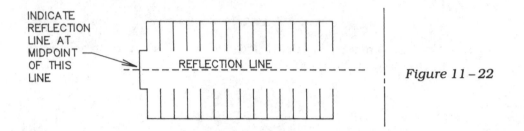

Figure 11 – 22

Step 1 – Pick the **Mirror** option, found in the EDIT menu.

Step 2 – Press [**Shift**] **X** and set the Object Snap to **Mid Pnt**.

Step 3 – Press mouse button **3** to quit out of the OBJECT SNAP menu and back into the **Mirror** option.

Step 4 – Object snap to the midpoint of the line shown in FIG. 11-23, to define the starting point of your reflection line.

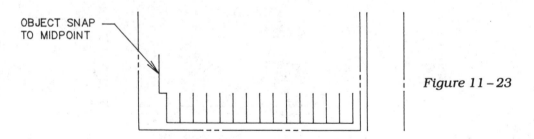

Figure 11 – 23

Step 5 – Pick the second point for your reflection line, making sure the line is straight on the X axis, as in FIG. 11-24. (Ortho mode helps you do this.)

Step 6 – Make sure the **Area** option is active.

Step 7 – Also make sure the **AndCopy** option is active.

Step 8 – Pick for the first and second corner points to indicate a rectangle

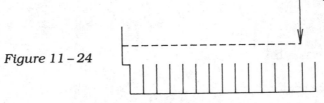

PICK A SECOND POINT
FOR YOUR LINE, USING
"ORTHO" MODE

Figure 11 – 24

around the area you wish to copy. Make sure you include only a part of the line you used to object snap to for your reflection line, as indicated below.

Any line that is only partially included in your rectangle will not be copied! Only lines completely surrounded by the rectangle will be mirrored. (FIG. 11-25.)

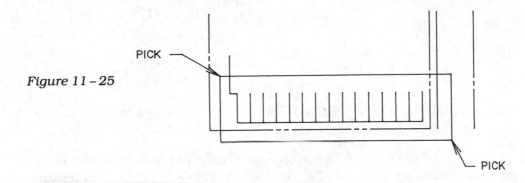

PICK

Figure 11 – 25

PICK

Step 9 – The copy is created, as illustrated in FIG. 11-26.

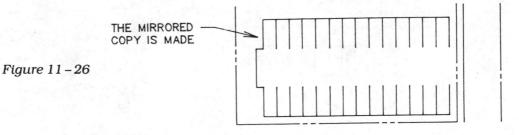

THE MIRRORED
COPY IS MADE

Figure 11 – 26

Step 10 – Use object snap to connect the fourth line to the seventh line of the mirrored pattern, as indicated in FIG. 11-27 on page 208.

Making a partial erase

Step 1 – Press **E** to erase.

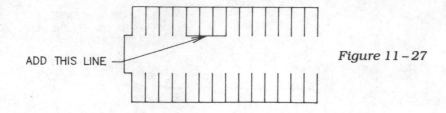

ADD THIS LINE

Figure 11 – 27

Step 2 – Pick the **Partial** option.

Step 3 – Pick the line indicated in FIG. 11-28. This is the line you will erase only a part of.

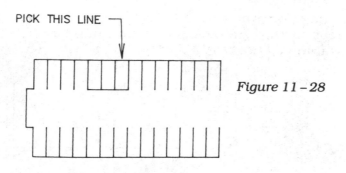

PICK THIS LINE

Figure 11 – 28

Step 4 – Make sure your OBJECT SNAP menu is set to **Intsect**, and that **Mid Pnt** is inactive.

Step 5 – Object snap to the intersections of the fourth and seventh line, as indicated in FIG. 11-29. This will define the part of the line you want to get rid of.

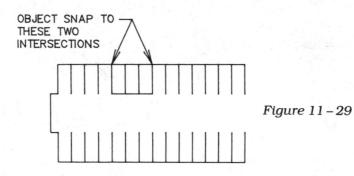

OBJECT SNAP TO THESE TWO INTERSECTIONS

Figure 11 – 29

Step 6 – The line will be cut and erased! (FIG. 11-30.)

One line trim

Step 1 – Pick the **CleanUp** option, found in the EDIT menu.

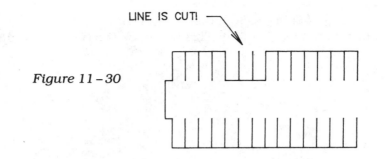

LINE IS CUT! —

Figure 11 – 30

Step 2 – Pick the **1LnTrim** option.

Step 3 – Make sure ***Entity** is active.

Step 4 – Also make sure ***LyrSrch** is active.

Step 5 – Pick the bottom line of the building, as indicated in FIG. 11-31. This is the line you will want to trim to.

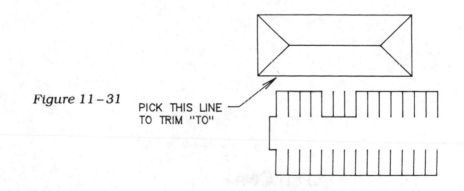

Figure 11 – 31

PICK THIS LINE —
TO TRIM "TO"

Step 6 – Pick anywhere on the other side of the line, where you don't want the line drawn, as indicated in FIG. 11-32.

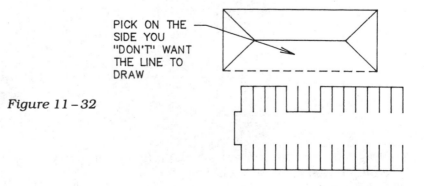

PICK ON THE —
SIDE YOU
"DON'T" WANT
THE LINE TO
DRAW

Figure 11 – 32

Step 7 – Pick the *Entity option, then pick the lines you want trimmed (or in this case, extended). This would be the two lines indicated in FIG. 11-33.

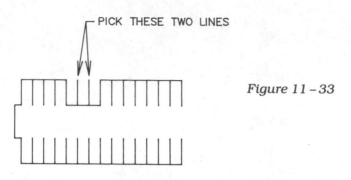

PICK THESE TWO LINES

Figure 11 – 33

Step 8 – The lines you pick will be stretched, or extended, to the building. (FIG. 11-34.)

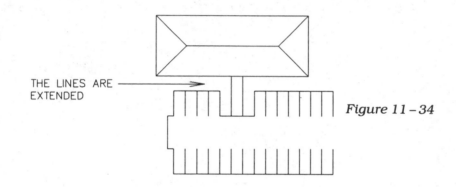

THE LINES ARE EXTENDED

Figure 11 – 34

Adding lines for the driveway

Step 1 – Object snap to the end of the line indicated in FIG. 11-35.

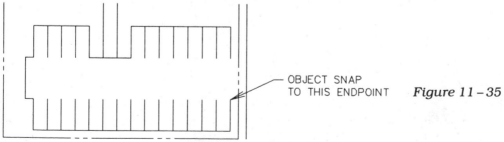

OBJECT SNAP TO THIS ENDPOINT   *Figure 11 – 35*

Step 2 – Drag a horizontal line out, overlapping the property line as indicated in FIG. 11-36. You will trim this later.

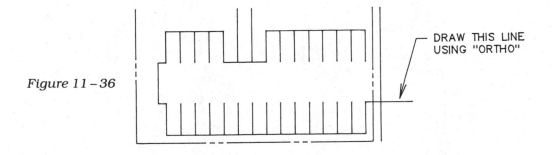

Figure 11 – 36

DRAW THIS LINE
USING "ORTHO"

Step 3 – Press **M** to **Move** this line to the other side of the driveway.

Step 4 – To define a moving distance, object snap to the first endpoint, then to the second, as indicated in FIG. 11-37.

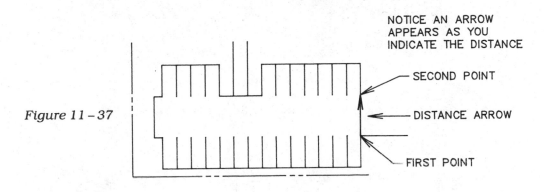

Figure 11 – 37

NOTICE AN ARROW
APPEARS AS YOU
INDICATE THE DISTANCE

SECOND POINT

DISTANCE ARROW

FIRST POINT

Step 5 – Make sure ***AndCopy** is active.

Step 6 – Pick the line to copy, and the copy is created! (FIG. 11-38.) Turn off **AndCopy**.

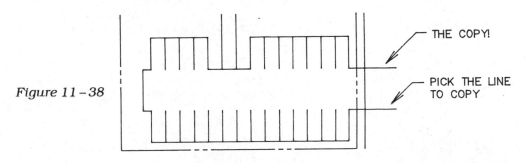

Figure 11 – 38

THE COPY!

PICK THE LINE
TO COPY

Step 7 – Use the **1 Line Trim** procedure to trim back the overlapping lines of your driveway, as shown in FIG. 11-39.

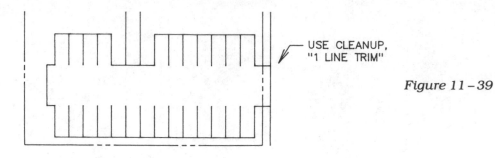

USE CLEANUP,
"1 LINE TRIM"

Figure 11 – 39

Creating the fillets

Fillets are the little arcs used to round the corners of the parking lot.

Step 1 – Pick **Cleanup**, found in the EDIT menu.

Step 2 – Pick the **Fillets** option.

Step 3 – Pick the **Radius** option.

Step 4 – Set the radius of the fillet to **2** feet.

Step 5 – Pick the first line of the "corner" to fillet, as indicated in FIG. 11-40.

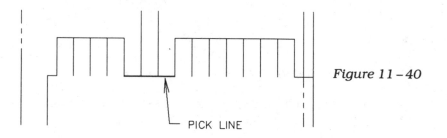

PICK LINE

Figure 11 – 40

Step 6 – Pick the second line of the corner to fillet. (FIG. 11-41.)

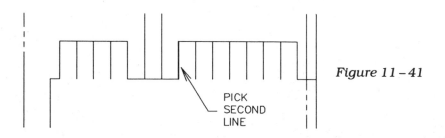

PICK
SECOND
LINE

Figure 11 – 41

Step 7 – Your fillet will be created. (See FIG. 11-42.)

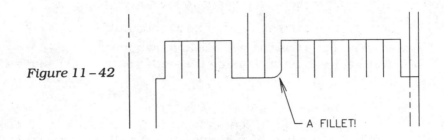

Figure 11 – 42

A FILLET!

Step 8 – Continue picking lines of the corners you wish to fillet, until your drawing is completed.

Step 9 – Using **3-D View, Prspect** option, create a bird's-eye view of your drawing, setting the **EyePnt Z** to **50** feet. Save this image and **Move** it to a desirable location. Create a **NewLayer**, calling this layer: **Birdseye**.

Adjust this 3-D view, if necessary, until it is positioned correctly. This is illustrated in FIG. 11-43.

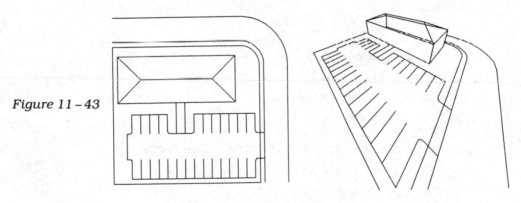

Figure 11 – 43

If you need a quick review of 3-D perspectives . . .

Just in case you are unable to recall the steps you went through to create your 3-D view, look back at the lesson called: Creating 3-D Views, or look in the Views - 3-D section of your *DataCAD Operations Guide*, Creating a birds-eye perspective view.

Step 10 – Save your file by pressing [**Shift**] **F**.

DataCAD exercise 11

Please complete the following exercise by reading each question carefully, then circling the letter that corresponds to the correct answer.

1. Before starting to create your project, you should:

   a. Preplan the steps you will use in drawing it.
   b. Not waste time preplanning the steps you will take in drawing it.

2. Part of the preplanning stage consists of:

   a. Creating the walls in your drawing.
   b. Looking for repeated patterns, and the "best" way to create your drawing.
   c. Looking for repeated patterns in your drawing. There is never a "best" way to create it.

3. To copy geometry in a repeated pattern, in the X and Y directions, you use the:

   a. **Move, AndCopy** options.
   b. **Copy, RectArry** options.
   c. **Copy, Repeat** options.

4. To reflect entities, or copies of entities, to another location, you use the:

   a. **Reflect** option.
   b. **Mid Pnt** option.
   c. **Mirror** option.

5. When defining an area to copy, items that are included only partially in the rectangle will:

   a. Not be copied.
   b. Will be copied.
   c. Will only be copied if the **Include** option is active.

6. To delete a gap out of a line only, you use the:

   a. **CleanUp, Partial** options.
   b. **Erase, Partial** options.
   c. **CleanUp, 1LnTrim** options.

7. To extend, or stretch, a line to another line, you use the:

   a. **Erase, Partial** options.
   b. **CleanUp, Stretch** options.
   c. **CleanUp, 1LnTrim** options.

8. If you wish to define a distance for placing a single copy of an entity by picking two points, you use the:

a. **Move** option, pick two point defining the move distance, make sure the **AndCopy** option is active, then pick the item(s) to copy.

b. **Move, Drag** options, pick two points defining the move distance, make sure the **AndCopy** option is active, then pick the item(s) to copy.

c. **Stretch** option, pick two points defining the move distance, make sure ***AndCopy** is active, then pick the item(s) to copy.

Some review questions

9. Default drawings allow you to:

a. Change the type of drawing you are going to create, but not the scale or drawing borders.

b. Preset several different "drawing formats" (blank drawing sheets) for the types and scales of drawings you will be creating. This includes setting up special layers for your drawings also.

c. Have the correct title block already set in your drawing only. The layers and scale cannot be preset in the default drawing.

10. To change your default drawing, you must retrieve the Drawing list (either by starting DataCAD, or using the **File I/O, New Dwg** options), then:

a. Enter the name of your default drawing.

b. Change the current directory using the **New Path** option.

c. Pick the **Default** option and pick the name of your default drawing.

11. Three possible choices for angle types are:

a. Normal, Cartesian, and Bearings.

b. Relative, Cartesian, and Bearings.

c. Normal, Compass, and Bearings.

12. Different lines (such as solid, dashed, dot-dash, etc.) are called:

a. Line Weights.

b. Linetypes.

c. Line Scales.

13. To set the angle type to Bearings, you use the:

a. [**Insert**] key.

b. [**Space bar**].

c. SETTINGS menu, **AngleTyp** option.

14. To set the input mode to Relative Polar, you use the:

a. [**Insert**] key.

b. [**Space bar**].

c. SETTINGS menu, **AngleTyp** option.

15. Before you use a relative input mode, you should:

    a. ALWAYS pick a start point.
    b. NEVER pick a start point.
    c. Only pick a start point if the drawing tells you to.

16. The quickest way to turn from lines to walls, or from walls to lines, is to use the:

    a. **Menu** option choices.
    b. [<] "less than" key.
    c. [=] "equal" key.

17. In order to define a reference point, you press the:

    a. [**Space bar**].
    b. ~ key.
    c. **X** key.

18. To clean up wall intersections after you create them, you:

    a. Press [**Alt**] **C**, to enter the CLEANUP menu.
    b. Press **A**, to enter the CLEANUP menu.
    c. Pick the CLEANUP menu, and use the **T** or **L** **intersection** options.

19. To erase the last item you created, you use the:

    a. **Delete** option.
    b. < less than key.
    c. > greater than key.

20. To erase an entire area at one time, you use the:

    a. **E** key to enter the ERASE menu, then pick the **Area** option.
    b. [**Shift**] < keys together.
    c. [**Shift**] > keys together.

Lesson 12
Detail drawings

What you will be doing

You will create details and add them to a detail sheet. Details are first drawn true size, scaled, then made into symbols for use in all of your detail sheets.

Objectives

Your lesson objectives are:

- Set up a default drawing for your $1^1/_2'' = 1'$ details
- Create a hatch boundary
- Define a hatch pattern and a scale for the pattern
- Explode the dimensions in your detail
- Reduce the size of the detail

Remember to refer to *The DataCAD Operations Guide* when instructed.

Defining the default drawing for your detail

The detail you will be drawing is shown in FIG. 12-1.

Before you begin your detail, you will want to set up a default drawing. You will be able to use this default for all of your details that are $1^1/_2'' = 1'$ scale. Of course, you will set up other default drawings to create details in different scales.

This section is a good review of lesson 2 - Drawing setup. You might wish to reference this lesson for further explanation.

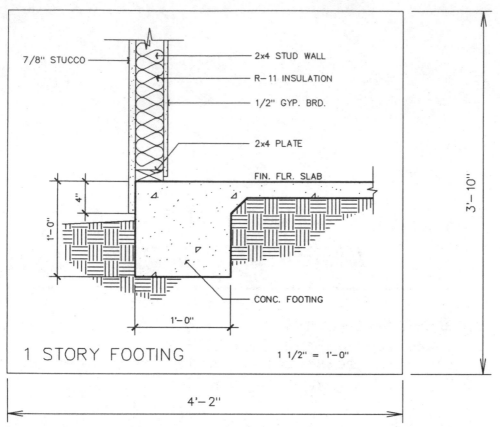

7/8" STUCCO

2x4 STUD WALL

R-11 INSULATION

1/2" GYP. BRD.

2x4 PLATE

FIN. FLR. SLAB

CONC. FOOTING

4"

1'-0"

1'-0"

3'-10"

1 STORY FOOTING

1 1/2" = 1'-0"

4'-2"

Figure 12-1

Step 1 – Retrieve the DataCAD drawing list, either by starting DataCAD, or by using **File I/O, New Dwg**.

Step 2 – You will want to change to the "Default" path (directory) that holds your default drawings. This way you can edit the default drawing just like any other drawing. Pick **New Path**.

Step 3 – Type in **Default**, and press [**Enter**], or press [**F2**] to select .. and then pick **Default** off the menu.

Step 4 – Now your default drawing names are displayed in the drawing list, as in FIG. 12-2.

Step 5 – To start a new default, you might want to use an existing default as a basis, or begin without any defaults. Because this drawing will be a new scale and type of default, you can begin without the help of an existing default. To clear out any previously chosen default, pick the **Default** option.

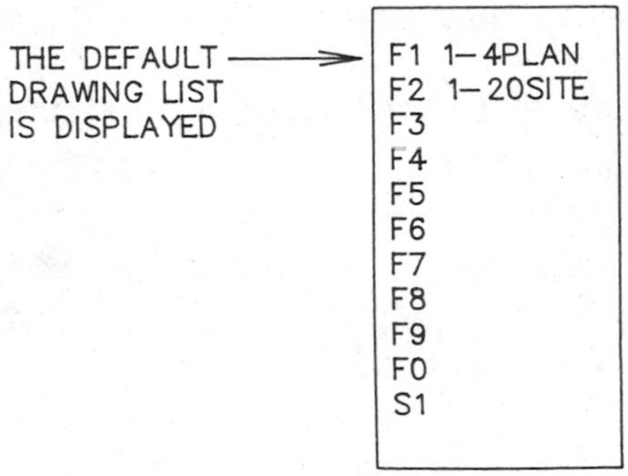

```
                    THE DEFAULT ─────▶  ┌──────────────┐
                    DRAWING LIST         │ F1  1─4PLAN  │
                    IS DISPLAYED         │ F2  1─20SITE │
                                         │ F3           │
                                         │ F4           │
                                         │ F5           │
                                         │ F6           │
      Figure 12 – 2                      │ F7           │
                                         │ F8           │
                                         │ F9           │
                                         │ F0           │
                                         │ S1           │
                                         └──────────────┘
```

Step 6 – Press the [**Space bar**] once. This will clear any name on the text
line.

Step 7 – Now press [**Enter**] to leave the DEFAULT menu and return to the
opening menu to start a new drawing.

Step 8 – Type in the new name of your default drawing: **det1-1-2**. This will
stand for: Detail $1^{1/2}''$ scale.

Setting your grid snap

The grid snap (mouse button 1 picking grid) can be set differently for every
layer you create. If you set the grid snap BEFORE creating your new layers,
all new layers will have the new grid setting! Then you can change only the
layers you wish to have a different setting.

Step 1 – Press **S** to Set your grid Snap. (UTILITY, GRIDS, SETSNAP
menus.) Make sure your CAPS LOCK is not on, and that you are
pressing the small s.

Step 2 – Press the [**F2**] key to pick **1/2"**, or type in **0.0.1/2** and press [**Enter**].

Step 3 – Press [**Enter**] again to except the same value for both the X and Y
directions.

Step 4 – Make sure the S is capital in SWOTHLUD. If it isn't, press the X
key to turn on grid "snap" pick. Now you can create your layers.

Adding new layers

Step 1 – When your new drawing file is displayed, press the **L** key to go to
the LAYERS menu.

Step 2 – Use the **NewLayer** option, to add 8 layers (9 layers total).

Step 3 – Name these layers, as indicated in the following list:

> **Walls**
> **Wood**
> **Concrete**
> **Earth**
> **Insul**
> **Dims**
> **Notes**
> **Misc**
> **Box**

A fast way to give the layer colors

You will keep the Walls layer color set to white, but the rest of your layers will have other colors associated with them.

Step 1 – Press [**Tab**] until the **Wood** layer is active.

Step 2 – Press the **K** key until the current color is set to **Brown**.

Step 3 – Press the [**Tab**] key until the **Concrete** layer is displayed.

Step 4 – Press the **K** key until the yellow is set.

Step 5 – Continue until all of the layers are assigned colors:

Walls	= **White**
Wood	= **Brown**
Concrete	= **Yellow**
Earth	= **Brown**
Insul	= **Lt Mgta**
Dims	= **Green**
Notes	= **Green**
Misc	= **Lt Cyan**
Box	= **Yellow**

Setting the dimension variables

Since dimensions are *Descriptive* items in your drawing, you need to adjust the variables to the correct settings for $1^{1}/_{2}'' = 1'$ scale.

The options you will be setting for your dimensions are illustrated in FIG. 12-3.

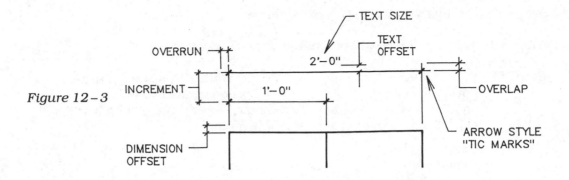

Figure 12-3

Step 1 – From the EDIT menu, select the **Dimension** option.

Step 2 – Pick the **Linear** option.

Step 3 – Select **TextStyl**.

Step 4 – Pick **TextSize**.

Step 5 – Turn to the DataCAD Scales & Sizes section of appendix B *Data-CAD Reference Guide*, and find the correct size for "Text Size Notes" at a $1^{1}/_{2}$" scale.

Step 6 – Change the current text size to the size you found in this section:

   1"

Step 7 – Change the text **Offset** option to **1"** also. This will set the offset to $^{1}/_{8}$".

Step 8 – Pick the **Color** option, and change it to **Green**.

Step 9 – Press the mouse button **3** to quit back to the DIMENSION menu, and pick **Dim Styl**.

Step 10 – Change the **Offset** to **1"**.

Step 11 – Change the **Overlap** to **1"**.

Step 12 – Change the **Incrment** to **4"**.

Step 13 – Pick **FixdDis** until the option is off (no star *****).

Step 14 – Press mouse button **3** once to quit back to DIMENSION menu, then pick **ArroStyl**.

Step 15 – Change the arrow style to **Tic Marks**.

Step 16 – Change the **Weight** of the drawn tic marks to **1**.

Step 17 – Pick **Color**, and change the color to **White**. This way, you can have a wider pen stroke the tic marks once, instead of having a smaller width pen stroke the tic mark several times which will slow down the plot (if you have a pen plotter).

> **Color**
> **White**

Step 18 – Press mouse button **3** to quit out of DIMENSIONS.

Detail box

You will draw a detail box that will hold your detail. Again, this is a descriptive item, and you will have to draw it in accordance with the final scale of the drawing.

Refer to the DataCAD Available Drawing Sheet Areas section in the *DataCAD Reference Guide*. The size you will use for the detail box is listed under the Typical Detail Box column. The sizes described here will result in a $6^1/_4'' \times 5^3/_4''$ box when scaled for plotting.

Step 1 – Make sure the **Box** layer is active.

Step 2 – Press the **Z** key, to change your Z-base and Z-height.

Step 3 – Change the base and height to **0**.

Step 4 – Return to the EDIT menu, and pick the **Polygon** option.

Step 5 – Pick the ***Rectangl** option until it is active.

Step 6 – Pick a start point for your box, then use the Relative cartesian coordinate input mode to enter the X and Y values for your detail box. (See FIG. 12-4.)

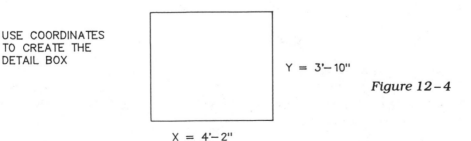

USE COORDINATES
TO CREATE THE
DETAIL BOX

Y = 3'– 10"

X = 4'– 2"

Figure 12 – 4

Step 7 – If necessary, recalculate the extents of your window, using the /
key.

Setting the object snap menu

You will want to set all of your object snap options in the default drawing
so that you don't have to do it every time you draw a detail.

Step 1 – Press the (capital) [**Shift**] **X** keys.

Step 2 – Make sure the following options have a star by them:

> ***End Pnt**
> ***Mid Pnt**
> ***Intsect**
> ***LyrSnap**

Step 3 – Press mouse button **3** to quit.

Step 4 – Save your default drawing and return to the Drawing list, using
the **File I/O, New Dwg, Yes** options.

> **File I/O**
> **New Dwg**
> **Yes**

Returning to your original drawing list

Now the drawing list for the Default drawings is displayed. You will want to
change the directory to your own drawing list.

Step 1 – Pick the **New Path** option.

Step 2 – Type in the directory pathname for your drawing (remember you
used your first or last name), and press [**Enter**]. OR—press or
pick [**F2**] to select the .. option, then pick your drawing directory
pathname from the list and press [**Enter**].

Step 3 – Now your drawings should appear (PLAN1, SITE1, and any other
drawing you may have created during your lessons).

If they do not appear, and you get the message "**Path 'name' does
not exist. Create it?**", pick the **No** option. Then check the spelling
of the pathname you are typing in. It should match the name you
defined in lesson 3—Basic drafting techniques *exactly*.

Step 4 – Once your drawing names appear, you can define which default
drawing you want active. Pick the **Default** option.

Step 5 – Pick the name of the detail Default Drawing: **DET1-1-2**.

Step 6 – Now type in the new name for your drawing: **DETAIL1**.

Creating the detail

Once the detail box (defined in the Default drawing) is displayed on the screen. You can begin drawing your detail. See FIG. 12-1.

Step 1 – Apply the skills you have learned in your previous lessons to create the detail, following the procedure illustrated in FIG. 12-5.

Saving your drawing

It is a wise idea to always "save" your drawing before you create the hatch pattern. In fact, you should always save your drawing before you begin a process that requires a lot of computing. You should also make a habit of saving it at least every hour!

Step 1 – Press the [**Shift**] **F** keys to quickly save your drawing.

Creating the hatch boundary

Texture patterns, called "crosshatching," are created in DataCAD using the **Hatch** option.

Before you create your hatch, you must first define a hatch "boundary." You can think of the boundary as a fence that contains your hatch. There are three ways to define your boundary:

1. Select existing items as your boundary. For example, you can use the four lines that define a wall in your detail as a boundary.
2. Create temporary items to use as a boundary. If you are creating a tiled floor area in a bath, you may want to create a temporary boundary around the sink, toilet, tub, and other items, plus an additional boundary around the word BATH. The boundary will keep the tile from crossing over the items. Then you can delete this boundary later, or turn off the layer it is on.
3. Use the **Boundary** option in the HATCH menu. This very helpful option allows you to create a temporary "invisible" boundary to use for your hatch. However, once you leave the HATCH menu, the boundary would have to be created again if you needed to change the hatching.

The important factor to remember is that the boundary should be CLOSED (no gaps). While some hatch patterns are trickier than others, the best results will occur when the hatch boundary is completely closed. Otherwise, the hatch lines could "flow out," as in FIG. 12-6 on page 226.

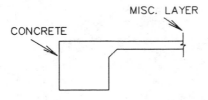

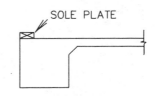

1. CHANGE TO THE CONCRETE
   LAYER, ADD CONCRETE OUTLINE
   USING CORRECT COORDINATES.
   GRID PICK IS VERY HELPFUL.

2. USE POLYGON TO CREATE
   THE RECTANGLE SOLE PLATE
   ON THE WOOD LAYER.

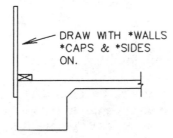

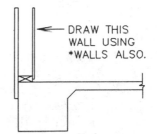

3. TAB TO WALL LAYER, AND
   USE ARCHITECT MENU TO ADD
   .0.7/8 WIDTH WALL FOR STUCCO.

4. CHANGE WALL WIDTH TO
   .0.1/2 AND DRAW GYP
   BOARD.

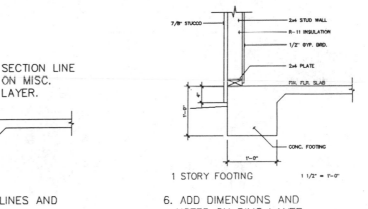

5. DRAW GROUND LINES AND
   BREAK LINES.

6. ADD DIMENSIONS AND
   NOTES ON DIMS LAYER.

Figure 12-5

Another problem with hatching can occur if you use a line that over-laps the desired area as part of your boundary. Sometimes this can cause your hatch lines to turn off and on in the wrong places. If this occurs, try redefining your boundary.

Step 1 – Remember to [**Tab**] to your Earth layer.

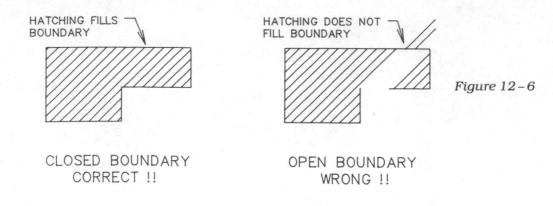

CLOSED BOUNDARY
CORRECT !!

OPEN BOUNDARY
WRONG !!

Figure 12–6

Step 2 – Press **H** to go to the HATCH menu, found in the UTILITY menu.

Step 3 – Pick the **Boundary** option, and draw the boundary as shown below in FIG. 12-7. Be sure to use object snap to make the boundary match the existing concrete lines. You may want to turn off Ortho mode by pressing the **O** key.

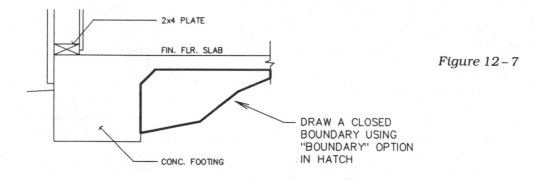

Figure 12–7

Step 4 – When the boundary is closed, press mouse button **3** to return to the main HATCH menu.

Step 5 – Pick the **ScrlFwrd** option (Scroll Forward) until the **Earth** option is displayed.

Step 6 – Pick **Earth**.

Step 7 – Now pick the **Scale** option, to adjust the size of the pattern.

Step 8 – The true size of the hatch pattern is approximately $1/32''$, as indicated in FIG. 12-8. You will want to scale it up, in order for it to look right in the drawing.

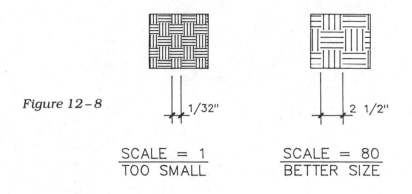

Figure 12-8

1/32"

2 1/2"

SCALE = 1
TOO SMALL

SCALE = 80
BETTER SIZE

Step 9 – The scale of your patterns will vary according to the plot scale. Hatch patterns are *descriptive*. Hatch patterns, however, do not rely on a particular formula for sizing. You will depend upon your own experimentation with the finished results for approximate scale sizes.

A 80 value for the scale size will result in an approximate pattern size of 2", which looks very nice in this detail. Type in **80** and press [**Enter**].

Caution: Always watch how your hatch comes in when you pick "**Begin**." If it comes in very small, as shown in FIG. 12-9, STOP THE HATCH IMMEDIATELY by pressing the [**Delete**] key.

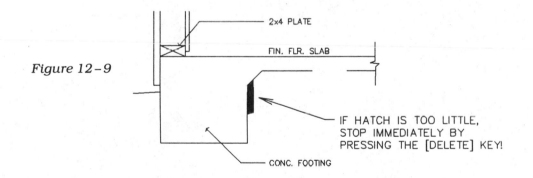

Figure 12-9

2x4 PLATE

FIN. FLR. SLAB

IF HATCH IS TOO LITTLE, STOP IMMEDIATELY BY PRESSING THE [DELETE] KEY!

CONC. FOOTING

If you allow the hatch to continue, it can add a very large amount of memory to your file. This problem usually occurs when there has been a mistake in the scale that you are using. Check the **Scale** option before picking **Begin** a second time!

Step 10 – Pick **Begin** to start the crosshatching process.

Step 11 – The boundary area will fill in with the earth texture pattern, as in FIG. 12-10.

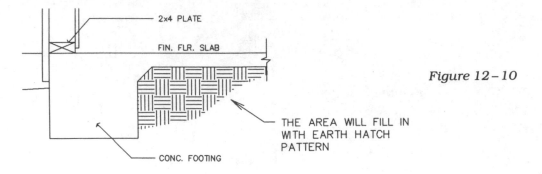

Figure 12 – 10

Step 12 – If there is an error in the crosshatching (because of the wrong scale or an overflow outside of the boundary), you will want to delete the hatch and start again.

If the pattern overflowed the boundary, or has "holes" in it as in FIG. 12-11, there is a gap somewhere in your boundary. This can occur if you use existing geometry as your boundary.

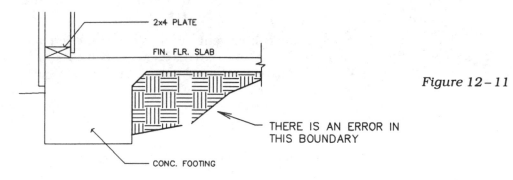

Figure 12 – 11

IF YOUR HATCH HAS AN ERROR -

Press [**Shift**] < to erase the last group.

-or-

Press the **E** to enter the ERASE menu.

Make sure the ***Group** option is active, then pick a line of the crosshatching. The hatching will disappear.

If necessary, fix the boundary or the scale, and try creating the crosshatching again.

Step 13 – If you used a temporary boundary to create your earth cross-hatching (you did not use the **Boundary** option in Hatch), you will want to delete it. Be sure to use the ERASE menu, ***Group**

option, in order to erase the boundary in one pick as a group, if possible. (See FIG. 12-12.)

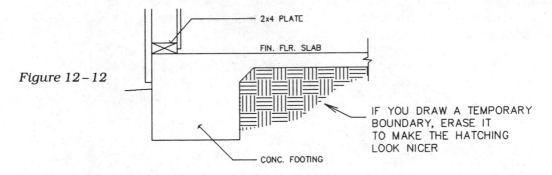

Figure 12–12

Step 14 – Continue making all of the hatching for your detail, as indicated in FIG. 12-13. You can use the wall outlines for the boundary of your "cement" hatch:

1. In the HATCH menu,
2. simply [**Tab**] to the Walls layer,
3. press the **K** key to change the color to **Dk Gray**,
4. turn off **LyrSrch**,
5. and use ***Area** to surround the walls.
6. The wall lines should become gray and dashed, indicating that they are selected for the hatch boundary.
7. Now adjust the **Scale** and the **Pattern**, then **Begin**.
8. Continue with this procedure to hatch the concrete foundation.

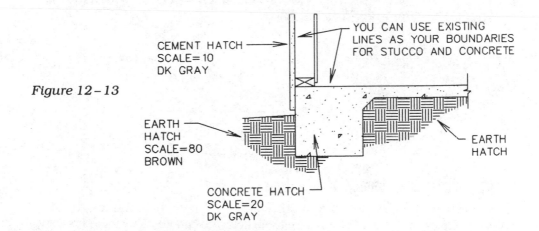

Figure 12–13

Creating the insulation

Now you are ready to create the insulation in your detail drawing. The insulation is created by using the Insul linetype.

A linetype is a *descriptive* item. You will need to adjust the size of your linetype. However, the exact size of insulation is more dependent on the size of your wall than on the final plot scale. You will probably want your insulation to fit inside the wall snugly. You will use the wall width as your sizing guide.

The size of a linetype is adjusted using the "spacing" option. The term "spacing" refers to the measurement from the start of the pattern, to the end of the pattern. This is illustrated in FIG. 12-14. Notice that one-half of the width of the insul linetype is equal to one pattern spacing.

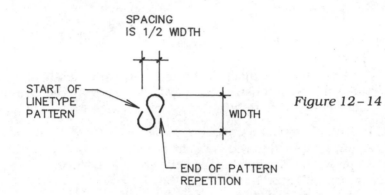

Figure 12–14

Finding the proper spacing for insulation

As shown in FIG. 12-14, the "insul" linetype spacing can be accurately adjusted by calculating the desired final width of the pattern, and dividing it by two. We know that the width of the wall, as indicated by the width of the sole plate, is 4 inches. (See FIG. 12-15.) This means you will define the spacing for your linetype as 2″.

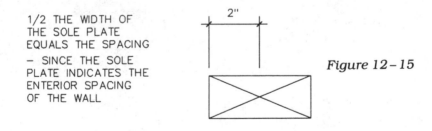

Figure 12–15

Measuring the length of a line

To double check the sole plate width, you can "measure" the length of a line in your drawing. (As you learned earlier, you also can use the **Identify** option.)

Step 1 – Press [**Alt**] **X** to quickly enter the MEASURES option from the UTILITY menu.

Step 2 – Select the **Line** option, to measure the length of a line.

Step 3 – Pick the top line of the plate, as indicated in FIG. 12-16.

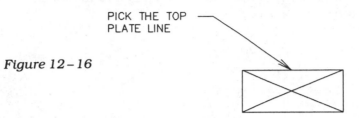

PICK THE TOP
PLATE LINE

Figure 12 – 16

Step 4 – What does the message say the length of the line is? Look at your message, as indicated in FIG. 12-17.

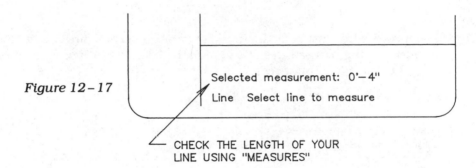

Figure 12 – 17

Selected measurement: 0'—4"

Line   Select line to measure

CHECK THE LENGTH OF YOUR
LINE USING "MEASURES"

Step 5 – If you originally created the line at 4″ (2 × 4 PLATE), then this line would now be 4″. If it is different than this, it might be you created the sole plate at it's real size of $3^1/_2$ × $1^1/_2$″. If you have a different size, make sure you write it down to use in the next steps.

Step 6 – Divide the size of your sole plate in half. If it is now 4″, then half of that would be 2″. If your sole plate is another size, then divide that in half, and use it in the next steps.

Setting up the linetype

Step 1 – Pick the **LineType** option, from the EDIT menu.

Step 2 – Pick the **Insul** linetype from the menu.

Step 3 – Pick the **Spacing** option.

Step 4 – Change the spacing to the appropriate value. If your plate was 4″, then you would enter **0.2**.

Step 5 – Make the ***MidPnt** option active in the OBJECT SNAP menu. Remember how to get into the OBJECT SNAP menu?

Step 6 – Object snap to the midpoint of the top line of the sole plate, as indicated in FIG. 12-18.

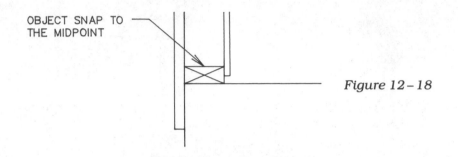

OBJECT SNAP TO
THE MIDPOINT

Figure 12 – 18

Step 7 – Draw the line, using Ortho mode to create a vertical line, as in FIG. 12-19, using mouse button **1** to pick the second point of your line. (If Ortho is NOT on, press **O** until it is.)

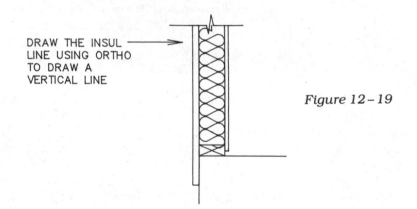

DRAW THE INSUL
LINE USING ORTHO
TO DRAW A
VERTICAL LINE

Figure 12 – 19

Preparing the detail for becoming a scaled symbol

To prepare the detail for adding it to the template as a symbol, you will make a copy of it and shrink the copy in size. Then the copy of the original detail will be scaled and ready to be made into a symbol.

The reason you will scale a copy of the detail instead of the original is so that you can retain the original for changes and additions that are easier to make in real size. Also, when you make a symbol, the items you make it from disappear into the template. Using a copy to use as a symbol, then, becomes a safe-guard from losing your original detail with all of it's layer information. (Symbols added to your drawing are now only one layer.)

Copying the detail

To prepare your detail for becoming a symbol, you will first copy it.

Step 1 – Press **C** to quickly go to the COPY menu, found in EDIT.

C

Step 2 – To use the copy function, all you have to do is pick "from" and "to" points. In other words, you are defining the new copy's location. This function works similar to **"Move,"** but it makes a copy at the same time.

Pick at the upper left corner of the detail box, as indicated in FIG. 12-20. This will be your "from" point.

OBJECT SNAP
HERE FOR YOUR
"FROM" POINT

Figure 12 – 20

Step 3 – Pick a point below the detail box, as indicated in FIG. 12-21. This will be your "to" point.

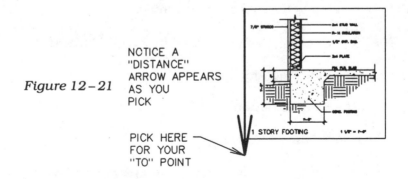

NOTICE A
"DISTANCE"
ARROW APPEARS
AS YOU
PICK

Figure 12 – 21

PICK HERE
FOR YOUR
"TO" POINT

Step 4 – Make sure ***Area and *LyrSrch** is active, then pick a box surrounding the entire detail box, as indicated in FIG. 12-22.

Step 5 – The copy is made! You may have to use the Window In key "/" and **Extends** to see both details. (See FIG. 12-23 on page 234.)

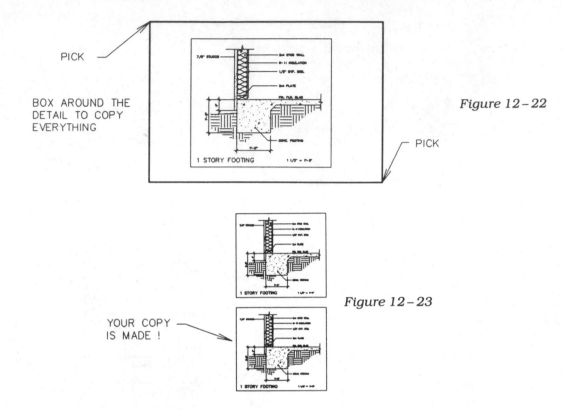

PICK

BOX AROUND THE
DETAIL TO COPY
EVERYTHING

Figure 12–22

PICK

Figure 12–23

YOUR COPY
IS MADE !

Exploding the dimensions

Before you scale the detail (reduce its actual size), you will explode the
dimensions. This will allow the dimensions to keep the original dimension
text, and not change to the new reduced dimensions.

Step 1 – Pick the **Dimension** option, found in the EDIT menu.

Step 2 – Pick the **Linear** option.

Step 3 – Pick the **Explode** option.

Step 4 – Make sure ***Area** is active.

Step 5 – You can [**Tab**] to the Dims layer, or use **Layer Search** to pick the
dimension entities.

Step 6 – Indicate two points to box in the entire drawing, as shown in FIG.
12-24. This will capture all dimensions. The prompt will be displayed "**3 items selected**." *If no entities were found*, then either
the Dims layer was not active, or Layer Search was not on.

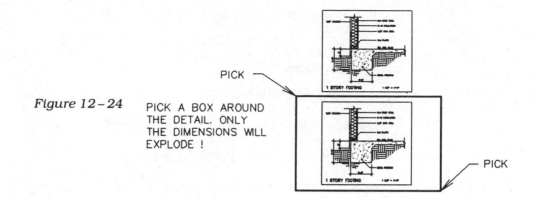

PICK

Figure 12–24 PICK A BOX AROUND
THE DETAIL. ONLY
THE DIMENSIONS WILL
EXPLODE !

PICK

Scaling the detail

Once you have created the detail drawing, and exploded the dimensions, you are ready to reduce it to the finished plotting scale. This new size will allow the detail to be added easily in many different detail sheets.

Step 1 – Pick the **Enlarge** option, found in the EDIT menu.

Step 2 – Pick anywhere around the center of your drawing for the "Center of Enlargement," shown in FIG. 12-25. This pick will indicate the "stationary point" of the detail (the point of the drawing that will not move when the enlargement or reduction is made).

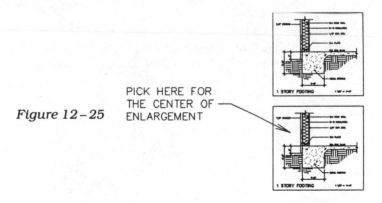

PICK HERE FOR
THE CENTER OF
ENLARGEMENT

Figure 12–25

Step 3 – Pick the **Enlrgmnt** option.

Step 4 – Pick **Set All** to set the enlargement factor so that the X, Y, and linetype shrink proportionately.

Step 5 – Referring to the scales formulas found in the DataCAD Scales &

Sizes section of appendix B, find the correct "Enlargement Factor" for a 1½" detail.

"Anticipated Plot Scale" = 1.½"
"Detail Enlargement Factor" = .125

Step 6 – Type in the Enlargement factor of **.125**

Step 7 – Press mouse button **3** to return to the ENLARGE menu.

Step 8 – Make sure the ***Area** option and ***LyrSrch** are active.

Step 9 – Pick two points to indicate a rectangle around the entire detail, including the detail box, as shown in FIG. 12-26.

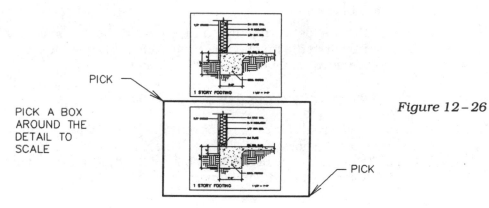

PICK →

PICK A BOX
AROUND THE
DETAIL TO
SCALE

Figure 12 – 26

PICK

Step 10 – The drawing will be reduced in size, as in FIG. 12-27. Now you have two details. One to keep as a real size detail for easy editing, and another one scaled and ready to make into a symbol!

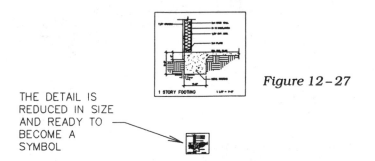

THE DETAIL IS
REDUCED IN SIZE
AND READY TO
BECOME A
SYMBOL

Figure 12 – 27

Step 11 – You may want to use the / key to **Recalc** your drawing window.

Step 12 – Press **[Shift] F** to save your drawing, or use the **File I/O, Save Dwg** option. Now you are ready to proceed to the next lesson.

Additional assignments

Included here are two more detail assignments for you to complete: Assignment 6 (FIG. 12-28) and Assignment 7 (FIG. 12-30). You may want to use the DET1-1-2 default to create them. However, notice that they are both 1″ = 1′-0″ scale. You will have to make just a few changes when you bring up your drawing file.

ASSIGNMENT #6

Figure 12-28

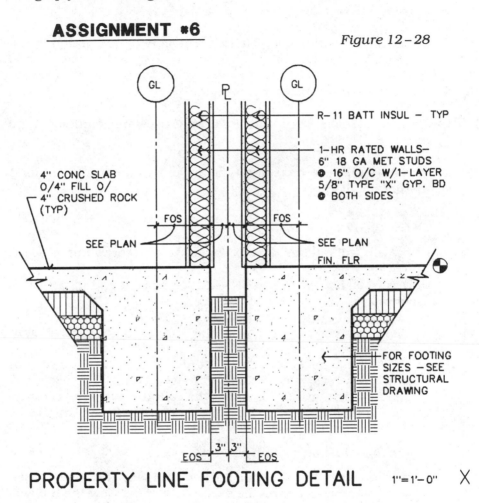

4" CONC SLAB O/4" FILL O/ 4" CRUSHED ROCK (TYP)

R-11 BATT INSUL – TYP

1-HR RATED WALLS– 6" 18 GA MET STUDS @ 16" O/C W/1-LAYER 5/8" TYPE "X" GYP. BD @ BOTH SIDES

FOS   FOS

SEE PLAN   SEE PLAN

FIN. FLR

FOR FOOTING SIZES – SEE STRUCTURAL DRAWING

3" 3"

EOS   EOS

PROPERTY LINE FOOTING DETAIL   1"=1'-0"   X

Step 1 – Return to your DataCAD drawing list, by either starting up Data-CAD, or if you are already in DataCAD, use **New Dwg**.

Step 2 – Pick **Default**.

Step 3 – Pick the **DET1-1-2** default (unless someone has made a DET-1 for you!).

Step 4 – Type in the name for your assignment: **Assig-6**. Press [**Enter**].

Step 5 – The first thing you will want to create is a new detail box. Because these details are larger, your box will be larger also.

Delete the existing box by using the **Erase, *Area, *LyrSrch** options.

Step 6 – [**Tab**] to the Box layer.

Step 7 – Press [**Alt**] **R** to quickly go to the **Rectangle** option, found in the POLYGON menu in EDIT.

Step 8 – Pick a start point for your rectangle.

Step 9 – Press the [**Insert**] key until Relative Cartesian Coordinates are set.

Step 10 – Press the [**Space bar**], and type in the real measurement for a larger detail box:

X = .10.3/4
Y = .10.1/2

Step 11 – Now you will Enlarge the box so that you can draw in real scale.

Step 12 – Press [**Alt**] **E** to go to the ENLARGE menu, found in the EDIT menu.

Step 13 – Pick in the center of the box for the centerpoint of enlargement.

Step 14 – Pick the **Enlargmnt** option, and **Set All**. Change the Enlargement factor to the size specified in the DataCAD Scales & Sizes section found in appendix B, under the column called the Descriptive Symbol Enlargement. The factor is **12**, which is the enlargement for 1″ = 1′-0″.

Type in **12** and press [Enter]

Step 15 – Press mouse button **3** to quit back to the ENLARGE menu, then use ***Area** to box around the entire detail box. Now the box will be enlarged to accommodate your 1″ details.

Note: This procedure is very helpful if you decide to create your own detail box size. Create the box in the correct scaled size, say 7″ × 10″, then enlarge it using the table shown on the DataCAD Scales & Sizes section found in appendix B. Now your detail box can be ready to draw in, in full size!

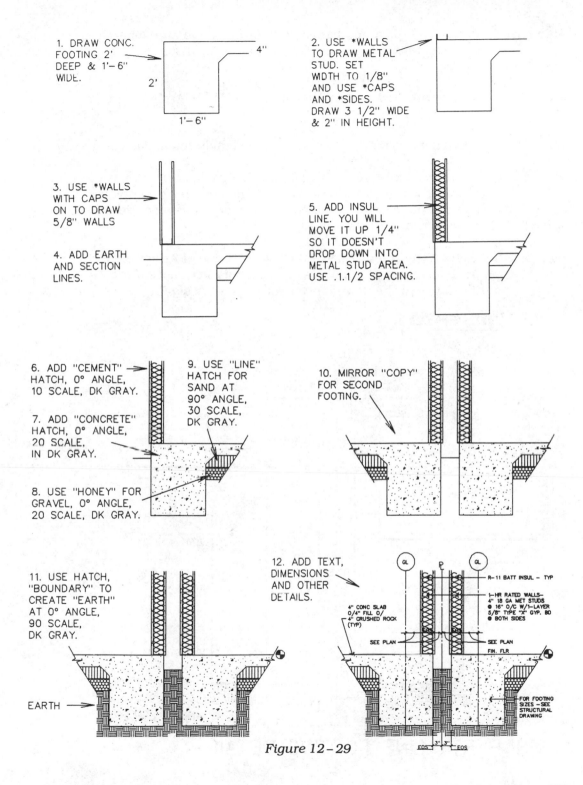

1. DRAW CONC. FOOTING 2' DEEP & 1'-6" WIDE.

4"

2'

1'-6"

2. USE *WALLS TO DRAW METAL STUD. SET WIDTH TO 1/8" AND USE *CAPS AND *SIDES. DRAW 3 1/2" WIDE & 2" IN HEIGHT.

3. USE *WALLS WITH CAPS ON TO DRAW 5/8" WALLS

4. ADD EARTH AND SECTION LINES.

5. ADD INSUL LINE. YOU WILL MOVE IT UP 1/4" SO IT DOESN'T DROP DOWN INTO METAL STUD AREA. USE .1.1/2 SPACING.

6. ADD "CEMENT" HATCH, 0° ANGLE, 10 SCALE, DK GRAY.

7. ADD "CONCRETE" HATCH, 0° ANGLE, 20 SCALE, IN DK GRAY.

8. USE "HONEY" FOR GRAVEL, 0° ANGLE, 20 SCALE, DK GRAY.

9. USE "LINE" HATCH FOR SAND AT 90° ANGLE, 30 SCALE, DK GRAY.

10. MIRROR "COPY" FOR SECOND FOOTING.

11. USE HATCH, "BOUNDARY" TO CREATE "EARTH" AT 0° ANGLE, 90 SCALE, DK GRAY.

EARTH

12. ADD TEXT, DIMENSIONS AND OTHER DETAILS.

R-11 BATT INSUL - TYP

1-HR RATED WALLS— 4" 18 GA MET STUDS @ 16" O/C W/1-LAYER 5/8" TYPE "X" GYP. BD @ BOTH SIDES

4" CONC SLAB O/4" FILL O/ 4" CRUSHED ROCK (TYP)

SEE PLAN

SEE PLAN

FIN. FLR

FOR FOOTING SIZES —SEE STRUCTURAL DRAWING

EOS

3" 3"

EOS

Figure 12-29

Step 16 – Use this same page to change your Dimensions and Text variables to the values for 1″ scale. A ¹/₈″ value, for instance, is 1¹/₂″ in a 1″ scale.

Step 17 – Now you can draw your first additional detail Assignment 6, shown in FIG. 12-28.

Step 18 – The instructions for drawing this detail is included in FIG. 12-29.

Step 19 – Remember to follow the appropriate steps to "Prepare your detail for becoming a scaled symbol." When you have completed this detail, there should be a copy of the detail as a scaled version in the same file!

Step 20 – To create Assignment 7 (FIG. 12-30), save a copy of Assignment 6 under a new name. To do this, use the **File I/O** menu, **Save As** option. Type in the new name of your detail: **Assig-7**.

ASSIGNMENT #7

Figure 12–30

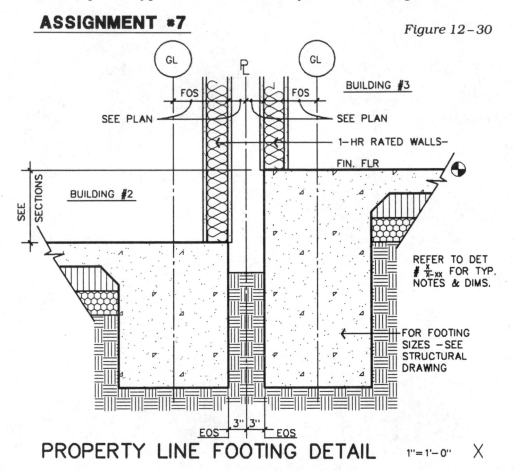

PROPERTY LINE FOOTING DETAIL   1″= 1′–0″   X

Step 21 – Once the copy has been saved, use the **New Dwg** option to save the first assignment and pull up the second assignment, Assig-7, to modify it.

Step 22 – The instructions on changing the details are shown in FIG. 12-31.

DataCAD exercise 12

Please complete the following exercise by reading each question carefully, then circling the letter that corresponds to the correct answer.

1. When you are creating a drawing, you should make it a practice to "save" the drawing using **File I/O**, every:

   a. Day.
   b. Time you quit DataCAD.
   c. At least every hour, or before a major change in your drawing, such as adding hatching.

2. Before creating the hatching pattern in your drawing, you must:

   a. Create an open or closed boundary.
   b. Create a closed boundary.
   c. Delete any existing boundaries.

3. If your hatch boundary is open:

   a. Your hatch pattern may flow out of the "fence."
   b. Your hatching will turn out okay anyway.
   c. The system will prompt you to close it.

4. If you wish to delete the hatch pattern, you should use the:

   a. **Erase, *Entity** option.
   b. **Erase, *Group** option.
   c. [,] key.

5. Hatch patterns reduce:

   a. Differently than the rest of your entities, and so should be created after you scale the detail.
   b. At a 1/2 scale than the rest of your drawing. You must use a special formula when scaling them.
   c. Perfectly with your drawing, and can be added before you scale it.

6. To reduce your detail, you use the:

   a. ENLARGE menu.
   b. SCALE menu.
   c. REDUCE menu.

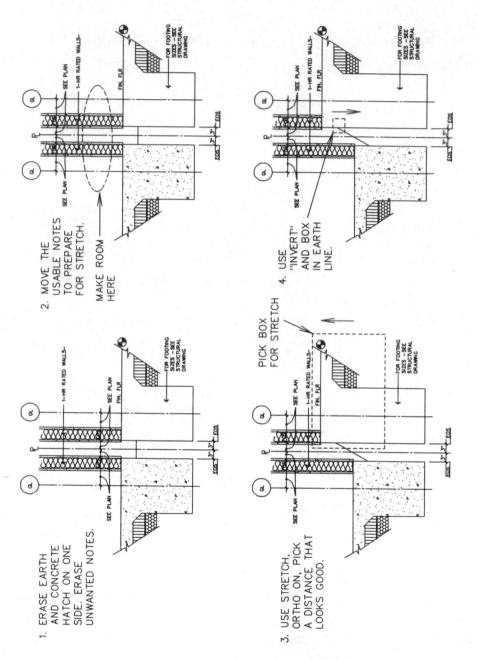

1. ERASE EARTH AND CONCRETE HATCH ON ONE SIDE. ERASE UNWANTED NOTES.

2. MOVE THE USABLE NOTES TO PREPARE FOR STRETCH.

3. USE STRETCH, ORTHO ON, PICK A DISTANCE THAT LOOKS GOOD.

4. USE "INVERT" AND BOX IN EARTH LINE.

5. FINISH BY ADDING EARTH HATCH BACK IN, AND BY ADDING THE ADDITIONAL NOTES.

Figure 12–31

242   Lesson 12

7. Linetypes:
    a. Should be added after you scale your detail, because their size is determined by "spacing."
    b. Reduce perfectly, and can be added before you scale your detail.
    c. Must be exploded before reducing.

8. Associated dimensions should always be:
    a. Created after you scale your detail.
    b. Exploded before reducing the size of your detail. Otherwise, dimensions will change to the new line sizes.
    c. Reduced along with the rest of your detail, without having to explode them.

9. When you explode dimensions by area, you can:
    a. Indicate an area around your whole drawing. It will only explode dimensions.
    b. Only indicate an area around the dimensions. You must be careful so you do not explode the objects in your drawing.

10. To find the length of a line, you use the:
    a. LENGTH menu.
    b. MEASURES menu.
    c. DISTANCE menu.

Lesson 13
Creating
templates and symbols

What you will be doing

You will create a new template, and define symbols to add to that template. You will also add report information to the template and symbol, then extract a report and add it to your drawing.

Objectives

Your lesson objectives are to:

- Create a template.
- Add a record field to the template report.
- Add your detail to the template as a symbol.
- Give the symbol an "item name," and other information for your report.
- Add the new symbol to your drawing.
- Extract a sample report and add it to your drawing.
- Modify a report field.

Remember to refer to *The DataCAD Operations Guide*.

Templates and symbols

You have already used templates and symbols in the earlier lesson Adding symbols. In this lesson, you will learn the steps to create your own templates, and how to make symbols out of items in your drawings to add to your template.

To create symbols, you have to:

1. Create the drawing that contains your symbols, and have the drawing displayed on the screen.
2. Create your new template. (Or call up an existing template you will be using.)
3. Add your symbols to the template.

You will create a template called FOOTINGS (Footing Details). This template will hold your footing details. See FIG. 13-1.

YOUR SYMBOLS →
ADDED TO YOUR
FOOTING TEMPLATE

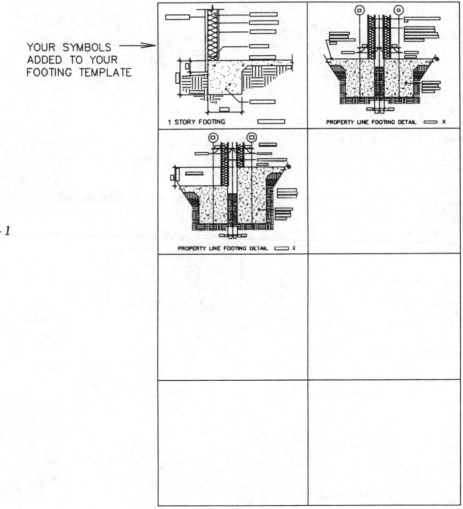

Figure 13–1

Template directory

When you create your template (which in essence is a series of boxes that will later hold your symbols), you will put it in your TEMPLATE directory, called TPL. This directory resides in the MTEC directory, so it is a "subdirectory" of MTEC, (a folder in your MTEC drawer) as indicated in FIG. 13-2.

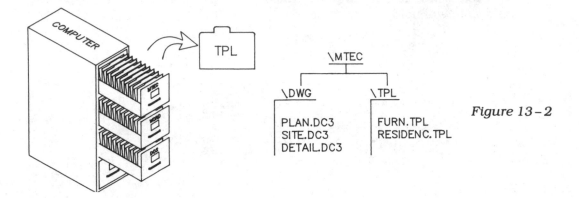

Figure 13-2

Step 1 – Make sure the footing detail drawing you created in the previous lesson is displayed on your screen. This is the detail you will be adding as a symbol to your template. (FIG. 13-3.)

Use the Window key [/] to zoom into the scaled detail.

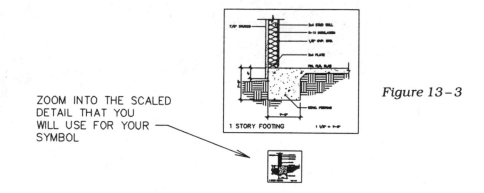

ZOOM INTO THE SCALED DETAIL THAT YOU WILL USE FOR YOUR SYMBOL

Figure 13-3

Creating a new template

Step 1 – Press **T** to enter the TEMPLATE menu.

Step 2 – Pick the **New Path** option.

Step 3 – Check that your directory pathname is set to: \ **mtec** \ **tpl** \ . If this directory path is already set, simply press [**Enter**] to continue. If it isn't set to this path, then type in: **TPL** (and press [**Enter**]). Or, if you wish, you can simply pick the path options from the menu.

(This will automatically change your directory to \ MTEC \ tpl.)

Step 4 – If you had to type the directory path in, and if this is a new directory, pick **Yes** to create it.

Step 5 – The user message prompts you to: **"Enter file name:"** for your template. Type in and [**Enter**] the name for your new template.

FOOTINGS

Step 6 – Because this is a new template, the message will say: **"file 'c: \ mtec \ tpl \ footings.tpl' does not exist. Create new file?"** Pick **Yes** to create it.

Template fields

Now you will be prompted to add any additional fields to the template form. "Fields" refer directly to the information areas in the schedules that you are able to attain for the symbols in your drawing. Fields 1 through 6 are already defined. They are:

1. Item name
2. Manufacturer
3. Model number
4. Remark 1
5. Remark 2
6. Cost

An example of a report containing these fields is illustrated in FIG. 13-4.

You will probably not use any kind of report for details, especially since you will explode the details when you bring them into your detail

```
Title
Item Name   Manufact   Model No    Remark 1    Remark 2    Qty.  Unit Cost   Total Cost
-----------------------------------------------------------------------------------------
Recliner  | La-Z-Boy| L385-12  | Stock    | Leather |   1|   995.00|     995.00
Sofa      | Stylus  | STY336-2| Custom   | Fab./Oak|   2|  1595.00|    3190.00
Coffee Ta| Stylus  | STY184-3| Custom   | Oak/Glas|   2|   295.00|     590.00
Tub/Showe| Am.Std. | 2146.223| Stock    | Fbrgls  |   1|   790.00|     790.00
W/C       | Am.Std. | 2109.405| Stock    | China   |   1|   140.00|     140.00
Lavatory | Am.Std. | 0470.039| Stock    | China   |   1|   187.00|     187.00
Oven/Rnge| GE      | JB600GH | Stock    | Electric|   1|   799.00|     799.00
Dbl.Sink | Am.Std. | 7018.012| Stock    | Cst.Iron|   1|   499.00|     499.00
Refrig.  | GE      | TA7SG   | Stock    | 6.6 c.f.|   1|   259.00|     259.00
-----------------------------------------------------------------------------------------
                              TOTAL ITEMS:     11
                                         TOTAL COST:      7449.00
                                          Tax (4%):        297.96
                                       GRAND TOTAL:       7746.96
```

Figure 13–4

sheet. However, you will want to use reports for door schedule symbols, electrical symbols (outlets, switches, etc.) and other symbols that you might want to pull quantity and costs estimates from.

The following steps 7 through 9, are just for your practice. These are steps that would come in handy if you designed your own reports.

Step 7 – To practice creating your own field, you will add one called "Steel Square Inch." Type in **Steel Square Inch** for "Field 7 Field name." Press [**Enter**].

Step 8 – Pick the **Number** option to define the field type.

Step 9 – Press mouse button **3** to quit defining fields.

Step 10 – Your new template will appear, as shown in FIG. 13-5.

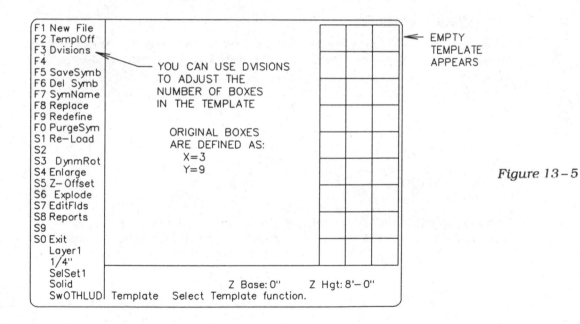

Figure 13–5

Adjusting the number of template boxes

You can easily define the number of boxes that appear in the template by adjusting the X number of boxes (columns across the X direction), and the Y number of boxes (rows in the Y direction).

Step 1 – Pick the **Dvisions** option, as shown in FIG. 13-5.

Step 2 – Type in the number **2** for the X division, and press [**Enter**].

Step 3 – Type in the number **5** for the Y division, and press [**Enter**].

Step 4 – Ten boxes will now be displayed.

Symbols and the symbol directories

Just like templates, symbols reside in a special directory. This helps keep your symbols properly organized. This is very important, because the template file needs to know where the symbols are. This is done by directories and pathnames. The main directory for all of your symbols is called SYM. (FIG. 13-6.)

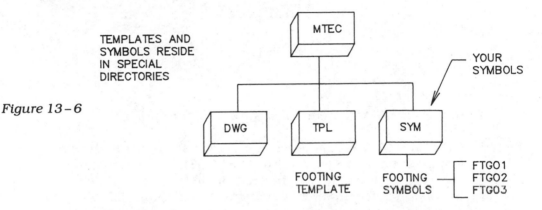

TEMPLATES AND
SYMBOLS RESIDE
IN SPECIAL
DIRECTORIES

YOUR
SYMBOLS

Figure 13 – 6

Your symbols are further organized under the SYM directory, into their own specific directory for the template they are attached to. This second "subdirectory" *must match the template name!* This organization is very important in the correct operation of your DataCAD template and symbols. (See FIG. 13-7.)

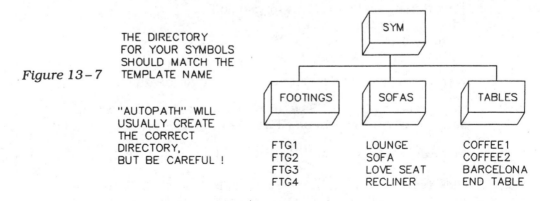

THE DIRECTORY
FOR YOUR SYMBOLS
SHOULD MATCH THE
TEMPLATE NAME

Figure 13 – 7

"AUTOPATH" WILL
USUALLY CREATE
THE CORRECT
DIRECTORY,
BUT BE CAREFUL !

The creation of the correct directories for your symbols is done automatically for you, using **Autopath** option!

Adding a symbol to your new template

Step 1 – The template you will be adding the symbol to must be displayed on your screen, as in FIG. 13-8.

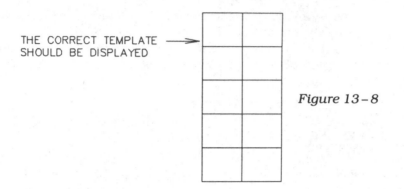

THE CORRECT TEMPLATE ⟶
SHOULD BE DISPLAYED

Figure 13 – 8

Step 2 – In the TEMPLATE menu, pick the **SaveSymb** option.

Step 3 – Make sure ***AutoPath** is active. When you use AutoPath, the directory path for your symbols are SUPPOSED to be automatically adjusted for you. The subdirectory in SYM should match your template name. However, sometimes this feature doesn't work correctly. You should always check the displayed path at the user message of your screen. Right now, it should read: Symbol files will be saved to **SYM \ FOOTINGS ** .

Step 4 – If the path displayed in the message is NOT correct, follow these steps:

1. Pick the **AutoPath** until it is turned OFF.
2. Pick the **NewPath** option.
3. Type in: **sym \ footings** (and press [**Enter**]).
4. If this is a new pathname, pick **Yes**.

Now the path will be corrected, but leave AutoPath OFF.

Step 5 – You are prompted to "**Save to which symbol file:**". Type in the name of your new symbol: **FTG1** (Footing 1).

Step 6 – Make sure the ***Area** and ***LyrSrch** options are active.

Step 7 – Pick two points to indicate a rectangle around the entire scaled detail, EXCLUDING THE DETAIL BOX, as indicated in FIG. 13-9.

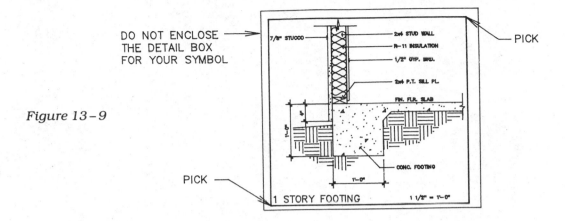

DO NOT ENCLOSE
THE DETAIL BOX
FOR YOUR SYMBOL

7/8" STUCCO

2x4 STUD WALL

R-11 INSULATION

1/2" GYP. BRD.

2x4 P.T. SILL PL.

FIN. FLR. SLAB

CONC. FOOTING

1'-0"

PICK

1 STORY FOOTING   1 1/2" = 1'-0"

PICK

Figure 13–9

Step 8 – Your detail will become dashed. Make a visual check that all pieces of your detail are included, and that the detail box is NOT included. FIG. 13-10 illustrates this.

THE ENTIRE SYMBOL
WILL BECOME GRAY
AND DASHED, EXCEPT
FOR THE DETAIL BOX

Figure 13–10

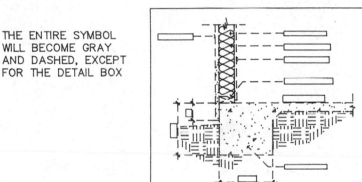

Step 9 – If everything is correct, continue to the next step. If parts of your detail DID NOT become gray and dashed, you must press mouse button **3** and start over.

Step 10 – Now you will be prompted to **"Enter reference point for your symbol."** Object snap to the lower left hand corner of your detail box, as in FIG. 13-11 on page 252. This will be the point you will use to place your symbol whenever you use it in your detail sheets.

Step 11 – Your symbol is added to the new template. (FIG. 13-12 on page 252.)

Step 12 – Now you are prompted to enter the item name for the symbol. This is the name that will appear when you hold your cursor on

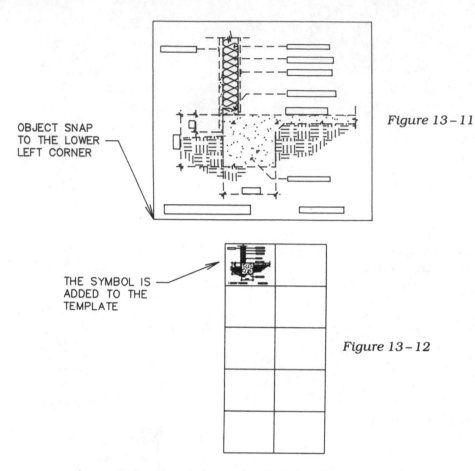

OBJECT SNAP
TO THE LOWER
LEFT CORNER

Figure 13 – 11

THE SYMBOL IS
ADDED TO THE
TEMPLATE

Figure 13 – 12

the template box where the detail is. Type in: **1 Story Footing** (and press [**Enter**]).

Adding report information

Although it was mentioned earlier that you will not want to use reports for your details, you will want to know the steps to enter report information for when you do need a report. Just for your practice, then, the following steps walk you through the report procedure. Try these steps just for the fun of it!

Step 13 – The first field was "item name." The next field is Manufacturer. For an example, you can type in **Conc Ctr** for Concrete Contractor. You are limited to 8 characters for this field.

Step 14 – Now the field is Model number. Type in: **N/A**, because footings typically do not have a model number.

Step 15 – For Remark 1, type in: **1 #4 T&B** for 1 number 4 reinforcing bar at the top and bottom. Again, you are limited to 8 characters for this field.

Step 16 – For Remark **2**, type in: **2000 PSI** for concrete strength. There is an 8 character limit.

Step 17 – The next field is Cost. Type in **200**. This field will only allow you to add numbers (no text), and will also display total costs. You may want to put your own, more accurate cost estimate here.

Step 18 – The last field is the new one you added: Steel Square Inch. Type in **.40**. Again, this field is limited to numbers.

Step 19 – Now you are prompted to save the next symbol. Notice that the name is automatically changed to ftg2. At this point, you would save your second detail if you had one, following the same procedure.

Step 20 – Press mouse button **3** to quit, because you are through making a symbol out of your detail.

Step 21 – Notice that when you move your cursor to the template box that contains your new symbol, the coordinate readout now says: **1 Story Footing**. This is the "Item name" you gave your symbol. If you do not use reports, you would still want to give your symbol an item name. This way, you can always tell what the symbol is by placing your cursor on the template box! (FIG. 13-13 on page 254.)

Referring to the DataCAD Operations Guide

You will want to turn to the Templates and symbols section of appendix A, the *DataCAD Operations Guide.*

This section guides you through the creation of templates and adding symbols to the templates, in easy-to-read steps. It also provides you with the steps you would follow to change a symbol in a template, replacing symbols on your drawing with new symbols, and other important operations.

Retrieving reports

You may want to see what your report looks like. You must add some symbols to your drawing before you can run a report.

Step 1 – In the TEMPLATE menu, make sure that the **Explode** option IS

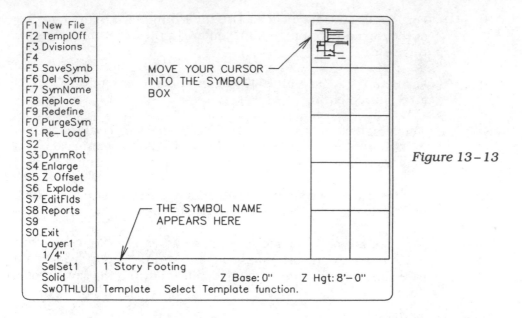

```
F1 New File
F2 TemplOff
F3 Dvisions
F4
F5 SaveSymb
F6 Del Symb          MOVE YOUR CURSOR
F7 SymName           INTO THE SYMBOL
F8 Replace           BOX
F9 Redefine
F0 PurgeSym
S1 Re-Load
S2
S3 DynmRot
S4 Enlarge
S5 Z Offset
S6 Explode
S7 EditFlds
S8 Reports
S9                   THE SYMBOL NAME
S0 Exit              APPEARS HERE
   Layer1
   1/4"
   SelSet1    1 Story Footing
   Solid                    Z Base: 0"      Z Hgt: 8'-0"
   SwOTHLUD  Template   Select Template function.
```

Figure 13-13

NOT active. If it is, your symbols will come in without any report information!

Step 2 – Pick the template box that contains your new footing detail symbol, and then pick 2 or 3 places on your drawing to add this detail symbol, as in FIG. 13-14.

Figure 13-14

Step 3 – Once a few symbols have been added, pick the **Reports** option.

Step 4 – The available reports should be listed. (FIG. 13-15.)

Step 5 – If the reports are not listed, you will have to change the pathname. This is done by selecting **New Path**, then typing in **FRM** and [**Enter**].

(This changes the pathname to \ **mtec** \ **frm**.)

```
AVAILABLE  ──────────▶      F1 DCADCOST
REPORTS                     F2 DCADLIST
ARE  LISTED                 F3 DCADQTY
                            F4 ELECLS
                            F5 ELECSKD
                            F6
        Figure 13-15        F7
                            F8
                            F9
```

Step 6 – Once your report forms are listed, you may pick one. Pick the report called **DCADCOST**.

Step 7 – The report will be displayed on your screen. Notice how each of your inputs appear in the correct box. Notice also that the item name: 1 Story Footing, does not fit in the Item Name box. Count the number of characters that did fit. You will find that this area is probably limited to 9 characters. (FIG. 13-16.)

```
Title
Item Name  Manufact  Model No  Remark 1  Remark 2   Qty. Unit Cost  Total Cost
--------------------------------------------------------------------------------
1Story Fo| Concrete|  N/A    | 1 #4 T&B| 2000 PSI|   3|  200.00|    600.00
--------------------------------------------------------------------------------
                                       TOTAL ITEMS:   3
                                               TOTAL COST:     600.00
                                                  Tax (4%):     24.00
                                             GRAND TOTAL:      624.00

       └── NOTICE THE FULL ITEM NAME DID
           NOT FIT
```

Figure 13-16

Step 8 – Press the [**Space bar**] to continue.

Step 9 – Now you are given options for the destination of the report. Pick the **ToDrwing** option.

Step 10 – Drag the cursor out on your screen. Notice that the cursor has changed to represent the text size of your report, as in FIG. 13-17 on page 256. You may want to pick the **Size** option to make the text bigger or smaller.

Step 11 – Once the text Size is adjusted to what you desire, pick a place for your report on your drawing. Keep in mind that your pick will indicate the upper left-hand corner of the report, as in FIG. 13-18 on page 256. The report will be added to your drawing.

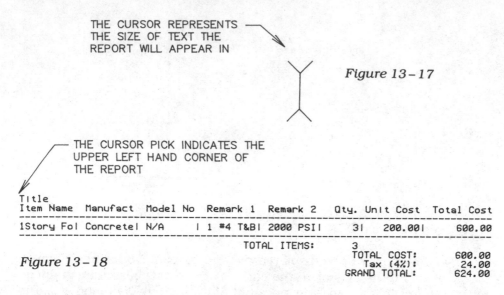

THE CURSOR REPRESENTS
THE SIZE OF TEXT THE
REPORT WILL APPEAR IN

Figure 13-17

THE CURSOR PICK INDICATES THE
UPPER LEFT HAND CORNER OF
THE REPORT

```
Title
Item Name  Manufact  Model No   Remark 1   Remark 2    Qty. Unit Cost  Total Cost
------------------------------------------------------------------------------
1Story Fo| Concrete| N/A      | 1 #4 T&B| 2000 PSI|    3|   200.00|     600.00
------------------------------------------------------------------------------
                                 TOTAL ITEMS:    3
                                                 TOTAL COST:    600.00
                                                    Tax (4%):    24.00
                                                 GRAND TOTAL:   624.00
```

Figure 13-18

Step 12 – Press the mouse button **3** to quit back to the TEMPLATE menu.

Correcting report information

It is an easy task to correct the field information in your report. You will want to change the text in the "Item name" field so that it will fit in 8 character spaces. If you will not be using reports, you do not have to change the item name. You would keep it as "1 Story Footing." For practice, however, you will modify it.

Step 1 – Pick the **EditFlds** option from the TEMPLATE menu.

Step 2 – Pick the template box that contains the footing detail, as in FIG. 13-19.

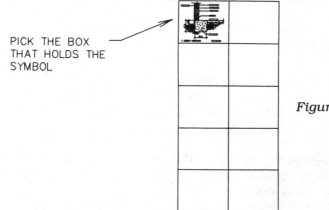

PICK THE BOX
THAT HOLDS THE
SYMBOL

Figure 13-19

Step 3 – Pick the **ItemName** option.

Step 4 – Type in and [**Enter**] a shortened name for your detail: **1 St Ftg**. This name is 8 characters long (spaces included).

Step 5 – Press mouse button **3** to quit back to the TEMPLATE menu.

Step 6 – Pick the **Reports** option. You can add the same report, or try another type of report for your drawing, if there is one. Notice that the Item Name is corrected. (FIG. 13-20.)

```
Title
Item Name  Manufact  Model No  Remark 1  Remark 2   Qty. Unit Cost  Total Cost
--------------------------------------------------------------------------------
1 St Ftg | Concrete| N/A     | 1 #4 T&B| 2000 PSI|   3|   200.00|     600.00
--------------------------------------------------------------------------------
                                    TOTAL ITEMS:     3
                                                      TOTAL COST:      600.00
                                                         Tax (4%):      24.00
                                                      GRAND TOTAL:     624.00
```

Figure 13 – 20

Exploding existing symbols

Sometimes you may add a symbol to your drawing that you later wish to explode. Exploding a symbol allows you to change the entities, such as deleting something, changing the color, or editing the text. DataCAD has provided a way to do this by giving you a macro called SYMEXP (Symbol Explode). You can try using this macro by exploding some of your detail symbols you have added to your drawing!

IMPORTANT After you explode a symbol, you can no longer extract report information, and you will not be able to work on the symbol using the "Replace" or "Redefine" options (see appendix A: *The Data-CAD Operations Guide*, Templates and Symbols). However, you really would want a detail symbol exploded anyway, in order to make changes to it.

Step 1 – Press [**Shift**] **M** (capital M) to quickly enter the MACROS menu, found in the EDIT menu.

Step 2 – The list of macros will be displayed, as in FIG. 13-21 on page 258.

Step 3 – Pick the macro called **SYMEXP**. If you have purchased more macros than have been supplied with DataCAD, and there is more than 1 page of macros listed, you may not see the SYMEXP on the first page. To get to the second page of listings, pick **SrlFrwd**. Once you find **SYMEXP**, pick it.

Step 4 – The SYMEXP menu will be displayed, as in FIG. 13-22. This is a

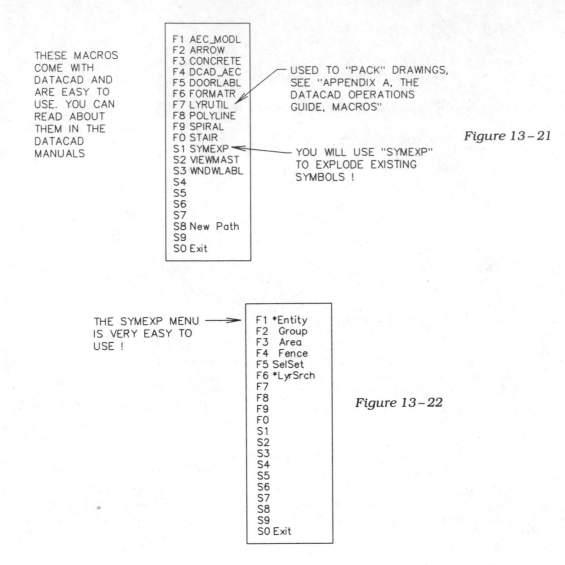

THESE MACROS
COME WITH
DATACAD AND
ARE EASY TO
USE. YOU CAN
READ ABOUT
THEM IN THE
DATACAD
MANUALS

F1 AEC_MODL
F2 ARROW
F3 CONCRETE
F4 DCAD_AEC
F5 DOORLABL
F6 FORMATR
F7 LYRUTIL
F8 POLYLINE
F9 SPIRAL
F0 STAIR
S1 SYMEXP
S2 VIEWMAST
S3 WNDWLABL
S4
S5
S6
S7
S8 New Path
S9
S0 Exit

USED TO "PACK" DRAWINGS,
SEE "APPENDIX A, THE
DATACAD OPERATIONS
GUIDE, MACROS"

Figure 13-21

YOU WILL USE "SYMEXP"
TO EXPLODE EXISTING
SYMBOLS !

THE SYMEXP MENU
IS VERY EASY TO
USE !

F1 *Entity
F2 Group
F3 Area
F4 Fence
F5 SelSet
F6 *LyrSrch
F7
F8
F9
F0
S1
S2
S3
S4
S5
S6
S7
S8
S9
S0 Exit

Figure 13-22

simple menu that allows you to pick a symbol to explode, and that's all there is to it.

Step 5 – Using the ***Entity** option, pick one of your detail symbols. It will blink, and will be exploded back into its original entities. You can test this by trying to erase part of it.

Step 6 – To exit a macro, you can either press mouse button **3** to quit out, or press a fast key, such as **E** to erase. The fast keys will exit you out of macros!

Leaving this drawing

Now you will want to exit this drawing file and retrieve the next detail to make into a symbol. But you have made such a mess out of this file, you certainly will not want to save any of these changes. Remember, then, to **Abort** detail files once you have made symbols out of them.

To get your next drawing and to Abort your current drawing changes, you can use the FILE I/O menu, **New Dwg** option. Aborting will not affect your new detail template symbol, as symbols are saved as soon as they are added to the template. And it will not affect your detail, because you have already saved this file!

Step 1 – Press [**Alt**] **N** to quickly go to the **New Dwg** option found in the FILE I/O menu.

Step 2 – Pick the **Abort** option.

Step 3 – You will be prompted "**Are you sure?** (Current changes will NOT be saved!) Pick **Yes**, or type in **Y**.

Additional assignments

Now you can add your detail assignments 6 and 7 to your Footings template.

Step 1 – Follow the steps in this lesson, applying them to your two assignment details: ASSIG-6 and ASSIG-7.

Step 2 – Make sure you check the symbol path before adding the new detail symbols!

Step 3 – You can skip the steps mentioned to create report information.

Step 4 – Make sure you end each session by Aborting the file changes.

DataCAD exercise 13

Please complete the following exercise by reading each question carefully, then circling the letter that corresponds to the correct answer.

1. A "template" is a:
   a. Series of boxes that will hold your symbols.
   b. Special directory for your forms.
   c. Report form.

2. When you make a template, you:
   a. Shouldn't put it in any special directory.
   b. Should put it in the TPL directory by defining a pathname.
   c. Should put it in the SYM directory by using the **AutoPath** option.

3. When you make a symbol, you:

   a. Should put it in the TPL directory by defining a pathname.
   b. Should put it in the SYM directory by using the **AutoPath** option.
   c. Don't have to worry about directories at all.

4. When using the **AutoPath** option, you:

   a. Should check that the symbol path is correct before saving your symbols.
   b. Don't have to worry – **AutoPath** will always give you the correct path.
   c. Shouldn't pay attention to the pathname. It doesn't make a difference where your symbols go.

5. When you create a symbol that is on more than one layer, you should make sure:

   a. **LyrSnap** is active in the OBJECT SNAP menu.
   b. All but one layer is turned off.
   c. **LyrSrch** is active in the SAVESYMB menu.

6. If you enter the TEMPLATE menu to pick a new template file, do not have a template active, and no template names are displayed in the menu area, you should:

   a. Call someone for help before you do anything.
   b. Check the current pathname, by picking **New Path**.
   c. Do nothing. All of your templates are deleted.

7. When you have a template active, and wish to get another template, you use the:

   a. **New File** option in the TEMPLATE menu.
   b. **New Template** option in the TEMPLATE menu.
   c. TEMPLATE menu. The template names are automatically displayed.

8. Template fields are:

   a. Information areas for reports that you are able to attain from the symbols in your drawing.
   b. An area in your drawing used in landscaping.
   c. Information that cannot be added to your drawing.

9. You can output the report in 3 ways. They are:

   a. To drawing, to plotter, and to printer.
   b. To drawing, to file, and to printer.
   c. To file, to printer, and to plotter.

10. In order to create a name for your symbol that can be read when you move your cursor to the symbol box in the Template, you:
    a. Define an "item name" for your symbol after adding it to the template. This name can be changed later if you wish.
    b. Have to give the symbol a name that you want before adding it to template. This name cannot be modified.
    c. Define an "item name" for your symbol after adding it to the template. This name cannot be changed once you define it.

11. To reduce your detail, you use the:
    a. ENLARGE menu.
    b. SCALE menu.
    c. REDUCE menu.

12. Linetypes:
    a. Should be added after you scale your detail, because their size is determined by "spacing."
    b. Reduce perfectly, and can be added before you scale your detail.
    c. Must be exploded before reducing.

13. Associated dimensions always should be:
    a. Created after you scale your detail.
    b. Exploded before reducing the size of your detail. Otherwise, the dimensions will change to the new line sizes.
    c. Reduced along with the rest of your detail, without having to explode them.

14. If you want to save a 3-D view with hidden lines removed, you must:
    a. Remove the lines, then pick the **SavImage** option.
    b. Remove the lines, then pick the **SaveView** option.
    c. Pick the **SavImage** option first, then remove the lines.

15. To display the plan view of your drawing after creating a 3-D view, you use the:
    a. **PlanView** option.
    b. **Ortho** option.
    c. Mouse button **3**. The plan view is automatically displayed.

16. To have text that is plotted at $1/8$ inch when you are plotting at a $1/4$ inch scale, you have to create the text at the size of
    a. $1/8$ inch.
    b. 1 foot.
    c. 6 inches.

Lesson 14
Creating
your default drawings

What you will be doing

You will create your standard default drawings during this lesson. Earlier, you developed basic default drawings. During this lesson, you will learn about the other common settings that can be predetermined and standardized for your daily use. The first steps presented during this lesson are the most common settings used for a 1:40 SITE plan.

During this lesson, you should begin to incorporate the standards for your own office, customizing the drawing variables for the most efficient use.

Objectives

Your lesson objectives are to:

- Preplan your default drawing.
- Create and attribute the layers for your drawings.
- Define the scale type, angle type, and other Settings values.
- Adjust the dimension standards.
- Set the text size.
- Set the display options.
- Adjust the Grid and snap values.
- Define the linetype spacing.
- Set typical **Object Snap** options.
- Preset common options in other menus (Polygon/rectangle, Walls/width/side, Z-base/Z-height, etc.)
- Create Borderline work and title block.
- Adjust the plotter settings.

Remember to refer to *The DataCAD Operations Guide* when instructed.

Default drawings

Default drawings save you steps, increase through-put, and help to eliminate errors. They also help to establish consistent standards in all of your CADD drawings!

This means increased productivity for your company. In fact, well planned default drawings can save you over 100 steps in creating a drawing.

Default drawings are simply drawing files that have certain switches and settings predefined in them for ease of use. You have learned the use of Default drawings in your previous lessons, and have created some basic ones.

A typical, well planned default drawing can contain the following:

1. Plotting settings, such as Scale, Paper size, and Pens.
2. **Scale Type, Angle Type,** and other options found in the Settings menu predetermined.
3. Dimension standards set.
4. Text font and size defined.
5. Layers named and attributed.
6. Display options set.
7. Grids and Grid Snap defined.
8. Linetype spacing set.
9. Object Snap settings activated.
10. Other typical defaults set in each menu, such as:
    Polygon/Rectangle
    Walls/Width/Side or Center
    Z-Base and Height
11. Borderline work
12. Title block, if not brought in as a symbol.

As you already know, default drawings reside in the MTEC\ DEFAULT directory. Before you create a new drawing, you pick a Default Drawing, which will serve as a base, or foundation for your new drawing.

How many default drawings do you need?

You will need at least one *default drawing for every different scale* you will be plotting in (e.g., 1/4" = 1', 1/8" = 1'), and for *different layer naming schemes*. The idea of a default drawing is to save you steps, and these two general types of changes (scale and layering schemes) entail a large number of steps!

Your "1:40 site" default drawing

The first default drawing you will create in this lesson can be used for your 1″ = 40′ site layouts. This default drawing will be similar to the one you created for the 1:20 site layout, but with greater detail paid to the default settings.

The default checklist

Before you begin a default drawing, you should preplan it. To help with this planning, a default checklist is provided so that you can quickly see what is involved in this preplanning. This checklist is shown in FIG. 14-1A, 14-1B, 14-1C. The checklist for your 1:40 site default drawing has been filled out for you in FIG. 14-1D, 14-1E, and 14-1F.

Take the time now to examine what was filled out on the checklists for the 1:40 site default. You can use the checklists that are not filled out to copy and create your default drawings. At the end of this lesson, you will find a checklist filled out for a ¹/₈″ scale commercial floor plan default drawing (FIGS. 14-7, 8, and 9).

Changing the pathname to your default drawings

You must remember to change the pathname to DEFAULT, *before* creating your default drawing.

Step 1 – Pick the **New Path** option.

Step 2 – Type in and [**Enter**] the pathname for your default drawing.

     default

Step 3 – Now, only the default drawings will be displayed. The default drawings currently on your system include:

     1-4PLAN - ¹/₄″ **= 1**′ scale plan layout
     1-20SITE - **1**″ = 20′ scale site layout
     DET1-1-2 - 1¹/₂″ = 1′ detail

Turning off the current default drawing

As before, you will first "turn-off" the current default drawing that may be assigned. You do not have to follow this part of the procedure every time you set a new default drawing. If you already had the same type of default drawing created, you could name it as your default drawing for creating the new one! This way, all of your layers would already be named properly and other desired settings would already be active.

However, this lesson will guide you from scratch. This way, all of the

LAYER CHECKLIST

DEFAULT DRAWING NAME: _____

Description: _____

Layer Names	Color	Description
1 _____	_____	_____
2 _____	_____	_____
3 _____	_____	_____
4 _____	_____	_____
5 _____	_____	_____
6 _____	_____	_____
7 _____	_____	_____
8 _____	_____	_____
9 _____	_____	_____
10 _____	_____	_____
11 _____	_____	_____
12 _____	_____	_____
13 _____	_____	_____
14 _____	_____	_____
15 _____	_____	_____
16 _____	_____	_____
17 _____	_____	_____
18 _____	_____	_____
19 _____	_____	_____
20 _____	_____	_____
21 _____	_____	_____
22 _____	_____	_____
23 _____	_____	_____
24 _____	_____	_____
25 _____	_____	_____
26 _____	_____	_____
27 _____	_____	_____
28 _____	_____	_____
29 _____	_____	_____
30 _____	_____	_____
31 _____	_____	_____
32 _____	_____	_____
33 _____	_____	_____
34 _____	_____	_____
35 _____	_____	_____
36 _____	_____	_____
37 _____	_____	_____
38 _____	_____	_____
39 _____	_____	_____
40 _____	_____	_____

Figure 14–1A

PAGE ___ OF ___

MENU CHECKLIST #1 OF 2

DEFAULT DRAWING NAME: _____

MENU	OPTION	SUGGESTED	YOUR SETTING
ARCHITCT	WALLS	ON	_____
	SIDES	ON	_____
	CENTERS	OFF	_____
	CLEAN	OFF	_____
	CAP	OFF	_____
	HILITE	OFF	_____
	WIDTH	6"	_____
-DOORSWNG	DRW JAMB	OFF	_____
	SIDES	ON	_____
	CNTRPNT	ON	_____
	CUTOUT	ON	_____
	IN WALL	ON	_____
	LYRSRCH	ON	_____
	JAMBWDTH	0	_____
	ANGLE	90	_____
	THICKNSS	1"	_____
	HEAD HGT	6'-8"	_____
	SINGLE	ON	_____
-WINDOWS	DRW JAMB	OFF	_____
	SIDES	ON	_____
	CNTRPNT	ON	_____
	CUTOUT	ON	_____
	IN WALL	ON	_____
	LYRSRCH	ON	_____
	JAMBWDTH	0"	_____
	OUT SILL	0"	_____
	IN SILL	0"	_____
	GLASSTHK	1/2"	_____
	SILL HGT	3'-0"	_____
	HEAD HGT	6'-8"	_____
Z VALUES	Z BASE	0"	_____
	Z HEIGHT	8'-0"	_____
SETTINGS	SAVEDLAY	30	_____
	DRWMRKS	ON	_____
	BEEPS	ON	_____
	BIG CURS	OFF/10	_____
	NEGDIST	ON	_____
	SHOW Z	ON	_____
	FIXDREF	OFF	_____
	DISSYNC	OFF	_____
	TXTSCAL	ON	_____

MENU	OPTION	SUGGESTED	YOUR SETTING
OBJ SNAP	END PNT	ON	_____
	MID PNT	ON	_____
	INTSECT	ON	_____
	CENTER	ON	_____
	MISSDIST	10	_____
	LYRSRCH	ON	_____
	QUICK	OFF	_____
	APERTUR	OFF	_____
TEXT	SIZE	1/8"	_____
	ANGLE	0°	_____
	WEIGHT	1	_____
	SLANT	0	_____
	ASPECT	1	_____
	FONTNAME	ROMAN2	_____
	FACTOR	1.1	_____
	LEFT	ON	_____
-ARROWS	SIZE	1	_____
	STYLE	OPEN	_____
	ASPECT	.75	_____
DIMENSION	HORIZNT	ON	_____
	ASSOC	ON	_____
-TEXTSTYL	TEXTSIZE	1/8"	_____
	WEIGHT	1	_____
	SLANT	0	_____
	ASPECT	1	_____
	FONTNAME	ROMAN2	_____
	IN HORZ	OFF	_____
	OUTHORZ	OFF	_____
	ABOVE	ON	_____
	OFFSET	(1/16")	_____
	COLOR	GREEN	_____
-DIM STYL	LINE 1	ON	_____
	LINE 2	ON	_____
	OFFSET	(1/8")	_____
	OVERLAP	(1/8")	_____
	INCRMENT	(3/8")	_____
	OVERRUN	(1/8")	_____
	FIXDDIS	OFF	_____
	LIMITS	OFF	_____
	TOLERNC	OFF	_____
-ARROSTYL	TICMRKS	ON	_____

Figure 14-1B

PAGE ___ OF ___

DEFAULT DRAWING NAME: _____

MENU	OPTION	SUGGESTED	YOUR SETTING
−ARROSTYL	SIZE	1	_____
	WEIGHT	1	_____
	COLOR	GREEN	_____
PLOTTER	SCALE	<VALUE>	_____
	PAPERSIZ	CUSTOM	_____
	PENWIDTH	(20)	_____
	LAYOUT	SET	_____
	CLRPLOT	ON	_____
	PENSORT	ON	_____
	SET PENS:	WHITE	_____
		RED	_____
		GREEN	_____
		BLUE	_____
		CYAN	_____
		MAGENTA	_____
		BROWN	_____
		LT GRAY	_____
		DK GRAY	_____
		LT RED	_____
		LT GRN	_____
		LT BLUE	_____
		LT CYAN	_____
		LT MGTA	_____
		YELLOW	_____
	ROTATE	OFF	_____
−LYOUTSET	LYOUT SZ	50	_____
	LYOUTDIV	2,2	_____
POLYGON	CNTRPNT	OFF	_____
	RECTANGL	ON	_____
GRIDS	SNAP ON	ON	_____
	DISP1ON	ON	_____
	DISP2ON	ON	_____
−GRIDSIZE	SET SNAP	<VALUE>	_____
−GRIDCOLOR	SETDISP1	LT RED	_____
	SETSISP2	LT BLUE	_____
	−MARKSIZE	3	_____
DISPLAY	SHOWTXT	ON	_____
	SHOWDIM	ON	_____
	SHOWHTCH	ON	_____
	SHOWWGT	ON	_____

MENU	OPTION	SUGGESTED	YOUR SETTING
	USERLIN	ON	_____
	OVERSHT	OFF	_____
	SHOWINS	ON	_____
	SHOWATRS	ON	_____
	CRVCTRS	ON	_____
	DIMMPTS	ON	_____
	*SMALLTXT	2	_____
	BOXCOLOR	MAGENTA	_____
	*SMALLSYM	3	_____
	*ARCFACTR	1	_____
* IF YOU ARE USING A DISPLAY LIST:			
	SMALLTXT	1	_____
	ARCFACTR	10	_____
−DISPLIST	RGNWARN	OFF	_____
	WNDWSIZE	4	_____

2D GO TO VIEWS

VIEWS	NAME	DESCRIPTION
1	_____	_____
2	_____	_____
3	_____	_____
4	_____	_____
5	_____	_____
6	_____	_____
7	_____	_____
8	_____	_____
9	_____	_____
10	_____	_____

3D GO TO VIEWS

VIEWS	NAME	DESCRIPTION
1	_____	_____
2	_____	_____
3	_____	_____
4	_____	_____
5	_____	_____
6	_____	_____
7	_____	_____
8	_____	_____
9	_____	_____
10	_____	_____

Figure 14−1C

PAGE ___ OF ___

LAYER CHECKLIST

DEFAULT DRAWING NAME: <u>1:40SITE</u>

Description: <u>1:40 SCALE SITE PLAN</u>

	Layer Names	Color	Description
1	LAYOUT	YELLOW	PLOT CENTER SNAP POINT
2	BORDER	YELLOW	DRAWING AREA
3	BRDRTXT	GREEN	TITLE BLOCK, SHEET NOS, ARROW, TEXT, REVS
4	PROPRTY	LT MGTA	PROPERTY LINES
5	STREET	CYAN	STREET
6	EASEMNT	LT GRN	EASEMENTS
7	SETBACK	BROWN	SETBACKS
8	UTILITY	LT GRAY	UTILITIES
9	DRAINAG	LT GRAY	DRAINAGE DIRECTIONS
10	FTPRINT	WHITE	BUILDING FTPRINTS
11	PARKING	GREEN	PARKING LINES
12	TRASH	LT CYAN	TRASH ENCLOSURES
13	SIGNS	LT RED	SIGNS, ETC.
14	SITDIMS	BROWN	SITE DIMENSIONS
15	STATS	GREEN	SITE STATISTICS
16	LEGEND	GREEN	LEGEND NOTES
17	LEGSYMS	GREEN	LEGEND SYMBOLS
18	VICYMAP	LT RED	VICINITY MAP
19	LANDSCP	GREEN	LANDSCAPING
20	SPRINKL	LT GRAY	SPRINKLERS, RUNS
21	MISC	MGTA	MISCELLANEOUS ITEMS
22			
23			
24			
25			
26			
27			
28			
29			
30			
31			
32			
33			
34			
35			
36			
37			
38			
39			
40			

Figure 14-1D   PAGE <u>1</u> OF <u>3</u>

DEFAULT DRAWING NAME: *1:40 SITE*

MENU	OPTION	SUGGESTED	YOUR SETTING		MENU	OPTION	SUGGESTED	YOUR SETTING
ARCHITCT	WALLS	ON	OFF		OBJ SNAP	END PNT	ON	✓
	SIDES	ON				MID PNT	ON	✓
	CENTERS	OFF				INTSECT	ON	✓
	CLEAN	OFF				CENTER	ON	✓
	CAP	OFF				MISSDIST	10	✓
	HILITE	OFF				LYRSRCH	ON	✓
	WIDTH	6"				QUICK	OFF	✓
–DOORSWNG	DRW JAMB	OFF				APERTUR	OFF	✓
	SIDES	ON			TEXT	SIZE	1/8"	✓
	CNTRPNT	ON				ANGLE	0°	✓
	CUTOUT	ON				WEIGHT	1	✓
	IN WALL	ON				SLANT	0	✓
	LYRSRCH	ON				ASPECT	1	✓
	JAMBWDTH	0				FONTNAME	ROMAN2	✓
	ANGLE	90				FACTOR	1.1	✓
	THICKNSS	1"				LEFT	ON	✓
	HEAD HGT	6'–8"			–ARROWS	SIZE	1	✓
	SINGLE	ON				STYLE	OPEN	✓
–WINDOWS	DRW JAMB	OFF				ASPECT	.75	1
	SIDES	ON			DIMENSION	HORIZNT	ON	✓
	CNTRPNT	ON				ASSOC	ON	✓
	CUTOUT	ON			–TEXTSTYL	TEXTSIZE	1/8"	✓
	IN WALL	ON				WEIGHT	1	✓
	LYRSRCH	ON				SLANT	0	✓
	JAMBWDTH	0"				ASPECT	1	✓
	OUT SILL	0"				FONTNAME	ROMAN2	✓
	IN SILL	0"				IN HORZ	OFF	✓
	GLASSTHK	1/2"				OUTHORZ	OFF	✓
	SILL HGT	3'–0"				ABOVE	ON	✓
	HEAD HGT	6'–8"	↓			OFFSET	(1/16")	2'-6"
Z VALUES	Z BASE	0"	0			COLOR	GREEN	✓
	Z HEIGHT	8'–0"	0		–DIM STYL	LINE 1	ON	✓
SETTINGS	SAVEDLAY	30	✓			LINE 2	ON	✓
	DRWMRKS	ON	✓			OFFSET	(1/8")	5'
	BEEPS	ON	✓			OVERLAP	(1/8")	5'
	BIG CURS	OFF/10	✓			INCRMENT	(3/8")	15'
	NEGDIST	ON	✓			OVERRUN	(1/8")	5'
	SHOW Z	ON	✓			FIXDDIS	OFF	✓
	FIXDREF	OFF	✓			LIMITS	OFF	✓
	DISSYNC	OFF	✓			TOLERNC	OFF	✓
	TXTSCAL	ON	✓		–ARROSTYL	TICMRKS	ON	✓

Figure 14–1E

PAGE 2 OF 3

MENU CHECKLIST #2 OF 2

DEFAULT DRAWING NAME: 1:40SITE

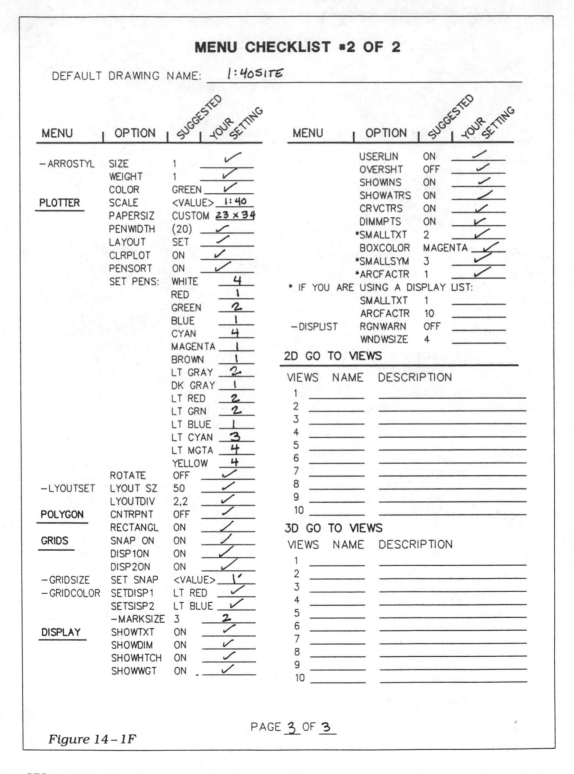

MENU	OPTION	SUGGESTED	YOUR SETTING
—ARROSTYL	SIZE	1	✓
	WEIGHT	1	✓
	COLOR	GREEN	✓
PLOTTER	SCALE	<VALUE> 1:40	
	PAPERSIZ	CUSTOM 23 × 34	
	PENWIDTH	(20)	✓
	LAYOUT	SET	✓
	CLRPLOT	ON	✓
	PENSORT	ON	✓
	SET PENS:	WHITE	4
		RED	1
		GREEN	2
		BLUE	1
		CYAN	4
		MAGENTA	1
		BROWN	1
		LT GRAY	2
		DK GRAY	1
		LT RED	2
		LT GRN	2
		LT BLUE	1
		LT CYAN	3
		LT MGTA	4
		YELLOW	4
	ROTATE	OFF	✓
—LYOUTSET	LYOUT SZ	50	✓
	LYOUTDIV	2,2	✓
POLYGON	CNTRPNT	OFF	✓
	RECTANGL	ON	✓
GRIDS	SNAP ON	ON	✓
	DISP1ON	ON	✓
	DISP2ON	ON	✓
—GRIDSIZE	SET SNAP	<VALUE> 1'	
—GRIDCOLOR	SETDISP1	LT RED	✓
	SETSISP2	LT BLUE	✓
	—MARKSIZE	3	2
DISPLAY	SHOWTXT	ON	✓
	SHOWDIM	ON	✓
	SHOWHTCH	ON	✓
	SHOWWGT	ON	✓

MENU	OPTION	SUGGESTED	YOUR SETTING
	USERLIN	ON	✓
	OVERSHT	OFF	✓
	SHOWINS	ON	✓
	SHOWATRS	ON	✓
	CRVCTRS	ON	✓
	DIMMPTS	ON	✓
	*SMALLTXT	2	✓
	BOXCOLOR	MAGENTA	✓
	*SMALLSYM	3	✓
	*ARCFACTR	1	✓
* IF YOU ARE USING A DISPLAY LIST:			
	SMALLTXT	1	
	ARCFACTR	10	
—DISPLIST	RGNWARN	OFF	
	WNDWSIZE	4	

2D GO TO VIEWS

VIEWS	NAME	DESCRIPTION
1		
2		
3		
4		
5		
6		
7		
8		
9		
10		

3D GO TO VIEWS

VIEWS	NAME	DESCRIPTION
1		
2		
3		
4		
5		
6		
7		
8		
9		
10		

PAGE 3 OF 3

Figure 14–1F

steps you need to follow will be documented here. You can easily refer to this lesson for creating all of your default drawings.

Step 1 – Start DataCAD, and display the drawing list. *If you are currently working on a drawing in DataCAD*, use the **File I/O, New Dwg** options to start a new drawing.

Step 2 – When the drawing list is displayed, pick the **Default** option.

Step 3 – Press the [**Space bar**] once, to clear any current default drawing, then press [**Enter**].

Step 4 – The new name for your site layout will be **1-40SITE**, which stands for 1:40 scale site layout. Type in and [**Enter**] this new name for your default drawing.

Setting up your snap grid

The "Snap Grid" can be set to a different value for each layer. Whatever the present value is will be given to all new layers that you create. After the layers are created, you will be able to go into the different layers and change the values as desired. Remember, the snap grid is for your ease of "picking" with mouse button number 1, and should be used as often as possible for maximum productivity. (Of course, typing in coordinates is sometimes faster and more accurate, depending on how close you are zoomed in and how large of an increment your snap is set to.)

Step 1 – Press **S** to enter the Set Snap mode.

Step 2 – Type in **1** in order to set a 1 foot increment, and press [**Enter**].

Step 3 – Now you can add new layers to your drawing, and all of the new layers will come in with a 1 foot increment. You will only have to change the snap on the layers that require a different increment.

Creating the layers

Follow these steps to create your layers.

Step 1 – Press **L** to enter the LAYERS menu.

Step 2 – Pick the **NewLayer** option.

Step 3 – Pick the **20** option, and [**Enter**].

Step 4 – Pick the **Name** option, to name your layers.

Step 5 – Pick **Layer1**.

Step 6 – Type in and the new name for this layer: **Layout** and press [**Enter**].

Step 7 – Pick **Layer2**.

Step 8 – Type in and the new name for this layer: **Border** and press [**Enter**].

Step 9 – Continue naming the layers for your default drawing, as indicated below.

Layer 1 = **Layout**
Layer 2 = **Border**
Layer 3 = **BrdrTxt**
Layer 4 = **Proprty**
Layer 5 = **Street**
Layer 6 = **Easemnt**
Layer 7 = **SetBack**
Layer 8 = **Utility**
Layer 9 = **Drainag**
Layer 10 = **FtPrint**
Layer 11 = **Parking**
Layer 12 = **Trash**
Layer 13 = **Signs**
Layer 14 = **SitDims**
Layer 15 = **Stats**
Layer 16 = **Legend**
Layer 17 = **LegSyms**
Layer 18 = **VicyMap**
Layer 19 = **Landscp**
Layer 20 = **Sprinkl**
Layer 21 = **Misc**

Step 10 – Press mouse button **3** to quit back to the LAYER menu.

Step 11 – Using the [**Tab**] key to change your layers, and the **K** key to change the colors, give each layer the colors listed below.

Layout   = **Yellow**
Border   = **Yellow**
BrdrTxt = **Green**
Proprty = **Lt Mgta**
Street   = **Cyan**
Easemnt = **Lt Grn**
SetBack = **Brown**

```
Utility  = Lt Gray
Drainag  = Lt Gray
FtPrint  = White
Parking  = Green
Trash    = Lt Cyan
Signs    = Lt Red
SitDims  = Brown
Stats    = Green
Legend   = Green
LegSyms  = Green
VicyMap  = Lt Red
Landscp  = Green
Sprinkl  = Lt Gray
Misc     = Mgta
```

Defining the "settings"

Step 1 – From the UTILITY menu, pick the **Settings** option.

Step 2 – Pick the **ScaleTyp** option.

Step 3 – Pick the ***Decimal** option until it is active.

Step 4 – The only other option that should be active is ***Units**.

Step 5 – Press mouse button **3** to quit back to the SETTINGS menu.

Step 6 – Pick the **AngleTyp** option.

Step 7 – Change the type to ***Bearing**.

Step 8 – Pick the **StrtAngl** option to indicate a north direction.

Step 9 – Pick a start point in the drawing area of your screen.

Step 10 – Making sure your Ortho mode is ON (large O in SwOTHLUD), pick the second point indicating the north direction of your site plan. An arrow will follow your cursor. Make sure you pick UP in the Y direction, and that your line is perfectly VERTICAL. (It doesn't matter how long the line is.)

Step 11 – Quit back to the SETTINGS menu, and pick the **MissDist** option. This option allows you to set the distances you can miss an object by and still be able to pick it.

Step 12 – Pick the number **10** (10 screen pixels), and press [**Enter**]. This number will be the approximate distance described by the size of your cursor.

Step 13 – Pick the **ScrlDist** option. This is the distance the viewing window changes when you press the arrow key.

Step 14 – Change this distance to **50**. This will move the viewing window 50% when you press the arrow key.

Step 15 – Pick the **SaveDlay** option, to set the timed intervals between the automatic saves.

Step 16 – Change the number of minutes to **20**.

Step 17 – Pick the **BigCurs** option TWICE (until the CURSOR SIZE menu is displayed). This will allow you to adjust the size of your screen cursor.

Step 18 – Change the number of pixels to **10**. This way the size of your cursor will be the same as the Miss Distance.

Step 19 – Pick ***NegDist** until it is active. This option makes the coordinate display show the negative sign (–) when you are moving the cursor in the minus direction.

Step 20 – Pick ***Show Z** until it is active also. This option will display the current Z-base and Z-height settings in the message area of your screen.

Step 21 – Now pick the ***Beeps** option until it is active. Setting this option makes your computer beep when you pick an item!

Step 22 – Pick the **TxtScal** option until it is active. This option allows you to set the text size in relation to the plot scale that is set in the Plotter menu.

Step 23 – Check your menu before you exit; ONLY the following items should be active:

*Beeps
*NegDist
*Show Z
*TxtScal

Defining the grids

Step 1 – Press **G** to enter the GRIDS menu.

Step 2 – Pick the **GridSize** option.

Step 3 – Pick the **Set Snap** option.

Step 4 – This menu has the same effect as using the **S** key to set your snap. You only need to change the snap settings on the layer that are different than 1′. (This is because all layers are set to 1′ at this point.) Press [**Tab**] until the Proprty layer is active.

Step 5 – Because the snap setting for your property should be set at 10′, and there is not a 10′ option in the list, you will want to pick the **Custom** option and type in the correct value.

Step 6 – Type in **10** and press [**Enter**] twice for both the X and Y grid snap.

Step 7 – Pick **Set Snap** again. Notice that the rest of your settings are displayed on the setting list. Now you can simply [**Tab**] to the correct layer and pick the setting required. Because you are picking off the list, you can remain in the **Set Snap** mode to set all layers.

Step 8 – Press [**Tab**] until **FtPrint** is active.

Step 9 – Pick the **6″** option.

Step 10 – Continue setting the snap for just the layers that require a change from 1′, as shown below in the layer list.

Layout	=	**1′**
Border	=	**1′**
BrdrTxt	=	**1′**
Proprty	=	**10′**
Street	=	**1′**
Easemnt	=	**1′**
SetBack	=	**1′**
Utility	=	**1′**
Drainag	=	**1′**
FtPrint	=	**6″**
Parking	=	**1′**
Trash	=	**6″**
Signs	=	**1′**
SitDims	=	**6″**
Stats	=	**6″**
Legend	=	**1′**
LegSyms	=	**1′**
VicyMap	=	**1′**
Landscp	=	**6″**
Sprinkl	=	**6″**
Misc	=	**1′**

Step 11 – When all of the snaps have been set, press mouse button **3** to quit back to the GRIDS menu.

Step 12 – Pick the **SetDisp1** option. This option allows you to define the display characteristics of the small grid.

Step 13 – Pick **Custom** to enter a custom spacing.

Step 14 – Enter the spacing size of **10** for both X and Y small grid.

Step 15 – Pick **SetDisp2** to define the large grid.

Step 16 – Pick **Custom**.

Step 17 – Set the X and Y large grid to **40**.

Step 18 – Press mouse button **3** once to exit back to the original GRIDS menu.

Step 19 – Pick the **GridColr** option.

Step 20 – You could use this menu to change the color of the grid, which is presently set to light red for small grid, and light blue for large grid. However, you won't be changing the color. Instead, you will use this menu to adjust the displayed "mark" size of the large grid (size of the displayed "+").

Pick the **SetDisp2** option.

Step 21 – Pick the **MarkSize** option.

Step 22 – Set the mark size (in pixels) of large grid to **2**.

Step 23 – Press mouse button **3** to quit.

Setting the display variables

Step 1 – From the UTILITY menu, pick the **Display** option.

Step 2 – The following options should be active:

> ***ShowTxt**
> ***ShowDim**
> ***ShwHtch**
> ***ShowWgt**
> ***UserLin**

*ShowIns
*DimmPts
*CrvCntr

Step 3 – The other options should be set to:

SmallTxt = 3
BoxColor = NoChange
SmallSym = 3
ArcFactr = 1

Step 4 – *Notice*: If you have display list processing set up for your computer, you will see an option in this menu called **DispList**. If it appears, you will want to follow these next steps.

1. Pick the **DispList** option.
2. Pick the **RgnWarn** (display regeneration warning) until it is OFF (no star). This will turn off the annoying regeneration warning that appears as you zoom in and out. You may want to turn the warning back on when your drawing becomes large and a regeneration becomes time consuming. However, leave it off in your default, since it will be used for a new drawing (that is not large yet).
3. Pick the **WndwSize** option. Change this setting to 4 to maximize the display list window and to reduce the number of regens while panning and zooming.
4. Quit back to the DISPLAY menu by pressing mouse button **3**.
5. Now change the **SmallSym** and **SmallTxt** option settings to zero. You may want to change this in the future, but try this setting for now. This will keep your text and symbols from looking like boxes when you zoom in.
6. Change the Arc Factor to **5**. This will keep your arcs looking smooth when you zoom in without having to regen.

OBJECT SNAP menu

It is a good idea to set the most used options in this menu.

Step 1 – Press **[Shift] X** to enter the OBJECT SNAP menu.

Step 2 – Make sure only the following options are active:

*End Pnt
*Mid Pnt
*Intsect
*LyrSnap

Dimension variables

You can set the variable once, in the LINEAR menu, and they will be set for all of the dimension types.

Step 1 – Press **D** to enter the DIMENSION menu.

Step 2 – Pick the **Linear** option.

Step 3 – Pick **TextStyl**.

Step 4 – Pick **TextSize**.

Step 5 – Type in the final size you wish your dimension text to be, and press [**Enter**]. With the **TxtScale** option active in the SETTINGS menu, this size will be ⅛″. Without using the **TxtScal** option, the text size would be 5 feet, as shown in appendix B, *DataCAD Reference Guide*, DataCAD scales & sizes.

Step 6 – Pick the **Weight** option, to adjust the line weight of your text.

Step 7 – Make sure the weight is set to **1**.

Step 8 – Pick the **Color** option.

Step 9 – Change the text color to **White**.

Step 10 – Make the **＊Above** and **＊Auto** options active.

Step 11 – Press mouse button **3** once, then pick the **DimStyl**.

Step 12 – Pick **Offset**, to adjust the gap that will be drawn in the extension line of the dimension, as shown in FIG. 14-2.

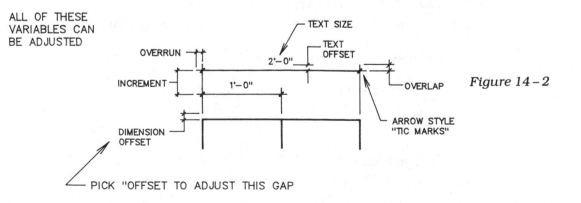

Figure 14 – 2

Step 13 – Change the offset to **5** feet, which will be plotted at an ¹/₈-inch gap.

Step 14 – Pick the **Overlap** option. This option adjusts the amount the extension line will overlap the dimension line. (FIG. 14-3.)

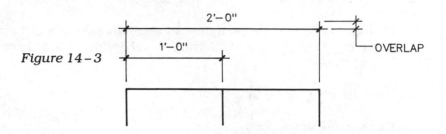

Figure 14 – 3

Step 15 – Change the overlap size to **5** feet.

Step 16 – Pick the **Incrment** option, which adjusts the space between stacked dimensions, as shown in FIG. 14-4.

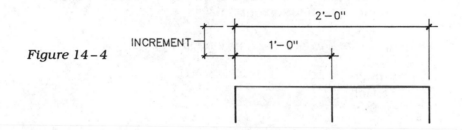

Figure 14 – 4

Step 17 – Change the increment spacing to **20** feet, which will be plotted at ¹/₂".

Step 18 – Pick the **OverRun** option. This describes the distance the dimension line will over-run the extension line, as in FIG. 14-5.

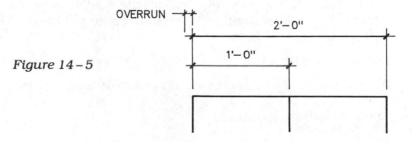

Figure 14 – 5

Step 19 – Set the overrun to **5** feet, to plot at ¹/₈ inch.

Step 20 – Press mouse button **3** once to return to the LINEAR menu, then pick the **ArroStyl** option.

Step 21 – Make the **TicMrks** option active.

Step 22 – Pick the **Size** option, to adjust the size of the tic marks.

Step 23 – Change the size of the tic marks to **.75**. This size is in a relative percentage to the text size. Setting it to .75 will create a tic mark $3/4$ the size of the text.

Step 24 – Pick the **Weight** option.

Step 25 – Change the weight to **1**.

Step 26 – Pick the **Color** option.

Step 27 – Change the tic mark color to **Green**, and press [**Enter**].

Step 28 – Press mouse button **3** once to quit back to the variables options, and pick the **AutoStyl** option.

Step 29 – Make sure the following options are active:

*Strngli
*PtsOnly
*LyrSrch

Setting up the text for notes

Step 1 – Pick the **Text** option from the EDIT menu.

Step 2 – Because you have set the ***TxtScal** in the SETTINGS menu, you will notice that the option called **TxtScal** in this menu is active also. This option allows you to select the final size your text will appear once it is plotted, so it works in conjunction with the set size in the PLOTTER menu.

Pick the **Size** option.

Step 3 – Type in **1/8″** for your text size, and press [**Enter**]: **0.0.1/8**.

Step 4 – Pick the **Arrows** option.

Step 5 – Change the **Size** of the arrows to **1**. This will produce an arrow with the width adjusted to the same size as text. (FIG. 14-6.)

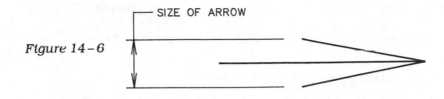

Figure 14–6

SIZE OF ARROW

Step 6 – Pick **Aspect**. This option allows you to adjust the relative length and width of the arrow.

Step 7 – You can change the **Aspect** to **1** and press [**Enter**]. This will result in an arrow head having 45 degree lines, as illustrated in FIG. 14-7. To have a more pointed arrow, you can increase the aspect. To have a flatter arrow, you might want to try .75 as a value.

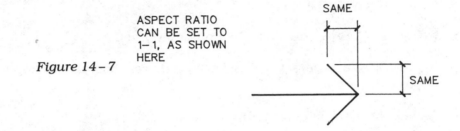

ASPECT RATIO CAN BE SET TO 1–1, AS SHOWN HERE

Figure 14–7

SAME

SAME

Changing the linetype spacing

The measurement in repeated patterns of a linetype, such as centerline, is adjustable for your own standard at your office. You can find the suggested formulas for this spacing in appendix B, *The DataCAD Reference Guide*, in the DataCAD Linetypes chart.

Step 1 – Press **f** (small f) to enter the LINETYPE menu, **Spacing** option.

Step 2 – Referring to the spacing formula for the **Propline** (Property Line), change the spacing value to **160**. This will give you a 2-inch spacing in the final plotted drawing. If you wish to have a 2¹/₂″ or 3″ spacing, use 240 or 280, respectively.

Step 3 – Use the mouse button **3** to quit.

Changing the Z-base and height

This is a good time to change the Z-base and height, BEFORE you draw your drawing border!

Step 1 – Press the **Z** key.

Step 2 – Type in **0** (zero) for the Z-Base, and press [**Enter**].

Step 3 – Type in **0** again for the Z-Height, and press [**Enter**].

Creating the drawing boundary

In appendix B, *The DataCAD Reference Guide*, Scales and Sizes, find the Border Enlargement column. Look up the enlargement factor for a 1:40 border. This factor will allow you to easily draw a border at the real size (D 24″ × 36″ size for example), and then you can enlarge it by this factor to enable a scale plot of your drawing. (How else could you draw a 700 foot property line in a 24 × 36 ″ border?)

Step 1 – From the EDIT menu, select the **Polygon** option.

Step 2 – Pick the **Rectangl** option.

Step 3 – Use the [**Tab**] key to make the Border layer active.

Step 4 – Press [**Insert**] to set the **Relative cartesian coordinates** input mode.

Step 5 – Pick the start point for your rectangle.

Step 6 – Refer to FIG. 14-8, which shows a regular D size drawing sheet, with the drawing area and the title block. This example is for communication purposes only, and you can use your own sheet for this lesson.

Using your drawing skills, draw the "drawing area" of the sheet (Not including the title/company/revision block area) on the Border layer. For this example, you can use the 23″ × 32″ drawing area in FIG. 14-8.

$$X = 0.32$$
$$Y = 0.23$$

Step 7 – Tab to the **BrdrTxt** layer, and add the rectangles indicating the revision, company, and title areas, as shown in FIG. 14-8. If you are creating your own sheet for your company, refer to an existing format to follow.

Step 8 – If you want to add text to your border, turn off the **TxtScal** option. Because your drawing is not enlarged to a 1:40 size, you would want to add the text relative to the size of the drawing, not to the plot scale.

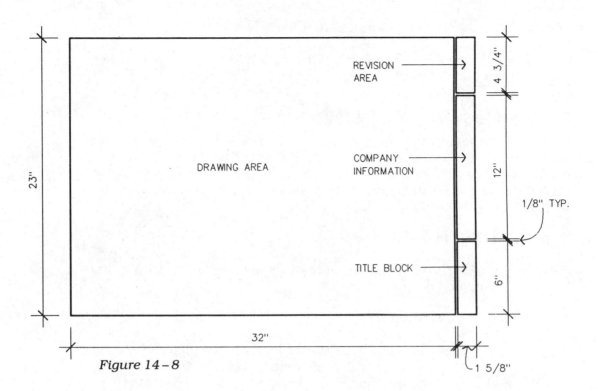

REVISION
AREA

COMPANY
INFORMATION

DRAWING AREA

TITLE BLOCK

4 3/4"

12"

1/8" TYP.

6"

23"

32"

1 5/8"

Figure 14–8

Remember to turn on the ***TxtScal** option after adding the text, and return the text size to ¹/₈″ if you changed it.

Step 9 – Once your rectangles are created, press [**Alt**] **E** to go to the ENLARGE menu.

Step 10 – Pick the lower left corner of the rectangle for the center of enlargement.

Step 11 – Pick the **Enlrgmnt** option.

Step 12 – Pick **Set All**.

Step 13 – Type in the Border Enlargement value for a 1:40 size drawing, and press [**Enter**].

      480

Step 14 – Quit back to the ENLARGE menu by pressing mouse button **3**.

Step 15 – Using ***Area** indicate a box around the entire border. It will enlarge to the correct size for your drawing!

Step 16 – Quit by pressing mouse button **3**.

Step 17 – Use the **/** key to **Recalc** your viewing window so that you can see the drawing area.

Getting ready for the plot layout

Now that you have drawn on your border, you will add a snap point that allows you to object snap your plot layout EXACTLY in the middle of your border rectangles. This snap point is especially helpful if you wish to use preprinted sheets, as you can get the same plotter pen positioning every-time you plot.

Step 1 – [**Tab**] to the Layout layer.

Step 2 – Press [**Alt**] **G** to quickly enter the **Geometry** option from the UTIL-ITY menu.

Step 3 – Pick the **Divide** option.

Step 4 – Check in the message area of your screen to see that the current number of divisions = **2**. If it doesn't, pick the **Dvisions** option and change the number of divisions to **2**, then press [**Enter**].

Step 5 – Object snap to the lower left corner of the drawing area, then to the upper right corner of the revision area, as indicated in FIG. 14-9.

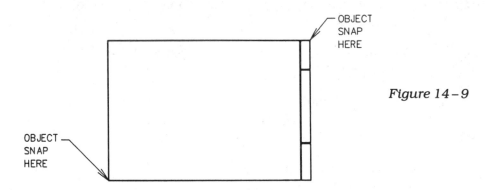

Figure 14 – 9

Step 6 – Your object snap point will appear in the middle of the border areas, as indicated in FIG. 14-10.

Presetting the plot specifications

Step 1 – Pick the **Plotter** option from the UTILITY menu.

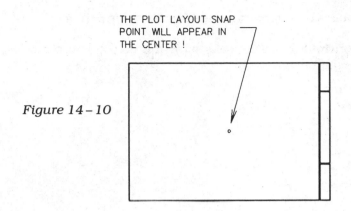

THE PLOT LAYOUT SNAP
POINT WILL APPEAR IN
THE CENTER !

Figure 14 – 10

Step 2 – Pick the **Scale** option.

Step 3 – Pick the **1:40** option.

Step 4 – Pick the **PaperSiz** option.

Step 5 – For a regular D size sheet (24×36), you will want your plotting limits of the paper as close to the edge as possible. Most plotters will allow you to get as close as 1/2″ to 3 edges, and 1¹/2″ to the fourth edge, which can be set to be the left side of your sheet. Because this is where the stapling or binding occurs, this kind of measurement works out well, and will give you a final plotting area of 23″×34″.

If you use the predefined DataCAD 24×36 D choice, you will only get a 21″×33″ plottable area. You can use this choice if you want, but if you want to get the full area of your plotter limits, you will have to type in a special size. To do this, pick **Custom**.

Step 6 – Type in **23** for 23 inches in the height and press [**Enter**].

Step 7 – Now type in **34** for the width, and press [**Enter**].

Step 8 – Press the mouse button **3** to return to the PLOTTER menu.

Step 9 – Pick the **Layout** option.

Step 10 – Drag the layout box over to your rectangle, and object snap to the rectangle centerpoint.

Step 11 – Now pick the **Set Pens** option, to define which pens will be used with which colors.

Step 12 – Pick **White**.

Step 13 – Enter the appropriate number for your pen: **4**.

Step 14 – Continue defining pens with the colors you are using, as described below:

White   = **4**
Red   = **1**
Green   = **2**
Blue   = **1**
Cyan   = **4**
Magenta = **1**
Brown   = **1**
Lt Gray = **2**
Dk Gray = **1**
Lt Red   = **2**
Lt Grn   = **2**
Lt Blue = **1**
Lt Cyan = **3**
Lt Mgta = **4**
Yellow   = **4**

These pen numbers will later be associated with appropriate pens in the plotter. The recommended pen widths that could be used with this type of numbering are (in point size for wet ink pens):

1 = **.25**
2 = **.35**
3 = **.50**
4 = **.75**

Step 15 – Once the numbers are defined, press button **3** to quit back to the PLOTTER menu.

Step 16 – Check to make sure the following options are active:

*ClrPlot
*PenSort

Step 17 – Press mouse button **3** to quit.

Setting miscellaneous options

It is a good idea to go into other menus and set defaults that are the most commonly used. This adds convenience to using the default drawing. As you use the system, you will become aware of many options you use frequently, that could be preset. Later, you can go back into the default drawing and make changes.

Step 1 – Press [**Tab**] until the Proprty layer is active.

Step 2 – Press the **Q** key to quickly change to the property linetype.

Step 3 – Press [**Insert**] twice to change the input mode to Relative Polar.

Step 4 – Check that the **W** in SWOTHLUD is small, indicating that you are NOT drawing walls. If it is capitalized, press the = key until the W appears in lowercase (SwOTHLUD).

Saving your default drawing

Step 1 – Pick the **File I/O** option, found in the UTILITY menu.

Step 2 – Pick **New Dwg**

Step 3 – Pick **Yes** to save your default drawing.

USER REMINDER – *Do* NOT *pick* ABORT, *or you will trash the settings you just created!*

Step 4 – The Default Drawing list is displayed. Notice that your default drawing is added to this list.

Getting back the drawing file list

Once your default drawings are filed (using the **File I/O, New Dwg, Yes** options), you are ready to begin drawing. To do so, you will want to bring back the original drawing list. This is done by changing the *pathname* again.

Remember, the pathname is a way to describe to the system "what drawer to look in," or what *directory*, for your drawings. Currently, you set your pathname to the DEFAULT directory, which exists in the MTEC drawer. This means that only the default drawings are displayed.

Step 5 – Pick the **New Path** option, to change the drawing file path back to the original setting.

Step 6 – Type in the name of your desired drawing file path. For example, to return to the DWG path, you would type in **dwg**.

-or-

You can pick the "**..**" option shown in **F2**. The subdirectories under the MTEC directory will be displayed. Pick the **DWG** option. The path "**C:\MTEC\DWG** will now be displayed in the message area of your screen. Press [**Enter**] to accept it. The DWG drawing list will be displayed.

Examples of default checklists

The following examples (FIGS. 14-11, 14-12, and 14-13) show a completed checklist for a $1/8''$ scale commercial floor plan default. These examples are included to illustrate how a default can be organized for $1/8''$ scale plan drawings. You will want to design your own defaults to meet your office requirements. For instance, you might not need all of the layers listed in this checklist. Only create the layers you want to use. You might also want to call the layers names using your own conventions. The important idea is to keep consistencies and standards, and to save you time by using default drawings.

Checklists for default drawings

Formula for common scales: (Can be used for Text and Dimension line sizes).

Plotted at	Created at	Resulting size	Plotted at	Created at	Resulting size
$1/8$ scale	1 foot	$1/8$ inch	1:20 scale	2.5 feet	$1/8$ inch
	2 feet	$1/4$ inch		5 feet	$1/4$ inch
	4 feet	$1/2$ inch		10 feet	$1/2$ inch
	8 feet	1 inch		20 feet	1 inch
$1/4$ scale	6 inches	$1/8$ inch	1:40 scale	5 feet	$1/8$ inch
	1 foot	$1/4$ inch		10 feet	$1/4$ inch
	2 feet	$1/2$ inch		20 feet	$1/2$ inch
	4 feet	1 inch		40 feet	1 inch

LAYER CHECKLIST

DEFAULT DRAWING NAME: 1-8 PLANC

Description: 1/8" SCALE - COMMERCIAL FLOOR PLAN

	Layer Names	Color	Description
1	LAYOUT	YELLOW	PLOT CENTER SNAP POINT
2	BORDER	YELLOW	DRAWING AREA
3	BRDRTXT	GREEN	TITLE BLOCK, SHEET NOS, TEXT, REVS
4	COLUMNS	LT MGTA	COLUMNS & GRID
5	EXTWALL	WHITE	EXTERIOR WALLS
6	INTWALL	WHITE	INTERIOR WALLS
7	LOWALL	LT GRAY	PARTITIONS - LOW WALLS
8	EXTWDWS	LT CYAN	EXTERIOR WINDOWS
9	INTWDWS	LT CYAN	INTERIOR WINDOWS
10	EXTDOOR	GREEN	EXTERIOR DOORS
11	INTDOOR	GREEN	INTERIOR DOORS
12	DIMS	BROWN	DIMENSIONS
13	NOTES	GREEN	NOTES
14	LABELS	CYAN	ROOM LABELS
15	SYMBOLS	GREEN	SECTION SYMBOLS, NOTE SYMBOLS
16	CORE	WHITE	CORES
17	ELEVTR	WHITE	ELEVATORS
18	LAVATRY	WHITE	MENS/WOMENS ROOMS
19	ELECTRL	LT BLUE	ELECTRICAL
20	REFCEIL	RED	REFLECTED CEILING
21	UTILITY	LT RED	UTILITY LOCATIONS
22	HVAC	LT RED	HEATING, VENTING & AIR CONDITIONING
23	PLUMBING	LT RED	PLUMBING
24	MISC	MGTA	MISCELLANEOUS ITEMS
25			
26			
27			
28			
29			
30			
31			
32			
33			
34			
35			
36			
37			
38			
39			
40			

Figure 14–11

PAGE 1 OF 3

MENU CHECKLIST #1 OF 2

DEFAULT DRAWING NAME: <u>1-3PLANC</u>

MENU	OPTION	SUGGESTED	YOUR SETTING	MENU	OPTION	SUGGESTED	YOUR SETTING
<u>ARCHITCT</u>	WALLS	ON	✓	<u>OBJ SNAP</u>	END PNT	ON	✓
	SIDES	ON	✓		MID PNT	ON	✓
	CENTERS	OFF	✓		INTSECT	ON	✓
	CLEAN	OFF	✓		CENTER	ON	✓
	CAP	OFF	✓		MISSDIST	10	✓
	HILITE	OFF	✓		LYRSRCH	ON	✓
	WIDTH	6"	0.5.1/2		QUICK	OFF	✓
–DOORSWNG	DRW JAMB	OFF	✓		APERTUR	OFF	✓
	SIDES	ON	✓	<u>TEXT</u>	SIZE	1/8"	✓
	CNTRPNT	ON	✓		ANGLE	0°	✓
	CUTOUT	ON	✓		WEIGHT	1	✓
	IN WALL	ON	✓		SLANT	0	10
	LYRSRCH	ON	✓		ASPECT	1	✓
	JAMBWDTH	0	✓		FONTNAME	ROMAN2	ARCWY2GP
	ANGLE	90	✓		FACTOR	1.1	
	THICKNSS	1"	0.2		LEFT	ON	✓
	HEAD HGT	6'–8"	✓	–ARROWS	SIZE	1	✓
	SINGLE	ON	✓		STYLE	OPEN	✓
–WINDOWS	DRW JAMB	OFF	✓		ASPECT	.75	✓
	SIDES	ON	✓	<u>DIMENSION</u>	HORIZNT	ON	✓
	CNTRPNT	ON	✓		ASSOC	ON	✓
	CUTOUT	ON	✓	–TEXTSTYL	TEXTSIZE	1/8"	✓
	IN WALL	ON	✓		WEIGHT	1	✓
	LYRSRCH	ON	✓		SLANT	0	10
	JAMBWDTH	0"	✓		ASPECT	1	
	OUT SILL	0"	0.2		FONTNAME	ROMAN2	ARCWY2GP
	IN SILL	0"	0.1		IN HORZ	OFF	✓
	GLASSTHK	1/2"	✓		OUTHORZ	OFF	✓
	SILL HGT	3'–0"	✓		ABOVE	ON	✓
	HEAD HGT	6'–8"	✓		OFFSET	(1/16")	0.6
<u>Z VALUES</u>	Z BASE	0"	✓		COLOR	GREEN	✓
	Z HEIGHT	8'–0"	✓	–DIM STYL	LINE 1	ON	✓
<u>SETTINGS</u>	SAVEDLAY	30	✓		LINE 2	ON	✓
	DRWMRKS	ON	✓		OFFSET	(1/8")	1
	BEEPS	ON	✓		OVERLAP	(1/8")	1
	BIG CURS	OFF/10	✓		INCRMENT	(3/8")	3
	NEGDIST	ON	✓		OVERRUN	(1/8")	1
	SHOW Z	ON	✓		FIXDDIS	OFF	✓
	FIXDREF	OFF	✓		LIMITS	OFF	✓
	DISSYNC	OFF	✓		TOLERNC	OFF	✓
	TXTSCAL	ON	✓	–ARROSTYL	TICMRKS	ON	✓

Figure 14–12

PAGE <u>2</u> OF <u>3</u>

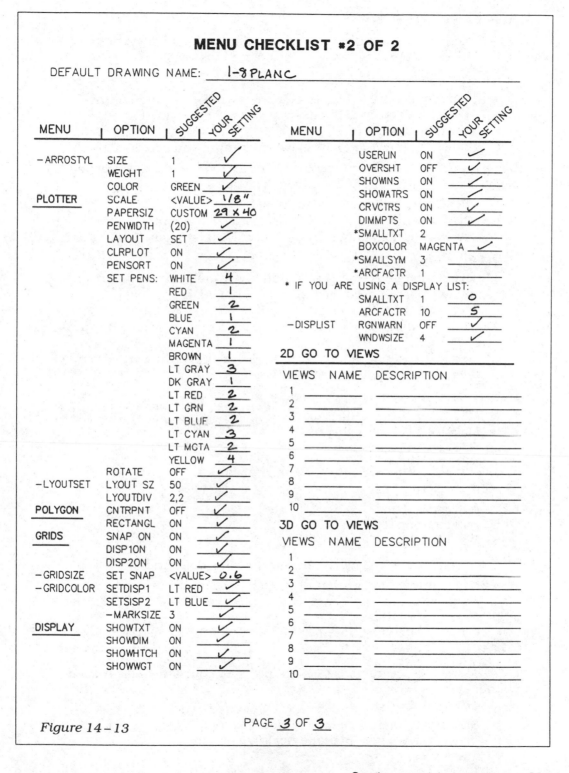

MENU CHECKLIST #2 OF 2

DEFAULT DRAWING NAME: <u>1-8 PLANC</u>

MENU	OPTION	SUGGESTED	YOUR SETTING
—ARROSTYL	SIZE	1	✓
	WEIGHT	1	✓
	COLOR	GREEN	✓
PLOTTER	SCALE	\<VALUE\>	1/8"
	PAPERSIZ	CUSTOM	29 X 40
	PENWIDTH	(20)	✓
	LAYOUT	SET	✓
	CLRPLOT	ON	✓
	PENSORT	ON	✓
	SET PENS: WHITE		4
	RED		1
	GREEN		2
	BLUE		1
	CYAN		2
	MAGENTA		1
	BROWN		1
	LT GRAY		3
	DK GRAY		1
	LT RED		2
	LT GRN		2
	LT BLUE		2
	LT CYAN		3
	LT MGTA		2
	YELLOW		4
	ROTATE	OFF	✓
—LYOUTSET	LYOUT SZ	50	✓
	LYOUTDIV	2,2	✓
POLYGON	CNTRPNT	OFF	✓
	RECTANGL	ON	✓
GRIDS	SNAP ON	ON	✓
	DISP1ON	ON	✓
	DISP2ON	ON	✓
—GRIDSIZE	SET SNAP	\<VALUE\>	0.6
—GRIDCOLOR	SETDISP1	LT RED	✓
	SETSISP2	LT BLUE	✓
	—MARKSIZE	3	✓
DISPLAY	SHOWTXT	ON	✓
	SHOWDIM	ON	✓
	SHOWHTCH	ON	✓
	SHOWWGT	ON	✓

MENU	OPTION	SUGGESTED	YOUR SETTING
	USERLIN	ON	✓
	OVERSHT	OFF	✓
	SHOWINS	ON	✓
	SHOWATRS	ON	✓
	CRVCTRS	ON	✓
	DIMMPTS	ON	✓
	*SMALLTXT	2	
	BOXCOLOR	MAGENTA	✓
	*SMALLSYM	3	
	*ARCFACTR	1	
* IF YOU ARE USING A DISPLAY LIST:			
	SMALLTXT	1	0
	ARCFACTR	10	5
—DISPLIST	RGNWARN	OFF	✓
	WNDWSIZE	4	✓

2D GO TO VIEWS

VIEWS	NAME	DESCRIPTION
1		
2		
3		
4		
5		
6		
7		
8		
9		
10		

3D GO TO VIEWS

VIEWS	NAME	DESCRIPTION
1		
2		
3		
4		
5		
6		
7		
8		
9		
10		

Figure 14–13

PAGE <u>3</u> OF <u>3</u>

DataCAD exercise 14

Please complete the following exercise by reading each question carefully.
Circling the letter that corresponds to the correct answer.

1. You should create:

   a. 5 default drawings. This is as many as anyone would ever need.
   b. At least 1 for every different scale you will need, and for different layer naming schemes.
   c. 10 default drawings. This is the maximum you can create.

2. To change into another directory in order to access other drawing files (such as the DEFAULT directory), you use the:

   a. DIRECTORY menu. **New Dir** option.
   b. **New Dir** option, found in the DRAWING list menu.
   c. **New Path** option, found in the DRAWING List menu.

3. Default drawings are created in order to:

   a. Save many steps, increase productivity, help eliminate errors, and establish consistency in all of your CADD drawings.
   b. Save many steps, increase productivity, and help eliminate errors. However, it it impossible to establish consistency in your CADD drawings.
   c. Increase the time-consuming steps in every drawing. Using Default drawings is not recommended.

4. Your default drawings should reside in the:

   a. MTEC \ DEFAULT directory.
   b. MTEC \ DWG directory.
   c. MTEC \ SYM directory.

5. To create additional layers in your drawing, you use the LAYERS menus, then the:

   a. **AddLayer** option.
   b. **NewLayer** option.
   c. **On/Off** option.

6. Once you have added layers to your drawing, you should:

   a. Use the **Snap** option found in the LAYERS menu to define a snap setting for each layer.
   b. Name your layers.
   c. Leave the LAYERS menu. The layers will be named automatically.

7. To define Architectural or Decimal units for your drawing, you use the:

   a. SETTINGS menu, then pick the **ScaleTyp** option.
   b. SETTINGS menu, then pick the **Units** option.
   c. UNITS menu, then pick the **ScaleTyp** option.

8. The **MissDist** option defines the:

   a. Distance the viewing window changes when you press the arrow keys.

   b. Gap that is created between lines when you object snap to another line.

   c. Distance you can miss an object by, and still be able to pick it or object snap to it.

9. The **ScrlDist** option defines the:

   a. Distance the viewing window changes when you press the arrow keys.

   b. Gap that is created between lines when you scroll to another line.

   c. Distance you can miss an object by, and still be able to pick it.

10. The **NegDist** option:

   a. Allows you to move the cursor in a negative distance.

   b. Allows you to input negative (−) coordinates and angles.

   c. Makes the coordinate readout display a minus sign (−) when you are moving the cursor in the negative direction.

11. The **SaveDlay** option sets the:

   a. Delay time of the coordinate readout display.

   b. Minutes between automatic saves.

   c. Delay time of the **File I/O**, **Save** option.

12. The **ScaleTyp**, **AngleTyp**, **MissDist**, **ScrlDist**, **SaveDlay**, and **NegDist** options are all found in the:

   a. SETTINGS menu.

   b. UNITS menu.

   c. DEFINITIONS menu.

13. The "snap spacing" refers to:

   a. How you have set the spacing in the OBJECT SNAP menu.

   b. The increments your cursor jumps to when the "Snap" mode is on (e.g., 1′, 4′, 6″, etc.).

   c. The spacing between the grids.

14. To define the snap spacing, you use the:

   a. **Snap Spc** option, found in the GRID menu.

   b. **Set Grid Snap** option, found in the OBJECT SNAP menu.

   c. **GridSize, Set Snap** options, found in the GRID menu.

15. Snap spacing can:

   a. Be different for each layer.

   b. Not be different for each layer.

   c. Not be changed once you set it.

16. The actual size of the drawing:

   a. Is determined once you define a plot scale in your default drawing. All walls and lines are drawn full scale as you create them, then are plotted at the appropriate scale. Only descriptive items are scaled as you draw them.

   b. Effects the way you create walls and other lines. These types of entities must be scaled as you draw them.

   c. Is defined in the SETTINGS menu.

17. To define the pens your plotter will use as the drawing is plotted, you use the:

   a. LAYER menu, **Color** and **Set Pens** options.

   b. PLOTTER menu, **Set Pens** option.

   c. PLOTTER menu, **Color** option.

18. Different pens are associated with different entities in your drawing by defining:

   a. Linetypes.

   b. Color.

   c. Line Widths.

19. When setting your Dimension variables, you:

   a. Have to define variables for all the different types of dimensions.

   b. Only have to define the variables for Linear and Angular dimensions.

   c. Only have to define the variables for Linear dimensions. These variables will then be set for all of the dimension types.

20. The Text Size that you define in your default drawing is set at:

   a. The appropriate size in relation to the plotting scale. (e.g., If the drawing is to be plotted at $1/4''$, text created 6 inches high will be plotted at $1/8''$ high.) The **TxtScal** option helps to automate the step.

   b. The size you want it plotted. It will always turn out the correct size, regardless of the plotted scale.

21. The text size must be adjusted in:

   a. The TEXT menu only.

   b. Both the TEXT and DIMENSIONS menu.

   c. The TEXT, DIMENSION, and PLOTTER menus.

22. The most important thing to know about your drawings BEFORE you create your default drawings, is the:

   a. Text size.

   b. Paper size.

   c. Plot scale.

Lesson 15
The DataCAD modeler

What you will be doing

You will use the DataCAD 3-D Modeler program to create a modeled building during this lesson. If you do not have the Modeler, you might have an older version of DataCAD. Starting with DataCAD 4.0, the Modeler is included with the basic software. (Now would be a good time to update your DataCAD!)

Although you have always drawn in 3-D with DataCAD, you have been pretty much restricted to drawing "planar" to the plan view. The one exception was when you used 3-D Line to draw in a parallel view. Also, all of your drawing entities have been perpendicular to the plan view (so they are flat on the top and bottom). For instance: walls are perpendicular to the plan view. You have probably discovered by now that walls are actually two lines drawn together, and are represented as two parallel planes in 3-D.

The Modeler, as you will see, allows you to create entities that are convoluted, or complex. What this means is that you are no longer restricted to having your walls flat on the top and bottom, and that you can also create curved 3-dimensional items. Walls will be drawn as slabs, and you can manipulate these slabs to create cathedral ceilings or archways. You will punch holes in the modeled walls so that you can see inside the building. If you were going to use a rendering package, such as Velocity, you could give the windows added to these holes a transparent quality in order to see in a room, or for a special effect.

Objectives

Your lesson objectives are to:

- Create a horizontal slab for a floor
- Draw vertical slabs for walls
- Define window and door slabs
- Process the window and door slabs into voids, which become holes in your walls
- Use inclined slabs to create a gable and hip roof
- Stretch the wall slab to meet the gable roof
- Use plane snap to transfer your working coordinates to the inclined roof plane
- Create a rectangular slab on your roof and process it into a void
- Add a mesh surface and manipulate it to curve it
- Use edit plane to change your working coordinates
- Use the 3-D Edit menu commands to move, copy, and manipulate your entities in 3-D

Typical 3-D model building procedure

The generic steps listed in this lesson will help you build your first 3-D model, but will also act as a general outline in building any 3-D residence or commercial building.

Creating a new drawing

To start this model, you will use a new drawing without using a default drawing. Follow these steps then, to set up your drawing:

Step 1 – Start DataCAD, or use the **New Dwg** procedure if you are already in a drawing. The drawing list should be displayed.

Step 2 – If you wish to change project directories, select the **New Path** option, and type in the name of the desired directory, then press [**Enter**], or use the picking technique to change your directories.

Step 3 – Type in the new name for your drawing: **model1**, and press [**Enter**].

Setting up your drawing

Because you did not use a default drawing, you must define your layers and perform the other steps needed to set up your drawing file. These settings are listed next, along with reminders on how to accomplish them.

Step 1 – Set Snap Grid to 6″ (press **s**).

Step 2 – Define 5 layers, naming and setting a color for each layer. (Press **L**, use NEW LAYER. Press **K** to change colors.):

1. **Floor (Light Cyan)**
2. **Walls (White)**
3. **Roof (Light Red)**
4. **Windows (Yellow)**
5. **Doors (Brown)**

Step 3 – In DataCAD 2-D SETTINGS menu, make sure the following is set:

1. ***Show Z**
2. **SaveDlay = 30**

Step 4 – In OBJECT SNAP menu (press [**Shift**] **X**), make sure the following is set:

1. ***End Pt**
2. ***Mid Pt**
3. ***Center**
4. ***Intsect**
5. ***LyrSnap**
6. **Fast3-D OFF!**

Step 5 – In 3-D SETTINGS menu (press **j**), make sure the following is set:

1. **QuickSrch OFF!**
2. ***Dynamic**
3. ***MeshGrd**
4. ***MeshPnt**

The two modeler menus

Like the 2-D side of DataCAD, there are two menus for 3-D (Modeler) Data-CAD. They are the 3-D EDIT menu and the 3-D ENTITY menu. These menus are illustrated in FIG. 15-1.

To access these menus, you can either find the **DCAD 3-D** option in the 2-D EDIT menu, or simply press the small **j** or capital **J** (written [**Shift**] **J**). The small **j** puts you in the 3-D EDIT menu, and the capital **J** puts you in the 3-D ENTITY menu.

Once you enter into the 3-D Modeler, you can use mouse button **3** to switch back and forth between these two menus.

Step 1 – Press **j** to go to the DataCAD 3-D (MODELER) menus.

Step 2 – Notice that the message area of your screen indicates that you are in the 3-D EDIT menu. Also notice that the **S0** option in the menu is 3-D Entity. Because your third mouse button selects S0 for you,

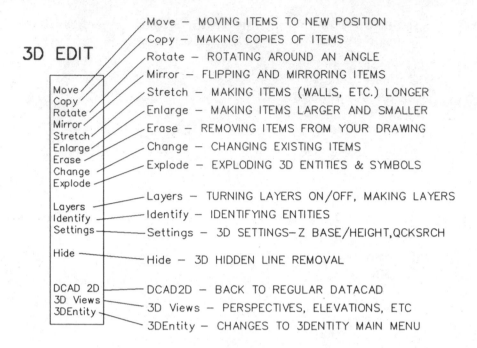

3D EDIT

Move	Move — MOVING ITEMS TO NEW POSITION
Copy	Copy — MAKING COPIES OF ITEMS
Rotate	Rotate — ROTATING AROUND AN ANGLE
Mirror	Mirror — FLIPPING AND MIRRORING ITEMS
Stretch	Stretch — MAKING ITEMS (WALLS, ETC.) LONGER
Enlarge	Enlarge — MAKING ITEMS LARGER AND SMALLER
Erase	Erase — REMOVING ITEMS FROM YOUR DRAWING
Change	Change — CHANGING EXISTING ITEMS
Explode	Explode — EXPLODING 3D ENTITIES & SYMBOLS
Layers	Layers — TURNING LAYERS ON/OFF, MAKING LAYERS
Identify	Identify — IDENTIFYING ENTITIES
Settings	Settings — 3D SETTINGS—Z BASE/HEIGHT,QCKSRCH
Hide	Hide — 3D HIDDEN LINE REMOVAL
DCAD 2D	DCAD2D — BACK TO REGULAR DATACAD
3D Views	3D Views — PERSPECTIVES, ELEVATIONS, ETC
3DEntity	3DEntity — CHANGES TO 3DENTITY MAIN MENU

Figure 15–1

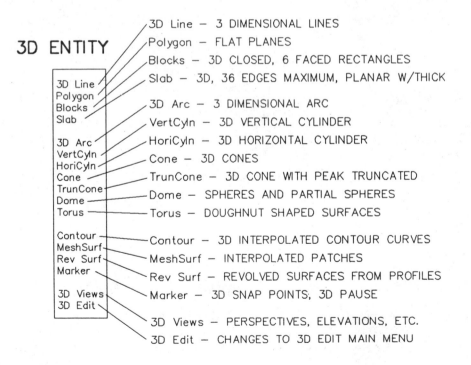

3D ENTITY

3D Line	3D Line — 3 DIMENSIONAL LINES
Polygon	Polygon — FLAT PLANES
Blocks	Blocks — 3D CLOSED, 6 FACED RECTANGLES
Slab	Slab — 3D, 36 EDGES MAXIMUM, PLANAR W/THICK
3D Arc	3D Arc — 3 DIMENSIONAL ARC
VertCyln	VertCyln — 3D VERTICAL CYLINDER
HoriCyln	HoriCyln — 3D HORIZONTAL CYLINDER
Cone	Cone — 3D CONES
TrunCone	TrunCone — 3D CONE WITH PEAK TRUNCATED
Dome	Dome — SPHERES AND PARTIAL SPHERES
Torus	Torus — DOUGHNUT SHAPED SURFACES
Contour	Contour — 3D INTERPOLATED CONTOUR CURVES
MeshSurf	MeshSurf — INTERPOLATED PATCHES
Rev Surf	Rev Surf — REVOLVED SURFACES FROM PROFILES
Marker	Marker — 3D SNAP POINTS, 3D PAUSE
3D Views	3D Views — PERSPECTIVES, ELEVATIONS, ETC.
3D Edit	3D Edit — CHANGES TO 3D EDIT MAIN MENU

try pressing it. You should be able to easily change to the 3-D ENTITY menu.

Step 3 – To quickly return to DataCAD 2-D, press the **;** key.

Modeler project

The project you will be creating during this lesson is shown in FIG. 15-2.

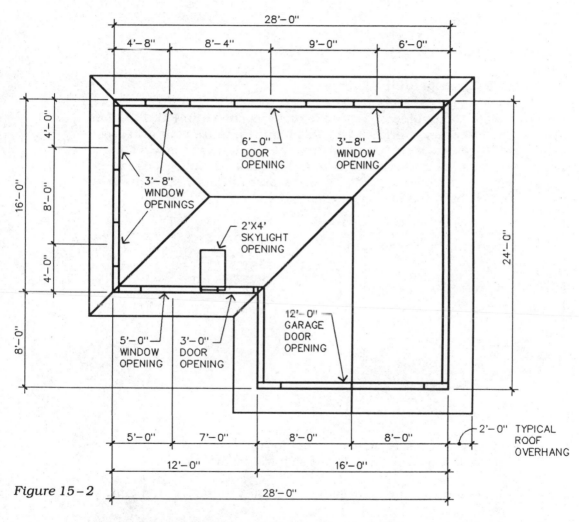

Figure 15 – 2

Creating the floor slab

You will use the 3-D ENTITY menu during the next few steps. You will use the Slab functions to create a 4″ floor slab for the foundation of your building.

Step 1 – [**Tab**] to the Floor layer.

Step 2 – Press **Z** and set the base to **–0.4** and the height to **0**.

Step 3 – Make sure grid snap is ON (S̲woTHLUD). If it isn't, press **x** until the message says "**Snap is on.**"

Step 4 – Press [**Shift**] **J** to enter the 3-D ENTITY menu.

Step 5 – Pick **Slab**.

Step 6 – Pick **Horizntl**.

Step 7 – Pick ***Bse/Hgt** until it is active.

Step 8 – Create the outline of the foundation, as shown in FIG. 15-3. You can either use a grid picking technique (because your grid is set to 6″), or use relative cartesian to type in dimensions. Creating a slab is similar to defining a fence. You draw all of the sides except for the last one. The **S0** option becomes "Close," so you press mouse button **3** to close the last side.

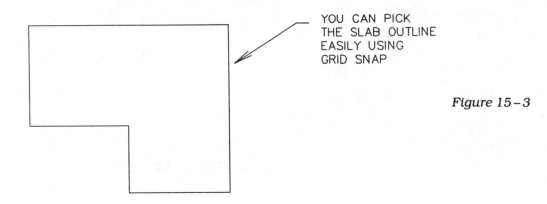

YOU CAN PICK
THE SLAB OUTLINE
EASILY USING
GRID SNAP

Figure 15–3

Step 9 – When your floor is drawn, except for the last side, press mouse button **3**. It will close and your slab will be drawn.

Step 10 – Press mouse button **3** again to quit back to the SLAB menu.

Drawing the walls

You can use the Slab function to draw your walls, too. This is important, since you can punch holes in slabs and manipulate them into different shapes.

Step 1 – [**Tab**] to the Walls layer.

Step 2 – Press **Z**, and change the Z-Base to **0**, and Height to (**9.10**).

Step 3 – Still in the SLAB menu, pick **Vertical**.

Step 4 – Pick the **Thicknss** option.

Step 5 – Change the thickness of your walls (wall width) to (**.6**), and press [**Enter**].

Step 6 – Make sure the ***Bas/Hgt** option is still active.

Step 7 – Pick the ***Left** option. This will produce a wall that is fattened out to the left, as you draw the wall up vertically (in the positive Y direction). You will draw the walls counterclockwise, so they will flatten out to the inside of your building.

Step 8 – Object snap at the first two corners, as indicated in FIG. 15-4.

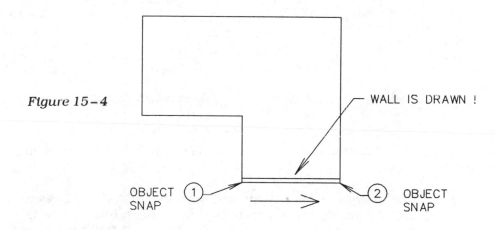

Figure 15 – 4

WALL IS DRAWN !

OBJECT SNAP ① ② OBJECT SNAP

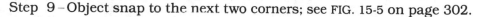

Step 9 – Object snap to the next two corners; see FIG. 15-5 on page 302.

Step 10 – Continue building your wall slabs, using the object snap technique as in steps 8 and 9. See FIG. 15-6 on page 302.

Step 11 – Save your drawing before continuing, by pressing capital **F**.

Quick 3-D view check

It is important to keep a visual 3-D check on your model. This is so that you can monitor your progress as you create your building. It will also help

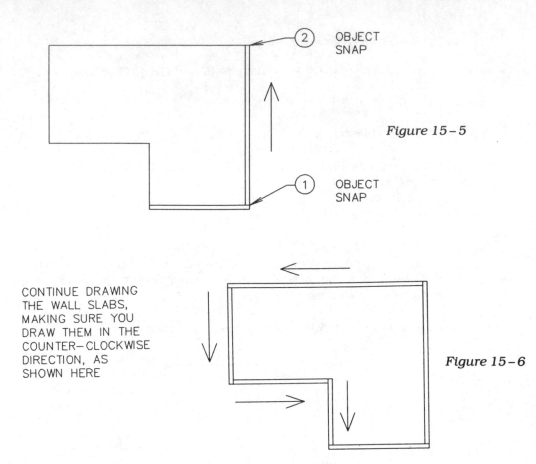

2 OBJECT
   SNAP

Figure 15–5

1 OBJECT
   SNAP

CONTINUE DRAWING
THE WALL SLABS,
MAKING SURE YOU
DRAW THEM IN THE
COUNTER–CLOCKWISE
DIRECTION, AS
SHOWN HERE

Figure 15–6

to give you a good feeling about working in 3-D, which you will be doing soon.

Step 1 – At the bottom of all 3-D menus, you will find the **3-D Views** option. It appears in all menus so that you can manipulate the view of your model easily and quickly. Pick the **3-D Views** option.

Step 2 – Pick the **Isometrc** option.

Step 3 – If necessary, use **/** and **Extends** to get a full view of your model so far. Notice that it has a flat top, just like when you used regular DataCAD (FIG. 15-7). This will change later, once you've added a roof. But for now, you will put some windows and doors in.

Step 4 – Pick the **Ortho** option to return to the plan view of your drawing.

Step 5 – Press mouse button **3** to return to the SLAB menu.

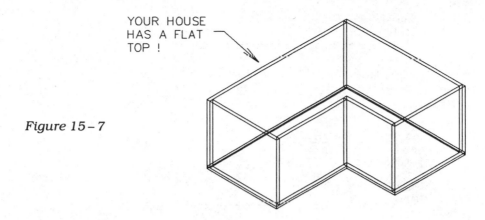

YOUR HOUSE
HAS A FLAT
TOP !

Figure 15 – 7

Creating the window slabs

To define a *Hole*, you must first create a slab inside your wall. Then you will convert that slab into a hole, or what DataCAD calls a *void*. You will be drawing the slabs for your openings at the following Z bases and heights:

Doors   Z Base = **0.2**
             Z Height = **6.8**

Windows   Z Base = **3.0**
             Z Height = **6.8**

Garage   Z Base = **0.0.1/8**
             Z Height = **7.0**

Step 1 – Press the **Z** key, and set your base to 0.2, and the height to 6.8, in order to create the doors.

ZBase = **0.2**
ZHeight = **6.8**

Step 2 – Change your snap to 2″ by pressing **s**, and typing in **0.2** and [**Enter**].

Step 3 – Still using the **Slab/Vertical/Left** options, create your own door openings, for both the front door and rear slider. You must create the slabs for your voids in the same direction as the wall was created. See FIG. 15-8 on page 304.

Step 4 – Once the door openings are complete, press **Z** to change your Z base and height to the following values, in order to create the windows.

ZBase = **3**
ZHeight = **6.8**

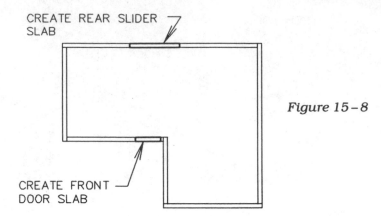

CREATE REAR SLIDER SLAB

CREATE FRONT DOOR SLAB

Figure 15 – 8

Step 5 – Now create your window slabs, making sure that they are drawn in the same directions as your walls, also. (See FIG. 15-9.)

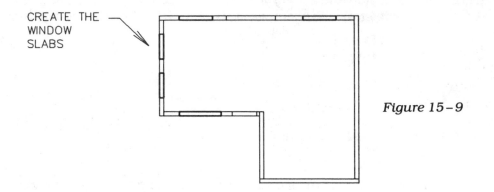

CREATE THE WINDOW SLABS

Figure 15 – 9

Step 6 – Finally, change your Z base to 0.0.1/8 and height to 7.0, and create your garage openings, as in FIG. 15-10.

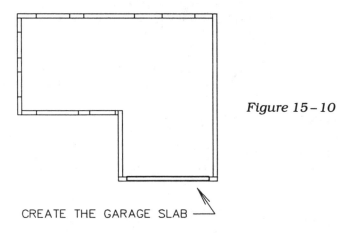

CREATE THE GARAGE SLAB

Figure 15 – 10

Step 7 – Pick the **3-D Views** option, and pick **Isometrc**. Do your windows, doors, and garage look correct? See FIG. 15-11. If they do not look correct, crase them and follow the steps again.

CHECK THAT
ALL OF YOUR
SLABS LOOK
CORRECT

Figure 15 – 11

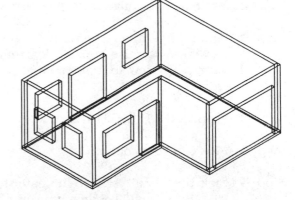

Step 8 – Save your drawing before continuing, by pressing capital **F**.

Performing a hide "before" voids

So that you can better understand how a void works, you can quickly perform a hide on your model "before and after" you define voids. Plus, it's fun to see how converting a slab into a void makes it "hide" different!

Step 1 – Press [**Shift**] **Y** to quickly enter the HIDE menu.

Step 2 – Make sure the **SavImag** option is OFF. You do *not* want to save this image.

Step 3 – Pick **Begin**.

Step 4 – Notice that the walls do not have any holes in them, yet. See FIG. 15-12.

"HIDE" LEAVES
LINES FOR
OPENING, BUT
NO "HOLES" !

Figure 15 – 12

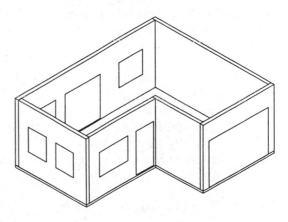

Step 5 – Press [**Shift**] **J** to return to 3-D ENTITY.

Converting slabs into voids

Now you are ready to convert the slabs into voids.

Step 1 – You could actually perform this operation in your 3-D iso view. However, because you are learning, you will want to return to your plan view to make things easier. To do that, press [**Alt**] **0** (zero!, not "oh").

Step 2 – From the 3-D ENTITY menu, return to **Slabs**.

Step 3 – Pick the **Voids** option.

Step 4 – Pick the "Wall" slab to indicate the "master slab," as shown in FIG. 15-13. It will become gray, and might appear dashed. (Sometimes vertical walls don't show up as dashed.)

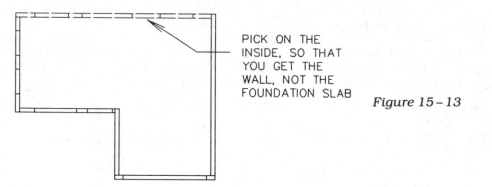

PICK ON THE
INSIDE, SO THAT
YOU GET THE
WALL, NOT THE
FOUNDATION SLAB

Figure 15 – 13

Step 5 – Make sure the ***AddVoid** is active!

Step 6 – Use ***Area** to select all of your window and door openings that are on this wall, at once. They will become gray and dashed also. See FIG. 15-14.

Step 7 – Press mouse button **3** once. The slabs will be processed at this point. Notice that all slabs are processed correctly. You will know if there's been an obvious problem (such as creating a hole the wrong direction), because at this point a "wrong way" void would actually jump outside the wall. If you get a problem like this, you must delete the void (use ***ErsVoid**), and recreate it in the correct direction.

Step 8 – Now pick the next master wall slab, as shown in FIG. 15-15.

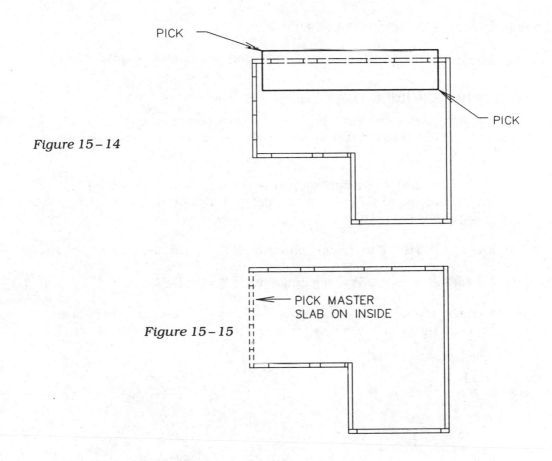

PICK

PICK

Figure 15 – 14

← PICK MASTER
SLAB ON INSIDE

Figure 15 – 15

Step 9 – Using ***Area** and ***AddVoid**, select the opening slabs along this wall, as shown in FIG. 15-16.

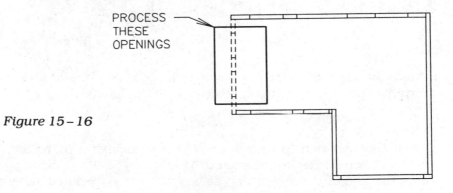

PROCESS
THESE
OPENINGS

Figure 15 – 16

Step 10 – Continue converting the opening slabs into voids, until all walls have been processed.

Step 11 – Press mouse button **3** to quit.

Step 12 – Save your drawing before continuing, by pressing capital **F**.

Performing a quick hide "after" voids

Now that you have converted the opening slabs into voids, they are really holes in the wall. Just so that you can see what is happening, you can try a hide again!

Step 1 – Pick the **3-D Views** options (at the bottom of all Modeler menus), and pick **Parallel**. The last parallel view will be displayed, which was your isometric view.

Step 2 – Press [**Shift**] **Y** to quickly enter the HIDE menu.

Step 3 – Making sure the **Savimag** option is OFF, pick **Begin**.

Step 4 – Did the holes in your walls process correctly? They should appear as though you could look right into the room, as in FIG. 15-17.

NOW, YOUR
HOUSE HAS
HOLES !

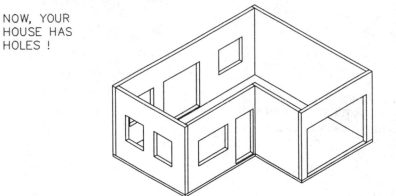

Figure 15 – 17

If the voids did not hide correctly—It might be because the slabs were not drawn right. The most common problems with opening slabs are:

1. The opening slabs were not drawn in the same direction as the master slab
2. They were drawn "upside down" (Z base was higher than Z height)
3. They were created at the same Z base or height as the master slab. Boundaries for the opening slab cannot be coincident with any boundary of the master slab

Rules for opening slabs

In conclusion, the following rules apply to creating the opening slabs for voids in your walls:

1. Must be created in the same direction as "master" slab
2. Should not be "upside-down" (Z-height lower than Z-base)
3. Must be "inside" master slab
4. Cannot touch or cross each other

Drawing the roof

You will be adding a roof to your model that has both hip and gable sections. Before creating a roof, you must calculate the Z base (lower edge of eave) and Z height (upper right height) of the roof.

There are some very good third-party packages available for DataCAD (special macros that you can buy) that are for building roofs. These macros allow you to pick the pitch of your roof (such as 4 in 12), and define a starting "Z-base." Then they automatically calculate the Z height for you. But, you can calculate on your own by following the simple instructions here. (See FIG. 15-18.)

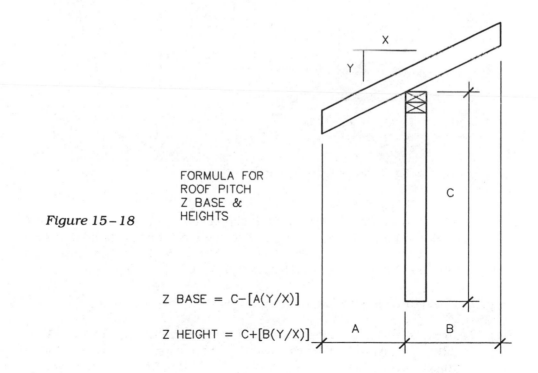

Figure 15-18

FORMULA FOR
ROOF PITCH
Z BASE &
HEIGHTS

$$Z\ BASE = C-[A(Y/X)]$$

$$Z\ HEIGHT = C+[B(Y/X)]$$

An example of this formula is worked out for the model you are creating during this lesson, based on an 8 in 12 pitch, in FIG. 15-19. Of course, you must convert all measurements to inches.

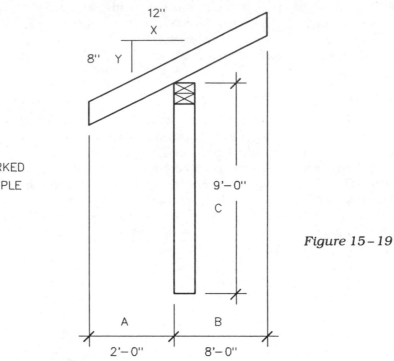

FORMULA WORKED
OUT FOR SAMPLE
PROJECT

Figure 15 – 19

Z BASE = 118"–[24"(8/12)] = 102" or 8'–6"

Z HEIGHT = 118"+[96"(8/12)] = 182" or 15'–2"

You will use the **Slab** option called **Inclines**. This option allows you to build your slab on an incline, or angle. There are 5 types of inclines, two consisting of three (3) edges, and the other selections having four (4) edges. These incline slabs are illustrated in FIG. 15-20.

Step 1 – [**Tab**] to your Roof layer.

Step 2 – Press **Z** and set your Z Base to **8'-6"** and the Z height to **15'-2"**. The 8'-6" height will be the lowest point of your roof slope (including the overhang), and the 15'-2" is the height at the ridge of your roof.

EXAMPLES OF INCLINED SLABS

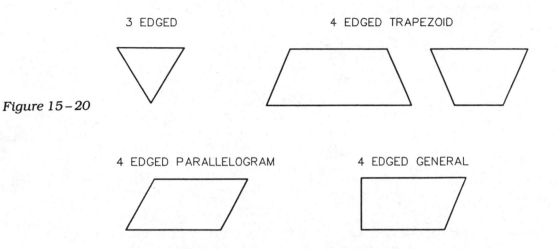

3 EDGED   4 EDGED TRAPEZOID

Figure 15–20

4 EDGED PARALLELOGRAM   4 EDGED GENERAL

Step 3 – In DataCAD 2-D (press **;**), draw the temporary hip lines for the hip side of the roof, as in FIG. 15-21. Be sure to use Ortho mode to draw exact 45 degree lines. Also draw a ridge line for the gabled roof over the garage.

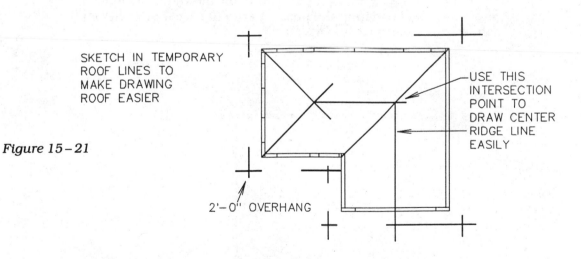

SKETCH IN TEMPORARY ROOF LINES TO MAKE DRAWING ROOF EASIER

USE THIS INTERSECTION POINT TO DRAW CENTER RIDGE LINE EASILY

Figure 15–21

2'– 0" OVERHANG

Step 4 – Press [**Shift**] **J** to go to the DCAD 3-D menu.

Step 5 – Pick the **Slab** option.

Step 6 – Pick the **Inclines** option.

Step 7 – Pick ***Vertical** until it is active. This option will set the edge line of your roof to be vertical, as shown in FIG. 15-22.

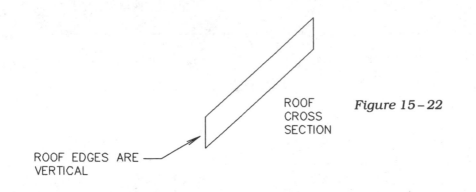

ROOF
CROSS
SECTION

Figure 15 – 22

ROOF EDGES ARE
VERTICAL

Step 8 – Pick the ***3EdgBot** option until it is active, which will create a 3 edged incline defined by the bottom edge first.

Step 9 – The rule of thumb for most of the incline slabs is that the first two picks indicate the lower edge (eave) of the roof, and the last pick(s) indicates the upper ridge. (The only exception to this rule is the **3EdgTop**, in which the first two picks indicate the top ridge edge.)
Knowing that the first 2 picks will indicate the lower edge of your roof, object snap to the first 2 overhang corners for the bottom edge, as indicated in FIG. 15-23.

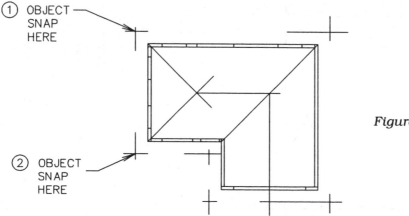

① OBJECT
SNAP
HERE

Figure 15 – 23

② OBJECT
SNAP
HERE

Step 10 – Now object snap to the ridge point of the hip roof, as indicated in FIG. 15-24.

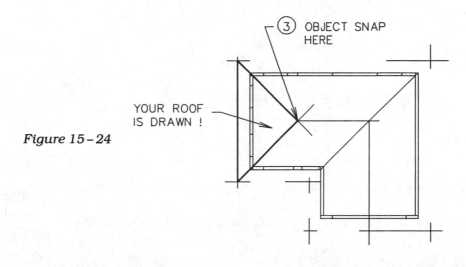

OBJECT SNAP HERE

YOUR ROOF IS DRAWN !

Figure 15–24

Taking a quick check in 3-D

As before, you might want to check on your progress by viewing your building in 3-D.

Step 1 – Pick the **3-D Views** option located at the bottom of the INCLINES menu.

Step 2 – Pick the **Parallel** option. Your last parallel view will be displayed, which was the isometric view. Check how your incline was created. Does the slope look correct? It may be too hard to see in this view, due to the temporary lines you drew. You might want to try an elevation view to see the slope better. See FIG. 15-25.

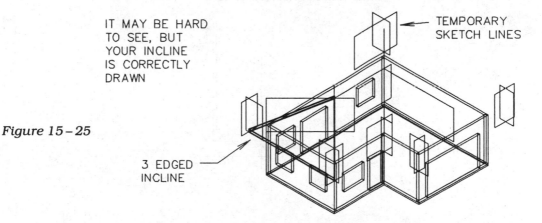

IT MAY BE HARD TO SEE, BUT YOUR INCLINE IS CORRECTLY DRAWN

TEMPORARY SKETCH LINES

Figure 15–25

3 EDGED INCLINE

Step 3 – Pick the **Elvation** option, and then pick **FrontElv**. Is the roof correct? If so, continue. If not, delete it and try again. See FIG. 15-26.

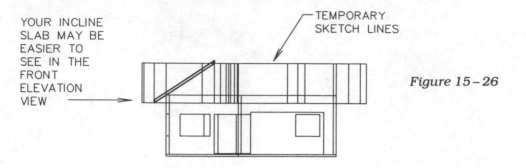

YOUR INCLINE
SLAB MAY BE
EASIER TO
SEE IN THE
FRONT
ELEVATION
VIEW

TEMPORARY
SKETCH LINES

Figure 15–26

Step 4 – Pick the **Ortho** option to return to the plan view of your drawing.

Step 5 – Press mouse button **3** to return to the INCLINES menu.

Drawing more roofs

Now you can use the other inclined slabs options to create the rest of your roof sections.

Step 1 – Pick the ***4EdgPar** option until it is active, to create a 4-edged parallelogram. A parallelogram defines a 4-edged surface that have the opposite side edges parallel to one another.

Step 2 – Object snap to the 2 lower corners of the overhang, indicating the bottom edge of the incline as indicated in FIG. 15-27.

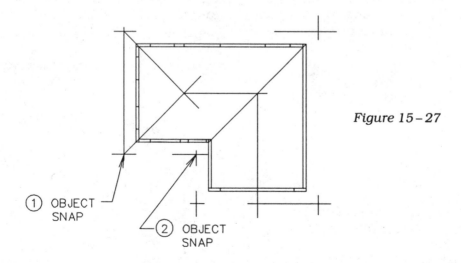

Figure 15–27

① OBJECT SNAP

② OBJECT SNAP

Step 3 – Move your cursor on the screen. Notice that when you move your cursor over to the first point that you picked, the parallelogram is easier to control. This first point (pick 1) indicates the controlling edge (or "leading edge"), of your 4-edge incline. You will get a better feel for this as you wiggle your cursor on the screen.

Object snap to the point indicating the ridge, as shown in FIG. 15-28.

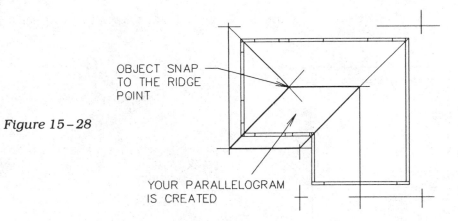

Figure 15–28

OBJECT SNAP
TO THE RIDGE
POINT

YOUR PARALLELOGRAM
IS CREATED

Step 4 – Now pick ***4EdgTrp** to create a 4-edged trapezoid. A trapezoid incline will result in a 4-sided polygon that has two opposite sides parallel, and the other two facing sides are angled opposite to each other, with equal angles. This seems wordy, but if you look back at FIG. 15-20 (which shows several examples of inclines), you can see how DataCAD defines a trapezoid.

Step 5 – Object snap to the two bottom edges of the overhang, as indicated in FIG. 15-29.

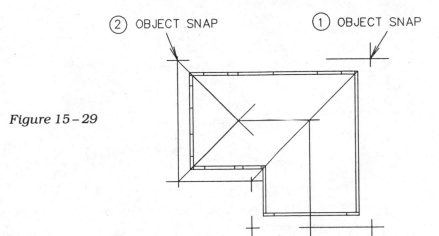

Figure 15–29

② OBJECT SNAP   ① OBJECT SNAP

Step 6 – Move your cursor around and notice how the trapezoid incline moves with sides angled opposite to one another. Also notice, that, as before, moving the cursor closer to the first pick makes it easier to control the slab. Again, the first pick defines the controlling edge.

Object snap to define the ridge edge, as shown in FIG. 15-30.

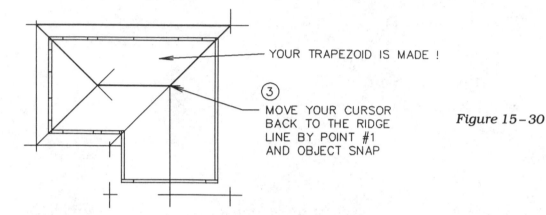

YOUR TRAPEZOID IS MADE !

③ MOVE YOUR CURSOR BACK TO THE RIDGE LINE BY POINT #1 AND OBJECT SNAP

Figure 15 – 30

Step 7 – The last two inclines will be created using the 4-Edged General incline, which allows you to define each of the edges separately. Pick ***4EdgGen** until it is active.

Step 8 – Object snap to the 2 bottom corners, as indicated in FIG. 15-31.

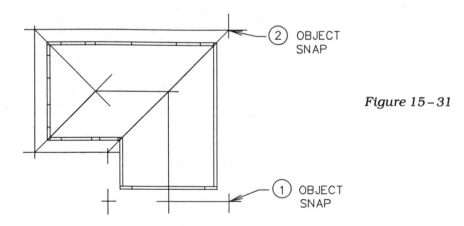

② OBJECT SNAP

Figure 15 – 31

① OBJECT SNAP

Step 9 – Object snap to the next point, which runs along the edge of the first pick, as indicated in FIG. 15-32.

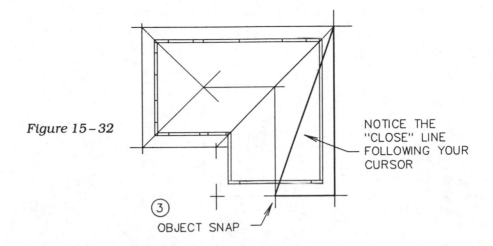

Figure 15-32

NOTICE THE
"CLOSE" LINE
FOLLOWING YOUR
CURSOR

③

OBJECT SNAP

Step 10 – Lastly, object snap for the final corner, as shown in FIG. 15-33.

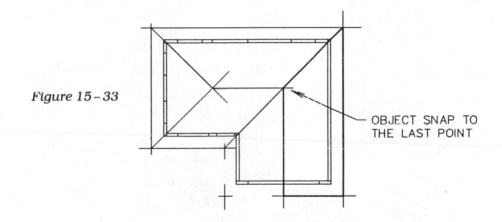

Figure 15-33

OBJECT SNAP TO
THE LAST POINT

Step 11 – Using the same technique of defining the bottom edge first, then defining the top edge, create the incline as in FIG. 15-34 on page 318. Follow the same pick order as illustrated.

Step 12 – Erase the temporary sketch lines, as in FIG. 15-35 on page 318.

Step 13 – Save your drawing before continuing, by pressing capital **F**.

Checking the roof in 3-D

Once your roof is completed, you will want to see how it looks in 3-D. Also, you can take advantage of your 3-D view to easily erase the temporary roof lines you created as a guide.

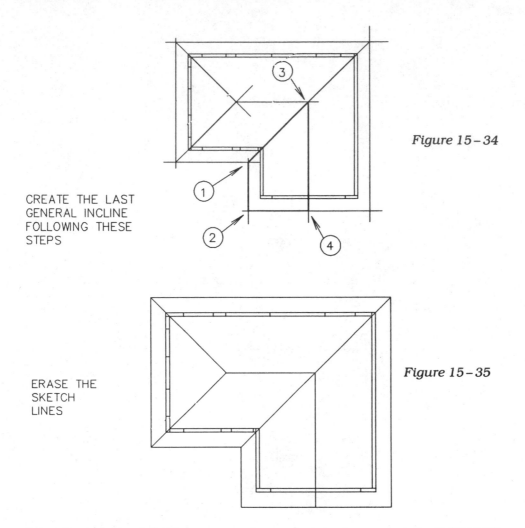

Figure 15 – 34

CREATE THE LAST
GENERAL INCLINE
FOLLOWING THESE
STEPS

Figure 15 – 35

ERASE THE
SKETCH
LINES

Step 1 – Pick the **3-D Views** option located at the bottom of the INCLINES menu.

Step 2 – Pick the **Isometrc** option. Check how your roof appears, as in FIG. 15-36. Do all of the slopes look correct? If so, continue. If not, delete the inclines, check your Z base and height settings, and try again. If there are still miscellaneous lines left over from the temporary sketch lines, you can erase them in this view if you want, by using the 3-D ERASE menu.

Step 3 – When you are through, pick the **3-D Views** option, and pick the **Ortho** option to return to the plan view of your drawing.

Step 4 – Press mouse button **3** until you return to the 3-D ENTITY menu.

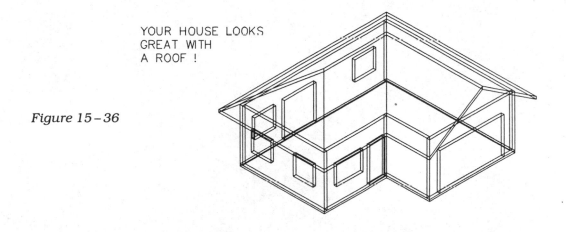

YOUR HOUSE LOOKS
GREAT WITH
A ROOF !

Figure 15–36

Turning off all but the active layers

To make the creation of the roof skylight easier, you will want to turn off all of the other layers.

Step 1 – Press **L** to go to the LAYERS menu.

Step 2 – Pick **ActvOnly**.

Step 3 – Pick the **Roof** layer. Now, only the roof layer will be displayed.

Step 4 – Quit, by pressing mouse button **3**.

Defining a new working plane

So far in your drawing, you have been creating geometry that is based on viewing from the Ortho, or Plan view. When in this view, the X and Y (and sometimes Z) coordinates have been very helpful in creating the items in your drawing. Up to now, you have used what is called "real world coordinates." In other words, X is running across the front of your building, Y is running up and down, and Z is running from the ground up to the height of your building. And, up until now, this is assumed to be a constant factor, as shown in FIG. 15-37 on page 320.

To help you draw easily in 3-D, the coordinates can be changed. What this means, is that, if you change your view to the front, you could still use the theory that across the "screen" is X, up and down the "screen" is Y, and running out of the "screen" is Z. This is called "working coordinates," and it is quite simple to use. This is illustrated in FIG. 15-38 on page 320.

There are two ways to define new working coordinates: Edit Plane and Plane Snap. Both of these options are found in the 3-D VIEWS menu.

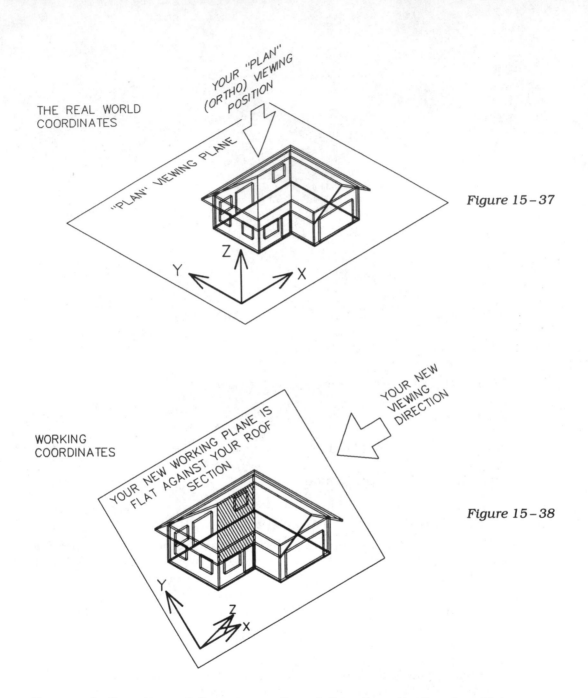

THE REAL WORLD
COORDINATES

YOUR "PLAN"
(ORTHO) VIEWING
POSITION

"PLAN" VIEWING PLANE

Figure 15 – 37

WORKING
COORDINATES

YOUR NEW WORKING PLANE IS
FLAT AGAINST YOUR ROOF
SECTION

YOUR NEW
VIEWING
DIRECTION

Figure 15 – 38

Because both options define a new plane (other than "ortho-plane") to
work in, the method is referred to as defining "Working Planes."

The first working plane you will define will be the inclined surface of
your roof. Once your working plane is on the same angle as your roof, you
can create the slab that you will convert into the skylight hole.

Step 1 – Pick the **3-D Views** option.

Step 2 – Pick the **Parallel** option, to get back to your isometric view.

Step 3 – What you will want to do now, is to move your view slightly until it is quite easy to pick the underneath roof edges of the front left roof plan. Window In by pressing / and pick a closer viewing window. Then pick in the area of the globe indicated in FIG. 15-39, to expose the necessary corners.

Step 4 – Once you get a clear view as shown in FIG. 15-39, pick the **PlneSnap** option.

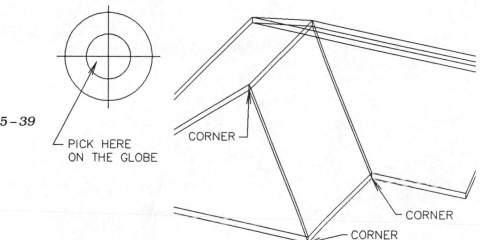

Figure 15 – 39

PICK HERE
ON THE GLOBE

CORNER —

CORNER

CORNER

Step 5 – Using Plane Snap allows you to pick 3 points to define a new working plane, by object snapping to existing endpoints in your drawing. When you move your cursor out to the screen, you will notice the familiar "XYZ" cursor, similar to the one you used when you created your "3-D Linc." (See FIG. 15-40.)

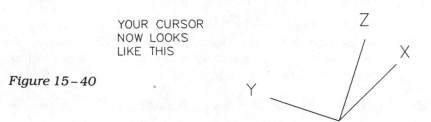

YOUR CURSOR
NOW LOOKS
LIKE THIS

Z

X

Figure 15 – 40

Y

Step 6 – When defining a 3 point working plane, the first and second pick defines the new X axis, and the last pick defines the Y axis, as shown in FIG. 15-41.

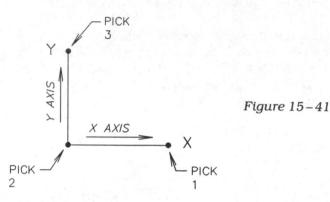

Figure 15–41

Step 7 – Object snap to the lower right edge, then the lower left edge, as indicated in FIG. 15-42.

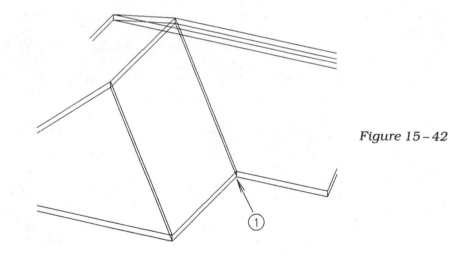

"OBJECT SNAP"
TO THE BOTTOM
OF THE FIRST
CORNER OF THE
ROOF

Figure 15–42

Step 8 – Now, object snap to the upper left edge, as shown in FIG. 15-43.

Step 9 – Your model will now be flipped up so that the roof is parallel to your screen. It is easy to work in this mode, because X is still across the screen, Y is still up and down, and Z is coming out at you. (See FIG. 15-44 on page 323.)

Creating the slab for the skylight void

Step 1 – Press [**Shift**] **J** to go to the 3-D ENTITY menu.

Step 2 – Pick the **Slab** option.

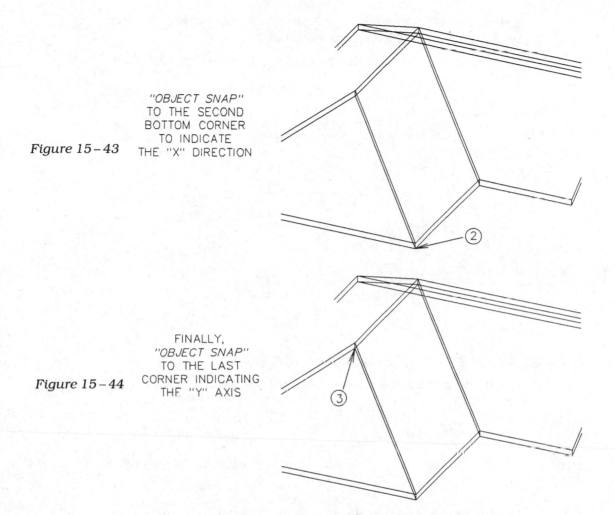

Figure 15–43   "OBJECT SNAP"
TO THE SECOND
BOTTOM CORNER
TO INDICATE
THE "X" DIRECTION

Figure 15–44   FINALLY,
"OBJECT SNAP"
TO THE LAST
CORNER INDICATING
THE "Y" AXIS

Step 3 – Pick the **Rectangl** option. This option allows you to easily create a
rectangular slab.

Step 4 – Check that your thickness is still 6″.

Step 5 – Make sure that the ***Bas + Thk** option is active.

Step 6 – Press **Z**, and set the Z Base to **0**. You do not have to change the Z
Height because you are only using the base setting.

Step 7 – Earlier, you created the roof slab by defining it from the left to the
right. Create your skylight rectangle in the same direction, as
illustrated in FIG. 15-45. This skylight is not dimensioned, so you
can pick anywhere that looks good. A standard skylight size

might be $2' \times 4'$ (22″ wide to fit between the studs). But, for this project, you can make it any reasonable size.

Pick with mouse button **1** to create the slab, or use relative cartesian coordinates.

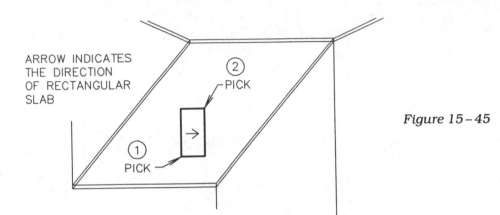

ARROW INDICATES
THE DIRECTION
OF RECTANGULAR
SLAB

Figure 15–45

Converting the skylight slab to a void

Step 1 – Quit by pressing mouse button **3** until you return to the SLAB menu.

Step 2 – Pick the **Voids** option.

Step 3 – Pick the master slab, in this case the roof section that contains the skylight.

Step 4 – Pick the skylight slab as the void to process.

Step 5 – Quit by pressing mouse button **3**. The void will be processed. You will notice that the slab's lower and upper edges move slightly as in FIG. 15-46. This is because the roof (master) slab's edges were defined as "vertical," and now the void's edges are "Vertical" too. This is fine, so don't worry. You'll be able to see it better when you check your skylight in the left elevation view. Quit back to the SLABS menu.

Step 6 – To check the void, pick the **3-D Views** option.

Step 7 – Pick the **Elevtion** option.

Step 8 – Pick **LeftElev**. The west side of your house will appear. Does the

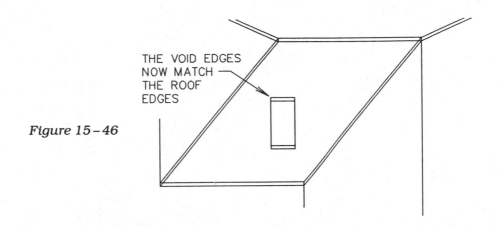

THE VOID EDGES
NOW MATCH
THE ROOF
EDGES

Figure 15 – 46

skylight look as though it was processed correctly (as in FIG. 15-47)? If not, delete the void and follow the steps to create the slab again, making sure you create it in the same direction as the roof slab. If it looks good, continue.

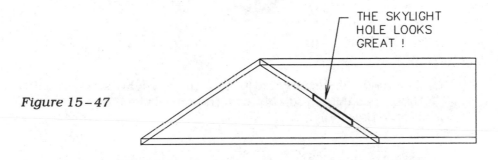

THE SKYLIGHT
HOLE LOOKS
GREAT !

Figure 15 – 47

Step 9 – Quit once, by pressing mouse button **3**, and pick **Isometrc** to return to your isometric view.

Defining another work plane

Now you will want to snap to the upper part of the skylight void for your working plane. This will allow you to create a mesh surface right on the top of the hole.

Step 1 – If necessary, window in for easier picking of the skylight corners, as shown in FIG. 15-48 on page 326.

Step 2 – Pick the **PlneSnap** option.

Step 3 – Object snap to define your new work plane, to the top side of the skylight hole. Follow the pick order shown in FIG. 15-49.

WINDOW IN
FOR EASIER
PICKING

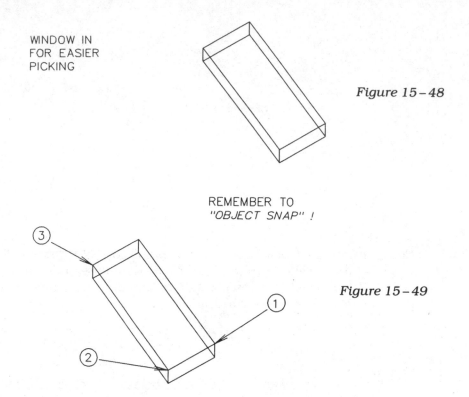

Figure 15–48

REMEMBER TO
"OBJECT SNAP" !

Figure 15–49

Step 4 – The model is now rotated so that the skylight hole is parallel to the screen (FIG. 15-50), but now the zero Z plane is on the top surface of the skylight.

YOUR NEW WORK PLANE ALLOWS YOU TO CREATE A MESH SURFACE ON THE TOP OF YOUR SKYLIGHT

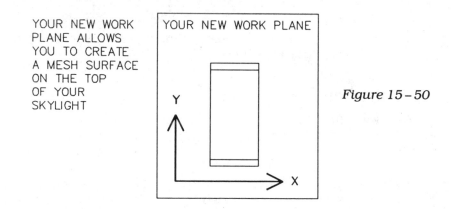

YOUR NEW WORK PLANE

Y

X

Figure 15–50

Creating the mesh surface

Step 1 – Press [**Shift**] **J** to return to 3-D ENTITY menu.

Step 2 – Pick the **Mesh Surf** option.

Step 3 – Pick **Rectangl**.

Step 4 – Pick the **DivDir1** (Divisions in Direction 1) option, change the setting to **10**, and press [**Enter**].

Step 5 – Pick the **DivDir2** (Divisions in Direction 2) option, change the setting to **10** also, and press [**Enter**].

Step 6 – Make sure the ***Z-Base** option is active. (The Z base should still be set to 0!)

Step 7 – Object snap to the void's diagonal corners, making sure to grab the top of the skylight hole, as indicated in FIG. 15-51.

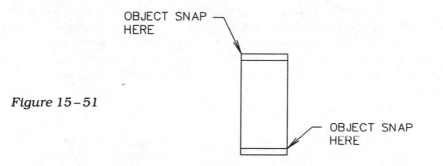

Figure 15 – 51

Step 8 – The rectangular mesh grid will be created, as shown in FIG. 15-52.

STAY IN THIS VIEW FOR THE NEXT STEP!!!

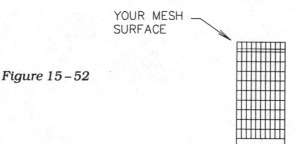

Figure 15 – 52

Curving the skylight "glass"

You will notice that the mesh contains a grid (as defined by DivDir1 and DivDir2), and you will also see that it contains 16 points, as shown in FIG. 15-53 on page 328. These points help you manipulate your surface, and are called *control points*.

At this point, your newly created mesh for your skylight is flat. Before

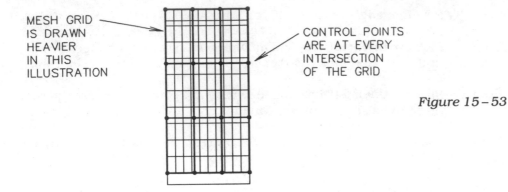

MESH GRID
IS DRAWN
HEAVIER
IN THIS
ILLUSTRATION

CONTROL POINTS
ARE AT EVERY
INTERSECTION
OF THE GRID

Figure 15 – 53

you leave this view, you can stretch the middle of the mesh up (out from the roof), resulting in a nicely curved surface, by stretching the "control points." A side view of a mesh is shown in FIG. 15-54. Notice that when you move the center control points, you actually define vectors, through which the mesh surface is forced tangent. This results in a smooth curve. How much the mesh is curved depends on the amount the control points are moved.

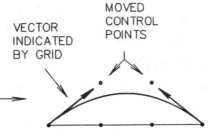

WHEN YOU MOVE A CONTROL POINT, THE MESH GENTLY CURVES THROUGH THE TANGENT VECTOR

VECTOR
INDICATED
BY GRID

MOVED
CONTROL
POINTS

Figure 15 – 54

HOW SHARP, OR "TIGHT" OF A CURVE DEPENDS ON HOW FAR THE CONTROL POINTS ARE MOVED — WHICH PROVIDES "MOMENTUM" TO THE CURVE

SIDE VIEW OF MESH, SHOWING THE ORIGINAL, FLAT POSITION, AND THE RESULTING CURVE AFTER MOVING THE CENTER 2 CONTROL POINTS

Step 1 – Press **J** to enter the 3-D EDIT menu.

Step 2 – Pick the **Stretch** option.

Step 3 – Pick **Z Dist**. (Do not use the "Z Only" option for this exercise. "Z Only" doesn't work with defined working planes, and would stretch your mesh in the true "real-world" Z direction.)

Step 4 – Type in and [**Enter**] the distance you want to stretch the mesh =

6″. Because the mesh is manipulated by its control point (which averages a move in order to smooth out the curve), your resulting curve after the stretch will be about 4″.

.6

Step 5 – Now, to get to the next menu, object snap to the SAME POINT TWICE. This will define a zero X and Y move. (See FIG. 15-55.)

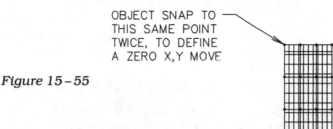

OBJECT SNAP TO THIS SAME POINT TWICE, TO DEFINE A ZERO X,Y MOVE

Figure 15 – 55

Step 6 – Make sure ***Box** is active.

Step 7 – Indicate a box around the four inside control points of the grid, as shown in FIG. 15-56. The mesh will blink.

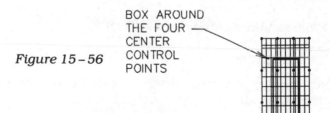

BOX AROUND THE FOUR CENTER CONTROL POINTS

Figure 15 – 56

Step 8 – Quit by pressing mouse button **3**.

Checking the mesh surface

Step 1 – Check your mesh by using the **3-D Views** option.

Step 2 – Pick the **Elevtion** option.

Step 3 – Pick the **LeftElev** option.

Step 4 – The mesh surface should appear like the one pictured in FIG. 15-57.

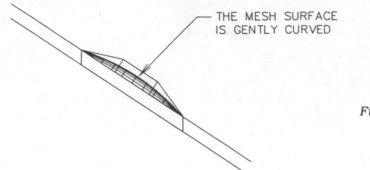

THE MESH SURFACE
IS GENTLY CURVED

Figure 15–57

Turning on and off the mesh grid and control points

Both the control points and the grid of the mesh can be turned on and off for displaying. You can turn them off when you are done manipulating the mesh surface, then turn them on again when you want to modify your mesh. (The grid and points will not plot. However, if you perform a "hide" with them on, they will be in the saved image as lines, and then they will plot.)

Step 1 – Press **J** to enter the 3-D EDIT menu.

Step 2 – Pick the **Settings** option.

Step 3 – Pick the **MeshGrd** option until it is OFF.

Step 4 – Pick the **MeshPts** option until it is OFF.

> ****Remember, you must turn these back on again in order to manipulate the mesh surface!**

Defining an edit plane

In order to have the wall "peak" up to the gabled roof, you will want to modify the wall slab in a working plane mode. You can use a second technique for defining a working plane, called "Edit Plane." (If you have ever used "New Elevation," you will find Edit Plane similar.) You define an Edit Plane using two points. The first defines the point of the plane, and the second pick defines a perpendicular point, which sets up the viewing direction and the working plane. This sounds complicated, but you will find it very easy to use.

Step 1 – Turn on all layers, by pressing **L**, and selecting **All On, Yes**.

Step 2 – Pick the **3-D Views** option.

Step 3 – Pick the **EditPlne** option.

Step 4 – Pick **Reset**, to return to the **Ortho** view.

Step 5 – Object snap to the front edge of the garage, as indicated in FIG. 15-58.

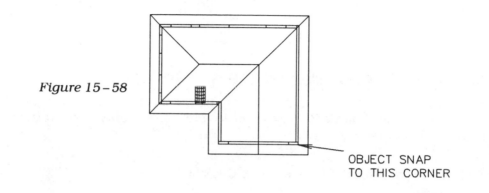

Figure 15 – 58

OBJECT SNAP
TO THIS CORNER

Step 6 – Move your cursor, and notice that an arrow is attached to it, and a line indicating a "working plane" moves along with the arrow. With Orthomode On (press O until the message says "**Orthomode is ON**"), the working plane will move to 45 degree increments. Move the cursor back into the garage, and pick so that the plane line is flat against the front of the garage, and the viewing direction is into the garage. (See FIG. 15-59.)

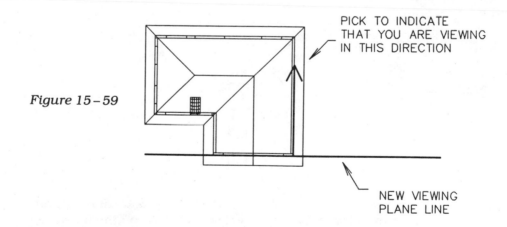

PICK TO INDICATE
THAT YOU ARE VIEWING
IN THIS DIRECTION

Figure 15 – 59

NEW VIEWING
PLANE LINE

Step 7 – The face of the garage will be flipped parallel to the screen, as in FIG. 15-60.

Step 8 – Quit by pressing mouse button **3**.

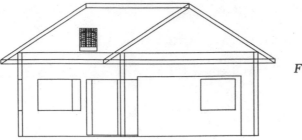

Figure 15 – 60

Modifying the wall slab for the gabled roof

You will use the function called "Partial" to modify the slab into a peaked wall. The option "partial" allows you to add, delete, and move vertices (corners) of your slabs.

Step 1 – Press [**Shift**] **J** to go to the 3-D ENTITY menu.

Step 2 – Pick **Slab**.

Step 3 – Pick the **Partial** option.

Step 4 – Pick the **AddVrtex** option.

Step 5 – Pick (do not object snap), somewhere around the middle of the top line defining the garage wall. (See FIG. 15-61.)

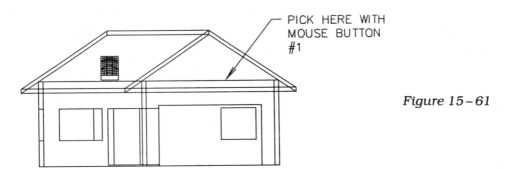

PICK HERE WITH
MOUSE BUTTON
#1

Figure 15 – 61

Step 6 – Move your cursor, and you will notice that you are dragging a new corner of the wall! The new vertex should be on the front wall of the garage, not the back wall. (This would be easy to tell, because the back wall extends the entire length of the house, while the front wall only is the size of the front of the garage.) Since your work plane is on the front wall, you probably would not have this problem. This is illustrated in FIG. 15-62.

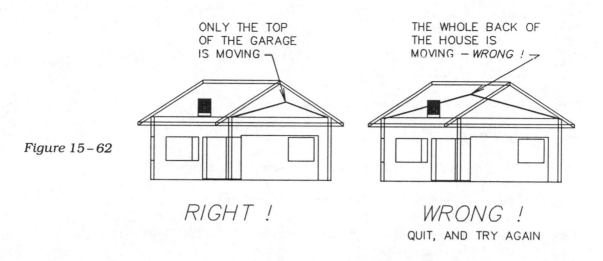

ONLY THE TOP
OF THE GARAGE
IS MOVING —

THE WHOLE BACK OF
THE HOUSE IS
MOVING — *WRONG !* —

RIGHT !

WRONG !

QUIT, AND TRY AGAIN

Figure 15–62

Step 7 – Now object snap to the roof peak, as shown in FIG. 15-63.

Figure 15–63

— OBJECT SNAP
TO FORM PEAK
IN WALL

Step 8 – Press mouse button **3** to quit.

Creating the final hide

Now you are ready to create the final hide of your house.

Step 1 – Press [**Shift**] **V** to go to the 3-D VIEWS menu.

Step 2 – Pick **SetPersp** to create a perspective view of your model.

Step 3 – Pick the **EyePtZ** option, and change the height of your eye point to **20**, then press [**Enter**].

Step 4 – You might want to press the [**Page Up**] key to move your viewing window out a bit.

Step 5 – Pick a standing point and a viewing point.

Step 6 – Once you have established a nice 3-D perspective, press capital **Y** to go to the HIDE menu.

Step 7 – Make sure the ***SavImag** option is active.

Step 8 – Pick **Begin**.

Step 9 – Once the hide is complete, pick the **NewLayer** option.

Step 10 – Name your new layer: **Hide1** and press [**Enter**].

Step 11 – Pick **On**, in order to leave your layer with the hidden view on.

Step 12 – Press [**Alt**] **E**, to return to DataCAD 2-D, and to go to the ENLARGE menu.

Step 13 – Enlarge your 3-D view as appropriate, then move it to a better location in your drawing. (See FIG. 15-64.)

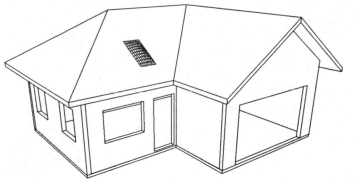

Figure 15 – 64

Step 14 – Press capital **F** to save your file.

Some additional notes on the modeler

The DataCAD Modeler is capable of doing many other functions than covered during this lesson. You will want to continue exploring the types of models that can be created using the Modeler. You can look in the *DataCAD User Manual* to find explanations of the other available functions. Have fun!

DataCAD exercise 15

Please complete the following exercise by reading each question carefully, then circling the letter that corresponds to the correct answer.

1. The quick key to go to the 3-D EDIT menu, is:
   a. **J**
   b. **V**
   c. **Y**

2. The quick key that takes you back to the 2-D EDIT menu, is:
   a. **S**
   b. **E**
   c. **;**

3. Before a hole can be punched in a slab wall, you must:
   a. Define a slab that will be processed as a hole.
   b. Rotate the slab into an edit plane.
   c. Create a working plane.

4. To process a slab into a hole, you use the:
   a. **Slab, Partial, *AddHole** options.
   b. **Slab, Voids, *AddVoid** options.
   c. **Holes, *Add** options.

5. The wall slab that will get the hole in it, is called the:
   a. Void slab.
   b. Master slab.
   c. Window slab.

6. The slab that becomes the hole, is called the:
   a. Void slab.
   b. Master slab.
   c. Window slab.

7. To easily create a roof, you use:
   a. Vertical slabs.
   b. Roof slabs.
   c. Inclined slabs.

8. To define the pitch of your roof, you:
   a. Define a Z base and height.
   b. Pick a pitch option, such as 4 in 12.
   c. Input an angle.

9. In order to draw something in a view other than the Ortho view, you use the:
   a. **Perspective** option.

b. **Edit Plane** or **Plane Snap** options.

c. **New View** option.

10. To make drawing in the new view easy, you use:

a. Real world coordinates.

b. Working plane coordinates.

c. New View coordinates.

11. In order to add a new corner to a slab, you use:

a. **Slab, Partial, AddVrtex**.

b. **Slab, Partial, NewCornr**.

c. **Corner, AddNew**.

Lesson 16
Detailing the model with doors and windows

What you will be doing

You will use the DataCAD AEC_MODL macro to create doors and windows. This new macro is provided with DataCAD, starting with the 4.0 release. It allows you to create fully detailed doors and windows. The use of this macro is explained in the *DataCAD User Manuals* (volume 3).

It is a very easy macro to use, as you will learn during this lesson. To give you an idea on how to use it, brief instructions are included here for adding windows, a door, and a French door.

Objectives

Your lesson objects are to:

- Create modeled windows
- Create modeled doors
- Create a French-look door

Starting the AEC_MODL macro

It is easy to start a macro. Like the SYMEXP macro, the AEC_MODL macro provides you with additional menus. These menus are designed to help facilitate the creation of modeled doors and windows.

Step 1 – Press [**Shift**] **M** capital **M** to go to the MACRO menu.

Step 2 – Pick the **AEC_MODL** macro.

Step 3 – The menu will appear for the macro. The two main choices on this menu are Doors and Windows. Notice that at the bottom of the menu, you can go to a 3-D VIEWS menu, and to a HIDE menu. Whenever you are in a macro, pressing a quick key or mouse button 3 will drop you back into regular DataCAD.

The first option you will use is to create windows. Pick the **Windows** option.

Step 4 – Now the WINDOWS menu is displayed. You are going to change a few of these settings before creating your window.

Pick the **UnitType** option, to set the type of window.

Step 5 – Pick ***Casement** until it is active.

Step 6 – Quit once (mouse button **3**) to return to the WINDOWS menu.

Step 7 – Pick the **Muntins** option.

Step 8 – Change the **PaneHorz** (number of panes horizontally) to **4**, and press [**Enter**].

Step 9 – Change the **PaneVert** (number of panes vertically) to **4**, and press [**Enter**].

Step 10 – Quit once (mouse button **3**) to return to the WINDOWS menu.

Step 11 – Pick ***In Plan** until it is active.

Step 12 – Change the **Head Hgt** to **6.8**, and press [**Enter**].

Step 13 – Change the **Sill Hgt** to **3.0**, and press [**Enter**].

Step 14 – [**Tab**] to the Windows layer.

Step 15 – Object snap to the first inside corner of a window opening, as indicated in FIG. 16-1.

Step 16 – Object snap to the next inside corner, as shown in FIG. 16-2.

Step 17 – Now, object snap to an outside window corner, as shown in FIG. 16-3.

Step 18 – Your window will be drawn! (FIG. 16-4 on page 340)

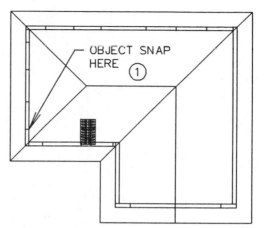

TO DRAW A
WINDOW, YOU
PICK THE TWO
INSIDE CORNERS,
THEN AN
OUTSIDE CORNER
(WHICH ALSO
INDICATES THE
WIDTH)

Figure 16 – 1

OBJECT SNAP
HERE
①

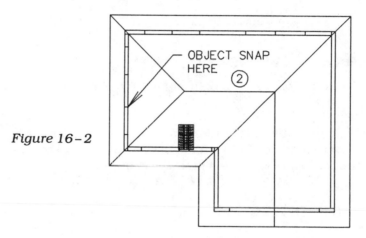

OBJECT SNAP
HERE
②

Figure 16 – 2

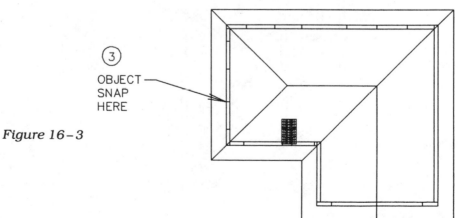

③
OBJECT
SNAP
HERE

Figure 16 – 3

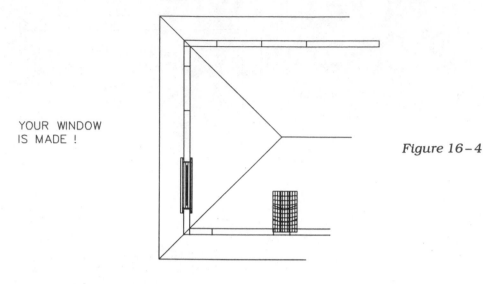

YOUR WINDOW
IS MADE !

Figure 16–4

Taking a 3-D view peek

Step 1 – Press [**Shift**] **V** to sneak into the 3-D VIEW menu without leaving the macro.

Step 2 – Pick the **Isometric** option. You might want to window in for a closer view. Notice the detail of the window. All of these items are models, so they "hide" great. See FIG. 16-5.

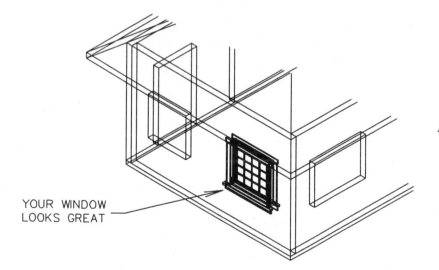

YOUR WINDOW
LOOKS GREAT

Figure 16–5

Step 3 – Pick **Ortho** to return to the plan view.

Step 4 – Press mouse button **3** to return to the WINDOWS menu.

Creating more windows

Step 1 – Continue creating the rest of the windows for your house, except for the front picture window. It should begin to look like the model pictured in FIG. 16-6.

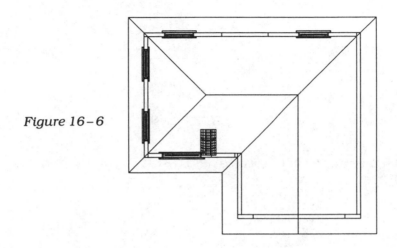

Figure 16–6

Step 2 – Once all windows are created, press mouse button **3** to return to the original menu that had the **Windows** and **Doors** options.

Creating the front door

Step 1 – Pick the **Doors** option.

Step 2 – Pick the **UnitType** option.

Step 3 – Pick the ***Single** option until it is active.

Step 4 – Pick the **%open** option, and make sure it is set to **0**. This will result in a door that is closed. Then press [**Enter**].

Step 5 – Quit (press mouse button **3**) once, to return to the DOORS menu.

Step 6 – Make sure the ***In Plan** option is active.

Step 7 – Change the **Head Hgt** to **6.8**, and press [**Enter**].

Step 8 – Change the **Sill Hgt** to **0.2**, and press [**Enter**].

Step 9 – [**Tab**] to the DOORS layer.

Step 10 – Follow the diagram below (FIG. 16-7) for the "object snap" procedure.

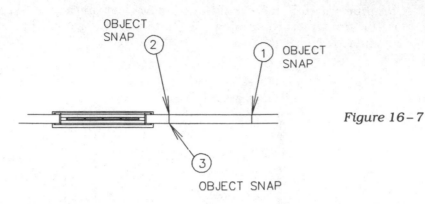

Figure 16 – 7

Step 11 – Your door will be created! (FIG. 16-8)

THE DOOR IS
CREATED, WITH
A KNOB !

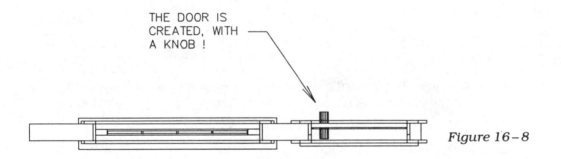

Figure 16 – 8

Taking a 3-D view peek

Step 1 – Press [**Shift**] **V** to sneak into the 3-D VIEWS menu without leaving the macro.

Step 2 – Pick the **Isometrc** option. You might want to window in for a closer view. Notice the detail of the door. All of these items are models, so they "hide" great. See FIG. 16-9.

Step 3 – Pick **Ortho** to return to the plan view.

Step 4 – Press mouse button **3** once to return to the DOORS menu.

Creating a French door

There is no easy way to create a French door using the **Doors** options. But, you can sneak in a French door by using the "**Windows**" options.

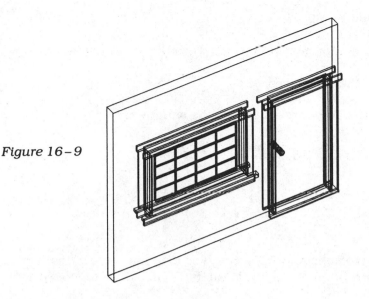

Figure 16–9

ALL OF THE
DOORS AND
WINDOWS ARE
MODELED

Step 1 – Return to the WINDOWS menu, by quitting once, and picking **Windows**.

Step 2 – You will have to change some of the settings before creating your French door.

Pick the **UnitType** option, to set the type of window.

Step 3 – Pick ***Casement** until it is active.

Step 4 – Quit once (mouse button **3**) to return to the WINDOWS menu.

Step 5 – Pick the **Muntins** option.

Step 6 – Change the **PaneHorz** (number of panes horizontally) to **3**, and press [**Enter**]. The vertical panes can remain set at 4.

Step 7 – Quit once (mouse button **3**) to return to the WINDOWS menu.

Step 8 – Change the **Sill Hgt** to **0.2**, and press [**Enter**].

Step 9 – Pick **Casing**.

Step 10 – Turn OFF **At Sill**.

Step 11 – Quit once (mouse button **3**) to return to the WINDOWS menu.

Step 12 – Pick the **Trim** option.

Step 13 – Turn OFF **At Sill**.

Step 14 – Quit once (mouse button **3**) to return to the WINDOWS menu.

Step 15 – [**Tab**] to the Windows layer.

Step 16 – Create the door just as you did the windows.

Step 17 – Press capital **F** to save your drawing.

Taking a 3-D view peek

Step 1 – Press [**Shift**] **V** to sneak into the 3-D VIEWS menu without leaving the macro.

Step 2 – Pick the **Isometrc** option. Notice how nice the French door looks. The illustration (FIG. 16-10) shows the French door, along with two casement windows.

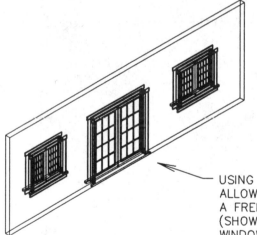

Figure 16 – 10

USING THE WINDOWS OPTION
ALLOWS YOU TO ALSO CREATE
A FRENCH DOOR LOOK
(SHOWN HERE WITH CASEMENT
WINDOWS)

The final hide

You might want to get a perspective view of your model and extract a hidden line removal image, as shown in FIG. 16-11. The results are very pleasant. A word of caution, though. If you have DataCAD 128, you will probably run out of room. Also, if you have a 286 computer, it can take a very long time to perform the hidden line removal. A 386 operating at 16 megahertz or while a faster machine will greatly reduce the time.

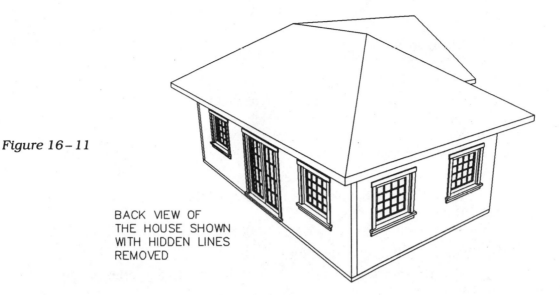

Figure 16–11

BACK VIEW OF
THE HOUSE SHOWN
WITH HIDDEN LINES
REMOVED

You might want to use less panes in the window description to speed your hide. Also, you can turn off some of the detailing (such as trims and jamb detailing).

Another note

When you use modeled windows and doors, you might want to create symbols out of them. This way, you can add them to your drawing fast and easy!

DataCAD exercise 16

Please complete the following exercise by reading each question carefully, then circling the letter that corresponds to the correct answer.

1. The quick key that takes you to the DataCAD menu, is:
   a. [**Alt**] **M**.
   b. [**Shift**] **M**.
   c. **D**.

2. The macro that facilitates the creation of modeled doors and windows, is called:
   a. DCAD_AEC.
   b. DRS&WNDW.
   c. AEC_MODL.

3. To change the type of window that you want to create, you use the:
   a. **UnitType** option.
   b. **WindwTyp** option.
   c. **Change** option.

4. To define the number of panes in your window, you use the:
   a. **Lites** option.
   b. **Muntins** option.
   c. **PaneNum** option.

5. To create a French door, you can use:
   a. Windows, and define Casement as the type.
   b. Door, and set *French.
   c. There is no way to create a French door.

6. When using the Hide function:
   a. It works real fast, no matter how many modeled entities in your drawing.
   b. The windows and doors don't hide.
   c. The more items you add, the slower it will work, so be careful, because a hide can take you hours.

7. Macros:
   a. Shouldn't be used very often, because they are so hard to use.
   b. Are a great way to save steps.
   c. Do not come with DataCAD.

Appendix A
The DataCAD
Operations Guide

Contents

This operations guide is a step-by-step "cookbook" designed to help you in your daily use of DataCAD. This guide is revised to DataCAD release 4.0.

Starting information

If you want to do this: Follow these steps:

Starting your computer

Starting your computer

1. Open diskette drive door. (Disk drive door should always be left open when not in use.)
2. Turn processor on.
3. Turn display screen on.

Starting DataCAD

Starting DataCAD

1. Type in and press [**Enter**]: **cd \ mtec**
2. Type in and press [**Enter**]: **rundcad**
3. Press the [**Enter**] key after reading copyright screen.
4. Pick a drawing from the drawing list, or type in and [**Enter**] a new drawing name.

Changing drawing lists

Changing to another drawing list (directory) by typing it in

1. Start DataCAD. The drawing list will be displayed.
2. Pick **New path**.
3. Type in the path name for your directory. Example: **dwg** *Notice:* If your drawing directory is NOT in the MTEC directory, put a \ before the name. If it is in another drive, put the drive name and a backslash. Example: **d: \ 893205**
4. Press [**Enter**].
5. If it is a new directory, pick **Yes**.

If you want to do this:	Follow these steps:
Changing to another drawing list (directory) by PICKING	1. Start DataCAD. The drawing list will be displayed. 2. Pick **New Path**. 3. Pick the **..** option to display the parent directory choices. -or- Pick the <**ROOT**> option to go to the root directory. 4. Pick the correct sub-directory(s) for your drawing list pathname. 5. Notice the pathname appears in the message area of your screen, in the text line. 6. Press [**Enter**] to accept the pathname. Your drawings will be displayed.

DataCAD menus

Switching EDIT and UTILITY menus	1. Press mouse button **3** to toggle between menus (or the right-most button). Mouse button **3** selects the S0 option, which is either Edit or Utility from the two main menus.
Picking a menu option	1. Move the mouse (cursor) to highlight the option: 2. Press mouse button **1**.
Exiting a sub-menu	1. Press mouse button **3** until the EDIT or UTILITY menu is displayed. (In most menus, the S0 option is Exit.)

Saving your drawing

Quick save	1. Press [**Shift**] **F**.
Temporary save (Automatic Save)	1. Pick **Settings** from the UTILITY menu. 2. Pick **SaveDlay**. 3. Type in the desired minutes between an automatic temporary save, and press [**Enter**]. Example: **30**

If you want to do this:	Follow these steps:

Exiting DataCAD

If you want to do this:	Follow these steps:
Exiting DataCAD and saving your drawing	1. Press [**Alt**] **Q**, or pick the **Quit** option, found in the UTILITY menu.
	2. Pick **Yes**, or type **Y**.
Exiting DataCAD and NOT saving any drawing changes	1. Press [**Alt**] **Q**, or pick the **Quit** option, found in the UTILITY menu.
	2. Pick **Abort**.
	3. Pick **Yes**, or type **Y**.

Retrieving the automatic save file

To access the "automatic save" file of your drawing	1. Start DataCAD.
	2. Pick the name of the drawing you were last working on from the drawing list.
	3. If there is an automatic save file for this drawing, you will be prompted: **WARNING: An autosave file (.ASV) for this drawing is present. Are you sure you want to continue?**
	4. Pick **Yes**.
	5. Pick **Yes** again to "**rename your file.**"
	6. Type in a new name for your .ASV file. It should not match the original file name. DO NOT add the DC3 extension, as the system does this for you. Example: Original file – **SITE001** rename .ASV file to – **SITE0012**
	7. Press [**Enter**].
	8. Press [**Enter**] again to continue.
	9. The drawing list is displayed, and the new drawing name you designated will now appear in the list.

DataCAD drawing operations (listed alphabetically)

If you want to do this:	Follow these steps:

Changing existing items

Changing the color of an existing item	1. Press [**Alt**] **c** (Edit/Change).
	2. Make sure ***Entity** is active (***** = active).

If you want to do this:	Follow these steps:
	3. Pick **Color**.
	4. Pick desired new color from menu.
	5. Pick entities to change to new color.
Changing the color of a group of items (many items created at one time)	1. Press [**Alt**] **c** (Edit/Change).
	2. Make sure ***Group** is active (***** = active).
	3. Pick **Color**.
	4. Pick desired new color from menu.
	5. Pick one entity indicating the group to change to new color.
Changing the color of many items in an area	1. Press [**Alt**] **c** (Edit/Change).
	2. Make sure ***Area** or ***Fence** is active (***** = active).
	3. Pick **Color**.
	4. Pick desired new color from menu.
	5. Pick two points indicating an area around the items you wish to change, or multiple points for your fence.
	6. If using Fence, press mouse button **3** to close it.
Changing other attributes of existing items (LineType, LineWgt, Color, Spacing, OverSht, Z-Base, Z-Height)	1. Press [**Alt**] **c** (Edit/Change).
	2. Make sure ***Entity, *Group, *Area,** or ***Fence** is active, as applicable.
	3. Pick and set the options that apply to the type of change desired. A star will appear by the options you have set.
	4. Pick items or area to change.
	5. If using Fence, press mouse button **3** to close it.
Changing existing items to match another existing item (Matching)	1. Press [**Alt**] **c** (Edit/Change).
	2. Pick ***Match** until it is active (***** = Active).
	3. Pick the options that will effectuate the type of change desired (LineType, LineWgt, Color, etc.), until a star appears by the option -or- Pick ***All** to match all attributes of the existing item.

If you want to do this:	Follow these steps:
	4. Select the item that has the attributes you WANT TO MATCH.
	5. Use ***Entity**, ***Group**, ***Area**, or ***Fence** to select the first item you WANT TO CHANGE.
	6. The second selected item will be changed to match the first selected item.
	7. If you want to pick more than one item or area TO CHANGE, pick **Match** to turn it OFF (no *****). This keeps all of the change information set to what you matched. Now continue to pick the items you wish changed.
Changing existing text to match other existing text	See TEXT, Matching existing text attributes
Changing the content of text	See TEXT, Editing existing text
Changing the size of text when changing a plotting scale	See TEXT, Changing the size of existing text - or- See TEXT, Relative text to plot scale
Changing the Layer of existing items	See MOVE, Moving items to another layer

Colors

Switching colors (Quick toggle)	1. Press **k** to scroll forward through the color list. 2. Press [**Shift**] **K** to scroll backward.
Assigning a color to a layer	1. Press [**Tab**] until the appropriate layer is displayed. 2. Press **k** to quickly change colors. This color will remain set on this layer until you change it.

If you want to do this:	Follow these steps
	Also see LAYERS, "Assigning a color to a layer, using the LAYER menu."
Changing the color of an item	See CHANGING EXISTING ITEMS, "Changing the color of an existing item."

Coordinate input

Definition of Cartesian coordinates (X,Y,Z)	1. Relative – MOST COMMONLY USED FROM a start point. X = across the screen, horizontal. Y = up and down, vertical. Z = coming out of the screen, depth (Height of walls). 2. Absolute – USUALLY NOT USED From the 0,0 origin. Same X,Y,Z as above.
Typing in format of feet-inches (Architectural units)	1 = 1'-0" 1.6 = 1'-6" .5 = 5" 1.4.$^1/_2$ = 1'-4$^1/_2$" .0.$^1/_8$"= $^1/_8$"
Definition of Polar coordinates (distance/angle)	1. Relative – MOST COMMONLY USED FROM a start point. Distance = along the angle, length of line. Angle = Degrees, Minutes, Seconds Z = coming out of the screen, depth (Height of walls). 2. Absolute – USUALLY NOT USED From the 0,0 origin. Same Distance/Angle as above.
Typing in format of angles (Normal or compass angle type)	1 1 degree 1.2 1 degree 2 minutes 1.2.15 1 degree 2 minutes 15 seconds

If you want to do this:	Follow these steps:
Definition of Polar angles	1. Normal – Counterclockwise movement. 0 horizontal at 3:00 position, 90 at 12:00, 180 at 9:00, 270 at 6:00. 2. Bearing – North, East, South, and West positions. 3. Compass – Clockwise movement. 0 at 12:00, 90 at 3:00, 180 at 6:00, 270 at 9:00.
Setting Normal or Compass Angle Type	1. Pick **Settings** from UTILITY menu. 2. Pick **AngleTyp**. 3. Pick **Normal** or **Compass** as applicable. 4. Press mouse button **3** to quit.
Setting Bearing Angle Type	1. Pick **Settings** from UTILITY menu. 2. Pick **AngleTyp**. 3. Pick **Bearing**. 4. Pick **Strt Angl**. 5. Pick two points to indicate a NORTH direction for your drawing. 6. Press mouse button **3** to quit back to SETTINGS menu. 7. Pick **ScaleTyp**. 8. Pick **Decimal** and **Units** until they are active (*****).
Typing in Cartesian relative coordinates	1. ALWAYS pick starting point. 2. Press [**Ins**] key until **Current input mode is relative cartesian (X,Y).** is displayed. 3. Press the [**Space bar**]. 4. Type in **X** (horizontal) distance, and [**Enter**].

If you want to do this:	Follow these steps:
	5. Type in **Y** (vertical) distance, and [**Enter**].
	6. Your new line/wall is drawn.
	7. Press the [**Space bar**] again to input next X,Y distance.
	8. This input mode will remain set until you change it.
Typing in polar angles (Normal or Compass Polar)	1. ALWAYS pick starting point.
	2. Press [**Ins**] key until **Current input mode is relative polar (distance, angle).** is displayed.
	3. Press the [**Space bar**].
	4. Type in distance, and [**Enter**].
	5. Type in angle, and [**Enter**].
	6. Your new line/wall is drawn.
	7. Press the [**Space bar**] again to input next distance and angle.
	8. This input mode will remain set until you change it.
Typing in angles (Bearings polar)	1. Pick starting point.
	2. Press [**Ins**] key until **Current input mode is relative polar (distance, angle).** is displayed.
	3. Press the [**Space bar**].
	4. Type in distance, and [**Enter**].
	5. Type in angle (ex. **N90E** would draw a horizontal line towards the right), and [**Enter**].
	6. Your new line/wall is drawn.
	7. Press the [**Space bar**] again to input next distance and angle.
Typing in format of angles (Bearing angle type)	n83.45.14e = north bearing 83 degrees 45 minutes 14 seconds due east s0.154w = south bearing 0 degrees 15 minutes 0 seconds due west
Using a reference point for coordinate input	1. Press [~] key.
	2. Pick point or corner to measure from (use OBJECT SNAP!).

If you want to do this:	Follow these steps:
	3. If necessary, use [**Ins**] key to set input mode.
	4. Press the [**Space bar**].
	5. Type in and [**Enter**] coordinates for the FIRST point of wall (or other item you are creating).
	6. Continue using the [**Space bar**] to type in your coordinates as needed.

Copying

Creating a single copy of an item or group of items	1. Press **c** key (EDIT/COPY menus).
	2. Pick two points indicating distance to move the new copy to.
	3. Pick **Entity** or **Group** until it is active (*), whichever is applicable.
	4. Pick item to copy.
Creating a copy of many items at once	1. Press **c** key (EDIT/COPY menus).
	2. Pick two points indicating distance to move the new copy to.
	3. Pick **Area** or **Fence** until it is active (*).
	4. Pick two diagonal points indicating a rectangle around items to be copied, or multiple points if using Fence.
	5. If using Fence, press mouse button **3** to close.
Creating multiple copies in one or two directions	1. Press **c** key (EDIT/COPY menus).
	2. Pick **RectArray**.
	3. Pick two points indicating the distance to move the new copies horizontally and vertically.
	4. Type in the TOTAL number of copies you want in the X direction (minimum = 1).
	5. Type in the TOTAL number of copies you want in the Y direction (minimum = 1).
	6. Pick **Entity**, **Group**, **Area**, or **Fence** until the desired option is active (*).
	7. Pick item(s) to copy.

If you want to do this:	Follow these steps:

Creating multiple copies on an angle

1. Press **c** (EDIT/COPY menus).
2. Pick **RectArry**.
3. Pick **Angular**.
4. Pick the first point to indicate a starting position for your copies.
5. Pick the second point to indicate the angle.
   -or-
   Use Relative Polar to type in angle. (Example: relative distance: 2 relative angle: 30 (Distance is arbitrary and is only being used to establish an angle.)
6. Pick to establish a distance.
   -or-
   Use Relative Polar to type in a distance, using same angle as established in step 5.
7. Use ***Entity**, ***Group**, ***Area**, or ***Fence** to select items to copy.

Making copies by dragging to position

1. Press **M** (EDIT/MOVE menus).
2. Pick **Drag**.
3. Pick **AndCopy** until it is active (*****).
4. Use ***Entity**, ***Group**, ***Area**, or ***Fence** until the desired option is active (*****).
5. Pick item(s) to copy.
6. Drag copies to position, and pick or object snap to place.

Copying items from one layer to another

1. Press **C**.
2. Pick **To Layer**.
3. Pick the layer you want to copy "to."
4. Pick items to copy by **Entity**, **Group**, **Area**, or **Fence**.
5. Press mouse button **3** to quit.

Crunching the drawing

See MACROS, Crunching the drawing using LYRUTIL

Default drawings

Creating the default drawing file

1. Start DataCAD, or start a new drawing so that the drawing list is displayed.

If you want to do this:	Follow these steps:

2. Pick **Default**.
3. Press [**Space bar**] once to clear any current default and press [**Enter**], -or- pick a default you wish to copy for your new default drawing (if necessary, pick **New Path**, and type in the default pathname to retrieve list: **default**).
4. When you are returned to your original drawing list, pick **New Path**.
5. Type in and [**Enter**] the name for the drawing default directory: **default**.
6. If this is a new directory, pick **Yes**.
7. Start a new drawing, giving it a descriptive name that defines the final plot scale and type. Example: **1-4PLAN** for a $1/4''$ plan type of drawing.
8. Define all necessary settings and defaults, create and name layers, plot scale and paper size, and other default drawing characteristics.
9. Pick **File I/O** from the UTILITY menu.
10. Pick **New Dwg**.
11. Pick **Yes** to save current drawing.
12. Pick **New Path** to return to your original drawing list.
13. Type in and [**Enter**] the name of your drawing directory. Example: **dwg**.

Using the default drawing

1. Start DataCAD, or if in DataCAD, pick **File I/O**, **NewDwg** to retrieve the drawing list.
2. Pick **Default** when the drawing list is displayed.
3. If necessary, pick **New Path**, and type in the default pathname, and press [**Enter**]: **default**
4. Pick the desired default drawing.
5. This default will stay set until you change it, or you quit DataCAD.

If you want to do this:	Follow these steps:

Dimensioning

Creating a single horizontal or vertical dimension	

1. Press [**Alt**] **d** (UTILITY/DIMENSION/ LINEAR menus).
2. Press [**Tab**] key until dimension layer is active.
3. If LyrSnap is not already active, Press [**Shift**] **X**, and pick **LyrSnap** until it is active (*****).
4. Pick **Horiznt** or **Verticl** until it is active (*****Horiznt).
5. Object snap to the first corner of wall or item to dimension from.
6. Object snap to next item to dimension to.
7. Pick location of dimension line, if **FixdDist** is not active.
8. Pick text position, if **AutoText** is not used.

Creating a string
line dimension
(horizontal or vertical)

1. Press [**Alt**] **d** (UTILITY/DIMENSION/ LINEAR menus).
2. Press [**Tab**] key until dimension layer is active.
3. If LyrSnap is not active, Press [**Shift**] **X**, and pick **LyrSnap** until it is active (*****).
4. Pick **Horiznt** or **Verticl** until it is active (*****Horiznt).
5. Object snap to the first corner of wall or item to dimension from.
6. Object snap to next item to dimension.
7. Pick location of dimension line, if FixdDist is not active.
8. Pick text position, if AutoText is not used.
9. Pick **Strnglin**.
10. Object snap to the *next item* to dimension.
11. Continue object snapping to items until all items are dimensioned.
12. When done with this stack of dimensions, quit by pressing mouse button **3**.

If you want to do this:	Follow these steps:
Creating a stringline dimension with an overall dimension	1. Follow steps 1 through 12 on page 360. 2. Press mouse button **3** once to quit back to the LINEAR DIMENSIONS menu, but *DO NOT LEAVE MENU*. 3. Pick the **Overall** option. 4. Use your cursor to place the overall dimension, and pick with mouse button **1**.
Dimensioning to the center of walls	1. Press [**Alt**] **g** (UTILITY/GEOMETRY menus). 2. Pick **Divide**. 3. Pick **Divisions**. 4. Type in **2**, and press [**Enter**]. 5. Object snap to the first line end point of the wall (first side of T intersection). 6. Object snap to the second line end point of the same wall (second side of T intersection). 7. A snap point will appear in the center of the wall end. 8. Follow steps 5 through 7 for all walls that will require dimensioning to the center. 9. Press [**Alt**] **d**. 10. Follow procedure for making dimensions, this time object snapping to wall center points.
Adding to existing dimensions	1. Additional rows of dimensions can be added by using the above techniques, but snapping to the tic marks of the existing dimension. This will also eliminate the gaps that result when using **Overall** option.
Creating rotated dimensions	1. Press **D** key (UTILITY/DIMENSION menu). 2. Pick the **Linear** option. 3. Press [**Tab**] until the dimension layer is active. 4. Make sure **LyrSnap** is active in the OBJECT SNAP menu.

If you want to do this:	Follow these steps:

5. Pick the **Rotate** option.
6. Type in the desired angle of rotation, and press [**Enter**] -or- Pick the **Match** option, then pick the line you will want the dimension to run parallel to. Press mouse button **3** to quit back to the DIMENSION menu.
7. The **Rotate** option will be active (***Rotate**).
8. Object snap to the first corner of wall or item to dimension.
9. Object snap to the next item.
10. Move your cursor away from the wall to place the text, if **FixdDist** is not active.

Setting dimension variables

1. Press **D** key (UTILITY/DIMENSION menu).
2. Pick **Linear**.
3. Pick **TextStyl**.
4. Adjust values in applicable options.
5. Make ***AutoTxt** active.
6. Press mouse button **3** once to quit.
7. Pick **DimStyl**.
8. Adjust values in applicable options.
9. Turn **FixdDist** OFF.
10. Press mouse button **3** once to quit.
11. Pick **ArroStyl**.
12. Adjust values in applicable options.
13. Press mouse button **3** once to quit.
14. Pick **AutoStyl**, if applicable.
15. Make ***Strngli**, ***PtsOnly**, and ***LyrSrch** active.
16. Press mouse button **3** to quit.

Changing the color of the dimension text in new dimensions

1. Press [**Alt**] **D**.
2. Pick **TextStyl**.
3. Pick **Color**.
4. Pick the color that you desire the text to appear in new dimensions.
5. If applicable, change the **Weight** of your text back to 1.
6. Quit by pressing mouse button **3**.

If you want to do this:	Follow these steps:
Changing the color of the dimension tic-mark in new dimensions	1. Press [**Alt**] **D**. 2. Pick **Dimstyl**. 3. Pick **Color**. 4. Pick the color you wish to have your tic-marks appear in new dimensions. 5. If applicable, change the **Weight** of the tic-marks back to 1.
Changing existing associated dimensions	1. Press [**Alt**] **D**. 2. Pick **Change**. 3. Pick **TextStyl**, **DimStyl**, or **ArroStyl** as applicable. 4. Adjust the variables you wish to change in the existing dimensions. 5. Quit back to the DIM CHANGE menu by pressing mouse button **3** once. 6. Use ***Entity**, ***Group**, ***Area**, ***Fence** as applicable to select the dimensions to change.
Changing the location of text in the existing associated dimension	1. Press [**Alt**] **D**. 2. Pick **Change**. 3. Pick **TxtPostn** (text position). 4. Pick the dimension that has the text you want to move. You can pick it at the center of the dimension line below the text, or by the tic mark. 5. Drag the text to a new location, using the cursor. 6. Pick to place the text.

Display settings

| Showing text as boxes | 1. Pick **Display** from the UTILITY menu.
2. Pick **ShowTxt** until it is OFF (no *****).
3. Pick **BoxColor**.
4. Select the color you would like the text boxes to appear in.
5. Press mouse button **3** to quit.
Note: When you are in the **Text** function and perform a redraw ([**Esc**]), or regeneration if you have display list processing (**u**), the boxes will appear as text again. |

If you want to do this:	Follow these steps:
Adjusting the size of text that will be shown as boxes	1. Pick **Display** from the UTILITY menu. 2. Pick **SmallTxt**. 3. Type in the size (in pixels) indicating how small your text can be before it will appear as a box, then press [**Enter**]. (Usually you can figure the size based on how little text is on the screen before you can't read it anymore.) Example: **10** 4. Pick **ShowTxt** until it is OFF (no *). 5. Pick **BoxColor**. 6. Select the color you would like the text box to appear in. 7. Press mouse button **3** to quit. *Note*: If you are using display list processing, the text box may not appear when the text is displayed small until a regeneration is performed.
Turning on and off the display of Dimensions	1. Pick **Display** from the UTILITY menu. 2. Pick **ShowDim** until the * is off. Your dimensions will disappear entirely until ***ShowDim** is turned on again. *Caution*: It is better to turn off the dimension layer, since people forget this setting is off. 3. The D will appear small in **SWOTHLUd** when ShowDim is off. 4. Press mouse button **3** to quit.
Turning on and off the display of Hatch	1. Pick **Display** from the UTILITY menu. 2. Pick **ShwHtch** until the * is off. Any hatching will disappear entirely until ***ShwHtch** is turned on again. *Caution*: It is better to turn off the Hatch layer if possible, since people forget this setting is off. 3. The H will appear small in **SWOThLUD** when ShwHtch is off. 4. Press mouse button **3** to quit.

If you want to do this:	Follow these steps:
Turning on and off the display of Line Weights	1. Pick **Display** from the UTILITY menu. 2. Pick **ShowWgt** until the * is off. All weighted lines will appear as weight 1 until ***ShowWgt** is turned on again. *Note*: Turn ***ShowWgt** back on before a plot, and to check that all lines have the proper weights as expected. 3. The L will appear small in **SWOTHIUD** when ShowWgt is off. 4. Press mouse button **3** to quit.
Turning on and off the display of Line Types	1. Pick **Display** from the UTILITY menu. 2. Pick **UserLin** until the * is off. All linetypes will appear as solid until ***UserLin** is turned on again. *Note*: Turn ***UserLin** back on before you plot, and to check that all lines have the proper linetypes as expected. 3. The U will appear small in **SWOTHLuD** when UserLin is off. 4. Press mouse button **3** to quit.
Turning on and off the display of Line Over shoots	1. Press – to turn on and off the display of overshoots. 2. Press [**Esc**] to redraw the screen, or **u** to regenerate the screen if you have display list processing. 3. This function can be found by picking **Display** from the UTILITY menu. Look for the ***OverSht** option. *Note*: Turn ON the display of overshoots before you plot and to check that all lines have the proper overshoots as expected.
Turning on and off the display of Insertion points (handle points)	1. Pick **Display** from the UTILITY menu. 2. Pick **ShowIns** until the * is off. All symbols handle points will be turned off until ***ShowIns** is turned on again. 3. Press mouse button **3** to quit.

If you want to do this:	Follow these steps:
Turning on and off the display of Curve center points	1. Pick **Display** from the UTILITY menu. 2. Pick **CrvCtrs** until the * is off. All circle and arc center points will be turned off from displaying until ***CrvCtrs** is turned on again. *Note*: Curve centers will plot. 3. Press mouse button **3** to quit.
Turning on and off the display of Associated Dimension handle points	1. Pick **Display** from the UTILITY menu. 2. Pick **DimmPts** until the * is off. All associated dimension handle points will be turned off from displaying until ***DimmPts** is turned on again. *Note*: DimmPts will plot and are intended to help you find the points for ease in stretching. 3. Press mouse button **3** to quit.
Adjusting the size of symbols that will be shown as boxes	1. Pick **Display** from the UTILITY menu. 2. Pick **SmallSym**. 3. Type in the size (in pixels) indicating how small your symbols can be before they will appear as a box, then press [**Enter**]. (Usually you can figure the size based on how little a symbol is on the screen before you can't see the details anymore.) Example **10** *Note*: The box color will appear as the color of the symbol handle point (active color when you placed the symbol). 4. Press mouse button **3** to quit.
Changing the resolution of curves on the screen	1. Pick **Display** from the UTILITY menu. 2. Pick **ArcFactor**. 3. Type in the size for the arc factor, then press [**Enter**]. The larger the number the finer the resolution. Going too fine can slow down the redraw of your display. If you are using display list processing, 10 will

If you want to do this:	Follow these steps:
	keep your arcs from looking like squares when you zoom in. Example: **10** 4. Press mouse button **3** to quit.
Setting the layer redraw order	1. Pick **Display** from the UTILITY menu. 2. Pick **LayerOrder**. 3. Pick ***First** to redraw the active layer first, ***Last** to redraw the active layer last, or ***InOrder** to redraw the layers in the defined order appearing in the layer list. 4. Press mouse button **3** to quit.
Turning off the display Regeneration Warning (Continue, Stop)	1. Pick **Display** from the UTILITY menu. 2. Pick **DispList**. 3. Pick **RgnWarn** until it is OFF (no *). 4. Press mouse button **3** to quit.
Adjusting your display list window size	1. Pick **Display** from the UTILITY menu. 2. Pick **DispList**. 3. Pick **WndwSize** until it is OFF (no *) 4. Type in 4 and press [**Enter**]. 5. Press mouse button **3** to quit.
Displaying the display list status	1. Pick **Display** from the UTILITY menu. 2. Pick **DispList**. 3. Pick **Status**. 4. The status will appear in the message area of the screen. 5. Press mouse button **3** to quit.

Doors

Adding doors	1. Press **A** key (EDIT/ARCHITCT menus). 2. Pick **DoorSwng**. 3. Pick **LyrSrch** until the layer list is displayed. 4. Pick the layer that the appropriate walls are on. This layer will remain set until you change it. 5. Pick hinge side on wall.

If you want to do this:	Follow these steps:

<table>
<tr><td></td><td>6. Pick strike side on wall.</td></tr>
<tr><td></td><td>7. Pick swing direction.</td></tr>
<tr><td></td><td>8. Pick outside of wall.</td></tr>
<tr><td></td><td>9. Your door will be created.</td></tr>
</table>

Adding doors using relative coordinate input

1. Press **A** key (EDIT/ARCHITCT menus

2. Pick **DoorSwng**.

3. Pick **LyrSrch** until the layer list is displayed.

4. Pick the layer that the appropriate walls are on. This layer will remain set until you change it.

5. Press [~] key.

6. Object snap to the inside corner you will reference the door placement from. This corner will become the 0,0 position.

7. Press [**Insert**] until the relative cartesian coordinates mode is set.

8. Press the [**Space bar**].

9. Type in the **X** coordinate for the door hinge, if applicable, and press [**Enter**] (X = horizontal, to the right). Use the - sign if the coordinate is toward the left.

10. Type in the **Y** coordinate for the door hinge, if applicable, and press [**Enter**] (Y = Vertical, up). Use the - sign if the coordinate is going down.
    Example: **X = 0.4**
    　　　　　Y = 0.0

11. Move your cursor to check that the door hinge is located in the correct area.

12. Press the [**Space bar**].

13. Type in the **X** coordinate to indicate the door swing (width of door), if applicable, and press [**Enter**] (X = horizontal, to the right). Use the - sign if the coordinate is toward the left.

If you want to do this:	Follow these steps:

14. Type in the **Y** coordinate, if applicable, and press [**Enter**] (Y = Vertical, up). Use the - sign if the coordinate is going down.
   Example: **X = 2.8**
             Y = 0.0
15. Pick swing direction.
16. Pick outside of wall.
17. Your door will be created.

Setting head height of doors

1. Press **A**.
2. Pick **DoorSwng**.
3. Pick **Head Hgt**.
4. Pick or type in head height of door.
5. Press [**Enter**].

Adding doors and windows on multiple story buildings

1. Press **Z**.
2. Change the Z-Base ad Z-Height to correct values for the walls on the story you will be adding doors and windows to.
3. Doors and windows will be inserted into the walls at that level.

Erasing Doors (Removing)

1. Press **a**.
2. Pick **DoorSwng**.
3. Pick **Remove**.
4. Pick two points to indicate a box around the door to remove.
5. Door is erased and walls are cleaned up.
   Caution: There is no UNDO. However, door may be recovered by pressing the > key, but wall will have to be cut again.
   Note: Windows and cut walls may also be removed with this option.

Erasing Windows (Removing)

1. Press **a**.
2. Pick **Windows**.
3. Pick **Remove**.
4. Pick two points to indicate a box around the window to remove.

If you want to do this:	Follow these steps:

5. Window is erased and walls are cleaned up.
Caution: There is no UNDO.
However, window may be recovered by pressing the > key, but wall will have to be cut again.
Note: Doors and cut walls may also be removed with this option.

Erasing Cuts in Walls (Removing)

1. Press **a**.
2. Pick **Cut Wall**.
3. Pick **Remove**.
4. Pick two points to indicate a box around the cut-out in the wall to remove.
5. Cut-out area is erased and walls are cleaned up.
Caution: There is no UNDO.
Note: Windows and doors may also be removed with this option.

Dividing snap points

See SNAP POINTS (MARKERS & DIVISIONS)

DXF formatted files

Notice: If you are transferring files to AutoCAD, make sure there are no spaces and no special characters in the names of your layers (! @ # $ % & * – _ + = ?), as these are reserved for special uses in AutoCAD.

Creating a DXF File from a DataCAD drawing

1. Have the drawing you wish to transfer displayed on your screen.
2. Press **L** (UTILITY/LAYERS menus).
3. Pick **On/Off**.
4. Check that your layer names do not have special characters in them (as mentioned in the above note).
5. Press mouse button **3** once.
6. Pick **All On**.
7. Pick **Yes**.
8. Press mouse button **3** to quit.
9. Pick **File I/O**.
10. Pick **WriteDXF**.
11. Pick ***Auto** to automatically adjust the

If you want to do this:	Follow these steps:
	line spacing for dashcd, *dotted, and dot-dashed linetypes.
	-or-
	Pick *Intract to type in your own line spacing values.
	12. Pick Begin.
	13. If you selected Intract, type in the values for the line spacing, pressing [Enter] each time.
	14. Pick New Path.
	15. Type in the correct path for your DXF files and press [Enter]. Example: dxf
	16. If it is a new directory, pick Yes to create it.
	17. Press [Enter] to accept present drawing name, or type in new name. Do NOT add the .dxf extension to the drawing name.
	18. The DXF file is created (filename.dxf). If you followed the example in step 15, your DXF file resides in the MTEC/DXF directory.
Retrieving a DXF file into DataCAD	1. Load DXF file into \MTEC\DXF directory.
	2. Start DataCAD.
	3. Start a new drawing.
	4. Pick File I/O.
	5. Pick Read DXF.
	6. When transferring AutoCAD drawings, make sure *Auto is active to turn off the user prompts, so that DataCAD will make best guesses for matching linetypes. If transferring from another CAD software, you may want to have *Intract active so that you can adjust the linetypes manually.
	7. Pick Scale.
	8. Type in 1, if the DXF file was originally creating in Feet/Inches/Fractions (1 = 1 foot). If the file was created as

If you want to do this:	Follow these steps:

Inches/Fractions (1 = 1 inch), type in .1, and press [**Enter**].

9. Pick **Begin**.
10. Pick **New Path**.
11. Type in and [**Enter**] the correct path for your DXF files: **dxf**
12. Pick the drawing you wish to convert to DataCAD.
13. If *Intract is being used, follow the prompts to define the linetypes.
    If *Auto, best guesses will be made for linetypes.
14. The drawing will be loaded into the present drawing file.
15. Check the size of your lines and that they came over in the correct scale. If there is a discrepancy, **Abort** the file and redo the procedure, this time trying a different scale. (It will usually be 1 or .1.)

Enlarging

Enlarging items

1. Press [**Alt**] **e** (EDIT/ENLARGE menus).
2. Pick to indicate the center of enlargement. This will be the enlargement stationary point.
3. Pick **Enlargmnt**.
4. Pick **Set All**.
5. Type in the applicable enlargement factor, and press [**Enter**].
   Example: **2** (will double the size)
6. Select items by *Entity, *Group, *Area, or *Fence.
7. If the enlargement resulted in undesired results, pick **Undo** BEFORE leaving option.

Undoing an enlargement if you already left the menu (last enlargement)

1. Press [**Alt**] **E**.
2. Pick **PrevCntr**.
3. Pick **Invert**.
4. Pick the entities to restore to the original size by *Entity, *Group, *Area, or *Fence, as applicable.

If you want to do this:	Follow these steps:
Finding the opposite calculation for a reduction (e.g., Enlarging a border for scale or enlarging a detail for plotting in a plan drawing)	1. Press [**Alt**] **E**. 2. Pick anywhere for the center. 3. Pick **Enlargmnt**. 4. Pick **Set All**. 5. Type in the factor (e.g., the plot scale), and press [**Enter**]. Example: $^1/_4''$ scale factor = .020833333 6. Quit back to the ENLARGE menu by pressing mouse button **3**. 7. Pick **Invert**. The opposite calculation will be displayed. Now you can enlarge your items, if applicable.

Erasing

Erasing entire areas	1. Press **E** (EDIT/ERASE menus). 2. Pick ***Area** or ***Fence** until it is active (*****). 3. Turn on or off the **LyrSrch** option as applicable. 4. Pick two points indicating a rectangle around the items you wish to erase, or multiple points if using Fence. 5. If using Fence, press mouse button **3** to close it.
Erasing picked items or groups	1. Press **E** (EDIT/ERASE menus). 2. Make sure ***Entity** or ***Group** is active, as applicable. (***** = active.) 3. Pick the items or group to erase.
Erasing the last line created	1. If necessary, press mouse button **3** to quit drawing lines. 2. Press the [,] (comma) key.
Erasing the last group created	1. Press the [**Shift**] and [<] keys simultaneously. 2. If the last items drawn were created as a group, they will be erased.
Restoring the last entity or group erased.	1. Press the [.] (period) key. 2. If the last item erased was an entity, it will be restored.

If you want to do this:	Follow these steps:
	3. If the last item erased was a group, it will be restored.
Erasing Doors	See DOORS and WINDOWS, "Erasing Doors (Removing)"
Erasing Windows	See DOORS and WINDOWS, "Erasing Windows (Removing)"
Erasing Cut Walls	See DOORS and WINDOWS, "Erasing Cut Walls (Removing)"

Grids

To define grids	1. Press **G**. (UTILITY/GRIDS menus)
	2. Pick **GridSize**.
	3. Pick **SetDisp1** for small grids.
	4. Pick **Custom**.
	5. Type in or pick from menu desired spacing for X grid. Example: **4**
	6. Press [**Enter**].
	7. Type in or pick from menu desired spacing for Y grid. Example: **4**
	8. Press [**Enter**].
	9. Pick **SetDisp2** for large grids.
	10. Pick **Custom**.
	11. Type in or pick from menu desired spacing for X grid. Example: **16**
	12. Press [**Enter**].
	13. Type in or pick from menu desired spacing for Y grid. Example: **16**
	14. Press [**Enter**].
	15. Press mouse button **3**.
	16. Pick **GridColr**.
	17. Pick **SetDisp1** for small grids.
	18. Pick desired color from menu. Example: **Lt Red**
	19. Pick **SetDisp2** for large grids.
	20. Pick **MarkSize**.

If you want to do this:	Follow these steps:
	21. Pick desired display size of large grid. Example: **2**
	22. Press [**Enter**].
	23. Pick desired color from menu. Example: **Lt Blue**
	24. Press mouse button **3**.
	25. Pick **Disp1On** until active (*Disp1On).
	26. Pick **Disp2On** until active (*Disp2On).
	27. Press mouse button **3** to quit.
Setting Grid Snap	See SNAP, Setting Increment grid snap.
Setting Ortho Mode Angles	See ORTHO, Setting ortho mode angles.

Grouping

SEE ALSO—SELECTION SETS

Making several entities into a group	1. Pick **LinkEnts** from EDIT menu.
	2. Pick **Entity**, **Group**, **Area**, or **Fence**, as applicable.
	3. Pick item(s) to group. They will become gray and dashed.
Ungrouping entities	1. Pick **LinkEnts** from EDIT menu.
	2. Pick ***Un-Link** until active.
	3. Pick **Entity**, **Group**, **Area**, or **Fence**, as applicable.
	4. Pick item(s) to ungroup. They will become gray and dashed.

Hatching

Defining a boundary using real geometry	1. Press [**Tab**] until correct layer that will hold hatching pattern is active.
	2. Draw outline for pattern, using **object snap** when applicable to match existing geometry.
	3. Make sure to **Object snap** to close boundary.
	4. Press **H** (HATCH/UTILITY menu).
	5. Use ***Entity**, ***Group**, ***Area**, or ***Fence** as applicable to select your boundary.

If you want to do this:	Follow these steps:
	6. Continue with hatching procedures as described below.
Defining the boundary using the temporary boundary feature	1. Press **H**.
Creating the hatch	1. Press **H**.
	2. Pick **Pattern**.
	3. Pick the desired hatch pattern.
	4. If necessary, pick **Scale**, and enter the desired scale of your pattern. Example: **80**.
	5. Pick **Group** until it is active (***Group**).
	6. Pick the boundary. It will become gray and dashed.
	7. Pick by entity if necessary to add to your boundary.
	8. When boundary is correct, pick **Begin**.
	9. Press mouse button **3** to quit.
Deleting the hatch	1. Press **E** (EDIT/ERASE).
	2. Make sure ***Group** is active.
	3. Pick Hatch to erase.
	4. Press mouse button **3** to quit.
Deleting the hatch if it was the last item created	1. Press the [**Shift**] <.
	2. The last group will be erased.

Identifying

Identifying an entity	1. Press [**Shift**] **I** (EDIT/IDENTIFY menus).
	2. Pick the item to identify. It will become gray and dashed.
	3. Notice the left column will display:

F1   Item type
F2   Layer
F3   Color
F4   Line type
F5 – F9 are setting values, and present settings for the selected item

If you want to do this:	Follow these steps:
	are displayed in the user message area of the screen.
Changing the current settings to match a selected item	1. Press [**Shift**] **I** (EDIT/IDENTIFY menus). 2. Pick the item you want to match. It will become gray and dashed. 3. Pick **Set All**. All of the current attribute settings will be changed to match the selected item, including: Layer Color Linetype Spacing Weight Z-Base Z-Height Over Shoot
Changing individual settings to match a selected item	1. Press [**Shift**] **I** (EDIT/IDENTIFY menus). 2. Pick the item you want to match. It will become gray and dashed. 3. Pick the option(s) you wish to set from the list in the left column. The picked attributes will be changed to match the selected item.

Increment snap

See SNAP

Layers

Defining Layers	1. Press **L** key. 2. Pick **NewLayer**. 3. Key in the number of new layers needed (ex. 5): **5** 4. Pick **Name**. 5. Pick layer to "name." 6. Key in new name for layer, and [**Enter**]. 7. Continue until all layers are named. 8. Press mouse button **3** to quit.
Changing active layers (Quick toggle)	1. Press [**Tab**] key to scroll forward. 2. Press [**Shift**] [**Tab**] to scroll backward.
Assigning a color to a layer, using LAYER menu	1. Press **L** key. 2. Press [**Tab**] until correct layer is active. 3. Pick **Color**.

If you want to do this:	Follow these steps:
	4. Pick the desired color from menu.
	5. Press mouse button **3** to quit.
Assigning a color to a layer, using Quick keys	1. Press [**Tab**] until correct layer is active.
	2. Press **K** key to scroll to correct color.
	3. Press [**Tab**] until next layer is active.
	4. Press **K** key to scroll to correct color.
	5. Continue until all layers have colors defined.
Turning on and off layers for viewing	1. Press **L** key.
	2. Pick **On/Off**.
	3. Pick layers to turn on or off for viewing. (* = Displayed, $ = Active.)
	4. Press mouse button **3** to quit.
Turning on all layers for viewing	1. Press **L**.
	2. Pick **All On**.
	3. Pick **Yes**.
	4. Press mouse button **3** to quit.
Turning off all layers but one	1. Press **L**.
	2. Pick **ActvOnly**.
	3. Pick the layer you wish displayed.
	4. Press mouse button **3** to quit.
	5. This layer becomes your active layer.
Saving a layer to a layer file	1. Display the drawing that contains the layer you wish to save.
	2. Press **L** key.
	3. Pick **SaveLayr**.
	4. Pick layer to save.
	5. Key in name for your layer file.
	6. A copy of your layer will be saved to file.
	7. Press mouse button **3** to quit.
Loading a layer file into a drawing	1. Display the drawing you wish to load the layers in, or create a new drawing.
	2. Press **L**.
	3. If necessary, use **NewLayer** to create the layers to hold the layer files.

If you want to do this:	Follow these steps:
	4. Press [**Tab**] until correct layer is active (empty layer that will hold the new layer file).
	5. Pick **Loadlayr**.
	6. Pick **Yes** (this will erase the original layer and layer name).
	7. Pick the name of the layer file you wish to load.
	8. The layer is added to your drawing.
	9. Continue adding all necessary layers.
	10. Press mouse button **3** to quit.
Moving items to another layer	See MOVE, Moving items to another layer
Copying items from one layer to another	See COPY
Erasing all items on a layer	1. Press **L**.
	2. Pick **ErseLyr**.
	3. Pick the layer that contains the items you wish to erase. *Caution*: All items on the layer will be erased!
	4. Pick **Yes**.
	5. Press mouse button **3** to quit.
Deleting a layer from the layer list	1. Press **L**.
	2. Pick **DelLayer**.
	3. Pick the layer you wish to remove from the list. *Caution*: All items on the layer will be erased also!
	4. Pick **Yes**.
	5. Press mouse button **3** once.
	6. Pick the **On/Off** option.
	7. Notice the layer is gone from the list.
	8. Press mouse button **3** to quit.

Notice: The following layer viewing techniques allow you to temporarily view layers. They may not be active, or even exist in the current drawing file. Do NOT attempt, then, to draw *until you have pressed the* [Esc] *key to refresh the screen!* This will return you to the true screen conditions.

If you want to do this:	Follow these steps:
Temporarily viewing one layer, with automatic window extends	1. Press **L**. 2. Pick **ViewLayr**. 3. Pick **Extends** and **LyrRfsh** until active (*). 4. Pick **Select**. 5. Pick the layer you wish to view. It will appear, and be automatically windowed to its extends. 6. Do NOT attempt to draw. 7. After viewing the layer, press the [**Esc**] key to return to the real screen conditions.
Temporarily viewing a saved layer file	1. Press [**L**]. 2. Pick **ViewFile**. 3. Pick **LyrRfsh** until active (*). 4. Pick **Select**. 5. Pick **New Path**. 6. Type in and [**Enter**] the pathname for your files: lyr 7. Pick the layer file you wish to view. It will be displayed on your screen. 8. Do NOT attempt to draw. 9. After viewing the file, press the [**Esc**] key to return to the real screen conditions.

Linetypes

Changing the current linetype using the quick key	1. Press **Q** key. 2. Linestyle will toggle forward through available types, and be displayed at the lower left hand corner of the DataCAD menu. 3. New items you create will be in active linestyle. 4. Press [**Shift**] **Q** to toggle backwards.
Changing the current linetype using the LINETYPE menu	1. Pick **LineTypes** from the EDIT menu. 2. Pick the desired linetype. 3. If the linetype is not displayed, pick the ScrolFwd option.

If you want to do this:	Follow these steps:
Adjusting the size of the linetype pattern	1. Pick **LineTypes** from the EDIT menu. 2. Pick the **Spacing** option. 3. Type in the new desired spacing. This spacing is relative to the plot scale. Example: 1:20 property line spacing = 20′ will result in a plotted spacing of 1″.
Setting a new line width	1. Press **W**. The new line weight value will be displayed in the user message area. 2. Press [**Shift**] **W** to scroll back.

If you want to do this:	Follow these steps:

Macros

Executing a Macro	1. Pick **Macros** from the EDIT menu. 2. Pick the macro you wish to execute, then press [**Enter**]. Example: **DCAD AEC**. 3. Press mouse button **3** to quit the macro.
Crunching your drawing using LYRUTIL	1. Display the drawing that you wish to crunch. (This procedure will compact the drawing file to make it contain less bytes, by eliminating gray space.) 2. Pick **Macros** from the EDIT menu. 3. Pick **LYRUTIL**. 4. Pick **SaveLyr**. 5. Type in a name that you will remember for your layers, and press [**Enter**]. This can be the same name as your drawing. The layers will be saved. Example: **flrpln1** 6. When the procedure is finished, press mouse button **3** to quit. 7. Press [**Alt**] **N** to begin a new drawing. 8. Pick **Yes**, or **Abort** as applicable. 9. When the drawing list is displayed, type in a new name for your crunched drawing. If you use a default drawing,

If you want to do this:	Follow these steps:

be aware that the layers will be appended onto the existing layers in the drawings. The unused layer names can be **deleted**, however.

10. Once the drawing file is created, pick **Macros** from the EDIT file.
11. Pick **LYRUTIL**.
12. Pick **LoadLyr**.
13. Pick the name you gave the layers in step 5, and press [**Enter**]. The layers will be loaded in your drawing. Example: **flrpln1**
14. Press mouse button **3** to quit.

Mirroring

Mirroring a copy of item(s)

1. Press [**Alt**] **M** (EDIT/MIRROR menus).
2. Pick or object snap 2 points to define a reflection line.
3. Pick ***AndCopy** until it is active.
4. Pick ***LyrSrch** until it is active, if items are on different layers.
5. Pick **Entity**, **Group**, **Area**, or **Fence** as applicable.
6. Pick desired item(s) to mirror a copy of.

Mirroring original item(s) (flipping)

1. Press [**Alt**] **M** (EDIT/MIRROR menus).
2. Pick or object snap 2 points to define a reflection line.
3. Pick **AndCopy** until it is OFF (no *****).
4. Pick ***LyrSrch** until it is active, if items are on different layers.
5. Pick **Entity**, **Group**, **Area**, or **Fence** as applicable.
6. Pick desired item(s) to flip.

Undoing the mirrored copy or flipped original

1. While still in MIRROR menu, pick **Undo**.

Move

Moving a single item or Group of items

1. Press **M** (EDIT/MOVE menus).
2. Pick two points indicating distance and direction to move (arrow will be displayed).

If you want to do this:	Follow these steps:

	3. Make correct layer active (press [**Tab**]), or pick ***LyrSrch** until it is active.
	4. Pick **Entity** or **Group** until it is active (***Entity**).
	5. Pick desired items or group to move.
Moving an area of items	1. Press **M** (EDIT/MOVE menus).
	2. Pick two points indicating distance and direction to move.
	3. Make correct layer active (press [**Tab**]), or pick ***LyrSrch** until it is active.
	4. Pick **Area** from menu.
	5. Pick two points indicating a rectangle around the items you wish to move.

Notice: If you attempt to **Drag** symbols or modeled entities, and there is so much detail in the item that your cursor jumps erratically, turn off the lines by picking **MaxLines**, and setting the number of lines to **0**. Now you will only get a box representing your symbol, and it will be easy to move!

Moving an item by dragging it	1. Press **M**.
	2. Pick **Drag**.
	3. Pick **Entity**, **Group**, or **Area** from menu.
	4. If copy is desired, pick ***AndCopy**.
	5. Pick item(s) or area to move.
	6. Pick the handle point to drag the item(s) by.
	7. Drag the items using the cursor to the new location.
Moving and copying items at the same time	1. Press **M**.
	2. Pick two points indicating the distance and direction of the move.
	3. Pick ***AndCopy** until it is active.
	4. Make correct layer active (press [**Tab**]), or pick ***LyrSrch** until it is active.
	5. Pick **Entity**, **Area**, or **Group** as applicable.
	6. Pick items or area to move and copy.

If you want to do this:	Follow these steps:

*Notice: The ***AndCopy** option will remain active until you change it. (Unless you are moving to a layer, at which time AndCopy is not applicable.)

Moving items in one layer	1. Press **M**. 2. Pick two points indicating distance and direction to move. 3. Press [**Tab**] until layer with items is active. 4. Pick **LyrSrch** until it is **INACTIVE** (LyrSrch). 5. Pick **Entity**, **Group**, or **Area** from menu. 6. Pick desired items or area to move.
Moving items to another layer	1. Press **M**. 2. Pick **To Layer**. 3. Pick the layer you want the items moved to. 4. Press [**Tab**] until the layer with the items is active, or pick **LyrSrch** until it is active. 5. Pick **Entity**, **Group**, or **Area** from menu. 6. Pick items or area to move.

Object snap

Setting the Object Snap modes	1. Press [**Shift**] **X**. (UTILITY/OBJECT SNAP menus) 2. Pick the desired settings for your Object snap, until they are active (*End Pnt). 3. Commonly used settings are: ***End Pnt** ***Mid pnt** ***Center** ***Intsect** These settings can all be on at the same time, to save steps later. 4. Press mouse button **3** to quit.
Picking the center of an arc	1. Press [**Shift**] **X**. 2. Pick **None**. 3. Pick **Center** until it is active (*Center). 4. Press mouse button **3** to quit.

If you want to do this:	Follow these steps:
	5. Move cursor to arc or circle, touching the actual perimeter of the arc or circle.
	6. Press mouse button **2** to object snap to the center.
Turning on Layer Snap (to grab items on different layers when Object snapping)	1. Press [**Shift**] **X** keys. (OBJECT SNAP menu)
	2. Pick **LyrSnap** until it is active (*LyrSnap).
	3. Press mouse button **3** to quit.
Making object snap points between two points	1. Press [**Alt**] **G** (UTILITY/GEOMETRY menus).
	2. Pick **Divide**.
	3. Pick **Dvisions**.
	4. Type in the number of points you will want between the two points you will pick, and press [**Enter**]. Example: **4**
	5. Pick the two points, or object snap to line endpoints. The snapping points will appear on the screen. These points can be moved, copied, or deleted like other pieces of geometry.
	6. Press mouse button **3** to quit.
Creating other object snap points	See SNAP POINTS (MARKERS & DIVISIONS)

Offsetting

Offsetting copies of lines, arcs, circles, and ellipses at a defined distance	1. Press [**Alt**] **g** (UTILITY/GEOMETRY menus).
	2. Pick **Offset**.
	3. Make sure **Dynamic** is OFF (no *)
	4. Pick **PerpDist**.
	5. Type in the distance, and press [**Enter**]. Example: **5.6**
	6. Pick the item to offset a copy from. It will become gray and dashed.

If you want to do this:	Follow these steps:

	7. Pick on a side of the selected item to indicate the side you want the offset to appear.
	8. Pick the next item to offset the same distance, if applicable, and pick the side to offset to.
	9. Press mouse button **3** to quit.

If you want do do this:	Follow these steps:

Offsetting copies of lines, arcs, circles, and ellipses dynamically	1. Press [**Alt**] **g** (UTILITY/GEOMETRY menus).
	2. Pick **Offset**.
	3. Pick ***Dynamic** until it is active (*****).
	4. Pick the item to offset. It will become gray and dashed.
	5. Notice a copy of the item will be connected to your cursor.
	6. Pick to place the copy.
	7. Press mouse button **3** to quit.

Ortho mode

Turning on Ortho mode	1. Press **O** until the message is displayed **Ortho Mode is ON**.
	2. The O will be capital in SWOTHLUD.

Adjusting the Ortho mode angles	1. Press **G** (UTILITY/GRIDS menus).
	2. Pick **SnapAngl**.
	3. Type in or pick the number of divisions of a circle you want to snap to, and press [**Enter**]. Example: **8 = 45 degree locks**.

Plotting

Key plotting steps (for quick reference)	1. Press [**Alt**] **P** (UTILITY/PLOTTER menus).
	2. Adjust **Paper Size**.
	3. Check **Layout** (place it on your drawing).
	4. Change **Scale** if necessary.

Typical Plotting procedure	1. Press [**Alt**] **P** (UTILITY/PLOTTER menus).
	2. Pick **PaperSize**.

If you want to do this:	Follow these steps:

3. Pick desired paper size, or enter a Custom size. Press mouse button **3** to quit back to PLOTTER menu.
4. Pick **Layout** to view the present paper location and relationship to your drawing. (The layout represents the plottable area of the sheet, NOT the outside edges of the sheet.)
5. —If the location of the layout is correct, press mouse button **3** to quit back to the PLOTTER menu.
—If you need to move the layout, move your cursor onto the screen. Notice a layout is connected to your cursor. Place the layout in the appropriate location.
6. If necessary, pick **Scale** to change the plotted size of your drawing (the present layout appears too small or too big). Then pick the desired scale value for your plot.
Note: The higher you pick on the list, the larger the drawing will be. The lower you pick, the smaller.
7. Check that the appropriate options are set:
*ClrPlot—''Color plot'' allows the plotter to make pen changes for the colors on your drawing.
*PenSort—To optimize your pen changes.
SetPens—To select which pens will be picked up for each color.
Note: DO NOT set **SnglPen** active unless you have a single pen plotter! (Otherwise, your plot will stop between pen changes, or a rasterized plot will stop altogether.)
8. When everything is OK, pick **Plot**.

Changing the Layout size (useful for rotated plots)

1. Press [**Alt**] **p**.
2. Pick **Lyout Set**.
3. Pick **Lyout Siz**.

If you want to do this:	Follow these steps:
	4. Type in new size value (percentage of layout to screen), and press [**Enter**]. Example: **20**
	5. Press mouse button **3** to return to PLOTTER menu.
Using the LPT1 port as a plotter connection	1. Follow steps 1 through 7 in **Typical Plotting Procedure** (pages 386 and 387).
	2. Pick **Configur**.
	3. Pick ***LPT1** until it is active (*****). Quit back to the PLOTTER menu.
	4. Pick **Plot**. *Note*: This setting is NOT retained with your drawing. Plotter port will change back to the main configuration everytime you start DataCAD.
Making the LPT1 a permanent plotting port choice	1. Quit DataCAD.
	2. Run the CONFIG.EXE program.
	3. Follow directions to configure DataCAD plotting for LPT1.
Defining new plot scales	SEE SCALES, Editing view and plot scales
Setting up the plot scale	1. Press [**Alt**] **P** (UTILITY, PLOTTER menus).
	2. Pick **Scale**.
	3. Pick the appropriate scale for your drawing.
	4. Press mouse button **3** to quit back to the PLOTTER menu.
	5. Pick **Layout**.
	6. Move the layout onto the screen with your cursor. Check that it fits your drawing, and place the layout with your cursor, by either picking or object snapping to a centerpoint.
Setting the pens	1. Press [**Alt**] **P**.
	2. Make sure ***ClrPlot** is active (Color Plot).
	3. Pick **SetPens**.

If you want to do this:	Follow these steps:

	4. Pick a color you are using. Example: **White**
	5. Pick a pen number for this color, and press [**Enter**]. Example: **4**
	6. Continue until all used colors are defined.

| Showing only the extents of your geometry for layout purposes | 1. Press [**Alt**] **P**.
2. Pick **LyoutSet**.
3. Pick ***Extents** until it is active (***** = Active).
4. Press mouse button **3** to quit back to PLOTTER menu.
5. Pick **Layout**.
6. A box will be displayed indicating the extents of your drawing. Place the layout as desired. |

| Rotating your plot | 1. Press [**Alt**] **p**.
2. Pick **Rotate**.
3. Pick in the center of your drawing for the rotation pivot point.
4. Type in the amount to rotate, and press [**Enter**].
Example: **90**
5. Place layout, if applicable. |

Reports

| Extracting reports from symbols in the drawing | 1. Press **T** (UTILITY/TEMPLATE menus).
2. Retrieve a template you wish to extract the report from.
Note: The template that is connected to the symbols that will be in your report must be displayed!
3. Pick **Reports** from the TEMPLATE menu, once the appropriate template is displayed.
4. Pick the type of report you wish to run.
Example: **DCADCOST**
5. The report will be displayed on your screen. |

If you want to do this:	Follow these steps:

—If the report is NOT displayed, check that you have the appropriate template that is connected to your symbols displayed. (The symbols must NOT be exploded.)

6. If the report is longer than can be displayed on the screen at one time, a **ScrlFrwd** option will appear in the menu. Pick **ScrlFrwd** to see the rest of your report if necessary.

7. Press [**Enter**] to continue.

8. Pick **ToDwg**, **ToFile** or **ToPrntr** as applicable.

9. If you have picked **ToDwg**:
—Change the size, font, aspect, etc., of your text as desired.
—Pick a start point on your drawing. This will be the upper left corner of your report.
—The report will appear. It can be edited like text as usual.

10. If you have picked **ToFile**:
—Pick NewPath to change to the appropriate directory.
—Type in the directory name, or pick the options from the menu. Press [**Enter**].
Example: **txt**
—Type in the name for your report text file, and press [**Enter**].
Example: **report1**
—The report will be written to a file with the extension of **.TXT**.

11. If you have picked **ToPrntr**, be sure that you have a printer connected to your computer, on line and ready to print.

Rotating

Rotating items using a typed in angle

1. Press **r** (EDIT/ROTATE menus).

2. Pick the point indicating the centerpoint that items will be rotated about.

3. If necessary, pick **NewAngle**, to

If you want to do this:	Follow these steps:
	indicate a new angle other than previously set.
	4. Type in desired angle, or pick from menu.
	5. Pick **Entity**, **Group**, or **Area** until active (*****), as applicable.
	6. Pick item(s) or area to be rotated.
Rotating items dynamically	1. Press **r**.
	2. Pick on the screen to indicate a rotation center point (pivot point).
	3. Pick ***Dynamic** until it is active (***** = active).
	4. Select the item(s) to rotate, using ***Entity**, ***Group**, ***Area**, or ***Fence**, as applicable.
	5. Pick to indicate a handle point for your rotation. (A point you will be able to drag the items by.)
	6. Now move the cursor to rotate your items. Ortho mode may be toggled on or off as necessary by pressing **o**.
	7. Once the desired angle is achieved, pick to place the items. *Note*: The **MaxLines** option has been added to help you specify the maximum amount of lines that can be shown while rotating the group. (Works like Move/Drag.) More lines shown will slow the rotation down. Less lines shown will turn the items into a "box" for rotation, but will be much faster.
Using a Previously defined center for your rotation	1. Press **r**.
	2. Pick **PrevCntr**, if the last rotation center defined will be used again.
	3. Continue using rotate as applicable.
Picking multiple items to rotate	1. Press **r**.
	2. Pick the center of rotation.
	3. Pick New Angle and type in the appropriate angle.

If you want to do this:	Follow these steps:
	-or- Pick ***Dynamic** until it is active. 4. Pick ***Multi** until it is active. 5. Use ***Entity**, ***Group**, ***Area**, or ***Fence** to select your items to rotate. 6. Notice you can now continue to select additional items to rotate. Continue picking items until all items you want to rotate are selected. 7. Pick **Begin**. The items will rotate to the defined angle, unless ***Dynamic** is active. —If ***Dynamic** is active, pick to indicate a handle point, then drag the items to a new rotation position.
Rotated Dimensions	See DIMENSIONING/Creating rotated dimensions
Rotating Symbols	See TEMPLATES & SYMBOLS/Rotating symbols as you add them
Undoing the last rotation	1. While still in the ROTATION menu pick **Undo**.
Undoing the last rotation if you've left the ROTATE menu	1. This will only work if you did NOT use **Dynamic**. 2. Press **r**. 3. Pick the **Prev Dist.** 4. Pick **Invert**. (Last angle will now invert.) 5. Pick same entity/group/area/or fence as before. It should revert to original position. If it is still not correct, pick **Undo** and try again.

Scales

| Editing view and plot scales | 1. Pick **Settings** in the UTILITY menu.
2. Pick **EditDefs**.
3. Pick **Scales.**
4. Pick **Change.**
5. Pick a scale you are not going to be |

If you want to do this:	Follow these steps:
	using for either *viewing or plotting*. Example: **1:1000**
	6. Type in a new name for the new scale, and press [**Enter**]. Example: **1:30**
	7. Type in the new scale, and press [**Enter**]. Example: **.00277777** (correct scale for 1:30)
	8. Pick **List** to check that your new scale fell in the correct place in the list.
	9. Press mouse button **3** to quit.
Saving a scale list to share with other drawings	1. Retrieve the drawing that has the scales you will want to save.
	2. Pick **Settings** from the UTILITY menu.
	3. Pick **EditDefs**.
	4. Pick **Scales**.
	5. Pick **SaveFile**.
	6. Type in the new name for the scale list, and press [**Enter**]. The entire scale list will be saved to a file. Example: **1-30SCL**
	7. Press mouse button **3** to quit.
Loading a scale list into another drawing	1. Retrieve drawing you want to load the new scale file into.
	2. Pick **Settings** from the UTILITY menu.
	3. Pick **EditDefs**.
	4. Pick **Scales**.
	5. Pick **LoadFile**.
	6. Pick the file that contains the scales you wish to load. Example: **1-30SCL**.
	7. Press mouse button **3** to quit.
	8. Pick List to check that the new scales have been added.
	9. Press mouse button **3** to quit.
Picking the scale for plotting	SEE PLOTTING, Setting up the plot scale.

If you want to do this:	Follow these steps:
Picking a scale for viewing	1. Pick **To Scale** from the UTILITY menu. 2. Pick desired scale from list. The view scale will change. 3. Press mouse button **3** to quit.

Selection sets

Defining a selection set	1. Press [**Shift**] **S** (Edit/EditSets) 2. Pick **Add To**. 3. Pick the selection set you will use. Example: **SelSet1** 4. Pick **Entity**, **Group**, **Area**, or **Fence**, as applicable. 5. Make ***LyrSrch** active if items are on different layers. 6. Select item(s) until they are gray and dashed. 7. Press mouse button **3** to return to EDITSETS menu. 8. Pick **Set Active**. 9. Pick the selection set you defined. Example: **SelSet1**
Naming a selection set	1. Press [**Shift**] **S**. 2. Pick **Name Set**. 3. Pick the selection set you wish to name. Example: **SelSet1** 4. Type in a new name for this set, and press [**Enter**]. Example: **ExtWall**
Using a selection set	1. The selection set MUST BE ACTIVE before it can be used (EditSets, Set Active). Follow steps in "Making a selection set." 2. When in the option you will be using (Erase/Move/Copy/etc.,) pick **Sel Set** as the selection mode. The current active selection set will be picked. 3. Proceed as applicable.

If you want to do this:	Follow these steps:
Creating a selection set by masking types	1. Press [**Shift**] **S**. 2. Pick **Add To**. 3. Pick the selection set you will use. Example: **SelSet1** 4. Make ***LyrSrch** active if items are on different layers. 5. Pick **Mask**. 6. Pick appropriate masking choice. Example: **Color** 7. Pick **All Off**. 8. Pick only the choices you will want added to the selection set. Example: **Red** 9. Quit once by pressing mouse button **3**. 10. A ***** should appear by the mask type you selected. 11. Press mouse button **3** to quit again. 12. Pick **Area**, **Fence**, or other applicable selection mode. 13. Select the items to add to your selection set. Example: If using ***Area**, Box around area you wish to add to your set. Only the masked items will be added, and they will become gray and dashed. 14. Press mouse button **3** once to return to EDITSETS menu. 15. Pick **Set Active**. 16. Pick the selection set you defined. Example: **SelSet1**

Stretching

Stretching item endpoints by indicating a box	1. Press [**Alt**] **S** (EDIT/STRETCH menus). 2. Pick two points to indicate a stretch distance. 3. Pick ***Box** until active. 4. Make ***LyrSrch** active also, if items to stretch are on different layers. 5. Pick two points to indicate a box around the ends of the items to stretch.

If you want to do this:	Follow these steps:
	6. If stretch resulted in undesirable results, pick **Undo**.
Stretching item endpoints by indicating a fence	1. Press [**Alt**] **S** (EDIT/STRETCH menus).
	2. Pick two points to indicate a stretch distance.
	3. Pick ***Fence** until active.
	4. Make ***LyrSrch** active also, if items to stretch are on different layers.
	5. Pick points indicating a multi-sided fence around the items you wish to stretch.
	6. Press mouse button **3** to close fence.
	7. If stretch resulted in undesirable results, pick **Undo**.
Stretching item endpoints using coordinate input	1. Press [**Insert**] until the input mode is set to **Relative cartesian coordinates**.
	2. Press [**Alt**] **S**.
	3. Pick a point on the screen.
	4. Press the [**Space bar**].
	5. Type in the desired X distance, if applicable, then [**Enter**].
	6. Type in the desired Y distance, if applicable, then [**Enter**].
	Example: **X = 5.0**
	Y = 0
	7. Make sure ***Box** is active.
	8. Make ***LyrSrch** active also, if applicable.
	9. Pick two points to indicate a box around the ends of item(s) to stretch.
Stretching item endpoints using coordinate input using "point"	1. Press [**Insert**] until the input mode is set to **Relative cartesian coordinates**.
	2. Press [**Alt**] **S**.
	3. Pick a point on the screen.
	4. Press the [**Space bar**].
	5. Type in the desired X distance, if applicable, then [**Enter**].
	6. Type in the desired Y distance, if applicable, then [**Enter**].
	Example: **X = 5.0**
	Y = 0

If you want to do this:	Follow these steps:
	7. Make sure **Box** is OFF (no *****).
	8. Make ***LyrSrch** active also, if applicable.
	9. **Object snap** to the endpoints you want stretched.
Undoing the last stretch if you've left the STRETCH menu	1. Press [**Alt**] **S**.
	2. Pick **PrevDist**.
	3. Pick **Invert**.
	4. Use ***Point**, ***Box**, or ***Fence** to select the same items you stretched earlier.
	5. If the results are incorrect, pick **Undo**.

Snap

Setting Increment Snap (Grid Snap)	1. Press **S** (UTILITY/GRIDS/ GRIDSIZE/SETSNAP menus).
	2. Type in the desired X value, then [**Enter**].
	3. Type in the desired Y value, then [**Enter**].
Turning on the Snap Mode	1. Press **X** until **Snap On** is displayed.

Snap points (markers & divisions)

Creating a reference snap point	1. Press [**Shift**] ~ (DCAD 3D/MARKER menus—sort of).
	2. Pick, type in coordinates, or Object snap to place the snap point.
	3. Press mouse button **3** to quit.
Creating object snap points in the center of walls, in order to facilitate dimensioning	See DIMENSIONING, Dimensioning to center of walls.
Dividing a line or arc with snap points	1. Press [**Alt**] **G** (UTILITY/GEOMETRY menus).
	2. Pick **Divide**. The number of Divisions will be displayed in the message area.

If you want to do this:	Follow these steps:

3. If you want to change the number of divisions:
   —Pick **Divisions**.
   —Type in the number wanted, then press [**Enter**].
4. Pick **Entity**.
5. Pick a line or arc to divide.

Dividing a circle with snap points

1. Press [**Alt**] **G** (UTILITY/Geometry menus).
2. Pick **Divide**. The number of Divisions will be displayed in the message area
3. If you want to change the number of divisions:
   —Pick **Divisions**.
   —Type in the number wanted, then press [**Enter**].
4. Pick **Entity**.
   Note: Where you pick the circle will become the start point of the divisions.
5. If you want the circle divided starting from a 45 degree angle (0, 90, 180, or 270 angle point):
   —Press [**Shift**] **X**.
   —Set the **Quadrant** object snap setting.
   Then press mouse button **3** to quit back to Divide.
   —bject snap to the circle to start the divisions.
6. If you want the divisions to start at the intersection of another item:
   —Press [**Shift**] **X**.
   —Set the **Intsect** object snap setting.
   —Then press mouse button **3** to quit back to Divide.
   – Object snap to the circle to start the divisions.
7. Or, pick the circle anywhere to start the divisions.
8. Press mouse button **3** to quit.

If you want to do this:	Follow these steps:
Dividing a line with snap points that have a defined distance between them	1. Press [**Alt**] **g**.
	2. Pick **Divide**.
	3. Pick **Divisions**.
	4. Type in the number of divisions you want, and press [**Enter**]. Example: **5**.
	5. Pick **Div & Dist**
	6. Type in the spacing value you want between the snap points, and press [**Enter**]. Example: **76**
	7. Object snap to the end of the line that you want the snap points to start.
	8. Object snap to the other end of your line.
	9. Press mouse button **3** to quit.

Symbols

See TEMPLATES AND SYMBOLS

Templates and symbols

Adding symbols to your drawing	1. Press **T**. (UTILITY/TEMPLATE menus).
	2. If the wrong template is active, pick **NewFile**.
	3. Pick the correct template name from menu.
	4. The template is displayed with the symbols.
	5. Press [**Tab**] until correct layer is active.
	6. Pick the appropriate symbol from the template.
	7. Pick the position for your symbol on your drawing and your symbol will be placed.
	8. Press mouse button **3** to quit placing the symbol.
Getting other template lists (Changing template directories)	1. Press **T**.
	2. If a template is displayed, pick **New File**.

If you want to do this:	Follow these steps:

	3. Pick **New Path** from the template list.
	4. Type in the pathname for the directory that contains the desired template list. Example: **tpl**
	5. The templates that are connected to the directory pathname will be listed.
Retrieving the templates and symbols that came with DataCAD	1. Press **T**.
	2. If a template is displayed, pick **New File**.
	3. Pick **New Path** from the template list.
	4. Type in *one* of the MTEC template pathnames, and press [**Enter**]. The proper names for these paths are: tpl \ furn tpl \ plumb tpl \ elec tpl \ mech tpl \ struct tpl \ dwg
	5. The templates that are connected to the directory pathname will be listed.
Creating new templates	1. Press **T**.
	2. If another is already displayed, pick **NewFile**.
	3. Type in new template name and [**Enter**].
	4. Pick **Yes**.
	5. Type in additional field information, if applicable.
	6. Press mouse button **3** to quit.
	7. Your new (empty) template is displayed.
Creating new symbols	1. Display drawing that has items for the new symbol.
	2. If you have just created these items, make sure that your drawing is SAVED BEFORE CONTINUING.
	3. Press **T**.

If you want to do this:	Follow these steps:
	4. If the wrong template is displayed, pick **New File**.
	5. Pick the correct template for your new symbols.
	6. Pick **SaveSymb**.
	7. Type in the file name for your new symbol (8 characters limit). Example: **ftg1**
	8. Make sure ***AutoPath** is active.
	9. Make sure ***LyrSrch** is active.
	10. Pick the items to be saved as a symbol by **Entity**, **Group**, **Area**, or **Fence**.
	11. All symbol components should become gray and dashed. If you missed some, press mouse button **3** and try again.
	12. Pick or object snap a reference point for later placing your symbol on your drawing.
	13. For "Item name," type in the name you wish to appear when you put your cursor over the template box for that symbol (or you wish to appear in your report), and press [**Enter**]. Example: **1 Story Footing**
	14. Fill in any applicable report fields.
	15. Press mouse button **3** to quit.
Changing the symbol name that appears when you place the cursor in the template box	1. Press **T**.
	2. If wrong template is displayed, pick **New File**.
	3. Pick **EditFlds**.
	4. Pick the symbol that will have the name changed.
	5. Pick **Item name**.
	6. Type in and [**Enter**] new name.
	7. Press mouse button **3** to quit to TEMPLATE menu.
	8. Pick **New File**.
	9. Pick the same template to reload the symbol names.
	10. Now move the cursor into the symbol

If you want to do this:	Follow these steps:
	box, and the new name will be displayed.
Changing symbols in a template (Redefine)	1. Display drawing with items for new symbol. 2. Press **T**. 3. If wrong template is displayed, pick **New File**. 4. Pick the correct template to display. 5. Pick **Redefine**. 6. Pick symbol in template box to change. 7. Pick the items to be saved as your new symbol by **Entity**, **Group**, or **Area**. (Symbols cannot be used!) 8. Pick **Continue**. 9. Pick reference point for new symbol. 10. The original symbol will be replaced with your new symbol. Any existing symbols that matched the original symbol on your drawing will be replaced also.

*Notice: Using **Del Symb** deletes the symbol from the Template box, and SHOULD NOT be used to delete the symbol from the drawing.

Deleting a symbol from a template	1. Press **T** and display the template with the symbol you wish to delete (see "Displaying a template"). 2. Pick **Del Symb**. 3. Pick symbol you want deleted from template. 4. Pick **Yes**. 5. Pick **Yes**. 6. Press mouse button **3** to quit.
Exploding existing symbols in your drawing	1. Press [**Shift**] **M** (MACROS/EDIT menus). 2. Pick **SymExp**. 3. Pick ***Entity**, ***Group**, ***Area**, or ***Fence** as applicable. 4. Select the symbols you wish to explode.

If you want to do this:	Follow these steps:
	Caution: DO NOT use this macro if your symbol has any polylines in it. It will turn the entire symbol into an unrecoverable dot.
Replacing symbols in your drawing (Updating)	1. Press **T** and display the template containing the new symbol (see "Displaying a template").
	2. Pick **Replace**.
	3. Pick the symbol on your drawing to indicate the type of symbol you will be replacing.
	4. Pick the new symbol from the template.
	5. Pick the symbols on your drawing that you want to replace by **Entity, Group, Area, or Fence.** -or- pick **All** to replace all of the symbols on the drawing that match the type of symbol you want to replace.
	6. Press mouse button **3** to quit.
Rotating symbols dynamically as you add them	1. Press **T** and display the desired template.
	2. Make ***DynmRot** active.
	3. Press [**Tab**] until correct layer is active.
	4. Pick the symbol from the template.
	5. Place the symbol. The handlepoint of the symbol now becomes the **pivot point.**
	6. Move the cursor until the desired rotation is achieved. You may want to turn on or off Ortho Mode by pressing **O**, as applicable.
	7. Pick to finish placing your symbol in the correct rotation.
	8. Press mouse button **3** to quit placing your symbol.
Rotating symbols to a defined angle	1. Press **T** and display the desired template.

If you want to do this:	Follow these steps:

2. Pick **DynmRot** until you can type in an angle.
3. Pick the appropriate angle of rotation from the menu, or type it in and press [**Enter**].
4. Press [**Tab**] until correct layer for the symbol is active.
5. Pick the symbol from the template.
6. Place the symbol. It will be rotated.
7. If you are through adding rotated symbols, pick **Rotate** and change the value back to **0′-0.**
8. Press mouse button **3** to quit placing your symbol.

Notice: The rotation value will stay until you change it. Remember to pick **0-0′** to take out rotation angle.

Turning off templates —Quick toggle	1. Press [**Alt**] and **B** keys simultaneously.

Turning off templates from "TEMPLATE" menu	1. Press **T**.
	2. Pick **TemplOff**.

Notice: The following section explains the beginning set-up for piping symbols. This is an advanced technique in DataCAD. It involves setting up the template correctly, then editing the actual text file of the template. Editing of the file is NOT performed in DataCAD, but by using EDLIN or other text editor. You should only attempt to pipe symbols if you are well versed in using EDLIN (the DOS text editor) or have the SNAP MENU text editor, or other non-document mode text editing capability.

Preparing symbols for piping	1. Create the symbol. This will be referred to as the "**actual symbol**."

2. Create the description you will use for piping. This could be text describing the actual symbol. This will be referred to as the "**descriptive symbol**."
3. Create the template that you will use, or display an existing one you will be adding to.
4. Use **SaveSymb** to save the **descriptive symbol** first.

If you want to do this:	Follow these steps:

5. Use **SaveSymb** to save the **actual symbol** second.
It is important that the **descriptive symbol** is immediately followed by the **actual symbol** in your template. (It will save a lot of typing for you.)
6. Once you have completed saving your descriptive and actual symbols, continue to the section in SYSTEM OPERATIONS called ''PIPING SYMBOLS.''

Text

Creating text, with text appearing at the cursor line in the message area of the screen while typing

1. Press [**Alt**] **T** (EDIT/TEXT menus).
2. Press [**Tab**] until correct layer is active.
3. Pick **Dynamic** until it is OFF (no *****).
4. Pick the start point.
5. Type in text.
6. Press [**Enter**].
7. Type in second line of text, if applicable.
8. Always press [**Enter**] before quitting, to enter the new line of text.
9. Once text has been entered, press mouse button **3** to quit.

Creating text, with text appearing on the drawing while typing

1. Press [**Alt**] **T**(EDIT/TEXT menus).
2. Press [**Tab**] until correct layer is active.
3. Pick ***Dynamic** until it is ON (***** = active)
4. Pick the start point.
5. Type in text.
6. Press [**Enter**] to add second line of text, if applicable.
7. Press mouse button **3** to quit.

Creating text with size relative to plot scale

1. Press [**Alt**] **p** (UTILITY/PLOTTER menus).
2. Pick Scale, and select the correct plot scale for your drawing.

If you want to do this:	Follow these steps:

	3. Press [**Alt**] **T** (EDIT/TEXT menus).
	4. Pick ***TextScal** until it is active.
	5. Pick **Size**.
	6. Type in the appropriate size of your text, as it will appear when plotted, and press [**Enter**]. Example: .**0.**$^1/_8$
	7. Pick the start point.
	8. Type in text.
	9. Press [**Enter**] to add second line of text, if applicable.
	10. Press mouse button **3** to quit.
Adjusting the size of text not using TextScal	1. Press [**Alt**] **T** (EDIT/TEXT menus).
	2. Pick **Size**.
	3. Type in a new text size, and press [**Enter**]. Example: .**6**
	4. Turn OFF **TextScal**.
	5. Pick the start point.
	6. Type in text.
	7. Press [**Enter**].
	8. Add second line of text, if applicable.
	9. Press mouse button **3** to quit.
Setting the angle of the text line	1. Press [**Alt**] **t**.
	2. Pick **Angle**.
	3. Type in the new angle you wish to have text appear on, then press [**Enter**]. Example: **90**
	4. Continue with procedure for adding text.
Setting text weight (for heavier letters)	1. Press [**Alt**] **t**.
	2. Pick **Weight**.
	3. Type in the weight you will want text to appear in, then press [**Enter**]. Example: **3**
	4. Continue with procedure for adding text.
Defining an italic slant for your text	1. Press [**Alt**] **t**.
	2. Pick **Slant**.

If you want to do this:	Follow these steps:
	3. Type in the slant you want the letters to be, in order to give them an italicized look, then press [**Enter**]. Example: **10**
	4. Continue with procedure for adding text.
Adjusting the width of text letters	1. Press [**Alt**] **t**.
	2. Pick **Aspect**.
	3. Type in a new text aspect to fatten or thin your text, and press [**Enter**]. (More than 1 makes letters thinner, less than 1 makes letters fatter.) Example: **1.2**
	4. Continue with procedure for adding text.
Adjusting the space between text lines	1. Press [**Alt**] **t**.
	2. Pick **Factor**.
	3. Type in the new spacing factor you want the lines to appear from each other, and press [**Enter**]. (More than 1 spaces lines farther apart, less than 1 makes them closer.) Example: **1.25**
	4. Continue with procedure for adding text.
Selecting a new text font (Type Face)	1. Press [**Alt**] **t**.
	2. Pick **FontName**.
	3. Select the new font you will want to use.
	4. Follow procedure for adding text.
Fitting text in an area	1. Press [**Alt**] **T**.
	2. Pick **Fit Text**.
	3. Press [**Tab**] until correct layer is active.
	4. Pick starting point of text.
	5. Pick end point of area.
	6. Pick point for height of area.
	7. Type in text.
	8. Press mouse button **3** to quit.

If you want to do this:	Follow these steps:
Saving current text style settings for future use or use in other drawings (Saves Size, Angle, Weight, Slant, Aspect, Factor, and FontName)	1. Press [**Alt**] **t**. 2. Set the desired text settings. 3. Pick **TxtStyls**. 4. Pick **SaveCurr**. 5. Type in the new name for your saved text settings, then press [**Enter**]. Example: **6INHAND** (6″ HAND LETTERING) 6. Press mouse button **3** to quit.
Getting saved text style settings (Will set Size, Angle, Weight, Slant, Aspect, Factor, and FontName)	1. Press [**Alt**] **t**. 2. Pick **TxtStyls**. 3. Pick **Load**. 4. Pick the name of text style you will want to use. 5. Press mouse button **3** to quit. 6. Continue with procedure for adding text.
Creating arrows	1. Press [**Alt**] **t**. 2. Pick **Arrows**. 3. Pick start of leader line close to text. 4. Pick elbow points, if desired. 5. Pick where arrow will be pointing. 6. Press mouse button **3** to quit. 7. Arrow will appear at last pick position.
Adjusting the size and look of your arrows	1. Press [**Alt**] **t**. 2. Pick **Arrows**. 3. Pick **Size**. 4. Type in the size you want your arrow to be (in relation to current text size), and press [**Enter**]. Example: **1** 5. Pick **Aspect**. 6. Type in the length value of the arrow head (in relation to the width), and press [**Enter**]. Example: **.75** 7. Pick **Style**. 8. Pick the type of arrow you wish to create.

If you want to do this:	Follow these steps:
	Example: **Open**
	9. Press mouse button **3** to return to the ARROW menu.
Example of settings for an architectural arrow (flat)	1. Size = 1 2. Aspect = .75 3. Style = Open
Example of settings for a mechanical arrow (pointy)	1. Size = .5 2. Aspect = 6 3. Style = Open
Example of settings for a site arrow (small, pointy, filled in)	1. Size = .25 2. Aspect = 6 3. Style = Closed 4. Set weight to 3 before creating arrow.
Changing current text settings to match existing text (Size, aspect, color, layer, font, etc.)	1. Press [**Shift**] **I** (EDIT/IDENTIFY menus). 2. Pick the text you want to match, at the LOWER LEFT CORNER point! Text will change to gray. 3. Pick **Set All**. 4. Press [**Alt**] **T** to go to text menu. 5. Continue creating new text.

Editing Text Features

Editing existing text.	1. Press [**Alt**] **C** (EDIT/CHANGE menus). 2. Pick **Text** from menu. 3. Pick **Content**. 4. Pick the text you wish to edit, at the LOWER LEFT CORNER point, or MIDDLE LOWER POINT, or LOWER RIGHT CORNER! 5. Type in new content. 6. Press [**Return**] or mouse button **3** to quit.
Changing the size of existing text.	1. Press [**Alt**] **C**. 2. Pick **Text**. 3. Pick **Size**. 4. Type in the new size for your existing text.

If you want to do this:	Follow these steps:
	5. Pick **Area** or **Fence** as applicable.
	6. Pick ***LyrSrch** if text is on different layers.
	7. Box around text to change, or entire drawing if applicable.
Changing the size of text to match existing text (Matching)	1. Press [**Alt**] **c**.
	2. Pick **Text**.
	3. Pick ***Match** to make it active (***** = active).
	4. Pick ***Size** to make it active.
	5. Select the text that you wish TO CHANGE, by ***Entity**, ***Group**, ***Area**, or ***Fence**.
	6. Select the text you wish to MATCH the size of. The text selected in step 5 will be changed.
	7. To continue selecting text to change to this new size: —Pick **Match** again to turn it OFF. —Continue selecting the text you want changed.
Changing existing text size relative to a new plot scale	1. Press [**Alt**] **p** (UTILITY/PLOTTER menus).
	2. Pick **Scale**
	3. Select the new plot scale for your drawing.
	4. Press [**Alt**] **t** (EDIT/TEXT menus).
	5. Pick ***TextScal** until it is active (***** = active).
	6. Pick **Size**, and type in the size you want the text to be in relation to the new plot scale, and press [**Enter**]. Example: **.0.**$^1/_8$
	7. Press [**Alt**] **c** (EDIT/CHANGE menus).
	8. Pick **Text**.
	9. Pick **Size**. The correct size will be displayed. Press [**Enter**].
	10. Select the text that you wish to change by ***Entity**, ***Group**, ***Area**, or ***Fence**.

If you want to do this:	Follow these steps:
Changing the size of text in associated dimensions	1. Press [**Alt**] **D** (EDIT, DIMENSION, LINEAR menus).
	2. Pick **Change**.
	3. Pick **TextStyl**.
	4. Pick **TextSize**.
	5. Type in the new size for your existing text.
	6. Pick **Area** or **Fence** as applicable.
	7. Pick ***LyrSrch** if text is on different layers.
	8. Box around dimension text to change, or entire drawing if applicable.

3-D views

See VIEWS-3D

Views (go to view)

Saving the current view (and layer settings, view scale)	1. Press **V** (UTILITY/GOTOVIEW).
	2. Pick **SaveView**.
	3. Pick one of the **View #** options from the menu.
	4. Type in the name of your view.
	5. The current view will be saved.
	6. Press mouse button **3** to quit.
Saving a windowed view	1. Press **V**.
	2. Pick **WindowIn**.
	3. Pick two points to indicate a rectangle around the area you wish to zoom into.
	4. Press mouse button **3** to quit back to GOTOVIEW menu.
	5. Pick **SaveView**.
	6. Pick one of the **View #** options from the menu.
	7. Type in the name of your view.
	8. The zoomed-in view will be saved.
	9. Press mouse button **3** to quit.
Recalling a view with layer settings reset to match original	1. Press **V**.
	2. Pick **LyrSet** until it is ACTIVE (*LyrSet).

If you want to do this:	Follow these steps:
saved view conditions	3. Pick the **Viewname** you wish to see from the menu.
	4. Your view will be displayed, and your settings (active layer, layers set on and off) will be reset to the conditions when the view was saved.
	5. Press mouse button **3** to quit.
Recalling a view without changing the current layer settings	1. Press **V**.
	2. Pick **LyrSet** until it is TURNED OFF (LyrSet).
	3. Pick the **Viewname** you wish to see from the menu.
	4. Your view will be displayed, and your settings will not be changed.
	5. Press mouse button **3** to quit.
Renaming a view	1. Press **V**.
	2. Pick **NameView**.
	3. Pick the **Viewname** you wish to rename from the menu.
	4. Type in the new name for your view.
	5. Press mouse button **3** to quit.
Recalling last window view	1. Press **P**.

Views-3D

Notice: Before creating your 3D views, turn off the layers you do not wish to view in 3D.

Creating a 3D perspective view at eye level	1. Press [**PgUp**] until drawing is reduced to approximately one-third the screen size.
	2. Press [**Arrow left**] and [**Arrow down**] until drawing is displayed over to the upper right hand corner.
	3. Press **Y** (EDIT/DCAD 3D/3D VIEWS menus)
	4. Pick **Prspect** from menu.
	5. Check that **EyePnt Z** and **CentPntZ** are set to **5'-0"**.

If you want to do this:	Follow these steps:
	6. Pick the eye point for the cone of vision, in lower left hand corner of screen.
	7. Pick **FixdCone** to turn it OFF, if applicable (NO *).
	8. Object snap to lower left corner of building or pick a point for picture plane placement.
	9. Your perspective will be displayed.
Creating a bird's-eye perspective view	1. Press [**Pg Up**] until drawing is reduced to approximately one-third the screen size.
	2. Press [**Arrow left**] and [**Arrow down**] until drawing is displayed over to the upper right hand corner.
	3. Press **Y** (EDIT/DCAD 3D/3D VIEWS menus).
	4. Pick **Prspect** from menu.
	5. Pick **EyePnt Z**.
	6. Change the eye point to a new height, and [**Enter**]. Example: **30'-0"**
	7. Pick **CentPntZ**.
	8. Type in and [**Enter**]: **5.0**
	9. Pick the eye point for the cone of vision, in lower left hand corner of screen.
	10. Pick ***FixdCone** until it is active.
	11. Object snap to lower left corner of building or pick a point for picture plane placement.
	12. Your bird's-eye view will be displayed.
	13. The bird's-eye settings (eye point and center point) will remain set until you change it.
Returning to PLAN view of drawing	1. Before leaving **3D View**, pick **Ortho**.
Quick Key for ortho view (plan)	1. Press [**Alt**] **0** (zero).

If you want to do this:	Follow these steps:
Saving a 3D view	1. Press **Y**. 2. Create desired view. 3. Pick **SaveImag**. 4. Pick **NewLayer**. 5. Type in the name of the new layer that will hold the 3D image. Example: **Persp1** 6. Pick **Yes** to display this layer or **No** to turn new layer off. 7. If necessary, move 3D view to better location (see MOVE: "Moving items in one layer" -or- Moving a group of items).

Walls

Turning on the walls drawing mode (Quick key)	1. Press [=] key ("Wall" key) until "Wall width" prompt is displayed. 2. Pick or type in wall width. 3. Press [**Enter**]. 4. Press [**Tab**] until correct wall layer is active. 5. Use cursor to pick placement, or use coordinate input (see COORDINATE INPUT).
Drawing walls dimensioned at the center (Example: interior walls)	1. Press **A** (EDIT/ARCHITECT menus). 2. Pick the ***Centers** option until it is active. 3. Press [**Tab**] until correct wall layer is active. 4. Pick the start and end points of your wall, or use coordinates. (The single line that is originally drawn represents the center-line of your wall.)
Placing walls dimensioned to a side (Exterior walls)	1. Press **A**. 2. Press ***Sides** until it is active. 3. Press [**Tab**] until correct wall layer is active. 4. Pick the start and endpoints of your wall, or use coordinates. (The single line that is drawn represents one side of your wall.)

If you want to do this:	Follow these steps:
	5. Pick to establish the other side of your wall. The wall will be fattened to the side you indicate with your pick. Example: Pick to the inside of the building if you are drawing exterior walls, which are dimensioned to the outside.
Creating an exterior wall with a thicker outside wall line (Highlighted)	1. Press **A**. 2. Make ***Sides** active to draw exterior walls. 3. Pick **Hilite**. 4. If you are using pen widths, pick **Width** and change it to **3**. 5. If you are going to use pen numbers: Pick **Color** and change it to the appropriate color that you will later match to a thicker pen. Pick **Width** and change it to **1**, *or whatever value you desire*, and press [**Enter**]. 6. Make ***Outside** active. 7. Press mouse button **3** to quit back to the ARCHITECT menu. ***Hilite** should be active. 8. Make sure ***Walls** is active, and draw your wall. The side you define as the *outside* will be highlighted.
Cleaning "T" wall intersections as they are created (Not recommended)	1. Press the [\] key until a prompt is displayed: **Wall "T" intersections will be cleaned**. (This sets the *Clean in the ARCHITECT menu.) 2. Be very careful when placing your walls, or the *wrong side may be cleaned*.
Cleaning up wall intersections after they are created	1. Pick **CleanUp** from the EDIT menu. 2. Pick **L-Intsct** (L-intersection) or **T-Intsct** (T-intersection), or **X-Intsct** (X-intersection), whichever is applicable.

If you want to do this:	Follow these steps:
	3. Press [**Tab**] until correct wall layer is active, or turn on ***LyrSrch**.
	4. Pick two points to indicate a rectangle around intersection.
	5. If "T-intersection," pick one line of wall to trim "to."
Connecting 2 co-linear walls	(See WALLS, Welding two walls together)
Defining wall height	1. Press **Z** key.
	2. Type in and [**Enter**] new "Z" base (bottom) and "Z" height (top).
	Example: **Z-Base = 0.0**
	Z-Height = 8.0
Picking wall placement	1. Move cursor with mouse.
	2. Watch coordinate readout.
	3. Press mouse button **1** for each end point of wall.
	4. Press mouse button **3** to quit or disconnect.
Using coordinates to create exterior walls	1. Press [**Insert**] until **Relative cartesian coordinates** is displayed.
	2. Press [**Tab**] until correct layer is active.
	3. Press **A** and make ***Walls** and ***Sides** active.
	4. Pick start point of wall.
	5. Press [**Space bar**].
	6. Type in the X length of your wall, if applicable. Press [**Enter**].
	7. Type in the Y length of your wall, if applicable. Press [**Enter**].
	Example: **X = 25.6**
	Y = 0
	8. A single line will appear on the screen. Pick to indicate the inside of the building. The second, inside wall line will appear.
	9. Press the [**Space bar**] and continue creating your walls using coordinates.

If you want to do this:	Follow these steps:
Welding 2 walls together (removing a hole from the wall)	1. Pick **Cleanup** from the EDIT menu. 2. Pick **WeldWall**. 3. [**Tab**] to the correct layer, or turn on ***LyrSrch**. 4. Pick 2 points to indicate a box around the hole in the wall, or the two wall ends that you wish to close.
Welding 1 wall line at a time	1. Press [**Alt**] **W**. 2. Pick the first line to weld. 3. Pick the second line to weld. 4. If they were not co-linear or were on an angle, a YES/NO will be displayed. Pick **Yes** if applicable.

Windows

Adding windows by sides	1. Press **A**. 2. Pick **Windows**. 3. Pick **LyrSrch** until the layer list is displayed. 4. Pick the layer that the appropriate walls are on. This layer will remain set until you change it. 5. Make ***Sides** active. 6. Press [**Tab**] until the window layer is displayed. 7. Pick one jamb side on wall. 8. Pick second jamb side on wall. 9. Pick outside of wall. 10. The window will be added.
Adding windows by centers	1. Press **A**. 2. Pick **Windows**. 3. Pick **LyrSrch** until the layer list is displayed. 4. Pick the layer that the appropriate walls are on. This layer will remain set until you change it. 5. Turn **Sides** OFF. 6. Press [**Tab**] until the window layer is displayed. 7. Object snap to center of inside wall. 8. Pick one jamb side on wall.

If you want to do this:	Follow these steps:

| | 9. Pick outside of wall. |
| | 10. The window is added. |

Adding windows by centers using coordinate input	1. Press **A**.
	2. Pick **Windows**.
	3. Pick **LyrSrch** until the layer list is displayed.
	4. Pick the layer that the appropriate walls are on. This layer will remain set until you change it.
	5. Turn **Sides** OFF.
	6. Press [**Tab**] until the window layer is displayed.
	7. Press [~] key.
	8. Object snap to outside corner the window is dimensioned from. This point will become 0,0.
	9. Press [**Insert**] until the relative cartesian coordinates mode is set.
	10. Press the [**Space bar**].
	11. Type in the **X** coordinate for the window center, if applicable, and press [**Enter**] (X = horizontal, to the right). use the - sign if the coordinate is toward the left.
	12. Type in the **Y** coordinate for the window center, if applicable, and press [**Enter**] (Y = Vertical, up). Use the − sign if the coordinate is going down. Example: **X = −8.0** **Y = 0.0**
	13. Move your cursor to check that the window center is located in the correct area.
	14. Press the [**Space bar**].
	15. Type in the **X** coordinate to indicate one jamb ($1/2$ width of window), if applicable, and press [**Enter**] (X = horizontal, to the right). Use the − sign if the coordinate is toward the left.
	16. Type in the **Y** coordinate, if applicable, and press [**Enter**] (Y = Vertical, up).

If you want to do this:	Follow these steps:
	Use the – sign if the coordinate is going down
	Example: **X = 3**
	Y = 0.0
	17. Pick outside of wall.
	18. Your window is added.
Adding doors and windows on multiple story buildings	1. Press **Z**.
	2. Change the Z-Base and Z-Height to correct values for the walls on the story you will be adding doors and windows to.
	3. Doors and windows will be inserted into the walls at that level.
Erasing Windows (Removing)	1. Press **a**.
	2. Pick **Windows**.
	3. Pick **Remove**.
	4. Pick two points to indicate a box around the window to remove.
	5. Window is erased and walls are cleaned up.
	Caution: There is no UNDO. However, window may be recovered by pressing the > key, but wall will have to cut again.
	Note: Doors and cut walls may also be removed with this option.

Windowing (view windows)

Zooming in (Windowing in)	1. Press the / key (has a ? on it).
	2. Pick two diagonal points to indicate a rectangle around the items you wish to "window-in" to.
	3. Press mouse button **3** to quit.
Getting a full view of your drawing	1. Press the / key.
	2. Pick **Extends**.
	3. If full view is not displayed, pick **Recalc**.
	4. Press mouse button **3** to quit.

If you want to do this:	Follow these steps:
Moving the viewing window to the right	1. Press the [**right arrow**] key.
Moving the viewing window to the left	1. Press the [**left arrow**] key.
Making the drawing smaller	1. Press the [**Page Up**] key.
Making the drawing larger	1. Press the [**Page Down**] key.
Returning to the previous window	1. Press the **P** key.

System operations

(Listed alphabetically)

DOS – drawing files management

Backups

Notice: Backups of all drawings on your hard disk should be made on a weekly basis. (Example: Every Friday at 4:30 p.m.) This is a safeguard against possible hard disk error.

Diskette backups of individual drawings should be made as "COPIES" (See COPYING DRAWINGS TO FLOPPY DISKETTES). However, if the drawing does not fit on 1 diskette, and therefore must be backed up on several diskettes, use Backup. "Backup" is the only command that allows you to split a drawing onto multiple diskettes.

Backing up all drawing files	
	1. Exit DataCAD and use DOS.
	2. *Important*: Make sure you are in the DOS root directory by typing in: **cd **
	3. Press [**Enter**].
	4. Now type in: **backup c: \ * .dc3 a:/s**
	5. Check that you typed in everything correctly, then press [**Enter**].
	6. Insert a formatted diskette into drive

If you want to do this:	Follow these steps:
	A, following the prompt, and press return.
	7. Continue following the prompts until all of your drawings are backed up.
	8. Label, date, and number all diskettes sequentially.
Restoring your backups	1. Exit DataCAD and use DOS.
	2. Make sure you are in the root directory by typing in: **cd** \
	3. Press [**Enter**].
	4. Now type in: **restore a: c:** \ ***.*/s**
	5. Check that the command is typed correctly, then press [**Enter**].
	6. Insert the 1 backup disk into drive A. If the diskette is NOT 1, you will be prompted to reinsert 1.
	7. Continue following the prompts until the restoration is completed.

Copying drawings to floppy diskette

Notice: A copy to diskette, of the current drawing you are working on should be made daily. (Example: At the end of the day's work on the drawing, copy it to diskette.) This is to safeguard possible errors, accidental changes, or deletion of the file on hard disk.

If the drawing does NOT fit on a single diskette, use Backup (see BACKUPS).

Copying one drawing to a diskette in drive A:	1. Exit DataCAD and use DOS.
	2. Type in **cd** (change directory) and the project directory pathname that holds your drawings. Be sure to use the \ key to separate the directory names. Example: **cd** \ **mtec** \ **proj01**
	3. Press [**Enter**].
	4. Insert a formatted diskette in drive A.
	5. Type in **copy**, the name of your drawing, and end the command with a: for drive specification. Separate each field with a space.

If you want to do this:	Follow these steps:

Example: **copy drawing1.dc3 a:**

6. Press [**Enter**].

Copying all the drawings in a directory to a diskette in drive A:	

1. Exit DataCAD and use DOS.
2. Type in **cd** (change directory) and the project directory pathname that holds your drawings. Be sure to use the \ key to separate the directory names. Example: **cd \ mtec \ proj01**
3. Press [**Enter**].
4. Insert a formatted diskette in drive A.
5. Type in:
   copy *.dc3 a:
6. Press [**Enter**].

Copying drawings from floppy diskette

Copying one drawing FROM a diskette in drive A:	

1. Exit DataCAD and use DOS.
2. Type in **cd** (change directory) and the project directory pathname that you want to copy your drawing to. Be sure to use the \ key to separate the directory names. Example: **cd \ mtec \ proj01**
3. Press [**Enter**].
4. Insert the diskette that contains the drawing you wish to copy to the hard disk, in drive A.
5. Type in **copy a:** and the name of your drawing. The drawing will be copied to the current directory. Separate the fields with a space. Example: **copy a:drawing1.dc3**
6. Press [**Enter**].

Copying all the drawings from a diskette in drive A: to the hard disk	

1. Exit DataCAD and use DOS.
2. Type in **cd** (change directory) and the project directory pathname that you want to copy your drawings to. Use the \ key to separate the directory names. Example: **cd \ mtec \ proj01**
3. Press [**Enter**].

If you want to do this:	Follow these steps:
	4. Insert the diskette that holds your drawings in drive A.
	5. Type in: **copy a:*.dc3**
	6. Press [**Enter**].

Piping template symbols

Notice: Prepare your symbols for piping using DataCAD (see TEM-PLATES & SYMBOLS).

Template piping is designed to make a template display faster, and so that it is easier to use. When a piped template is displayed, only text or other simple description for each symbol is shown in the symbol boxes. Once you place the symbol, the *actual symbol* appears.

The directions below assume that you are using, and have experience with, a text editor or EDLIN to change your template file.

Using a text editor to pipe your template symbols	1. Using your text editor, enter the template file you wish to pipe. (Contains both descriptive and actual symbols.)
	2. Notice that the **descriptive symbol** should be followed by the **actual symbol** on the next line! (Otherwise you will have to retype everything in.) An example of this file is below:
(title)	**DataCAD template file. version 01.10.**
(one blank line)	
(number of columns)	**2**
(number of rows)	**8**
	*
(symbol pathnames)	**sym \ furn \ tabltext**
	sym \ furn \ table
	sym \ furn \ sinktext
	sym \ furn \ sink
	sym \ furn \ lamptext
	sym \ furn \ lamp
	3. Edit the file, so the *descriptive symbol* is first, on the same line as the *actual symbol*, separated by a "|"

If you want to do this:	Follow these steps:
	as shown below. There should be NO spaces in the line (*Note: Tabltext* is the descriptive symbol, and *table* is the actual symbol.) **sym \ furn \ tabltext \ sym \ furn \ table**

4. Make sure you do not add an extra line or spaces in the template file. There should be *only one blank line*, and that is the one right after the title.
5. When you have condensed your file, you may want to edit the number of columns and rows to match.
6. Exit the editor when you are through, saving the changes you made to the template file.
7. Start DataCAD, and test your template.

Appendix B
The DataCAD
Reference Guide

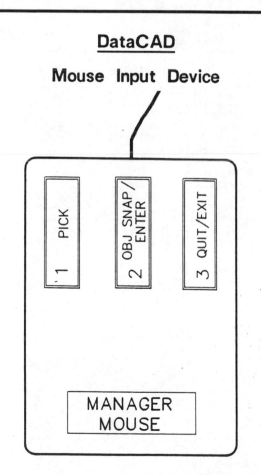

DataCAD Menu
Organization Edit Menu

F1 Move	F2 Copy	F3 Rotate	F4 Mirror	F5 Stretch
F1 Entity	F1 Entity	F1 Entity	F1 Entity	F1 Point
F2*Group	F2*Group	F2*Group	F2*Group	F2*Box
F3 Area	F3 Area	F3 Area	F3 Area	F3
F4 Fence	F4 Fence	F4 Fence	F4 Fence	F4
F5Sel Set	F5Sel Set	F5Sel Set	F5Sel Set	F5
F6 LyrSrch	F6 LyrSrch	F6 LyrSrch	F6 LyrSrch	F6 LyrSrch
F7	F7	F7	F7	F7
F8New Dist	F8New Dist	F8NewAngle	F8New Line	F8New Dist
F9Invert	F9Invert	F9Invert	F9*FixText	F9Invert
F0	F0	F0NewCentr	F0	F0
S1To Layer	S1To Layer	S1	S1	S1
S2 AndCopy	S2	S2 AndCopy	S2 AndCopy	S2
S3 Move Z	S3	S3	S3	S3
S4	S4RectArry	S4	S4	S4
S5Drag	S5CircArry	S5	S5	S5
S6	S6	S6	S6	S6
S7	S7	S7	S7	S7
S8	S8	S8	S8	S8
S9	S9	S9	S9	S9
S0Exit	S0Exit	S0Exit	S0Exit	S0Exit

F6 Enlarge	F7 Erase	F8 LinkEnts	F9 Cleanup	F0 Change
F1 Entity	F1 Entity	F1 Entity	F1Fillets	F1 Entity
F2*Group	F2*Group	F2*Group	F2Chamfer	F2*Group
F3 Area	F3 Area	F3 Area	F3	F3 Area
F4 Fence	F4 Fence	F4 Fence	F41Ln Trim	F4 Fence
F5Sel Set	F5Sel Set	F5Sel Set	F52Ln Trim	F5Sel Set
F6 LyrSrch	F6 LyrSrch	F6 LyrSrch	F6	F6 LyrSrch
F7	F7	F7	F7WeldLine	F7
F8Enlrgmnt	F8Undo	F8	F8	F8 LineTyp
F9Invert	F9Partial	F9	F9T Intsct	F9 LineWgt
F0Center	F0	F0 Un–Link	F0L Intsct	F0 Color
S1	S1Clr Undo	S1	S1	S1 Spacing
S2 AndCopy	S2	S2	S2	S2 OverSht
S3 Enlrg Z	S3	S3	S3	S3 Z–Base
S4	S4	S4	S4	S4 Z–Heigh
S5	S5	S5	S5	S5
S6	S6	S6	S6	S6Text
S7	S7	S7	S7	S7
S8	S8	S8	S8	S8
S9	S9	S9	S9	S9
S0Exit	S0Exit	S0Exit	S0Exit	S0Exit

DataCAD Menu
Organization Edit Menu

S1 Identify	S2 EditSets	S3 Architct	S4 Polygons	S5 Curves
F1EntType	F1Show	F1*Walls	F1No.Sides	F12 Pt Arc
F2Layer	F2Add To	F2*Sides	F2	F23 Pt Arc
F3Color	F3Del From	F3 Centers	F3*Dynamic	F3CentAngl
F4LineType	F4Clear	F4*Clean	F4*CntrPnt	F4Cent Arc
F5Spacing	F5Name Set	F5 Cap	F5*Vertex	F5CentChrd
F6LineWgt	F6	F6 Hilite	F6*Diametr	F6EndPtRad
F7OverSht	F7	F7Width	F7*Inscrib	F7EndPtAng
F8Z−Base	F8	F8	F8	F8StartDir
F9Z−Height	F9 Append	F9DoorSwng	F9	F9Tangent
F0	F0SetActiv	F0Windows	F0 Rectngl	F0
S1	S1	S1Cut Wall	S1	S1Rad Circ
S2	S2	S2	S2	S2Dia Circ
S3	S3	S3	S3	S33Pt Circ
S4	S4	S4	S4	S4
S5	S5	S5	S5	S5Ellipse
S6	S6	S6	S6	S6Polyline
S7Angle	S7	S7	S7	S7Bezier
S8Length	S8	S8	S8	S8B−Spline
S93D Views	S9	S9	S9	S9CurvData
S0Exit	S0Exit	S0Exit	S0Exit	S0Exit

S6 Text	S7 LineType	S8 DCAD 3D	S9 Macros	S0 Utility
F1Size	F1Solid	F13D Views	DCAD_AEC	F1To Scale
F2Angle	F2Dotted	F2Hide	F2	F2GotoView
F3Weight	F3Dashed	F33D Line	F3	F3Layers
F4Slant	F4Dot−Dash	3D Arc	F4	F4Template
F5Aspect	F5ElecLine	Settings	F5	F5Hatch
F6	F6Tel Line	F6	F6	F6Geometry
F7Arrows	F7Box	F7	F7	F7Measures
F8TextFile	F8PropLine	F8	F8	F8Dmension
F9	F9Insul	F9	F9	F9Freehand
F0Justify	F03/4Plywd	F0	F0	F0Settings
S1	S1	S1	S1	S1Grids
S2*Left	S2ScrlFwrd	S2	S2	S2Display
S3 Center	S3	S3	S3	S3Obj Snap
S4 Right	S4	S4	S4	S4
S5	S5*Factor	S5	S5	S5Plotter
S6Fit Text	S6LineWgt	S6	S6	S6File I/O
S7	S7Color	S7	S7	S7Directry
S8Factor	S8Spacing	S8	S8	S8WindowIn
S9FontName	S9OverSht	S9	S9	S9Quit
S0Exit	S0Exit	S0Exit	S0Exit	S0Exit

DataCAD Menu
Organization Utility

F1 To Scale	F2 GotoView	F3 Layers	F4 Template	F5 Hatch
F112"	F1View 1	F1On/Off	F1New File	F1*Entity
F26"	F2View 2	F2All On	F2TemplOff	F2 Group
F33"	F3View 3	F3SetActiv	F3Dvisions	F3 Area
F42"	F4View 4	F4ActvOnly	F4	F4 Fence
F51-1/2"	F5View 5	F5	F5SaveSymb	F5Sel Set
F61"	F6View 6	F6Name	F6Del Symb	F6 LyrSrch
F73/4"	F7View 7	F7Color	F7SymName	F7
F81/2"	F8View 8	F8	F8Replace	F8HtchType
F93/8"	F9View 9	F9NewLayer	F9Redefine	F9Pattern
F01/4"	F0View 10	F0ErseLayr	F0PurgeSym	F0Scale
S13/16"	S1	S1DelLayer	S1Re—Load	S1Angle
S21/8"	S2SaveView	S2	S2	S2Origin
S33/32"	S3NameView	S3SaveLayr	S3Rotate	S3
S41/16"	S4To Scale	S4LoadLayr	S4Enlarge	S4
S51: 20	S5WindowIn	S5	S5Z Offset	S5
S61: 40	S6*LayrSet	S6ViewLayr	S6 Explode	S6
S71: 100	S7	S7ViewFile	S7EditFlds	S7
S81: 1000	S8	S8	S8Reports	S8Begin
S9	S9	S9*LyrRfsh	S9	S9
S0NoChange	S0Exit	S0Exit	S0Exit	S0Exit

F6 Geometry	F7 Measures	F8 Dmension	F9 FreeHand	F0 Settings
F1Divide	F1Ref Pnt	F1*Horizntl	F1	F1Password
F2Intrsect	F2Snap Pnt	F2 Vertcal	F2	F2ScaleTyp
F3Offset	F3Line	F3 Aligned	F3	F3AngleTyp
F4Tangents	F4PntToPnt	F4 Rotated	F4	F4EditDefs
F5	F5Diameter	F5*Assoc	F5	F5MissDist
F6	F6Radius	F6Entity	F6	F6SmalGrid
F7	F7Chord	F7AutoDim	F7	F7ScrlDist
F8	F8ArcLnth	F8	F8	F8DistDlay
F9	F9Crcmfrnc	F9	F9	F9SaveDlay
F0	F0	F0	F0	F0
S1	S1InclAngl	S1	S1	S1 DrwMrks
S2	S2ExclAngl	S2	S2	S2*Beeps
S3	S3LineAngl	S3TextStyl	S3	S3 BigCurs
S4	S4	S4Dim Styl	S4	S4 NegDist
S5	S5Area/Per	S5ArroStyl	S5	S5*Show Z
S6	S6Takeoffs	S6AutoStyl	S6	S6 FixdRef
S7	S7	S7Explode	S7	S7 DisSync
S8	S8	S8Change	S8	S8
S9	S9	S9	S9	S9
S0Exit	S0Exit	S0Exit	S0Exit	S0Exit

DataCAD Menu
Organization Utility

S1 Grids	S2 Display	S3 Obj Snap	S4	S5 Plotter
F1*Snap On	F1*ShowTxt	F1 Nearest		F1Plot
F2*Disp1On	F2*ShowDim	F2*End Pnt		F2Backgrnd
F3*Disp2On	F3*ShwHtch	F3*Mid Pnt		F3To File
F4	F4*ShowWgt	F4 N Pnts		F4Scale
F5GridSize	F5*UserLin	F5*Center		F5PaperSiz
F6	F6 Ovrsht	F6 Quadrnt		F6PenSpeed
F7GridColr	F7*ShowIns	F7*Intsect		F7PenWidth
F8	F8*ShowAtrs	F8 Perpend		F8Partial
F9	F9	F9 Tangent		F9Layout
F0Snap Ang	F0SmallTxt	F0		F0Lyout Sz
S1Angle	S1BoxColor	S1 None		S1LyoutDiv
S2Grid Org	S2SmallSym	S2*FastSym		S2 Rotate
S3	S3ArcFactr	S3*Fast 3D		S3*ColrPlot
S4	S4	S4MissDist		S4Set Pens
S5	S5	S5*LyrSnap		S5*PenSort
S6	S6	S6*SrchHch		S6
S7	S7	S7 Quick		S7
S8	S8	S8 Sel Set		S8
S9	S9	S9 Apertur		S93D Views
S0Exit	S0Exit	S0Exit		S0Exit

S6 File I/O	S7 Directry	S8 WindowIn	S9 Quit	S0 Edit
F1New Dwg	F1Project	F1Extents	F1Abort	F1Move
F2SaveDwg	F2Employee	F2Re—Calc	F2	F2Copy
F3Copy Dwg	F3Rate	F3	F3	F3Rotate
F4	F4Deprtmnt	F4	F4	F4Mirror
F5Read DXF	F5Phase	F5	F5 Yes	F5Stretch
F6WriteDXF	F6Service	F6	F6 No	F6Enlarge
F7	F7	F7	F7	F7Erase
F8Copy	F8To File	F8	F8	F8LinkEnts
F9Delete	F9	F9	F9	F9Cleanup
F0Rename	F0ScrlFwrd	F0	F0	F0Change
S1 .BAK	S1	S1	S1	S1Identify
S2*.DC3	S2SymFiles	S2	S2	S2EditSets
S3 .FRM	S3	S3	S3	S3Architct
S4 .LYR	S4	S4	S4	S4Polygons
S5 .PLT	S5	S5	S5	S5Curves
S6 .SM3	S6	S6	S6	S6Text
S7 .TPL	S7Pause	S7	S7	S7LineType
S8 .TXT	S8Total	S8	S8	S8DCAD 3D
S9	S9	S9	S9	S9Macros
S0Exit	S0Exit	S0Exit	S0Exit	S0Utility

DataCAD Hatch Patterns

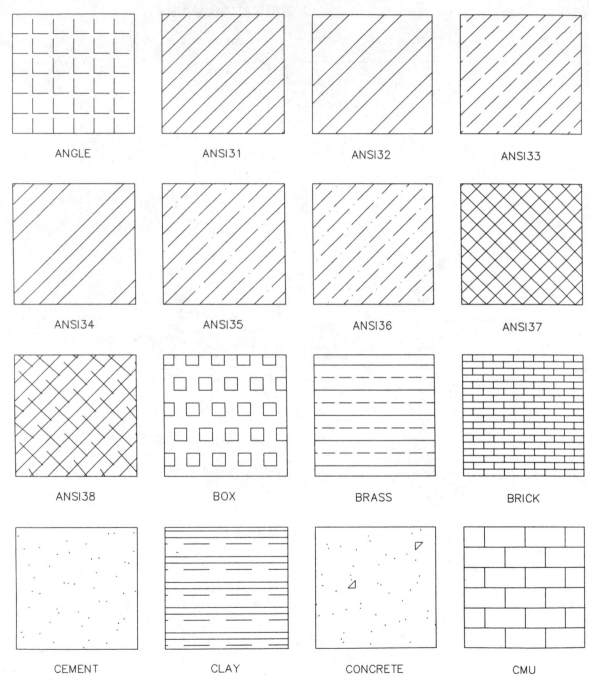

ANGLE   ANSI31   ANSI32   ANSI33

ANSI34   ANSI35   ANSI36   ANSI37

ANSI38   BOX   BRASS   BRICK

CEMENT   CLAY   CONCRETE   CMU

DataCAD Hatch Patterns

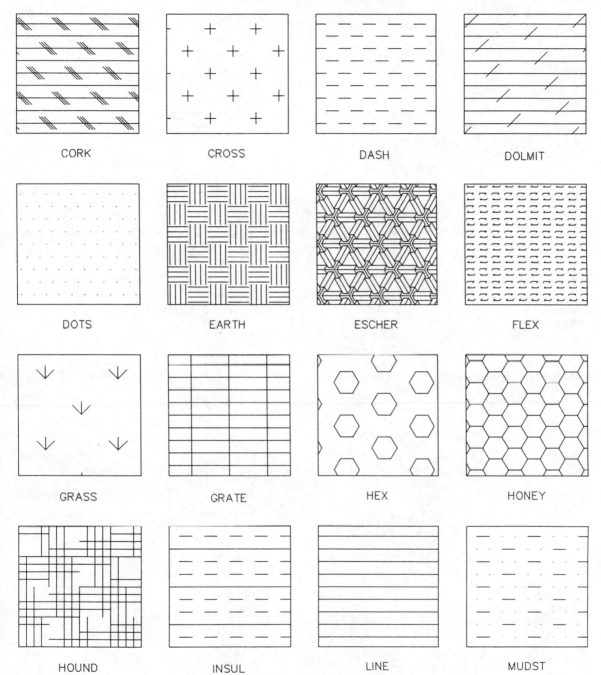

CORK

CROSS

DASH

DOLMIT

DOTS

EARTH

ESCHER

FLEX

GRASS

GRATE

HEX

HONEY

HOUND

INSUL

LINE

MUDST

DataCAD Hatch Patterns

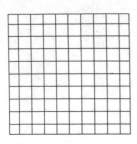

NET

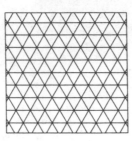

NET3

PLAST

PLASTI

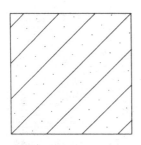

SACNCR

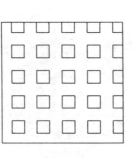

SQUARE

STEEL

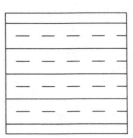

TRANS

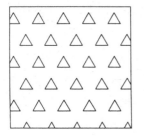

TRIANG

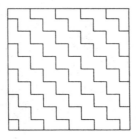

ZIGZAG

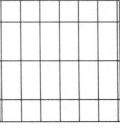

24X48TIL

48X24TIL

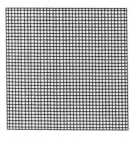

4X4TIL

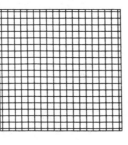

8X8TIL

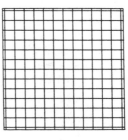

12X12TIL

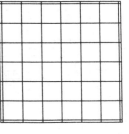

24X24TIL

DataCAD Drawing Outline

Job Name: _____ Job No: _____

Drawing Name (w/ path): _____

Drawing Description: _____

Layer Name:	Description:	Layer Name:	Description:
_____	_____	_____	_____
_____	_____	_____	_____
_____	_____	_____	_____
_____	_____	_____	_____
_____	_____	_____	_____
_____	_____	_____	_____
_____	_____	_____	_____
_____	_____	_____	_____
_____	_____	_____	_____
_____	_____	_____	_____
_____	_____	_____	_____
_____	_____	_____	_____
_____	_____	_____	_____
_____	_____	_____	_____
_____	_____	_____	_____
_____	_____	_____	_____
_____	_____	_____	_____
_____	_____	_____	_____
_____	_____	_____	_____
_____	_____	_____	_____

Go To View:	Description:	Go To View:	Description:
_____	_____	_____	_____
_____	_____	_____	_____
_____	_____	_____	_____
_____	_____	_____	_____
_____	_____	_____	_____

Descriptive

Sheet Size: _____ Plot Scale: _____ Symbols Scale: _____

Text Size (notes): _____ (titles): _____

Text Font (notes): _____ (titles): _____

Notes: _____

_____

_____

_____

DataCAD Template Outline

Template Name (w/ path):

_____

Template Description:

_____

Symbols:

Symbol Name (w/ path):   Description:

_____   _____
_____   _____
_____   _____
_____   _____
_____   _____
_____   _____
_____   _____
_____   _____
_____   _____
_____   _____
_____   _____
_____   _____
_____   _____
_____   _____
_____   _____
_____   _____
_____   _____
_____   _____
_____   _____
_____   _____
_____   _____
_____   _____
_____   _____
_____   _____

Notes:

_____
_____
_____
_____
_____
_____

DataCAD
Available Drawing Areas

Final Plot Scale	36" x 24" Actual Drawing Area	42" x 30" Actual Drawing Area	Typical Detail Box
12"	2'-8" x 1'-11"	3'-2" x 2'-5"	6 1/4" x 5 3/4"
6"	5'-4" x 3'-10"	6'-4" x 4'-10"	1'-1/2" x 11 1/2"
3"	10'-8" x 7'-8"	12'-8" x 9'-8"	2'-1" x 1'-11"
1.1/2"	21'-4" x 15'-4"	25'-4" x 19'-4"	4'-2" x 3'-10"
1"	32' x 23'	38' x 29'	6'-3" x 5'-9"
3/4"	42'-8" x 30'-8"	50'-8" x 38'-8"	8'-4" x 7'-8"
1/2"	64' x 46'	76' x 58'	12'-6" x 11'-6"
3/8"	85'-4" x 61'-4"	101'-4" x 77'-4"	16'-8" x 15'-4"
1/4"	128' x 92'	152' x 116'	25'-0" x 23'-0"
3/16"	170'-8" x 122'-8"	202'-8" x 154'-8"	33'-4" x 30'-8"
1/8"	256' x 184'	304' x 232'	50'-0" x 46'-0"
3/32"	341'-4" x 245'-4"	405'-4" x 309'-4"	66'-8" x 61'-4"
1/16"	512' x 368'	608' x 464'	100'-0" x 92'-0"
1:20	640' x 460'	760' x 580'	125' x 115'
1:40	1280' x 920'	1520' x 1160'	250' x 230'
1:100	3200' x 2300'	3800' x 2900'	625' x 575'

Formula:
X limit in feet = (Available width in inches)/Plot Scale
Y limit in feet = (Available height in inches)/Plot Scale

* When entering Custom Sheet Size in the Plotter menu use 32 & 23 for 24x36 sheets and use 38 & 29 for 30x42 sheets (inside border limits).

DataCAD
Suggested Colors/Pens Assignments

Color Number	Color Name	Pen Position In Plotter	Wet Ink Pen Size			
F1	White	0	1#	.50mm	.020"	(medium)
F2	Red	2	00#	.30mm	.012"	
F3	Green	3	0#	.35mm	.014"	(fine)
F4	Blue	4		.40mm	.016"	
F5	Cyan	5	1#	.50mm	.020"	(medium)
F6	Magenta	7	2.5#	.70mm	.028"	(bold)
F7	Brown	6	2#	.60mm	.024"	
F8	Lt Gray	1	000#	.25mm	.010"	(extra fine)
F9	Dk Gray	1	000#	.25mm	.010"	(extra fine)
F0	Lt Red	2	-- empty --			
S1	Lt Grn	3	0#	.35mm	.014"	(fine)
S2	Lt Blue	4		.40mm	.016"	
S3	Lt Cyan	5	1#	.50mm	.020"	(medium)
S4	Lt Mgta	7	2.5#	.70mm	.028"	(bold)
S5	Yellow	6	2#	.60mm	.024"	

DataCAD EditDefs Scales

Architectural

The following settings can be used to modify the scale settings in Datacad software for architectural drawings:

Scale:	Setting:
1/32" = 1'-0"	0.00260416
1/16" = 1'-0"	0.00520833
3/32" = 1'-0"	0.00781250
1/8" = 1'-0"	0.01041666
3/16" = 1'-0"	0.01562500
1/4" = 1'-0"	0.02083333
3/8" = 1'-0"	0.03125000
1/2" = 1'-0"	0.04166666
3/4" = 1'-0"	0.06250000
1" = 1'-0"	0.08333333
1 1/2" = 1'-0"	0.12500000
2" = 1'-0"	0.16666666
3" = 1'-0"	0.25000000
6" = 1'-0"	0.50000000
12" = 1'-0"	1.00000000
24" = 1'-0"	2.00000000

Formula:

To calculate the scaling value for additional architectural scales, express the fraction in decimal form, and divide by 12 to convert the feet to inches. For example, 1/4" = 1'-0" would be 0.25" = 1'-0", or 0.02083333" = 1".

DataCAD Editdefs Scales

Engineering

The following settings can be used to modify the scale settings in Datacad software for engineering drawings:

Scale:	Setting:
1:10	0.00833333
1:20	0.00416666
1:33 1/3	0.00250000
1:40	0.00208333
1:50	0.00166666
1:80	0.00104166
1:100	0.00083333
1:200	0.00041666
1:400	0.00020833
1:600	0.00013888
1:1000	0.00008333

Formula:

To calculate the scaling value for additional engineering scales, express the ratio in decimal form and divide by twelve to convert the feet to inches. For example, 1:10 would be 0.1/12 or 0.00833333.

DataCAD Scales & Sizes

Final Plot Scale	Text Size "Notes"	Text Size "Titles"	*Descriptive* Symbol Enlargement	Detail Enlargement Factor
12"	1/8"	1/4"	1	1
6"	1/4"	1/2"	2	.5
3"	1/2"	1"	4	.25
1.1/2"	1"	2"	8	.125
1"	1.1/2"	3"	12	.0833
3/4"	2"	4"	16	.0625
1/2"	3"	6"	24	.0417
3/8"	4"	8"	32	.0313
1/4"	6"	1'-0"	48	.0208
3/16"	8"	1'-4"	64	.0156
1/8"	1'-0"	2'-0"	96	.0104
3/32"	1'-4"	2'-8"	128	.0078
1/16"	2'-0"	4'-0"	192	.0052
1:20	2'-6"	5'-0"	240	.0042
1:40	5'-0"	10'-0"	480	.0021
1:100	12'-6"	25'-0"	1200	.0008

Formulas:

Text in inches   = ((12/(drawing scale)) x (desired text height))
Titles in inches   = ((12/(drawing scale)) x (desired title height))
Descriptive Symbol Enlargement Factor = (12/(drawing scale))
Detail Enlargement Factor = ((drawing scale)/12)

* NOTE – Roman text will plot at 3/32" high based on the above chart.
 – Roman titles will plot at 3/16" high based on the above chart.
 – Symbol enlargement size is designed only for *descriptive symbols* created at actual size (not building component symbols).

DataCAD Linetypes

Samples	Linetype	Spacing Formula
——————	Solid	Any scale.
··············	Dotted	(.125/plot scale) = spacing (feet)
– – – – – – –	Dashed	(.125/plot scale) x 2 = spacing (feet)
—— · —	Dot-dash	(.125/plot scale) x 16 = spacing (feet)
—·——·—	Elecline	(.125/plot scale) x 8 = spacing (feet)
—'——'—	Tel Line	(.125/plot scale) x 8 = spacing (feet)
—◇——◇—	Box	(.125/plot scale) x 8 = spacing (feet)
———– –	Propline	(.125/plot scale) x 16 = spacing (feet)
⬠⬠⬠⬠⬠	Insul	wall width/2 = spacing
▬▬▬▬▬	3/4 Plywd	3/4"
▬▬▬▬▬	1/2 Plywd	3/4"
∿∿∿∿∿	Hedge	height x 2 = spacing
—————– – —	Centrlin	(.125/plot scale) x 16 = spacing (feet)
—⌐⌐—	Section	(.125/plot scale) x 8 = spacing (feet)
◿◿	Shingles	exposed length x 2 = spacing
◿◿	LapSidng	exposed length = spacing
▭▭▭	Shiplap	length of 1 board = spacing
⊓⊓⊓⊓⊓⊓	Brick	8"
▭ ▭ ▭	4" Block	8"
▭ ▭	8" Block	8"
	12"Block	8"
▬▬▬▬	Rigid	Ins thickness = spacing
————————	Grass	height x 2 = spacing
———·——·—	Groundlin	(.125/plot scale) x 8 = spacing (feet)

Appendix C
Answers to exercises

Exercise 1 – Beginning DataCAD

1. a	6. b	11. a
2. b	7. c	12. b
3. c	8. a	13. c
4. a	9. b	14. a
5. b	10. c	

Exercise 2 – Drawing Setup

1. b	6. b	11. a
2. c	7. a	12. b
3. a	8. b	13. c
4. a	9. b	
5. b	10. c	

Exercise 3 – Basic Drafting

1. a	7. b	13. a
2. b	8. c	14. b
3. c	9. c	15. b
4. a	10. a	16. a
5. c	11. a	
6. a	12. b	

Exercise 4 – Windowing

1. b	3. b
2. a	4. c

5. b   9. c
6. a   10. a
7. b   11. b
8. b

Exercise 5 – Adding Symbols

1. a   7. c
2. c   8. b
3. b   9. c
4. b   10. a
5. b   11. c
6. a   12. a

Exercise 6 – Dimensions and Text

1. a   6. c
2. a   7. a
3. c   8. b
4. b   9. c
5. b   10. a

Exercise 7 – Viewing in 3-D

1. b   7. b
2. a   8. a
3. c   9. a
4. b   10. c
5. a   11. a
6. c

Exercise 8 – Plotting your Drawing

1. c   7. b   13. a
2. b   8. a   14. c
3. c   9. c   15. b
4. a   10. b   16. a
5. a   11. a   17. c
6. c   12. b   18. a

Exercise 9 – Initial Site Plans

1. b   5. b   9. c
2. b   6. b   10. a
3. b   7. c   11. a
4. c   8. a   12. b

13.	b	15.	c	17.	a
14.	c	16.	b	18.	b

Exercise 10 – 3-D Lines

1.	b	6.	a	11.	a
2.	a	7.	c	12.	c
3.	a	8.	b	13.	b
4.	c	9.	a	14.	a
5.	b	10.	b		

Exercise 11 – Copying Techniques

1.	a	8.	a	15.	a
2.	b	9.	b	16.	c
3.	b	10.	c	17.	b
4.	c	11.	c	18.	c
5.	a	12.	b	19.	b
6.	b	13.	c	20.	a
7.	c	14.	a		

Exercise 12 – Details

1.	c	6.	a
2.	b	7.	b
3.	a	8.	b
4.	b	9.	a
5.	c	10.	b

Exercise 13 – Templates and Symbols

1.	a	7.	a	13.	c
2.	b	8.	b	14.	b
3.	b	9.	a	15.	c
4.	c	10.	a	16.	c
5.	b	11.	b		
6.	a	12.	b		

Exercise 14 – Default Drawings

1.	b	9.	a	17.	b
2.	c	10.	c	18.	b
3.	a	11.	b	19.	c
4.	a	12.	a	20.	a
5.	b	13.	b	21.	b
6.	b	14.	c	22.	c

7. a	15. a	
8. c	16. a	

Exercise 15 – Final

1. b	11. c	21. c
2. c	12. b	22. a
3. b	13. a	23. c
4. a	14. b	24. b
5. a	15. b	25. b
6. b	16. a	26. a
7. a	17. b	27. b
8. a	18. a	28. a
9. a	19. b	29. a
10. b	20. c	30. c

Exercise 16 – Modeled Doors and Windows

1. b	6. c
2. c	7. b
3. a	
4. b	
5. a	

Index

Other Bestsellers of Related Interest

ADVANCED MANUFACTURING TECHNOLOGY—T.H. Allegri, P.E.

T.H. Allegri illustrates the many ways that various disciplines have been integrated in order to produce advancements in the technology of manufacturing. Digesting dozens of references, Allegri covers: CIM, CAD, CAE, management information systems, robotics, graphics and simulation, automated materials handling systems, quality control and product life cycle, flexible manufacturing systems, and more. 400 pages, 63 illustrations. Book No. 2746, $44.50 hardcover only

COMPUTER TOOLS, MODELS, AND TECHNIQUES FOR PROJECT MANAGEMENT—Dr. Adedeji B. Badiru and Dr. Gary E. Whitehouse

Badiru and Whitehouse provide you with practical, down-to-earth guidance on the use of project management tools, models, and techniques. You'll find this book filled with helpful tips and advice. You'll also discover ways to use your current computer hardware and software resources to more effectively enhance and project management functions. 320 pages, 112 illustrations. Book No. 3200, $32.95 hardcover only

BASIC MATHEMATICAL PROGRAMS FOR ENGINEERS AND SCIENTISTS
—H. Guggenheimer

Offering 40 tested BASIC programs, this book presents the background you need to understand the methods employed and the limitations inherent in every numerical method. Discussion includes three-dimensional geometry without linear algebra, high precision integration, variable step-size methods for differential equations, and the QR algorithm for eigenvalues of matrices. 243 pages, illustrated. Book No. 8225, $19.95 paperback only

DATA ACQUISITION AND CONTROL: Microcomputer Applications for Scientists and Engineers—Joseph J. Carr

This comprehensive overview of automated data systems for research and industrial applications describes the professional applications of transducers and components and covers the spectrum of measurable input. The author describes in detail the peripheral components essential to data transference and signal processing including op amps, electronic integrator and differentiator circuits, and more. 430 pages, 150 illustrations. Book No. 2956, $34.95 hardcover only

THE C4 HANDBOOK: CAD, CAM, CAE, CIM—Carl Machover

Increase your productivity and diversity with this collection of articles by international industry experts, detailing what you can expect from the latest advances in computer aided design and manufacturing technology. Machover has created an invaluable guide to identifying equipment requirements, justifying investments, defining and selecting systems, and training staff to use the systems. 448 pages, 166 illustrations. Book No. 3098, $44.50 hardcover only

ENGINEERING DESIGN: Reliability, Maintainability, and Testability
—James V. Jones

Today's economy demands low-cost, reliable products. To meet that demand, design engineers must be able to coordinate their efforts with those of end users, test technicians, manufacturing and support personnel, and other engineers. In this comprehensive guide, management and logistics expert Jim Jones presents a total, field-tested plan that will help you keep your customers satisfied and increase your chances for success. 334 pages, 188 illustrations. Book No. 3151, $39.95 hardcover only

HANDBOOK OF ARCHITECTURAL ACOUSTICS AND NOISE CONTROL
—Michael Rettinger

This handbook presents techniques for designing acoustically suitable structures. The author examines the physics of sound, noise sources, sound insulation, and acoustic design in detail, and supplies complete mathematical analysis of reducing noise from every conceivable source of a building's environment. Beginning with an overview of the scientific basis of sound, the author examines sound pressure, air-particle displacement, velocity, acceleration, sound intensity, energy density, and power. 272 pages, illustrated. Book No. 2686, $31.95 hardcover only

HUMAN FACTORS IN INDUSTRIAL DESIGN: The Designer's Companion
—John H. Burgess

This book presents a nonscientific introduction to human-factor considerations. It's directed specifically to the everyday needs of industrial designers, emphasizing the importance of creating products and equipment that are both safe and useful to their human users. Burgess explains the methods employed by human-factors specialists in determining the significance of human dimensions, capabilities, and limitations in designing everything from small hand tools to large, complex systems. 218 pages, illustrated. Book No. 3356, $27.95 hardcover only

Prices Subject to Change Without Notice.

Look for These and Other TAB Books at Your Local Bookstore

To Order Call Toll Free 1-800-822-8158
(in PA, AK, and Canada call 717-794-2191)

or write to TAB Books, Blue Ridge Summit, PA 17294-0840.

Title		Product No.	Quantity	Price

☐ Check or money order made payable to TAB Books

Charge my ☐ VISA ☐ MasterCard ☐ American Express

Acct. No. _____ Exp. _____

Signature: _____

Name: _____

Address: _____

City: _____

State: _____ Zip: _____

Subtotal $ _____

Postage and Handling
($3.00 in U.S., $5.00 outside U.S.) $ _____

Add applicable state and local
sales tax $ _____

TOTAL $ _____

TAB Books catalog free with purchase; otherwise send $1.00 in check or money order and receive a $1.00 credit on your next purchase.

Orders outside U.S. must pay with international money order in U.S. dollars.

TAB Guarantee: If for any reason you are not satisfied with the book(s) you order, simply return it (them) within 15 days and receive a full refund.   BC